A
Mind
at a
Time

Dr Mel Levine

SIMON &
SCHUSTER

LONDON • NEW YORK • SYDNEY • TOKYO • SINGAPORE • TORONTO • DUBLIN

A Mind at a Time is dedicated to the Board of Trustees and to the many other generous supporters of All Kinds of Minds, a non-profit institute for the understanding of differences in learning. These are extraordinary individuals whose dedication, wisdom, and sensitivity are helping to prevent the lethal misinterpretation and misuse of any mind at any time.

First published in Great Britain by Simon & Schuster UK Ltd, 2003
A Viacom Company

Copyright © 2002 by Mel Levine

1 3 5 7 9 10 8 6 4 2

Simon & Schuster UK Ltd
Africa House
64–78 Kingsway
London WC2B 6AH

www.simonsays.co.uk

Simon & Schuster Australia
Sydney

A CIP catalogue record for this book is
available from the British Library

ISBN 0-7432-3925-3

Printed and bound in Great Britain by
The Bath Press, Bath

Acknowledgments

The author would like to offer his gratitude to the many individuals who directly or indirectly contributed to *A Mind at a Time*. Mark Grayson, the talented and visionary CEO of All Kinds of Minds, was instrumental in conceiving the book, as was my brilliant and highly supportive literary agent, Lane Zachary. Also, Mr. Bob Bender at Simon & Schuster has been my idea of the perfect editor. Dr. Missy Wakely was most valuable in helping compile the readings and other resources. I also want to thank my many professional colleagues whose ongoing inspiration and intellectual fervor have energized my own career. These include: my closest friend, Dr. Bill Coleman, as well as Ann Hobgood, Dr. Steven Hooper, Dr. Desmond Kelly, Dr. Craig Pohlman, Stacy Parker Fisher, Tamara Nimkoff, and Dr. Carl Swartz. Additionally, I would like to acknowledge the remarkable work of Mary Dean Barringer and Marjorie Satinsky, who have been innovative leaders in our teacher training and clinical evaluation programs, respectively. Sally Bowles and Alexa Culwell have been staunch and wise allies in pursuing our missions. I also appreciate the high-quality work and dedication of my assistant, Pam McBane.

I am especially indebted to Charles and Helen Schwab for their confidence and support of my work. I also feel an enormous debt of gratitude to Bob and Mary Ann Eubanks. Bob has been the president of All Kinds of Minds; his brilliant thinking, extraordinary wit, and great friendship have been a highlight in my life in North Carolina.

I want to thank the University of North Carolina in Chapel Hill and the state of North Carolina for their unwavering support of my efforts. I am especially grateful to Dean Jeffrey Houpt of the University of North Carolina Medical School for his courageous tolerance of my kind of mind.

I feel compelled to thank as well our beloved family of animals who live with us on Sanctuary Farm. Their loyalty and their dazzling individual virtues and eccentricities constantly educate me about the unique value of all living things. I also want to acknowledge the extraordinary work of David Taylor, who often toiled on the farm while I was cultivating this book. Finally, and most important, I express my deepest appreciation to my spouse, Bambi, whose love and astute guidance have their imprint on every page of this book.

Contents

9   Relating to Relating:
Our Social Thinking System

10   When a Mind Falls Behind

11 Getting a Mind Realigned
(but Not Redesigned)

12   Raisin' Brain: *Homes for All Kinds of Minds*

13   The Right to Differ:
Schools for All Kinds of Minds   307

1

A Mind at a Time ❧

Introduction

Mind, *n.* A mysterious form of matter secreted by the brain. Its chief activity consists in the endeavor to ascertain its own nature, the futility of the attempt being due to the fact that it has nothing but itself to know itself with.

AMBROSE BIERCE, *The Devil's Dictionary*

Time is that wherein there is opportunity, and opportunity is that wherein there is no great time. . . . Healing is a matter of time, but it is also a matter of opportunity.

HIPPOCRATES, *Epidemics*

PLANET earth is inhabited by all kinds of people who have all kinds of minds. The brain of each human is unique. Some minds are wired to create symphonies and sonnets, while others are fitted out to build bridges, highways, and computers; design airplanes and road systems; drive trucks and taxicabs; or seek cures for breast cancer and hypertension. The growth of our society and the progress of the world are dependent on our commitment to fostering in our children, and among ourselves, the coexistence and mutual respect of these many different kinds of minds. Parents have a special responsibility and joy as they get to know well and to cultivate their children's individual minds. Tragic results are seen when we misconstrue and possibly even misuse a child's kind of mind! And that happens all the time.

I'm a pediatrician with a mission. I'm obsessed with helping children find success. Over the years, working in all sorts of settings, I have been struck by the despairing flocks of boys and girls out there trying to make a go of it but faltering badly and disappointing their teachers, their families, and, worst of all, themselves. It has to be hard, very hard, to be a disappointment. I have come to the conclusion that helping such children find their way is as much a part of pediatric care as curing asthma attacks and ear infections.

Kids who can't seem to operate their minds to meet expectations feel terrible about themselves, while their perplexed parents understandably lose sleep over their child who reads with little understanding or has trouble making friends or is out of focus in school. Teachers may feel exasperated and sometimes incompetent as they witness a student's inexplicable downward spiral.

Some children end up paying an exorbitant price for having the kind of mind they were born with. Through no fault of their own, they are the owners of brains that somehow don't quite mesh with the demands they come up against, requirements like the need to spell accurately, write legibly, read quickly, work efficiently, or recall multiplication facts automatically. When they grow up, they will be able to practice their brain's specialties; in childhood they will be evaluated ruthlessly on how well they do everything. Having seen so often the agony of those who taste failure at an early age, I have developed a fervent commitment to such kids and to their parents and teachers. All are well-meaning, innocent victims of a child's particular neurological circuitry.

On countless evenings I have driven home from work feeling emotionally depleted, dejected after listening to the sad tales of children who have come to equate education with humiliation. Many of them have been forced to accept labels for themselves, labels that mark them as somehow permanently deviant or dysfunctional, labels like ADD (attention deficit disorder) or LD (learning disability). Others have been placed willy-nilly on several drugs to somehow settle or sedate or soothe their kinds of minds. Adding to the torturous trails they navigate, many struggling students have been seriously wounded by the current testing mania in our society. Their intellectual identity has been shrunken down to a list of examination scores that will determine their destinies while shedding little light on their true strengths, weaknesses, and educational needs.

I have not been willing to stand by while these children suffer a battering of their self-esteem. Too many of them are misread, oversimplified, maltreated, or else falsely accused by the adult world. And you have to worry about what these innocent victims of their own wiring think of themselves. As one child lamented in a letter to me, "I can't do nothing rite. My mom and my teachers keep hollerin at me all the time. I feel like I'm the dumbest kid in my class. I guess I was boren to loose." No one should have to grow up feeling that way. And given all that recent research has revealed about differences in learning, no one needs to anymore.

The scenario is universal. Not every child is severely traumatized by a mismatching of his brain's wiring to current demands, but all of us sooner or later come up against expectations that cause us frustration and lead to some panicky feelings of inadequacy. No one is exempt. We can all recall times in our lives when we felt close to worthless compared to others. Luckily, most of us are reasonably resilient and so can bounce back from such feelings of inferiority. Some people, however, never recover from their failures.

Just think of the tragedy in the making when a child goes through life listening to such caustic refrains as "We know you can do better" or "He'll start succeeding when he makes up his mind to do so" or "She's got an attitude problem" when such statements are just plain untrue. They suggest that a child is somehow academically immoral, guilty in the first degree of his or her own undoing! Yes, they all can do better, but if and only if they are better understood by adults and then helped to succeed. There is much that parents and teachers can do to redeem such kids, all of whom possess remarkable strengths waiting to be tapped. That is what energizes me the most as I participate in their evolving biographies. They all can be helped once we identify the strengths of their minds as well as the potholes that get in the way of their success or mastery. We can cultivate their minds by addressing the weaknesses and strengthening the strengths.

A Mind at a Time sets out to accomplish multiple goals. In the course of describing the struggles of unsuccessful children, I will shed light on the brain's challenges that we all endure and see in our children over the years. Additionally, this book is intended to provide a road map for parents and teachers, enabling them to observe as children develop and mature through their school years the unfolding of important mind functions that play a leading role in school performance (and in career success). As such, this book might well be read by all parents and educators committed to the earliest possible detection of breakdowns in learning as well as the prompt identification of a child's assets. This is a book that could not have been written decades ago. It is only in recent years that, fortified with a wealth of research into learning, brain function, and school failure, we have been able to develop approaches to the understanding of children's minds.

A Mind at a Time is also a call to arms. I am beckoning parents, teachers, and policy makers to recognize how many kinds of young minds there are and to realize we need to meet their learning needs and strengthen their strengths and in so doing preserve their hopes for the future.

In writing this book, I decided to rely heavily on my own thirty years of experience as a pediatrician working in clinical programs and in schools of all types, from kindergarten through twelfth grade (with occasional forays into the early post–high school years). Over the course of these three decades I have been a collector and chronicler of case vignettes as well as direct quotations, the actual stories and words of real children's struggles. For me these kids have been like textbooks on learning and mind development. I can learn more about a child by getting to know her well than by reading a list of computer-generated test scores. In fact, whenever I participate in the clinical evaluation of a child, I see some facets of brain function that I have never before seen. In this book I want to share what I have learned from the students, their parents, and their teachers. Although I follow the research in the field very closely, I think it appropriate to write this book based purely on objective clinical observation, a volume in which children and their families and teachers tell most of the story (the names and identifying details all changed, of course).

To set the tone, before venturing any further, I would like to offer several illustrative examples of some of these clinical encounters. All were the children of good parents who were feeling desperate and seeking help from my colleagues and me. I start with Caleb.

Caleb, a boy living just outside of Boston, enters preschool at the age of nearly four. Over the next two years of his education, he is expected to relate amiably and cooperatively with his little classmates and accept the routines, rules, and other requirements of daily life at Happy Mountain Preschool and Kindergarten. His parents feel justifiably pleased and proud. At this age Caleb must show that he is acquiring a set of much needed early academic pre-skills, as they are often called. That means he is using a scissors with good results, forming letters legibly, counting beads, understanding adventure stories, and acting upon verbal directions. Caleb keeps up with the motor demands, but he is slow to follow directions and uninterested during storytelling. His parents become concerned because Caleb is starting to say that he hates school. He makes believe his belly is aching on many a school day. They worry about him but can't really pinpoint any kind of learning problem.

In first and second grades, Caleb is supposed to pick up some very basic math skills, which seem to come easily to him. He also must get his mind fully attuned to the sounds of the English language, so that he can tell them apart (like the difference between "bowl" and "ball") readily, and start matching sounds with symbols. The latter is the basis for reading. Out of the blue, Caleb announces one night at supper, "School stinks, and I hate it. I can't stand school. It's dumb and I'm the stupidest kid in my room." He flees to his bed in tears. Caleb is stumbling and beginning to fail academically because of his mind's language weaknesses, which include trouble appreciating distinctly the sounds that make up words. He looks around and sees his classmates cracking the language code for reading, and he feels terrible and panic-stricken. His mother and father wonder if he needs tutoring or testing but are told by their pediatrician that Caleb is bright and no doubt will outgrow his problem. In third and fourth grades the language requirements intensify with the call for rapid growth of vocabulary and the understanding and use of challenging grammar. Caleb falls further behind.

Now he plunges into an academic nosedive. He is virtually blocked when it comes to putting his thoughts into language and then down on paper, even though he can form letters neatly. His parents, now very worried about him, have me evaluate him in North Carolina, find out that he is struggling with some critical language weaknesses, and arrange for Caleb to get intensive help. Meanwhile, Caleb's math abilities are getting stronger, and he is discovered to be a terrific artist. He also has started trumpet lessons and is doing very well musically. Caleb competes well with his peers in sports, but does not seem to be a budding athletic talent. His parents come back to see me once a year and keep in touch by fax and e-mail.

As he makes his way through the notorious obstacle course we call middle school, Caleb's reading starts to catch up to expectations. With continuing help, by the middle of eighth grade he is at grade level in reading and is beginning to write a lot more. He is getting straight As in math and keeping pace in science too. However, a lot of the abstract terminology in social studies and science confuses him due to his lingering language weaknesses. Caleb is coping effectively with the relentless peer pressure that is the guiding force of middle school life. He is also contending successfully with the heavy surge of memory demand that takes place in middle school—all those scientific facts, historical dates, math processes, and geographic places you have to file away. He also satisfies the need to be organized with homework, with deadlines, with meeting other responsibilities. His parents are pleased and relieved. They believe he is out of the woods.

Alas, during ninth grade, his first year of high school, Caleb's grades take a terrible tumble. He has lost all interest in school, feels hopelessly overwhelmed, as if he could never succeed. He is lost amid 2,800 students and the overworked, underpaid, well-intentioned teachers, all of whom seem to have all they can do to learn the names of their students, much less understand their individual learning needs. Caleb has never read for pleasure and now he finds the reading load unbearable. Even his math work, Caleb's dependably strong suit, declines.

Ninth grade amounts to an academic famine; Caleb is starved for success, but he manages to get by. His parents are in a panic. They call me for advice, and I discuss his situation with Caleb on the phone several times. I also arrange for him to see a psychologist at the Children's Hospital in Boston. Caleb is denying he's having problems and refuses all help. "If you guys would just bug off and quit hassling me I'd do okay. Besides, I don't like any of my teachers, and none of my friends like their teachers either." His mother and father feel as if they have been on a roller-coaster ride for the last decade. His mother described Caleb as follows: "He's a doll. He's so good. He means well. He craves our respect, but he believes he doesn't deserve us. Now he feels so low, so blue all the time. And we know he's discouraged, very discouraged. So are we. We have no idea what's going on, why it is that school is defeating Caleb, and he is definitely surrendering."

When I meet with Caleb again he is belligerent. Talking to him is no fun. He won't make eye contact and insists that he's "stupid" and "lazy" and doesn't need Dr. Mel Levine to tell him that. Our assessment team proceeds to retest Caleb, who is now surprisingly cooperative—revealing that down deep in his heart, this boy desperately wants help. We are able to document some significant language problems that are still plaguing Caleb. It is evident that as the language demands of secondary school are skyrocketing, Caleb's mind is sputtering and stalling like a truck failing to make it up a steep grade. I take the time to remind Caleb of his language difficulty and how that relates to the troubles he has had in school over the years. It is miraculous to see the change overtaking his personality when I reassure him that he isn't "dumb" but has a very specific problem with the verbal parts of learning. His parents also look relieved. We then discuss ways of helping Caleb make more effective use of language, starting in subject areas that he enjoys. He loves anything connected with cars, especially racing cars. So he is encouraged to talk about cars and write about cars and read automobile magazines as much as possible. Often people like Caleb need to develop their language abilities in their areas of passion and expertise.

In tenth grade, Mr. Peters, Caleb's geometry teacher (coincidentally also the leader of the school band), takes a strong interest in him. The two form a bond; Caleb starts excelling in geometry and in the band. Mr. Peters serves as a friend and mentor to Caleb, which makes a vast difference. Mr. Peters and his wife take Caleb and some friends backpacking several times, and he loves the experience. In fact, he spends the following summer on an extended mountain trek. Caleb discovers himself. All his schoolwork gets handed in, and Caleb learns with gusto in eleventh and twelfth grades. He goes on to attend the state university as an engineering major and intellectually thrives as an undergraduate. His parents are beside themselves with pride. They're keeping their fingers crossed.

Caleb is now an acoustical engineer. He is a partner in a company that designs the sound properties of concert halls, theaters, and churches throughout North America. He loves his work. He's found his niche. In a letter Caleb wrote to me recently, he pointed out, "When I head for work in the morning, I can't wait to get there. I love what I do." His parents are ecstatic. Caleb's mom made a statement so moving that I recorded it verbatim in Caleb's chart. She said, "Seeing how proud he is tells me how pained he was."

Children like Caleb bring to school their unique kinds of minds, and the many circuits of their brain wiring get modified and refined over time. As I meet children like him, I can't escape the conclusion that different kinds of kids' minds are destined to lead different kinds of adult lives. Minds seek and should find their best ways of functioning during their school years, a period during which brains give off little signals that reveal what they are and are not wired for. Is anyone listening?

There's a lesson to be learned from Caleb's saga, namely that by keeping an informed eye and ear on the year-to-year performance of a child, we can tune in to the drama of his young mind in formation. Not only that, we are also able to have a positive influence over the dramatic plot (as Mr. Peters did) and how it turns out as adulthood approaches.

Then there's Carson, a boy who was told over and over by his parents that he would never amount to anything. His teachers echoed these gloom-and-doom prophecies. The adults around him were convinced that Carson's dismal school performance was attributable to plain and simple laziness, a moral lack for which Carson was repeatedly found guilty. By age thirteen this likable and handsome New York City boy was carousing and congregating with much older adolescents as a citizen of a culture that led him to become seriously drug- and alcohol-dependent. Carson felt flattered by his older friends' interest in him, especially since no one in the adult world was offering him anything resembling approval. On several occasions before his fourteenth birthday, his parents had to bail Carson out of jail. His father, who felt deeply anguished and depressed over his boy's self-destructive lifestyle, told him he was a "loser," a label Carson had come to accept as accurate.

But Carson's parents, teachers, and even Carson himself were all wrong. His was a misunderstood mind. He had always suffered frustrating problems with math and writing, even though this boy was a first-rate reader and a fertile source of perceptive thoughts during class discussions. Looking back it was clear that Carson had crippling trouble with tasks involving the heavy use of his memory. Math facts, spelling, even cursive writing and punctuation seemed to exceed his mind's storage capacity. He was totally unaware of his memory deficiencies; his parents were in the dark, as were Carson's teachers. In elementary school, he could have been taught strategies to improve his memory, such as forming images, associations, and examples of the facts he was memorizing. He could have been encouraged to use a calculator to solve math problems and taught keyboarding as early as possible to ease his writing trouble.

Carson nearly died of a drug overdose three weeks before his fifteenth birthday. He was in a coma for thirty-six hours, during which it was unclear whether he would ever come to.

I first met Carson about two months after he was discharged from the hospital and enrolled in a drug and alcohol rehabilitation program. School remained a threat to this beaten-down teenager. Carson confessed during his initial evaluation, "I'm sunk when it comes to learning. I'm so far behind I feel as if I'm drowning in the Pacific Ocean. I even have dreams about drowning—almost every night, and I see my teachers speeding by in a boat just as I'm going under." Carson's dad noted, "I think Carson is dealing with his substance abuse problems pretty well, but the thought of going back to school sends him into a tailspin. He's just plain afraid to fail again. And we're afraid for him. We've been hard on him for years and we wonder if we've been too hard."

Carson underwent testing at the Clinical Center for the Study of Development and Learning, which I direct at the University of North Carolina Medical School. Our evaluation team was able to confirm that this boy had some serious difficulties in math and in his writing. We also "diagnosed" his impressively strong language abilities, dazzling social skills, and a galaxy of other positive traits and capabilities, including his ability to come up with original and perceptive thoughts regarding current political and international issues. Carson pored over every inch of the daily newspaper and had an opinion on everything. But during my testing, when I gave him a list of numbers to repeat, Carson, this clearly brilliant boy, kept getting them out of order. Nor could he draw designs from memory, typically leaving out key details. Assessments of his long- and short-term memory revealed some huge gaps. It was hard to imagine this boy remembering quickly and accurately enough to do well on tests in school.

At the end of a morning of assessment, I had a chance to "demystify" Carson, to explain to him and his parents his strengths and weaknesses. I talked to Carson about his superb language functioning, his unusual creativity, and his phenomenal people skills. I pointed out his advanced reading performance and his razor-sharp critical thinking. I mentioned that I thought that at age sixteen he could hold his own on any college debating team. Watching his expression, I had the impression that Carson had never before heard anyone say anything favorable about his brain! He lit up like a Roman candle on the Fourth of July.

Then we talked about the areas of his mind that needed some work. I told him everyone has these. I explained to Carson that he was by no means stupid, that his communication skills and insightful thinking were signs of a really outstanding kind of mind. I then explained that I thought Carson was far better at understanding and explaining things than he was at remembering, that he had been struggling in school because of difficulty filing and retrieving information and certain kinds of skills in his long-term memory. I used a diagram I developed called "The Memory Factory" to show Carson what aspects of his memory were falling short of expectations. I gave him examples of different techniques he might try in order to become more systematic in memorizing facts and testing himself. I assured him that over time if he kept consciously thinking about his memory while studying, his capacity for remembering would likely grow. I also let him know that cramming tons of information into your memory happens a lot in school but that this isn't a major part of most careers. So the outlook for Carson could be excellent once he found his niche in an occupation. I then fueled his optimism by discussing with him all the exciting career options in which he could excel just by using the strengths he already possesses.

Carson's father telephoned me several days after his evaluation to report, "I can tell you this kid is on cloud nine, and he's even talking about possibly going back to school next week—it's as if he's come to see some genuine uses for himself. We're delighted."

Carson did go back to school (with understandable trepidation). We arranged for him to get the help he needed in math. He learned some good memory strategies. His teachers offered some humane accommodations. For example, his history teacher agreed to refrain from calling on him in class for factual questions that demanded an immediate response and instead would call on him to offer his opinion on an issue. Because of his writing problems Carson was helped with his keyboarding.

Carson is now at City College in New York. He has stayed away from drugs and alcohol, is majoring in journalism, and was elected editor in chief of the college paper. Carson has always loved to travel and wants to become a foreign correspondent. He came back to see me during his spring break. He said, "I think I have my act together. I still worry a lot about school and have trouble sometimes on quizzes, but I made the dean's list last semester. For the first time I'm really starting to feel like a winner." Carson knew that I am a pediatrician, but he asked if he could still come back to see me in Chapel Hill from time to time, just to check in. He seemed a little embarrassed to be making this request, but I was delighted. It's visits from the Carsons and Calebs that keep convincing me that we can help all kinds of minds thrive. Besides, often I identify so closely with these kids that I start feeling like their uncle.

One more true story, that of Nana from Illinois. She was a very active little girl who often got into hot water for doing too many things too quickly without thinking them through. She had a devilish personality but could cast her spell on absolutely anyone in her vicinity. Her infectious laughter, her bouncing coils of golden hair, and her zany sense of humor attracted the attention and affection of other children as well as adults. She succeeded with formal learning in school despite mostly subpar concentration and highly impulsive tendencies. Nana always did the first thing that came into her mind with little if any use of good judgment. As she told her teacher, "I have a jumpy brain. It keeps jumping into things without looking." That seemed to be part of an attention problem that had plagued her since her earliest toddler days.

One afternoon, when she was about nine years old, Nana had a fierce argument with a classmate Juanita as they were getting off the bus. Several moments after the vehicle pulled away, she impulsively pushed her friend into the street, where she was struck by a minivan. Juanita fractured her femur and her pelvis. She was hospitalized for several weeks and underwent surgery. Fortunately, she recovered, but had a noticeable limp long after the accident. Nana never recovered. She had bad dreams about her friend dying because of her. She would feel guilty and depressed whenever she saw Juanita limping across the playground.

During the first four grades of school Nana often got punished severely for her disruptive behavior but never got understanding or sympathy. Her parents could have considered some counseling for Nana had they realized that she was having trouble controlling her attention, a problem commonly accompanied by impulsive tendencies. With some coaching, Nana could have learned about the risks of being impulsive and been taught such techniques as stopping and counting and thinking before acting. She might also have benefited from medication to tighten her control over her attention.

Fortunately, now at age nineteen Nana has gotten some help from a local mental health professional who has explained to Nana the various aspects of her attentional dysfunction. She has recently started on medication, which is helping reduce her impulsivity, although she realizes that drugs are not the ultimate answer to gaining control over herself. Nana managed to get through high school and is now working in a beauty salon, where her great people skills have served her well. The psychologist who told me Nana's story reported that Nana is seriously considering attending college. She would like to become a social worker.

·❧ A Mind's Possibilities

It's taken for granted in adult society that we cannot all be generalists skilled in every area of learning and mastery. Nevertheless, we apply tremendous pressure on our children to be good at *everything*. Every day they are expected to shine in math, reading, writing, speaking, spelling, memorization, comprehension, problem solving, socialization, athletics, and following verbal directions. Few if any children can master all of these "trades." And none of us adults can. In one way or another, all minds have their specialties and their frailties.

Each of us is endowed with a highly complex, inborn circuitry—creating innumerable branching pathways of options and obstacles. While some of us have brains that are wired to handle a lot of information at once, others have brains that can absorb and process only a little information at a time (often with greater accuracy). While some of us have brains that store and retrieve from memory with precision and speed, others possess brains that access facts more slowly or with less precision. Some kinds of minds prefer to dream up their own original thoughts rather than drawing upon the ideas of others, and vice versa.

Although some of us have minds that are more comfortable and effective visualizing complex political or even religious ideas, others are apt to do much of their thinking in words and sentences. So it is that we all live with minds wired to excel in one area and crash in another. Hopefully, we discover and engage in good matches between our kind of mind and our pursuits in life.

Our abilities and inabilities are tested and challenged throughout our school years and in the course of every day of our careers. We all face the never-ending looming threat of failure to meet expectations—both the expectations that are imposed upon us and those we set for ourselves. An eleven-year-old who has never earned a grade below B+ on her report card suddenly sees her self-esteem plummet as she discovers she has a horrible time learning a foreign language. A young boy makes a fool of himself trying to serve a volleyball in physical education class—he can't get the ball over the net. His conspicuous gross motor shortcomings provoke humiliating jeers from his infuriated, ruthlessly judgmental fifth-grade teammates.

Some price, modest or substantial, must be paid any time a mind is forced or attempts to learn or perform something in a way for which it is not wired. This happens to all of us from time to time, but the outcome is tragic when the mismatching of a mind to a set of important tasks becomes a daily event and when that poor fit is not understood. This phenomenon takes place every day in schools everywhere.

✒ A PEDIATRIC PERSPECTIVE

To help you understand the roots of this book, I feel compelled to indulge in a modest outpouring of autobiographical detail. I have been what is called a developmental-behavioral pediatrician. This is a growing branch of pediatrics, one that deals with child development, behavioral issues, and learning. After my training at Harvard Medical School and at the Children's Hospital in Boston, I served as a captain and school physician at Clark Air Force Base in the Philippines. At that point I became fascinated with the remarkable ways in which pediatricians and educators could collaborate in helping kids find themselves in life. When that stint ended, I went back to Boston and directed outpatient clinics at the Children's Hospital. I was astounded by the large numbers of kids who came to see us, not with traditional diseases but with problems functioning, especially in school. They appeared to me to be neither emotionally disturbed, nor dumb, nor lazy; there was obviously something far more subtle and insidious going on inside them, something awaiting our detection and good management. I soon became obsessed with these "hidden dysfunctions" and ultimately based my whole career on trying to elucidate them in order to help kids. Subsequently, I became a professor of pediatrics and director of the Clinical Center for the Study of Development and Learning at the University of North Carolina Medical School, a position I currently hold.

In 1995 I was the co-founder (with Charles Schwab) of All Kinds of Minds, a nonprofit institute for the understanding of differences in learning. The institute is heavily involved in training teachers to understand and deal with differences in learning. It also is designed to work with parents, clinicians, and children in an effort to make sure that the many different kinds of minds of kids are well understood and educated. All Kinds of Minds has grown rapidly, and I am happy to relate that it is having a powerful impact on children throughout the world.

Like almost everyone, as a child I had to cope with my allotment of harrowing run-ins with my own brain wiring, although I was, for the most part, a good student. In preschool I could never stay within the lines when I colored. I was unable to use a scissors properly (and still can't). The exhilaration that comes from either drawing or cutting in a straight line was a thrill I could only watch my classmates experience. My artwork was substandard at every stage of my development, requiring me to bend over drawings and other works of art, so as to shield my products from the spying of my classmates. My artistic defeats no doubt were helped by the red-green color blindness I didn't discover until some years later. To this day I feel humiliated whenever I attempt to fold a sheet of 8½ × 11 paper so it will fit neatly in an envelope. Not only have I remained unable to accomplish this elusive feat, but I also marvel at how others do so! I'm about equally stumped when I have to fold a road map; it gets jammed like turkey stuffing in the glove compartment. Furthermore, while I'm confessing my personal disrupted wiring, I should add that from early kindergarten up to the present, I have never been able to operate a pencil sharpener. Again, I watch with gnawing envy as my peer group displays its effortless mastery; whenever I insert a pencil, the utensil comes out a blunt wooden stub.

I was never an athlete. While I was quite good at interpreting complicated language, I could not understand a thing a physical education teacher ever uttered in my presence (probably still couldn't). I hit neurodevelopmental rock bottom when we had square dancing, as there was no way I could transform verbal instructions into a gross motor pattern—I inevitably swung my partner in the wrong direction. What an embarrassment! I passed through childhood being picked last for teams. I sometimes felt as if I were in a police lineup during the selection process. Gym class was like a nuclear weapon in its destructive effect on my self-esteem. In middle school the nurse's office on gym mornings became my bomb shelter. I often retreated there strategically to complain of excruciating upper abdominal pain. And I really felt that pain. Catching or throwing a ball was well beyond my brain's inborn job description. When I was a teenager, my father talked me into taking some golf lessons. After several sessions, the golf pro politely suggested I might want to pursue some alternative form of recreation, as my swing was such that its arc seldom paused to make contact with the ball. So instead of sports, I opted to become the editor in chief of my high school newspaper (which did little to fortify my body image).

In fifth grade I had grave problems relating to my teacher, Miss Briggs. I was inept when it came to organizing my homework and writing neatly. I started to care only about my pets (a collie, a turtle, and a school of assorted tropical fish), all of whom I loved passionately. I felt out of place in school that year. Miss Briggs, who would criticize me brutally each day in front of my classmates, wanted to shackle me with retention in the fifth grade, but thank goodness my parents would not hear of it, in part because my achievement-test scores were very high in all areas. I went on to earn mostly As in sixth grade. Like so many others, I had suffered my share of horror and the pain of humiliation in school. Over the years I have worked hard to help alleviate that pain in thousands of unsuccessful students whose failed efforts have been in strictly academic areas or else in the demanding world of social life or even in their ability to live up to their parents' loving hopes and expectations for them. In the process I think I have acquired enormous respect for parents and teachers, and at the same time, I have come to view struggling children as modern day heroes and heroines re-peatedly wounded by the fact that their thwarted struggles to succeed are so widely misunderstood by grown-ups and also by themselves.

While studying and trying to help these unhappy kids I have found my-self opening some windows on learning. I have been educated in the uniqueness of individual minds. This, in turn, has forced me to think about "a mind at a time" and ultimately to write this book. This volume could have as its subtitle "What We Are Learning About Learning from Children Who Aren't Learning," since I have discovered unexpectedly that the study of problematic learning shines a floodlight on all learning and how it's sup-posed to work. My three decades of clinical observations, my many years of collaboration with schools all over the world, my extensive devouring of the neuroscientific literature, along with the research in which I have been involved, have helped me assemble a model of learning and, in particular, a model that tries to account for patterns of learning as I see them across the broad spectrum of kinds of minds. This model provides a means for under-standing and managing weak school performance whenever a child's brain functions can't keep up with demands.

When people, adults and children, learn about their own gaps, they fre-quently show, or actually report, a sense of relief, because for the first time in their lives they are able to understand exactly why they've been strug-gling to meet certain demands and how they can go about conquering or bypassing these challenges. They can forgive themselves and set about be-coming stronger people. When I explained to Caleb that he was having trouble understanding complicated language when his teacher was talking or while he was reading, he no longer felt as if he was hopelessly retarded compared to other kids. When I reviewed with Carson the fact that he was experiencing problems with his memory, his face lit up. "So that's what it is. And I thought I was born with bad brain damage," he proclaimed. When Nana learned what it means to be impulsive, she no longer felt evil. Insight is liberating—and forgiving.

2

The Ways of Learning ❧

The mosquito is an automaton. It can afford to be nothing else. There are only about one hundred thousand nerve cells in its tiny head, and each one has to pull its weight. The only way to run accurately and successfully through a life cycle in a matter of days is by instinct, a series of rigid behaviors programmed by the genes. . . . The channels of human mental development, in contrast, are circuitous and variable.

EDWARD O. WILSON, *On Human Nature*

FRITZ wore very thick lenses in his wire-rimmed spectacles. He was an awkward kid who mostly liked being by himself. At age eight he was becoming an insatiable glutton for the printed word, devouring all manner of written nourishment wherever he found it. At first, his parents were vexed by his marathon stays locked in the bathroom, until they found out that that was where their eccentric Fritz felt most comfortable savoring his reading. Fritz came to see me because of some motor problems, including difficulty writing, along with some seeming leaks in his memory.

On several occasions, his mom and dad mentioned that Fritz was fascinated with gadgets of any kind. He relished getting his hands on whatever seductive apparatus was within reach. In the car he would studiously detach or disassemble ashtrays, loudspeakers, and door handles. His extraordinarily tolerant father observed that Fritz was much more talented and enthusiastic when it came to taking things apart than when putting them together! But Mr. Powell did admit that his son was nothing short of remarkable at fixing objects around the house.

I was able to confirm this finding when one day I was doing a physical examination on Fritz in my office. He saw that one of the lights I use for examining ears (my otoscope) was not working. I told him it was broken and that I had changed the batteries and the bulb to no avail. I had also used a well-established, arguably primitive, Mel Levine technique; in vain, I had shaken it repeatedly and briskly. Anyway, Fritz pounced on my otoscope and immodestly proclaimed, "I'll fix it for you." Of course, I consented to the proposed surgery. Fritz then inspected the instrument, and thought out loud, "Let me see now, how is this supposed to work?" I never would have asked myself that question. Fritz then used his fingers and his voice to trace and talk through the way an otoscope is supposed to work. Only then did he go back and determine where the breakdown was occurring. In doing so, he encountered a loose connection in the switch, which he remedied with leverage from one of his handy talonlike fingernails. What struck me and what I never forgot after that was that Fritz was unwilling to repair my light without first determining how such lights were supposed to work. I have since applied the "Fritz Principle" in my career. That is to say, I should never try to understand and deal with differences in learning until I know how learning works when it's working. So I can't figure out why a kid is enduring serious grief in algebra unless I understand what it ordinarily takes to master algebra—in other words, how that kind of learning works.

§❧ How Learning Works

The most basic instrument for learning is something called a neurodevelopmental function. Our own minds and those of our children are like tool chests. They are filled with these delicate instruments, neurodevelopmental functions, the various implements for learning and for applying what's learned. Just as a carpenter might deploy different groups of tools to complete various projects or a dentist might use different sets of tools for different tooth tasks, our minds make use of different clusters of neurodevelopmental functions to learn specific skills and to create particular products. One committee of neurodevelopmental functions enables a student to master subtraction; another squad participates in the recitation of the Pledge of Allegiance, yet another neurodevelopmental task force makes possible riding a scooter.

A neurodevelopmental function may be one component of memory, such as the ability to recall things that have been seen in the past (i.e., visual memory), or it may be the awareness of where within the letter "g" your pencil is located during each instant while you form that letter. The capacity to store and retrieve chains of information, such as the alphabet or the events leading up to World War I, is another example of a neurodevelopmental function. As you can surmise, the brain's toolbox is vast, the total number of neurodevelopmental functions inestimable. On top of that, the range of different combinations of functions called upon to accomplish academic tasks is mind-boggling. In view of all these moving parts, it should not surprise us that breakdowns or specific weaknesses are commonplace. We call these deficiencies neurodevelopmental dysfunctions. We as well as our kids all live with our share of these flaws. Often the dysfunctions do not seriously obstruct roads to success. But sometimes they do.

Here are some examples of neurodevelopmental dysfunctions. Some children have difficulty writing, even though they have lots to say. They just can't seem to form letters quickly and accurately enough to keep up with their flow of ideas and words. So their writing is dramatically inferior to the richness of their thinking or speaking. When kids write, their brains assign specific muscles to specific aspects of letter formation; certain muscles are supposed to handle vertical movement, others create rotary movement, others assume responsibility for horizontal movement, while still others operate to stabilize the pencil so it won't fall on the floor while they write. Some kids endure agonizing difficulty with such motor implementation; they simply can't assign the proper muscles consistently. Therefore, writing looms as a tormenting problem for them. This inability to assign specific muscles to operate in the right way at the right time during letter formation is a perfect example of a neurodevelopmental dysfunction. Other kids have trouble finding the exact words they need when they talk, difficulty remembering the associations between sounds and symbols when they read, or trouble understanding complex sentences and thereby following directions quickly and precisely enough in the classroom. Each of these deficiencies is a specific neurodevelopmental dysfunction and in each instance the dysfunction is likely to interfere with learning.

All too often a neurodevelopmental dysfunction goes undetected—much like an unsolved crime. As was the case with Carson, the assumption may prevail that somehow a floundering student is not really trying, that he is lazy, unmotivated, or, perhaps, even worse, that he's "just not too bright." A child like Nana may be discovered to be daydreaming and fidgeting in class, dreadfully out of focus. She is told she needs to start paying attention in class or she'll get detention. She comes to believe she is somehow bad. No one seems to realize that her fragile concentration is a kind of mental fatigue or burnout; she has neurodevelopmental dysfunctions interfering with her mind's ability to turn on and keep up the flow of mental energy that she needs to concentrate in class. Her neurodevelopmental dysfunction is misread as a behavior problem when she has to combat serious mental fatigue. She's an innocent victim of her own wiring.

ᕙᕗ Eight Systems

Approximately 30 trillion synapses or nerve linkages exist within the human brain. That crowded network allows for plenty of strong connections, disconnections, and misconnections—in short, a nearly endless combination of neurodevelopmental possibilities. As we have seen, designated teams of neurodevelopmental functions join together to enable kids to acquire specific abilities. When one or more members of a team fail to show up or fail to do their share, performance suffers. Such negative results can bring on a backlash of emotional and motivational complications. Fortunately, we have the wherewithal and the knowledge to mend these problems before they get out of hand.

Schools and parents share the job of ensuring the healthy growth of vital neurodevelopmental functions. How then do we keep track of a mind's growth processes over the course of a child's school career? The answer is that caring adults need to know how these functions are supposed to be operating year by year—just as they might be tuned in to a child's ongoing nutritional needs or rate of growth. At first glance, staying on top of the many facets of a child's mind development might appear to be a daunting, unrealistic undertaking in view of the vast constellation of important neurodevelopmental functions. But don't despair; to aid us in our surveillance mission, all of the different neurodevelopmental functions can be sorted into eight manageable categories, or neurodevelopmental systems. In my work with schools and clinicians I have called these "the neurodevelopmental constructs," but they are perhaps more helpfully thought of as the systems of a mind.

In medicine we are accustomed to thinking about overall health as the sum total of the health of various systems, such as the cardiovascular system, the nervous system, and the gastrointestinal system. Similarly, we can think about your child's learning health in terms of the well-being of the eight learning systems I am about to describe. As with the systems that operate in our bodies, the neurodevelopmental systems are dependent on one another. They have to work together if learning is to occur, just as the cardiovascular system has to team up with the pulmonary system to promote the delivery of oxygen to various parts of our bodies.

These systems are like the major characters in an unfolding drama. As we watch our kids grow and develop over their school years, we need to focus on the progress of the eight systems. At any point, the strength of functions within each system directly influences performance in and out of school. Systems change in their capacities. The functions can grow in their effectiveness. They can level off. They can deteriorate. Therefore, it is important that caring adults keep an eye on the progress in each system, promptly detecting and dealing with any important impairments or signs of delayed development.

The eight neurodevelopmental systems are depicted in Figure 2-1. Individual chapters in this book focus on each system. But first, I will provide a brief description of each.

The Attention Control System   Jesse gets a traffic ticket for speeding; he's all riled up over it and defends (pardons) himself by proclaiming to his parents, "I just wasn't paying attention to the speedometer. I had other things on my mind." But Jesse often experiences such mind lapses, and has had a long-standing difficulty directing his attention. His mom once pointed out, "That's my Jesse. It's absolutely incredible how he can be doing one thing and thinking about three other things at the same time! He's concentrating on everything but what he's doing."

Attention is the administrative bureau of the brain, the headquarters for mental regulators that patrol and control learning and behavior. The attention controls direct the distribution of mental energy within our brains, so that we have the wherewithal to finish what we start and stay alert throughout the day. Other controls of attention slow down our thinking so we can

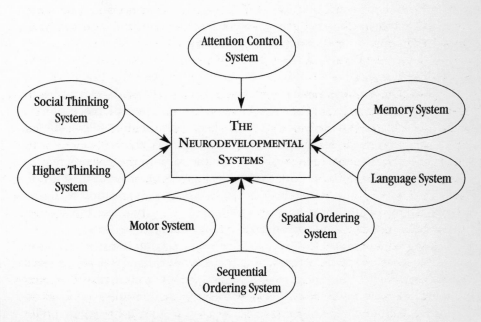

Figure 2-1.   The neurodevelopmental systems.

plan and complete tasks competently and efficiently. An example of attention control is a child's ability to resist the temptation to think about the party she's invited to tonight so she can concentrate on the word problem her math teacher is explaining. Attention keeps your child focused while filtering out distractions. Children vary widely in how often their attention controls function effectively.

The Memory System   Elsa keeps "bombing out" on tests or quizzes that force her to memorize and later answer questions that have only one correct response. She recently flunked a quiz on plant structure despite studying like a devout monk. "I thought I knew all that stuff, but it must have just leaked out of my brain while I was sleeping." Our school years involve more strenuous exercising of memory than at any other time in our lives. In fact, much more memory is needed for school success than is required in virtually any career. To varying extents, every course in school is a memory workout. And memory is downright complicated with countless little facets to go with the many different kinds of things we try to remember. Every student has memory compartments that serve him well, while other parts of memory bring on varying degrees of frustration. There are countless intellectually competent kids who unravel in school because they understand far better than they remember. Ironically, there are many students with superb rote memory who succeed with flying colors through their school years simply by regurgitating factual data. They may be far less successful during adult careers when memory plays much less of a starring role.

The Language System   Riley just received an A+ on a highly original short story; he's always gotten As in English and he loves to read and write. This guy makes most schoolwork look like the proverbial piece of cake. That's because school is a perfect fit for born linguists like Riley. The language ingredients of learning include, among other things, the ease with which a brain detects differences between the forty-four or so different English language sounds (an indispensable ingredient of reading skill), the ability to understand, remember, and start using new vocabulary, the capacity to express thoughts while speaking and on paper, and the speed of comprehension needed to keep pace with a seemingly supersonic flow of verbal explanations and instructions. Learning a second language is another example of an academic demand that calls for strong verbal capacity. Not surprisingly, kids who are good with language are more likely to succeed throughout school. On the other hand, those poor souls with even the mildest (often unapparent) language inefficiencies are apt to suffer agonizing pain trying to make it in our schools.

The Spatial Ordering System   Marcus's parents fret over his inability to distinguish left from right; more often than not, he puts his shoe on the wrong foot. Marcus's father once commented to me, "It's as if this kid is completely lost in space. He never remembers where he's left anything and he puts his shirt on backward more often than not—even when he thinks about it." Also, his confused drawings in school are a source of shame to Marcus. These shortcomings reveal his weak spatial ordering. The spatial ordering system is designed to enable us to deal with or create information arranged in a gestalt, a visual pattern, or a configuration. Through spatial ordering we perceive how parts of things fit together. We are able to study and later recognize familiar shapes, their relative positions, and what goes with what to make a pattern, such as the letter "h" or an octagon or your boyfriend's face. Spatial ordering also helps us organize the various material necessities of the day, such as pencils, notebooks, desks, locker contents, and other props needed for academic efficiency and proficiency. Spatial ordering calls for the use of closed circuits between our eyes and our brains, wiring designed to discern patterns and discriminate between them. People with strong spatial ordering are not likely to waste much time searching for lost objects; they know where things are. On a more complex level, spatial ordering enables us to think with pictures, so a child hearing a story about Robin Hood can visualize the dramatic events, while a student in art class can picture the steps needed to undertake a ceramics project.

The Sequential Ordering System   If you tell Suzanne to do three things in a row, she appears dazed and ends up fulfilling only the last step of the instruction. Her teacher describes her as "strictly a one-step processor." She has trouble recalling the steps required to tackle a long-division problem. This girl is contending with her inadequate capacity for sequencing. This system, a working partner of spatial ordering, helps us deal with the chains of information that come into or depart from our minds coded in a particular serial order or sequence. Throughout their day, kids are under attack by a furious onslaught of sequences, which range from the steps in balancing an algebraic equation, to the order of digits in a new friend's telephone number, to the chronology of events culminating in the election of a president. A teacher's directions are transmitted in a verbal sequence. But the most challenging and insidious sequence of all is called time. Sequential ordering forms the basis for time management, for understanding time, estimating time, allocating time, and being aware of time's passage. On a higher plane, sequential ordering is involved in many forms of reasoning, perhaps most vividly showcased in a tenth grader's geometric proof.

The Motor System   Alcindor is frustrated and exquisitely self-conscious about not being able to ride a two-wheeler when all of his buddies can do so effortlessly. He feels like a klutz. The poor kid is living with a breakdown in his motor system, at least at this point in his development. The motor system is supposed to govern the very precise and complex network of tight connections between the brain and various muscles all over the body. A child's motor functions determine whether or not she will excel in sports and, if so, whether it will be field hockey, tennis, or track. Other neuromotor functions make possible cursive writing, playing the fiddle, and guiding scissors. Motor coordination is important to children; being able to show off proficiency makes an important contribution to overall self-concept and confidence. Clumsy children may come to feel globally inferior to their agile classmates.

The Higher Thinking System   Melinda just can't seem to grasp the concept of mass in her high school physics class. The difference between velocity and acceleration, the meaning of resistance in a wire, and the phenomenon of static electricity have also eluded her. She willingly fesses up, "I don't get physics; I don't get it at all." Melinda is struggling with inadequate higher thinking, a system that represents the real summit, the very peak of our thinking abilities. Jackson can't seem to decipher the symbolism in a poem by T. S. Eliot but has no trouble with symbols in his advanced algebra class. He has a very specific breakdown in higher thinking when he is using language. Myrna is great at figuring out what's wrong when her computer isn't functioning but she has trouble figuring out the point of view expressed in an editorial on global warming. Higher thinking includes the ability to problem-solve and reason logically, to form and make use of concepts (such as mass in physics), to understand how and when rules apply, and to get the point of a complicated idea. Higher thinking also takes in critical and creative thinking.

The Social Thinking System   Bethany never gets invited to parties. The phone rings off the hook for her brother and sister, but never for her. At school she is picked on, jeered at, taunted, and avoided like a venomous snake by her classmates. She has no friends and is understandably crushed. Bethany is lacking in the kind of social thinking that is needed for maintaining successful relationships. Her mother laments, "Bethany would give her right arm to have a true friend, but it seems as if every time she comes close to having a satisfying relationship, she messes up. She either says or does something that upsets and puts off her new friend. And Bethany has no idea what she's doing wrong, no idea at all."

Children's social abilities occupy center stage in school. The social spotlights are glaring. They illuminate a galaxy of interpersonal strengths and shortcomings. Interactions with peers yield the bulk of the gratification or humiliation a student experiences in life. Some kids seem to be born with distinct social talents that allow for friendship formation and a solid reputation; others have to be taught how to relate. A child (or adult) may be strong in the seven other neurodevelopmental systems yet seem to fail in life because he or she is unable to behave in a way that fits appropriately with others of his age group. He may have trouble establishing new friendships and keeping old ones afloat, working collaboratively in groups, or coping tactfully with flammable conflicts involving classmates. Even the most brilliant child can end up frustrated if he is too shy, socially inept, or antisocial. School affords little or no privacy. Those who have stunted functions for social interaction are condemned to feel the pain of exposure and daily humiliation. They are likely to be the most downtrodden students in a school (and also the most anguished employees on the job).

Parents and teachers experience satisfaction watching children's neurodevelopmental systems expand in their capabilities over days, months, and years, especially when the functions are put to good use, exercised like limber muscles. Caring adults have to realize that a system deteriorates drastically when it is underutilized. For example, if a child almost never elaborates on ideas, rarely talks in complete sentences, and instead overindulges in words like "stuff" and "thing," or else in profanity, then his verbal skills will stagnate, fail to grow, and even diminish. If you never do any running, the neurodevelopmental functions needed for running are likely to starve, inevitably eroding your overall gross motor performance.

Your child's neurodevelopmental systems never get a chance to perform as soloists; they constantly join forces to accomplish good results. Memory partners with language to help your third grader recall the words to "Silent Night." Attention control reacts with gross motor ability to produce the sinking of a long putt on the eighteenth green. Sequencing, visual memory, and language combine with social awareness to let you explain to a friend the plot of the science fiction thriller you saw on TV last night.

❧ NEURODEVELOPMENTAL PROFILES

Every one of our children ambles down the highly judgmental corridors of school each day dragging along his mind's profile, a partly hidden spreadsheet of personal strengths and weaknesses. And throughout every moment of the school day that profile gets put to the test. Some of our children are blessed with profiles that are magnificently matched to expectations, while others are saddled with profiles that fail to mesh with demands—an all too common disparity that can arise at any age.

If a child you know has a profile that's not conforming to demands, don't give up and don't allow him to give up either. That very profile has a good chance of coming into its own sooner or later. That's because we know a pattern of strengths and weaknesses may operate particularly well at specific ages and in certain contexts but not nearly so optimally in other times and under alternative circumstances.

This was just the case with Toby. He was a kid who had a lot of trouble with the memory demands of both elementary and middle school. He had trouble remembering facts and skills quickly and automatically, and it was hard for him to hold several things in his mind at once while completing an assignment. As a result he was wiped out in algebra and had a very hard time with writing assignments. In the latter case, he kept forgetting what he was going to write whenever he paused to think about spelling. But Toby was brilliantly creative, and he was a phenomenal conceptualizer and a razor-sharp critical thinker. After barely surviving daily disgrace in elementary and middle school due to his memory shortfall, he rose like a ballistic missile when he was allowed to take advanced placement courses in history, English, and art in high school. A guidance counselor had been humane and perceptive enough to know that sometimes you fix a weakness by pursuing strengths. His honor classes all downplayed sheer memory work and stressed instead original and critical thinking. Graduating near the top of his class, Toby majored in political science at Brown University, and is now a Ph.D. candidate with an interest in the career pathways of successful national leaders. He has just written an important book on the subject of political motivation. He still claims to have trouble with his memory, but that doesn't seem to matter or interfere anymore. Computers have helped enormously. As he reflects, "My hard drive is sitting on my desk, so it doesn't need to be housed in my skull! Besides, no one around here gets tenure because of his memory."

I think a big part of teaching and parenting entails helping kids make it through periods when they feel inadequate. It happens to everyone once in a while. And that is why we need to think about how a particular mind is fitting in at a particular time of life. It means we need to consider "a mind at a time" (a second meaning of the title of this book).

Not only may a mind come into its own at any time, but also a profile that is perfectly set up for success in school may not be nearly so well fitted for career attainment. A kid's profile may win all sorts of praise throughout her elementary school years, but that in no way guarantees that her particular profile will satisfy career requirements at age twenty-three. Clearly then, some profiles work better at certain ages than at others. Sometimes the very same traits that jeopardize your kid in third grade could evolve into his prize assets during adulthood. Distractibility and daydreaming during reading class may be an attention deficit yet may also be early indicators of creativity and innovative thinking, "symptoms" that will bolster her career as a scriptwriter or music video producer. A student's trouble understanding language may cause him to do much less of his thinking with words, as a result of which he strengthens his visual and spatial thinking, destined to serve him well two decades later in his career as a mechanical engineer designing nuclear power plants.

When a child brings home disappointing grades, parents can take solace in the well-documented finding that report cards are notoriously poor at predicting how your child will eventually do in a career. In fact, sometimes when I see a child in my office who is failing or perhaps just floundering in school, I love to rev him up by saying something like this: "Hey, Reginald, when you go back to school on Monday, take a good look around your classroom and pick out a kid you really envy, someone who gets fantastic grades, is good-looking and is a super jock too, you know, a kid who always seems to do everything right. And who is popular. Look closely at that kid, and seriously consider the possibility that this may well be his finest hour! There is a good chance he'll be working for you someday." I guess that's another way of saying that different profiles are destined to make the grade at different times of life and when the conditions are right. Adult life offers many more opportunities for infinitely more kinds of minds than are available during child life. Parents need to find things to praise in a struggling child and make sure that he doesn't give up on himself and get depressed and distressed while waiting for his day to come.

Not only do different profiles have their day in the limelight eventually, but also children are capable of changing their strengths and weaknesses over time. Take heart, parents: neurodevelopmental profiles are not like computer hardware or fossils. They are resilient. One despondent mother confided, "My daughter Cathy is so sweet and kind. She will do anything for anyone. But school is such a frustration for her. I sometimes wish we could just trade in the learning part of her mind." Well, it turns out you can change your mind but not exchange it. For instance, some individuals plagued with language impairments in school become fluent and articulate speakers and have phenomenal reading comprehension by the age of thirty. They actually have built up their language system after having been nonverbal schoolchildren. Through extensive use of language (often within their chosen careers), they become respectable linguists. Of course, there may be some ceilings, limitations on how strong a weakness can become. If I, an inept athlete, were given batting lessons in baseball, I could improve some (there is a lot of room to do so), but no matter how dismal a season they were having, it is highly unlikely that I could ever play shortstop for the Boston Red Sox.

Many individuals grow up in homes that are dysfunctional, neighborhoods that are violent, environments that seem to starve their minds, yet somehow they manage to salvage their minds, to discover some ways of learning and succeeding despite biographical odds that are so stacked against them. Some of this resiliency may result from hidden neurodevelopmental strengths that they discover and ignite within themselves. There are well-known attorneys, preachers, and playwrights who grew up in poverty but had superior innate verbal wiring. Having a talent as an orator, actor, or comedian can be the wellspring of resiliency. Of course, sometimes hidden talents remain forever hidden and go to waste instead of triggering resiliency. That means parents and teachers have to be on a constant, diligent quest for buried treasure within children.

ᗡ᙭ How a Mind's Profile Comes to Be

What shapes your child's profile? Can you influence the process? These are thorny questions, ones we shall confront throughout this book. No doubt multiple forces interact to determine a child's strengths and shortcomings. And parents are in a pretty good position to influence most—but not all—of these forces.

Genes   For better or for worse, mothers and fathers don't get to select or reject the traits a child inherits. Sandy is just as absentminded and disorganized as her mom, who says, "How in the world am I supposed I help my daughter get her act together when I'm even more discombobulated than she is?" Many strengths and weaknesses appear to be inherited—either completely or in part. In the best of all possible worlds sharing aspects of your child's profile can make you a more sympathetic parent. You know what he's going through. In my experience, often when a child has a particular kind of learning weakness, much the same pattern will be plainly evident in one or both parents or else in a sibling. When parents observe us testing a child, it is very common to hear from a father or mother: "I had trouble with the same things he did!"

Joey, an absolutely delightful patient, came to me recently for a follow-up visit. This country boy with his close crew cut and his reversed baseball cap permanently bonded to his skull actually lives on a farm close to my own. Despite being only ten, Joey always talks like a venerable elder statesman.

During a recent visit to my office, when I inquired about how things were going in school, Joey replied, "Not so good, Doc." When I asked what he meant by that, he responded, "It's my handwriting, just my handwriting, same ole thing. My teacher, Mrs. Bailey, she says she can't read nothin' I write." I asked, "Well, Joey, what are you doing about it?" The boy reported in a slow, almost fatherly voice, "Well, Doc, I did what I needed to do. I had a long, long talk with her. I told her, Mrs. Bailey, you know my granddaddy wrote like that, and my daddy writes just like that, and I been writin' like that since I been six years old. Mrs. Bailey, in my family, that's as good as it gits." Joey was pleading for the weighty influence of genetic factors. With all due respect to Joey, genes are powerful but they don't prevent us from working on our weak spots, especially if we decide they're worth working on.

Family Life and Stress Level   Billy's family has been so overwhelmed with financial, marital, and other domestic problems that his mother has not been able to help him with schoolwork. She complains, "I have all I can do to get by, to earn some money, to keep our place looking decent, to feed the kids the right food, and to make sure the dogs get some exercise." She herself had a hard time in school and never got through ninth grade. Billy has no interest in school and derives little if any positive feeling from learning. Clearly when families feel as if they are buried beneath the stresses and strains of daily existence, it may be hard to foster a stimulating intellectual life through shared experiences and high-level discussions at the dinner table regarding current events. Cassandra's is a very different story. Cassie (to her friends) has a mother who is a dermatologist and a father who's a trial judge. At home there are frequent discussions about the world of ideas. Both parents love to read. They value their intellectual life and share it abundantly with their only daughter. They have infected their daughter with intellectual curiosity. Cassie excels academically and has an unquenchable thirst for new knowledge. Contrast her with Billy. Socioeconomic realities exert powerful influences on a child's development. Poverty has its risks, as does being overprivileged and overindulged. The neighborhood, the community, and local resources of many different kinds impinge upon a mind's evolving strengths and deficits.

Cultural Factors   Suzie comes from a family recently emigrated from Hong Kong. Her family has always had a very powerful work ethic dating back generations. All of her Chinese friends share the same background, one that takes education seriously. Suzie comes home from school and works for four to six hours without a break. She assumes that this is the way people are, even though her classmates are out playing volleyball and planning the weekend's parties. Suzie's neurodevelopmental capacities keep on getting stretched, perhaps even stretched to the limit. She has developed extraordinary powers of concentration and can exert mental effort whenever she needs to. Her teacher has marveled at Suzie's tenacity, as he comments, "This girl is the ultimate plugger. She won't give up ever until what she has produced is of the highest quality no matter how long it takes her." Her flawless honor grades testify to this. A student's cultural background may help determine which neurodevelopmental strengths get stronger and which ones do not. In some cultural settings athletic prowess is considered valuable; in others, sports are deemed trivial pastimes. Whether or not a teenager reads novels, does crossword puzzles, repairs jeeps, attends Italian opera, engages in household chores, or hunts white-tailed deer vividly reflects the culture in which he or she is growing up. These activities, in turn, profoundly influence a child's profile of strengths and weaknesses.

Friends   Christian has pretty much stopped doing any schoolwork. In ninth grade, he is very popular. Most of his friends feel that homework completion is not cool; rather it's a pursuit designed exclusively for geeks, dorks, and other weirdos. Christian, who savors his popularity like a rare vintage Burgundy, has caved in to the social pressure and is failing several subjects. According to his father, "My kid has been lost to his friends. They're all he cares about. I feel as if he has fled from our family and cares only for the approval of his peers. He performs for his friends like a puppet; he'll do whatever it takes to win their applause. And he's with kids who live only in the present. They couldn't care less about school and about their minds."

Friends play a dominant role in shaping the brains of their friends. Children who have no intellectual interests become negative role models for one another. Learning and succeeding in school may be perceived as some kind of social taboo. On the other hand, I have one patient, a thirteen-year-old boy from New York, whose friends and he have a strong interest in politics. They worked on a local campaign last summer and are incessantly talking politics, discussing editorials in the *New York Times*, and debating raging political issues. He told me they consider themselves "local political dissidents," as their views are pretty radical. In the meantime, they are developing extraordinary language, critical thinking, and reading ability, bolstering their minds' profiles. Their parents are in awe of these boys and girls. One mother confessed, "Half the time I don't even understand what they're talking about, but it sure sounds impressive—and a little intimidating. I love listening to them. I'm proud of them all. I think they are becoming the leaders of the future. They are really lucky to have each other and we parents are so fortunate to have them as our children."

Health   Deanna suffered a bad case of viral meningitis when she was fourteen months old. Following her illness she developed a seizure disorder, one that has been difficult to control ever since. She is delayed in reading and math. There is a strong suspicion that her medical history played a role in weakening certain neurodevelopmental functions important for acquiring basic skills. Deanna has noticeable gaps in language function and in certain parts of her memory, and she becomes frustrated in school. Her older sister, Beth, worries about her all the time. She always accompanies Deanna when she comes to see me in my office. Beth informed me once, "Deanna really feels dumb. Between her seizures and her trouble at school she feels like she just can't do anything right. I feel so bad for her." Numerous medical factors either foster or impede brain development during the school years. Nutrition, certain illnesses, and physical trauma all may play a role in the shaping of a profile.

Emotions   Geraldine has been depressed all year. Her parents got a divorce, she broke up with her boyfriend, and her grandmother died last summer. Her mother and father feel guilty, as they worry they have damaged their daughter permanently. Geraldine feels sad much of every day. She's lost interest in school; her grades show it. Students with anxiety or depressed feelings often lose all interest and become inhibited about performing in school, which then begins to stunt their academic and neurodevelopmental growth. Geraldine has closed her mind to new learning during a period of school in which kids ordinarily develop their ability to absorb and think about highly abstract terms such as creationism, symbolism, altruism, and imperialism. If her mind stays absent from school, this important growth spurt in higher-order thinking may fail to take place. Emotions and neurodevelopmental functions are like a two-way street: emotional problems may weaken the functions and weakened functions can cause emotional turmoil.

Educational Experience   Arturo had been in first- and second-grade classrooms in which there were forty-two students with one teacher and only an occasional aide. His parents are utterly frustrated. His mom complained to me at a conference where I spoke, "Arturo is lost, totally lost in that school. He's the kind of kid who doesn't make trouble for anyone but you might not even notice he's around. And he'll never ask for help. He pretends he does understand when he doesn't get it half the time. But the school's so big; they don't see that he's getting nowhere. I'm so nervous about him." Arturo's reading instruction was inadequate, and he fell further and further behind in math as well. Now in sixth grade he remains seriously delayed and has lost his drive, having given up on himself. He is starting to get some individualized help, which is just beginning to make a difference in his performance and his self-esteem. Hopefully, it's not too late. The quality of a child's teaching most certainly affects his or her mind profile. In fact, recent studies using sophisticated brain scans have shown vividly that good instruction can actually result in positive changes in brain structure. It is possible to see increases in brain tissue when parts of the brain get properly stimulated after having been neglected. Also, a child's educational track record profoundly affects motivation, as kids like Arturo, who have failed over and over again in the past, may be sapped of motivation and sink even further into failure. Success, on the other hand, has a way of breeding more success.

All of these forces interact to produce the profile of a nine-year-old child or an adult as seen in Figure 2-2.

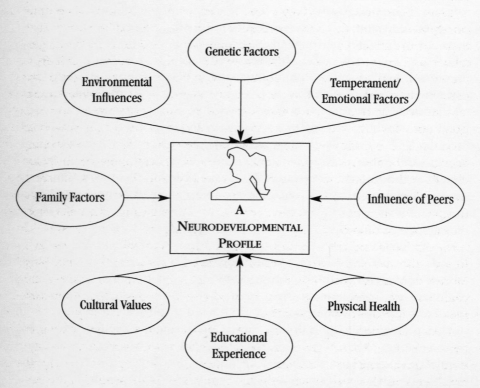

Figure 2-2.   The multiple forces determining a child's neurodevelopmental profile.

ᔰ How Lifestyles May Affect Learning Styles

Increasingly over the years, I've heard a succession of mothers, fathers, and educators grumble about contemporary children's ways of life and all the ways in which those ways of life are "dumbing them down." A middle school English teacher voiced her concerns as follows: "I feel I'm at a real disadvantage. The students I teach have spent so much of their lives on couches watching sitcoms and violent videos, all of which require negligible concentration, have only sparse details and no implications or hidden meanings in them, and resolve nearly instantaneously any conflicts in their trite plots. How can I then expect my kids to come in here and delay their gratification to wade through *A Tale of Two Cities* or write a creative short story of their own? So many of their brains are just plain out of shape for what I think they need to be doing, and even enjoying, in my English class." I had to agree. Rapidly paced entertainment can make school content seem like a colossal bore!

I have been finding in all my clinical work that many aspects of contemporary life can stunt the growth of key neurodevelopmental functions. First, there are the effects of all the electronic experiences children and teenagers take in and savor. Television is the most well established culprit. Aside from the violence that may model impulsive, acting-out behaviors, there is the passivity involved in watching most TV programs. Inactive information uptake while lying on your back and consuming buttery popcorn eclipses opportunities for creative thinking, brainstorming, and the development of products and hobbies—all more active and proactive mind-strengthening activities. For the most part, television shows offer stimulation in small chunks without much call for sustained attention and deep concentration. At times I think certain television shows serve as models of attentional dysfunction for their young viewers. Canned laughter during situation comedies is a major offender in my opinion and should probably be banned as a form of intellectual child abuse! Imagine being told when something is funny—the ultimate affront to language processing and higher thinking. Moreover, the verbal content of television tends to be woefully unsophisticated, and the stress is very much on vivid visual imagery rather than complex language use or interpretation.

Unsophisticated language is also a feature of much of the music that interests children. There was a time when a composer would hire a lyricist, a kind of poet, to fashion the words to his music. Lyricists are now mainly unemployed, as the person who creates the melody also produces the language accompaniment, which is often grammatically and semantically impoverished, simply everyday language rather than language that plays on words and cleverly turns a phrase. Thus, music no longer reinforces verbal abilities. Also, much of the music to which children are exposed tends to make use of very brief themes or melodic lines, which keep on coming back monotonously. As a result, the ability to retain patterns in memory is not strengthened through music (as I believe it once was).

Electronic games have also taken their toll, although sometimes they have a positive effect on eye-hand coordination and spatial ordering. Unfortunately the latter capacities do not make an enormous contribution to a child's intellectual development. One of my patients, a nine-year-old boy, let me know, "I love my games more than anything else. I hate to read because it's not as exciting and fun. I can beat all my friends and my big brother even when it's a new game. I would play all day and skip school if I could. That would be neat. When I grow up, I want to be a game designer."

Use of the Internet is a mixed blessing. On the one hand, leaning to surf the Internet for specific bits of information can become a powerful research skill. However, some students have made use of Web sites to download information without really understanding or integrating it. Thus, the process runs the risk of becoming a new mode of passive learning or perhaps even a way of acquiring plagiarizing skills.

Family life can also deter mind development. When families feel overwhelmed, life can be nothing short of frenetic at home. As one mother told me, "We barely see each other. We're always on the run or getting ready for some major event. I can't remember the last time we sat down and had a decent dinner table conversation. In fact, with my job and my husband's job, and all the kids' activities, most nights we don't even eat together." That makes it hard for family life to reinforce communication skills, doesn't it? The lack can be even more pronounced among the many single-parent families whose daily lives can be even more logistically consumed with little or no time for any mind-enhancing reflection and discussion. Frazzled lifestyle patterns can also cost something in terms of children's nutrition. Skipping breakfast, overindulging in convenient junk foods, and becoming addicted to empty calories of various sorts may be taking a hidden toll on brain development and mental energy.

Nightlife is yet another potential invader. I find that kids are orienting increasingly toward nighttime pleasures, often getting to sleep late and having trouble functioning in school the next day. TV, the Internet, social life, e-mail, instant messaging, and a multitude of other thrilling forms of nocturnal experience make homework and other educationally useful activities seem like impositions or chores to get over with as expeditiously as possible. And students who rush through their work derive little intellectual benefit or stimulation from it. As one mother recently exclaimed over the phone, "I'm not surprised he's having trouble staying awake in class, the kid's up until 2:00 A.M. listening to music, watching TV, and doing his instant messaging, and if we're lucky, rushing through his homework at the last second." I think that mother's right. Suddenly, more and more kids are becoming night people. What used to be the downtime of the day has now become for so many children the most stimulating and distracting interlude.

I sometimes refer to a state of mind (or body) that I call "visual-motor ecstasy." In this form of nirvana kids seem to derive excessive pleasure from the movement of their bodies through space. Activities such as skateboarding, Rollerblading, driving a car fast, or even skiing can become obsessive experiences for some kids. These are all nonverbal activities that are certainly good as somewhat mindless forms of entertainment, but they become hazardous to mind health when they are pursued in excess to the exclusion of learning. An excessive interest in sports may also qualify as a form of visual-motor ecstasy.

Contemporary culture values visual appearance, perhaps too much. Lots of students become preoccupied with their bodies and their physical appearance. As one father noted, "I can't believe it, my eleven-year-old son spends what seem like hours in the morning inspecting himself in the mirror and making all sorts of minor adjustments to his appearance, like making sure his dirty blue jeans and torn T-shirt look just right. I wish he'd expend that much time and energy on his homework."

Lifestyle issues also arise when a child becomes overly programmed. Schools that are highly and tightly structured so that there is little time for original thinking can short-circuit brainstorming in students. This is especially the case when a child is also heavily laden with scheduled activities after school and on weekends. One girl complained to me, "I have no free time at all. It's as if I'm in the army. Every day, I have to report somewhere at some time to do something I'm not sure I want to do or need to do. I keep wishing I had nothing to do." I think having nothing to do is plenty to do. I always admire kids who can entertain themselves for hours on end; that is an important strength, often the forerunner of creativity and resourcefulness.

Millions of teenagers have jobs after school, often for more than twenty hours a week. Frequently, these jobs entail little or no mind work. A cashier at a supermarket uses a scanner to do the math work and has only repetitious, rather undemanding verbal exchanges (e.g., "Paper or plastic?") for hours on end. A working student may be more likely to give homework short shrift and find school an irritant if he is trying to make money and save up for a car. It looks as if these kids should be working somewhat less than twenty hours a week if that's economically feasible.

Adolescence is also the time when kids are most prone to the effects of drugs and alcohol, both of which can have negative effects on brain growth and development. Teenagers need to be made aware of such risky addictions.

Clearly, there are plenty of kids who grow up in our contemporary culture with all its potential sidetracks and hidden traps yet thrive in school and go on to develop great kinds of minds. On the other hand, I have met so many others with subtle or not so subtle learning difficulties whose weaknesses have been further weakened as a direct result of some negative lifestyle forces such as the ones I have enumerated. In some instances students who have been frustrated in school seek refuge in intellectually void pursuits as they try to escape from the pain of their educational wounds. In all likelihood, television, visual-motor ecstasy, a strong interest in appearance, as well as the other distractions I have mentioned, are pretty benign until they start to occupy too much of a kid's time and focus, to the exclusion of essential mind-cultivating experience. That means that as parents you have an obligation to keep things in check, to gauge whether a cultural phenomenon is somehow out of control and then to make the critical adjustments. Contemporary lifestyles are desirable in moderation.

ᔕ SPLITTING RATHER THAN LUMPING

I've noticed that the people who study or work with kids can be divided into lumpers and splitters. I must confess to being a splitter, quite possibly a terminal case. That is to say, I am steadfastly unwilling to lump children into categories and then assume that all members of each category are pretty much alike. To the contrary, to me kids have more differences than resemblances. In fact, every time I meet a child in my office, I encounter some phenomenon that I have never seen before in any other child. Each kid unrolls an original mural of mind traits. The challenge is to understand his or her special wiring and its implications for parenting, counseling, and educating.

In *A Mind at a Time* I will advocate and demonstrate an approach that stresses close observation and accurate description instead of lumping kids together in a category (such as ADD). Teachers, parents, and even the children themselves need to be able to observe, talk about, and work with profiles. They need to locate those trouble spots where facets of a profile don't mesh with facets of school. In this way, we can understand what's blocking the way when a child is stymied.

The identification and celebration of strengths may well be even more important. I believe that when your child has strengths that are suppressed, abilities he is prevented from using while growing up, he becomes a virtual time bomb primed for detonation. Gerard was a fourteen-year-old from a small town in North Carolina. He was short and razor thin and looked more like ten than fourteen. Gerard harbored neurodevelopmental dysfunctions in language, memory, and his attention, but had brilliant mechanical problem-solving abilities, along with strong social skills. Nevertheless, he was in serious jeopardy in ninth grade. Gerard was a discipline problem. He often tried to act defiant, ultra-cool, and tough in class, probably to conceal his physical immaturity and academic humiliation. There were multiple charges against him, including that he would not remove his jacket in English class, chewed gum (a school felony), mumbled offensive language in front of his teachers, refused to "suit up" for physical education (protecting his undeveloped body from peer scrutiny), insisted on wearing his baseball cap permanently, and sported lewdly suggestive T-shirts. He had stopped submitting homework, and his report cards were saturated with acerbic moral condemnations.

Gerard's father was the manager of a service station. He commented to me that on weekends Gerard would come to work with him. He stated that Gerard "is no problem at all when he's with me on Saturdays and Sundays. In fact, that kid's the best worker I have. Folks come in and ask for Gerard when their car breaks down. That little guy can stick his blond head under a hood and figure out almost anything that's wrong, and you know, he never studied cars. He just senses how things work and why they don't work. He's got common sense but no book sense. I was just like him when I was young. He also has the best people skills, the best sense of humor. And he's real kind to everyone. Everybody wants to talk to Gerard. You know that boy has all he needs to be a successful grown-up, but to tell you the truth, I doubt I'm ever gonna get him there."

Gerard's mechanical aptitude and people skills were not valued or even recognized in his high school. But then Gerard's father had a brainstorm. He heard about a vocational school in the next town. Overcoming all kinds of red tape and bureaucratic barriers, he managed to get Gerard into that school for tenth grade. Gerard flourished in the auto mechanics class, but interestingly he started to make extraordinary gains in English and in math. In eleventh grade his terrific people skills got him elected to the student government. Now in twelfth grade, he recently told me, "This is a great school. I really fit in. I love cars, but I don't think I want to be a 'wrenchy' type forever. Someday I'm planning to design cars or be some kind of a sports car dealer." Gerard is finding his niche, and that is making all the difference. Discovering a place for your kind of mind, a place where your profile can thrive, almost always works wonders. Sadly, vocational schools, such as the one Gerard has been attending, are not as prevalent as they once were. This shortage discriminates against great minds like Gerard's. As his father relates, "This boy would be in jail now if he couldn't practice his specialty in school. He's so happy and so are we."

✌ The Early Detection of Dysfunction

It is a commonly held belief that the earlier you detect and deal with your child's dysfunctions, the more likely you are to prevent disastrous behavioral complications. I believe there is some truth to that. It might seem odd, therefore, that this book deals exclusively with school-aged children rather than beginning with infancy. In part, this is because my expertise is limited to school-aged children and adolescents. Additionally, so many of the neurodevelopmental functions needed for learning cannot be assessed until they are called for in school. Problems with memory, with time management, with the understanding of abstract language, along with hundreds of other breakdowns in learning are just not detectable until kids are actually attending school. As the demands keep changing, learning differences can and do crop up for the first time at all grade levels from kindergarten through the final year of college. I'm bothered by the fact that some academicians, policy makers, and early educators have maintained that if you don't fix a learning problem before age six, it will be impossible to deal with later on. This assertion is false. As we shall see, even adults can show remarkable improvement in one or more of their neurodevelopmental systems. It's never too late to understand and strengthen a mind.

✌ Some Adult Implications

Although this book concentrates on neurodevelopmental variation during the school years, any reader is likely to perceive its implications for adults. In fact, I daresay no one will be able to read this book without feeling as if he's gazing into a mirror while encountering the descriptions of individuals who struggle with the features of their wiring. The very same dysfunctions that trip up so many children often snare unsuspecting adults—in their careers, in their avocations, and in their functioning within families. Here are three examples:

Donna is a middle school principal. She is an efficient manager and a popular leader among the kids and teachers. But she has serious problems with public speaking. She chokes up and often feels she makes a fool of herself at PTA and school board meetings. As a student in school, she had always been very quiet. She doesn't realize she is battling a lifelong problem with her own wiring; Donna has serious difficulty transforming her ideas into words and sentences. She has timely things to say and excellent insights into key issues, but finding words and constructing sentences are painful brain activities for her. She suspects her problem is "just anxiety," but her apprehension is justified when it comes to oral presentations. As she puts it, "I get so uptight when I have to speak in public. My ideas come out sounding too simple or even distorted. Yet I can write well and I do just fine talking slowly in a conversation. But I can't find words fast and organize my thoughts when I give a speech, and that's a real problem in my job, especially since I'd like to be a superintendent someday."

Kathleen is a young CPA who entered her father's accounting firm last year. An only child in a closely knit loving family, she chose this career mainly to please her parents (something she had always sought to do). But her work has been uniformly poor, disappointing, and exasperating, especially for her dad. She consistently reveals her superb social and communication skills and is richly creative and affably energetic, but Kathleen is hopelessly distractible and tends to rush through every assignment she undertakes, often leaving behind a hazy cloud of careless mistakes and gaping oversights. She possesses the kind of mind that favors and savors the big picture while often glossing over smaller points. Her brain just abhors minute details, such as the ones on an accountant's spreadsheets. Kathleen is wired for conceptualizing, creating, and theorizing. She probably should not be a CPA, but she doesn't seem to understand and perceive the career implications of her brain's characteristics. Her remarkable strengths are going untapped. She is now showing classic signs of depression and says that her "everyday existence feels so meaningless and aimless."

Brad loved orthopedic surgery in medical school. He had always been a sports fanatic, and the lure of sports medicine as a career enticed him to endure medical school (which was tedious and difficult for him). He is now an orthopedic resident. Sadly, he has been totally incompetent, possibly hazardous, in the operating room. No one can fathom it; he was such a motivated medical student. It turns out that this bright guy lacks the spatial perception and nonverbal problem-solving skill (a form of mechanical aptitude) needed to function as a skilled orthopedic surgeon. He is struggling with an all too common insidious plight, namely the chaotic career of a person whose interests don't coincide with the wiring of his particular kind of mind. Brad is in pursuit of what he's unlikely to succeed at. He's unaware of this risky discrepancy. He has found no channel for his many assets. The chief of orthopedic surgery has recommended that he leave the department because of "persistent incompetence as a clinician."

Each of these individuals is highly capable. Each has a niche out there somewhere they can fit into. None of the three has much understanding of her or his profile, of its lack of fit with current demands. The cost of their lack of insight will be high for these three bright and motivated people. They have lots of company. There are countless highly competent people who contend with the same sorts of poor fit without knowing it. They would be on the road to recovery if only they could see clearly the mismatch of their occupations with their minds.

Now over the next seven chapters of *A Mind at a Time*, I will elaborate on the eight neurodevelopmental systems and the potent ways in which they affect lives.

3

Conducting a Mind ♪

Our Attention Control System

Darwin confessed that his brain was not constructed for much thinking and wisely gave up the attempt to use it for pursuance of his special subjects for more than an hour or so at a time. Had he not done so, much of his invaluable work might never have seen the light. If a man of Darwin's gigantic intellect found it impossible to concentrate his attention for any lengthy period without fatigue, surely allowance should be made for children who doubtless suffer as he did. Yet bright intelligent children are often expected to concentrate their attention for many hours at a time, and when they fail are regarded as simply lazy.

LEONARD G. GUTHRIE, *Functional Nervous Disorders in Childhood* (1909)

BEVERLY Samson, a mom who plays first viola in a prominent symphony orchestra, is in acute distress and exclaims during a phone call to me regarding her ten-year-old James, "His brain is like an out-of-control orchestra, full of the best, greatest, and most talented players, but there's no conductor. Different musicians in his mind just go off and play their own melodies without paying any attention to the score. There's absolutely no harmony, and no melody ever reaches its fanfare. Even though my James is never at a loss for brilliant thoughts, he accomplishes almost nothing, especially when it comes to schoolwork."

Mrs. Samson's analogy was fitting, for our minds are conducted very much like large musical groups. The performing brain systems are akin to the parts of an orchestra: the language, memory, and sequencing sections, when combined with the spatial section, are capable of melodious and precise harmony, but they require talented leadership with a mental baton, a competent mind conductor. The conducting of a child's mind is assigned to a team of brain functions I and my colleagues call the attention controls. From resisting the temptation to stare out the window while your teacher is talking to making sure you've zipped up your fly before heading for the bus, attention manages so much, from life's little details to its major priorities. Therefore, weaknesses of attention, or inadequate brain leadership, can have widespread unfortunate, embarrassing, and troublesome effects. Mrs. Samson, commenting further on James, pointed out, "If I don't keep an eye on things, he'll go charging off to school wearing two different-colored socks with his pants pretty much sliding down his hips because he forgot to put his belt on, and his lunch bag left abandoned on the kitchen floor." This is a kid who, like so many others, through no fault of his own, has poorly calibrated attention controls. If parents observed closely they might notice that their child was phasing in and out of focus and carrying out way too many actions at a frenetic rate or without much thought. Mrs. Samson picked up on this: "James is basically a kid on alternating current. He tunes in and tunes out all day like a flickering candle. There are times when I just have to hold him and speak directly into one of his ears to get him to connect with something I'm trying to tell him."

When the attention controls operate as they're supposed to, they help a student learn, they help her become productive, and they help her behave appropriately. She can pay close attention in class and think through the best way to solve a math problem instead of just impulsively initiating the first thing that crosses her mind. The results are gratifying. On the other hand, dysfunctions of the attention controls often lead to chaos in the learning process and also in the daily life of a family. As James describes it, "I just keep messin' up, and then everyone gets real mad at me, I mean real mad— like my teacher and my mom and my dad and all. It's like I do things and I do them so fast that later on I can't believe what I did—happens all the time. Like the time I threw that paper plane and it hit Miss Taylor right in the face. I didn't even think she might turn around by the time the plane got to her. But she did. I was in deep trouble, but that was nothing new." Luckily, children who struggle with their attention controls often possess some remarkable redeeming traits we can't afford to overlook. James is great at imaginary play and loves to design and build kites (to say nothing of misguided aircraft). He's also a funny storyteller and an articulate speaker.

Patterns of weak attention control vary from kid to kid; let's look at two typical stories as seen in two otherwise quite different patients of mine, Clark and April. They will then follow us around during this chapter.

Clark is a dreamer and a schemer. This nine-year-old with wavy blond

hair and freckle-spangled cheeks appears to be powered by internal turbines with inexhaustible boosters and seemingly limitless energy reserves.
Clark detonates his fuel surplus to create excitement at the drop of a hat.
One night he spread thick wads of multicolored toothpaste on his sister's
aqua bedsheets. Recently he transformed a family heirloom plate into a flying saucer (witnessing its shattering crash landing during this maiden
launch). Clark has succeeded in causing an uproar with his suggestive commentaries regarding the body contours of his older brother's girlfriend,
statements candidly broadcast in her presence. I couldn't possibly count the
number of times his mother called me to report Clark's latest unplanned and
misguided adventure or uncouth comment.

Clark is a child I respect greatly despite his aggravating antics. This guy is
well stocked with neurodevelopmental assets. He tantalizes us with his
mind's strengths while letting us down when it comes to his unpredictable
day-to-day behavior and productivity. No doubt about it, Clark marches to
the beat of his own drummer—for the most part, pretty much out of step
with the rest of us!

Clark is impulsive. This is fairly typical of many kids I meet with weak attention controls. They don't intend to be bad; actually, they are not at all
bad. But they annoy their embattled parents as well as their brothers and
sisters. That is because they lack the controls needed to slow down and
think about consequences before they do something. His mom once
pointed out to me, "Clark is forever going with the first thing that comes into
his mind—whether or not it's right to do it—and mostly it's not. It's as if he
has no choice. When a very bad notion pops up on his screen, he either
says it or does it instantaneously, and that gets him into serious hot water
much too often."

Clark harbors another trait found in many kids with weak attention controls; he is insatiable, aloft in an often-frenzied quest for stimulation, entertainment, new playthings, and golden opportunities to provoke excitement.
When conditions are blissfully placid on the home scene, Clark's mind steps
up and volunteers to get things going, to stir the pot, to cook up some stimulating feuding. When he thinks back, Clark regrets his family felonies. As a
result, in many respects Clark isn't very happy being Clark. Then too, his
parents aren't all that happy about being Clark's parents. They do love
him—very much. But a lot of times they don't like him.

This boy can be very kind. And I identify with his sensitivity regarding all
living things. He is exceptionally empathetic, and feels compassionately for
all creatures. He insists on rescuing spiders before his mother can obliterate
their webs. Clark will reach out to any kid in school who appears anguished
or frustrated. Clark has recently befriended a new girl in his class who is se-

riously developmentally disabled and hearing-impaired, helping her with lunch every day. I think Clark would make a super pediatrician.

Clark has a way with words and is a skillful sketcher with a pencil or a piece of chalk. At his young age he is creating comic strips about outer space heroes. His valued works adorn the yellow cinder-block walls of Springdale Elementary and are prominently featured at home as well. Sometimes, however, his images are found where they're not supposed to be, as Clark seems to have a natural affinity for graffiti.

Clark is a fast and accurate reader and speller. When he comes to my office, his backpack contains his current bundle of science fiction tomes, which he likes to share with me. His math work is adequate but not outstanding; he generally understands all the concepts but overlooks the details (plus signs, minus signs, and the like) in his rush to finish an assignment. It is common for kids with attentional problems to succeed with big ideas but have trouble dealing with little but critical details. Clark personifies the word "erratic" when it comes to submitting homework. Either he forgets to do it or he just can't get his body secured to a desk chair at home. This pattern is yet another common finding among those with weak attention controls.

Clark's teachers have become fed up with his behavior, but they are impressed by his insights and original creations. His parents are equally ambivalent. It isn't easy parenting Clark. The attention they've had to devote to Clark has hurt their marriage and caused them to neglect some important needs of their other two children. "Clark is like a full-time job," says his dad. "You feel you have to keep an eye on him all the time, and he seems to want you to. I've never met anyone who thrives on constant attention the way he does."

His peers enjoy Clark's antics and love to laugh with him, but he has no close friends and doesn't get invited to birthday parties. Like any number of others with attentional problems, this boy's lack of self-control ultimately is repellent to other children. Also, when he's with them, Clark insists on being in charge at all times; he demands to be the star of the show. That goes along with his insatiability, which the other children resent.

Clark is starting to learn about his attentional difficulties. He is beginning to recognize that these traits are not his fault, but that he definitely needs to work on them, to get them into better shape. He has been studying the attention controls and talking about techniques he might use to get more in control. For example, when his teacher gives instructions, Clark whispers them back to himself so he can be sure he is listening carefully enough. He also tries to go back over all his work to check for errors and plan his tasks ahead of time. He consciously asks himself, "What's the best way to do this?" or "Is this the best thing to do now?" before undertaking an activity. As Clark told me, "It's not easy and sometimes I forget, but I'm trying to look before I leap." He is beginning to perceive the negative impact he is having on teachers and classmates. He is also coming to understand how being out of control is making him feel unhappy, especially because other kids are starting to reject him. In order to improve his rapidly deteriorating self-esteem, we are helping Clark discover and make better use of his impressive strengths.

Now here's the tale of another child who struggles with the attention controls. April is fourteen and, like Clark, experiences problems with her attention. Like Clark she is refreshingly original, enticingly offbeat in her ways of thinking. She is petite and wears wire-rimmed spectacles, conveying an appealingly delicate, fragile image. Over the last three years, I've gotten to know her very well. This girl positively grows on you. Her parents find her a true delight. She is not at all a behavior problem in school or at home, and she enjoys plenty of enduring friendships. Although her serious gaps in attention impede her academic performance, they don't impair her behavior or her social life. She does not show the impulsivity and insatiability that Clark does.

April suffers from another problem, one all too common in kids with weak attention controls: writing is especially hard for her. Torture is a more accurate word for it. Despite good ideas, very nice handwriting, and fluent language, her written output is labored and seriously flawed. Writing is often a seemingly insurmountable threat to kids with attention problems, as it takes strong attention controls to conduct the orchestra needed to express thoughts on paper. You have to slow down, plan, organize your thinking, pace yourself, watch what you're putting on paper, and pay attention to all kinds of small details all at once (such as punctuation, spelling, capitalization, and use of grammar). These demands can be tough for those with weak attention controls. Writing is one of the largest orchestras a kid's mind has to conduct.

When April starts to write she feels overwhelmed. So she writes as little as she can get away with (and sometimes even less than she can get away with). She is often accused of being lazy and irresponsible. She isn't lazy at all. April once explained to me, "Whenever I try to write, I lose my ideas and I get all mixed up about them. Then when I see what I'm writing, it's all a big mess, and the ideas that come out are not the ones from my head. They look babyish and stupid. Then I'm afraid one of my friends will see what I wrote or my teacher will show it to everyone or my parents will get real mad and say I wasn't even trying. I hate to write." We are helping April to do her writing in stages, so first she brainstorms her ideas into a tape recorder, then takes a break, then writes down key ideas, takes another break, then organizes her ideas in the best order, then, after another break, writes a draft without worrying about neatness, spelling, or punctuation (these details will be added later). Using a computer for writing has been good for April; she likes to type fast and then go back and correct her mistakes, which are pointed out to her by the computer's word processing program.

In class April is a light sleeper. She regularly tunes out and misses salient information. She often looks as if she suffers from a crippling case of battle fatigue, which is due in part to the fact that she has a difficult time falling and staying asleep at night. Often she doesn't get to bed until 2:00 A.M.; even then her slumber is fitful. Problems regulating sleep and staying alert during the day are a common occurrence in kids with insufficient attention control. We call this a sleep-arousal imbalance. With advice from her pediatrician, she is trying to get into bed at the same time each night with white noise in the background. She reads as she tries to relax and doze off. If these measures don't work, she may need to take some medication for a few months in order to get a better night's sleep. There is a clear relationship in all of us between the quality and quantity of sleep and performance in school or at work the next day. April's sleep problems have taken their toll.

April's teachers comment on how erratic and unpredictable she is. There are days when she functions perfectly well, while on other occasions, she appears totally spaced out and unable to concentrate. Recently, during one of her off days, April commented, "This is one of those times when I've got the wrong lens on my brain. Everything seems blurry and fuzzy. It's like I don't hear what the teacher is saying, even though the sounds are coming at me. And I feel as if I'm half asleep when that happens. But that doesn't happen all the time. Sometimes I'm great at listening. I don't miss anything. But I never know when I go to school in the morning whether I'm going to have a bad listening day or not. That's a little scary, I guess." As we saw in Clark's case, performance inconsistency is a source of constant confusion and anxiety to kids with attention deficits as well as the adults in their lives. As her mom once inquired with an air of bewilderment, "Why does she function so beautifully some of the time and so abysmally at other times?" That question keeps coming up with respect to minds that are inadequately controlled.

As these two cases so vividly demonstrate, the very same kids who suffer lack of attention control are often remarkable people in their own right, displaying refreshingly unorthodox pathways of thought. I believe these children are challenging types of human variation rather than deviation, so parents should never believe that their child with attention deficits is necessarily abnormal or pathological. This is one reason I resist applying the stigmatizing letters ADD or ADHD. There's more that's right than wrong with most of these kids. What a crime to assume simply that all of these kids are damaged goods and therefore are destined always to be defective. After many years working with these individuals, I am impressed with how many of them turn out to be extraordinary adults. We just have to help get them there.

Attention is at work throughout the waking day. Parents can see these controls operating as their child interacts with others, behaves appropriately, and takes on schoolwork and learning. These are all highly regulated activities in which a child, without realizing it, takes aim at some goals and accomplishes them in a nicely regulated, reasonably efficient manner. Such goals might range from doing a homework assignment to following the rules during a football game to acting in a friendly manner with a group of classmates on the playground. In the model that I and my colleagues have developed based on our clinical work and research done on the subject, these and scores of other assorted activities are guided by three forms of control: control over mental energy, control over intake (of information and various other stimuli), and control over output (of work and behavior). Although in this chapter I will be defining the very specific jobs done by each form of attention control, it's important to remember that these forms of control have to work closely together if a child is to succeed as a learner and make a reasonable behavioral and social adjustment during his school years. As we shall see, each of the three forms of attention control has within it a small team of neurodevelopmental functions that take on specific roles.

It is absolutely vital for parents and teachers to understand these three forms of attention control. Knowing how they work and when they're not up to par can enable you to be a much more effective educator or parent. Knowledge of these areas has been indispensable for me professionally as a pediatrician trying to help children savor success in their lives. So, one by one, let's explore the three forms of attention control.

✒ THE MENTAL ENERGY CONTROLS

You don't get something for nothing. Whether you are engaged in weeding a vegetable garden, running a marathon, or paddling a kayak down the rapids, you are burning lots of calories, so that you can generate enough physical energy to do the job. In recent years, we have learned about similar processes that regulate the energy required for thinking and controlling behavior. These basically sedentary activities also consume high levels of energy, namely mental energy, so that there is a need for a steady supply of

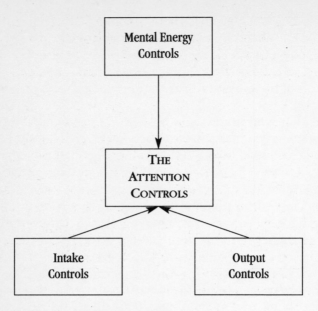

Figure 3-1.   The attention controls.

"fuel" to just the right regions of the brain at the right times. If your child is running for class treasurer and has to make a speech at an assembly this morning, he needs to have as much mental fuel as possible flowing to the language portion of his brain so that he can appeal to the yet undecided voters. What a waste it would be if way too much fuel was headed toward the visual-processing parts of his brain, so he kept looking out the window while he was speaking and therefore not really concentrating on what he was saying. That fuel supply not only must be delivered to the right parts of the brain at any moment, but also the flow has to continue long enough to get a job done. As a patient of mine once said, "My brain runs out of gas before I can finish my work; like when I try to do those stupid worksheets in math. I just sorta burn out. It's like my mind's got a dead battery or something. And I feel real tired and bored, so I just quit whatever I'm doing, even though it's not finished, and I find something new to do. Doing something new wakes me up." This boy was describing his losing battles over the control of mental energy, a campaign all children constantly engage in. Every one of them has trouble with it some of the time. Some have trouble with it too much of the time.

In controlling the flow of mental energy, attention makes use of four neurodevelopmental functions.

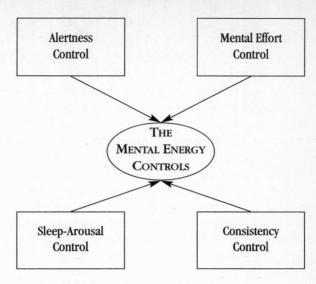

Figure 3-2.   The mental energy controls.

Alertness Control

Mental energy turns on and maintains your child's alertness. It enables a student to be vigilant in the classroom, to concentrate on important incoming information, to feel a sense of being engaged or tuned in during a school activity. It makes her or him a good listener—no minor asset. When mental energy is poorly controlled a child is likely to reveal a neurodevelopmental dysfunction affecting his ability to stay alert. Of course, even the most conscientious student may misplace his focus from time to time, lose interest, and experience intellectual brownouts, much like a big city during a serious energy crisis. Often when they try to concentrate, kids with attention control problems feel exhausted, as occurred in the case of April. Teachers commonly notice that some students show obvious signs of mental fatigue more often and with greater severity than do others. Their mental fatigue inevitably affects their learning as well as the quality of their schoolwork.

Kids who are having serious trouble sustaining alertness do not come home and proclaim to their parents, "I am having serious problems sustaining my level of alertness in the classroom." Rather, they announce (sometimes with smug pride), "School is boring."

It may seem odd, but many children react to their mental fatigue by becoming hyper. It is as if they have a need to substitute physical energy for their shortage of mental energy. As one mother put it, "My kid is sort of bizarre. He runs around all day, never slows down, and is always zooming like a torpedo. But I notice that he's yawning half the time. It's almost like he's racing all around so he can stay awake." She's right.

Nine-year-old Meg, who was referred to me at the suggestion of her principal, looks as if her joints have been replaced with mattress springs. She is a boundless bouncer. This agreeably agile but thoroughly distractible girl keeps yawning, fidgeting, and daydreaming while vital classroom information is being beamed to alert listeners. Fortunately, Mrs. Armstrong allows her to retreat strategically to the back of the room whenever confinement to a desk chair becomes unbearable for Meg. To help her meet the all-consuming need to discharge her surplus of physical energy, Meg is regularly assigned to run errands to the main office and other destinations. Instead of embarrassing Meg by calling on her when she's into her own wavelengths, Mrs. Armstrong has an inconspicuous way of tapping Meg's left shoulder as a way of resetting her alertness control. It works.

Mental Effort Control

It takes a lot of energy to do things you don't feel like doing! Attention control distributes and maintains the energy flow needed for a mind to get work done, to have the stamina to delay gratification and engage in thinking activities that are worthwhile and mentally demanding if not entertaining. Studying for a trigonometry test can be a lot of work; playing *Major Zappo and the Killer Zipper Zappers* on your video screen may be pure pleasure and demanding of virtually no mental energy. For some kids work seems to be too much work, while for others effort is effortless. Schools for generations have assigned effort grades (generally thinly disguised moral evaluations of their students). Such judgments are dubious distinctions, since we know there are some children for whom effort comes easily, in which case they should never be able to earn a commendable effort grade. Others, those for whom effort is almost insurmountably challenging, deserve strong effort grades when they put forth even a mini-erg of effort because that level of output is so difficult for them. Many children who are thought to be lazy are experiencing trouble generating and sustaining their mental effort. We should stop accusing them and start understanding and helping them develop ways of controlling their mental effort.

Homework is the classic challenge to mental effort. Being academically productive at home was a steep uphill battle for both Clark and April as it is for so many kids with attention deficits. Fierce and tense disputes over homework are waged regularly in many families. As they glare at the surface of a desk, some kids are overtaken with the paralyzing sensation that the effort demanded exceeds their brain's fuel reserves. But homework and studying also become the wellsprings for building greater mental effort capacity in all kids. Schools should teach kids how to learn, and parents should teach them how to work by establishing work rules and a work ethic at home. Many need help getting started with an assignment, a relatively distraction-free environment, and more frequent breaks.

Sleep-Arousal Control

A six-year-old boy can never seem to settle down at night; almost every evening he debates his worn-out parents about having to go to sleep at a reasonable hour as if he is appealing an unjust sentence. At bedtime he seems to have energy to spare, and his parents try to figure out how to burn off that excess. Much as they love time spent with their child, they really wouldn't mind having a little time to themselves. Unfortunately, he's raring to go when they're about ready to hit the sack.

The tight regulation of sleep and wakefulness is a crucial part of mental energy control. With it your child can fall asleep without too much difficulty and stay asleep through the night. He then is mentally energized for school. A good night's sleep (at least eight hours) is essential for optimal brain function in school. Some kids can't get the sleep they need and so come to school sleep-deprived, unable to operate mentally on all cylinders.

At the very base of the brain, in the brainstem, a kind of sleep thermostat permits our kids to wind down at bedtime. When that thermostat operates, a child's senses are quieted, allowing her to filter out ambulance sirens, dogs barking, and a neighbor's CD. At the same time, she can turn off any worry about what to wear to school tomorrow or whether she'll be invited to her friend's birthday party. By relaxing her mind, this little girl can experience friendly fatigue and drift into blissful somnolence. Then, the following morning, she rebounds at 6:30 A.M. and becomes sufficiently aroused and tuned into the day's events and stimuli. Her sleep-rejuvenated brain tones up and tunes in. She has achieved what I call healthy sleep-arousal balance.

Unfortunately, some kids, like April, have to contend with a sleep-arousal imbalance. Frequently children like her experience difficulty falling asleep at night. They tend to get far too little sound sleep on many a school night. And sometimes the slumber they do accumulate just isn't restful enough; their sleep is as turbulent as a bouncy airplane flight. Then the next day, much like April, their minds fail to operate on full throttle. They may display obvious mental fatigue and have a hard time concentrating on high-energy drainers such as lessons in grammatical construction. Often, to help these kids we have to intervene on the sleep side, trying various techniques to enable them to sleep more soundly, so that they can become more vigilant during their daylight hours.

Parents should not despair; some children with a sleep-arousal imbalance may turn out to be the next generation of night people. They may compose cello sonatas at 2:00 A.M., work the night shift at the BMW plant, or host an all-night radio rock show. Regrettably, during childhood, tomorrow's night owls are condemned to attend school with all the day kids. We don't yet offer night schools for night children.

Consistency Control

As we have noted, everyone has attentional difficulty some of the time. You have reason to be concerned when your child has trouble with his attention too much of the time and at moments that most call for control, such as when your adolescent is learning to drive a car. You may have a child for whom the flow of mental energy is just plain undependable or inconsistent; you never know if it will be there or not on any given day, at any given moment. Yet even those with the most severe attentional difficulties have periods when that energy appears to be flowing efficiently. Clark and April both live such puzzling lives of inconsistency. Ironically, their good times cause them grief by elevating the expectations of adults. But as Clark once exclaimed, "I have a real good brain, but it keeps having power failures! I sit in class and I'm really working and thinking the way I should, then whammo, another power outage in my head; it could last seconds or minutes or hours or days . . . who knows when the lights will go back on!"

Here's a typical scenario that affected April and stemmed from the misunderstanding of her performance inconsistency. On one particular Friday afternoon April recalled vividly that she took a mathematics quiz on which she succeeded with distinction. In fact, she scored higher than anyone else in her class. She paced herself nicely, worked accurately, checked her calculations, and came away with a stunning 99. The usually expressionless Mr. Rollins was visibly impressed. Sadly, he responded nearly vindictively: "Now we know she can do it. When April really sets her mind to it, she can get the work done. When she really tries, she can be successful." In the mind of her teacher, April's brief display of genius justified moral condemnation of prior and future bouts of inattention. He implied that all of the rest of the time she was guilty of not trying to do well, of not really putting in the effort.

Almost all kids with attention deficits manifest such disheartening performance inconsistency. Their erratic performance in life not only confuses everyone but brings on a heavy volley of unfair accusations, such as, "We know he can do the work, we've seen him do it. When he makes up his mind to succeed he can." Wrong! (Sometimes I feel like advising these oft misinterpreted children to be especially careful not to let anyone ever catch them doing something right, since it might well be held against them for-ever after.) If only parents and teachers would help children see that their inconsistency is not a crime but instead something they need to be working on. They could start to keep track of periods of good and poor performance and consciously try to increase the proportion of the time they are on target. Little by little (i.e., not overnight), they might then show greater consis-tency.

Performance inconsistency can extend well into adulthood. When it oc-curs among adults we call it "unreliability." "You can't really count on him. Sometimes he shows up and does an excellent job and then he may not even show up when you need him again. He is so undependable." In part as a result of their inconsistency, I have found that many of these kids come to the conclusion during adolescence that eventually they will need to be self-employed. They'll want and need to set their own hours.

I remember a young man I met during a visit to Putney, Vermont. He con-fided that he always had problems with his attention but that he has now come to terms with his challenging traits. He was living in the Green Moun-tains and constructing furniture. He boasted, "This furniture I make is first-rate. It is truly excellent. But I'll tell you one thing: there are lots of mornings when I get up and know for sure I'm not going to accomplish anything—so I go back to sleep. Other days I leap out of bed and feel fantastic, and I work for ten hours nonstop. I don't even have lunch. At the end of any month I've accomplished as much as anybody else around. But I have to work when I feel like working and I have to just chill out when I don't feel like working. If I had a regular job with a regular boss I would have been fired ages ago." Interestingly, that same kind of statement is made often by poets, sculptors, playwrights, and other immensely creative people who re-port that when they enter their studios in the morning, they may or may not have the mental energy to fuel their creative effort. That very same incon-sistency we fret over in some individuals actually may come bundled with a bunch of winning strengths. Ralph Waldo Emerson in his essay "Self-Reliance" noted, "I have never met a great man who wasn't inconsistent." Parents take note.

✌ THE INTAKE CONTROLS

Much information, both valuable and worthless, orbits around the minds of our kids in school. What are they supposed to do with it? How can they manage the daily data deluge? What needs to occur for a mind to choose the right information to process at the right time and then to concentrate deeply enough to extract some meaningful ideas and absorb enough of it? How does your child manage to arrive at an active enough state of mind to get the most out of what he's focused on? And how is he able to remain focused long enough to learn something but not so long that he becomes bogged down and can't switch over to the next relevant topic or activity? The answers to all these questions reside in part within the intake controls of attention, for it is their joint responsibility to prepare the mind for thinking, making the best use of available newly arrived or remembered facts, ideas, and experiences.

Five neurodevelopmental functions split the chores of intake control, as shown in Figure 3-3.

Selection Control

Jarring reverberating buzzers that seem nearly to break the sound barrier, irrelevant and irreverent comments from your friends, predictable cautions (or threats) from your teachers, and overstimulating bulletin boards blend together with far more cogent information during a typical day at school. Unconsciously, but with virtuous persistence, attention rapidly inspects all

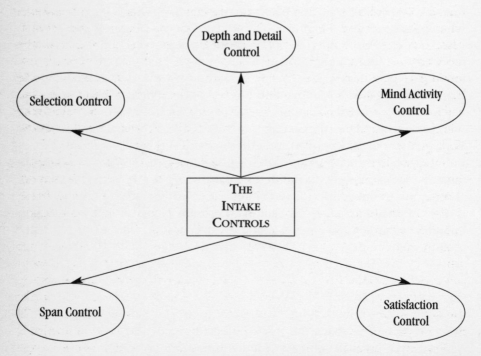

Figure 3-3.   The intake controls that regulate incoming information and other stimuli.

candidates for admission to the thinking brain, filters out and discards what it deems irrelevant, welcomes a chosen few stimuli into consciousness, and then invites the most timely and informative of these selections to penetrate deeply enough to be understood and/or remembered or else used right away.

Selection control disposes of worthless stimuli, such as the quiet hum of a fluorescent bulb or the mauve hue of your teacher's panty hose or totally irrelevant memories that may be competing for attention. Selection control does not actually interpret or put to use what we hear or see; it just picks out the very best items, the most important and currently relevant data. Selection control that works well is especially valuable in view of the fact that a mind has very little capacity from moment to moment for brand-new information. The entryway that leads to conscious awareness is narrow; space is limited. So selection control is obliged to be highly refined.

To succeed you need to focus on what can get you somewhere. A child falls behind in school when he can't seem to prioritize and concentrate on the most useful information rather than worthless trivia. Your daughter won't retain anything of value from that densely packed chapter on the Russian Revolution unless she can be selective and discriminate between what's important and what's not. There's no way she can remember all of it. Also, a distractible young scholar can't come close to absorbing all of the most critical information contained in an article while simultaneously attending to the whispers, the blue jeans, and the very cool guys that encircle her during a study hall. Therefore, there is a legitimate job for a reliable gatekeeper, for a selection process, for a way of determining which data will get welcomed into consciousness and which will be turned away at the door by the security guards of the input control system.

Some students have a hard time deciding on relative degrees of importance. Others focus on too many things at once. As Clark once lamented, "You know, my head is just like a TV set, but I have no remote control for it; so I get all the programs on my screen at the same time." I'm sure he does, and that makes for a rather noisy and cluttered mind.

Difficulty deciding what's important occurs at two levels. There are those who have trouble filtering out certain kinds of useless sensations or memories and those who focus on the right inputs but concentrate on the wrong aspects of those inputs. The former group are said to be distractible, while the latter suffer from problems with what I call "significance detection." I'll describe both of these patterns—don't be surprised if they sound familiar.

Some kids manifest predominantly visual distractibility. These happy wanderers pull into class in the morning and appear as if their heads are mounted on a very loose ball bearing or an unstable turret, as they are fever-only scanning their environment. Such a child comes up with the indisputable observation that there are three thumbtacks on the bulletin board, only two of which are being utilized at the moment. His keen sighting results in five minutes of internal speculation regarding the reasons for the underutilization of thumbtack three as well as its potential applications in the future. Meanwhile, some truly salient classroom information has been denied access at the borders of this boy's mind. One teacher in our educator training program, Schools Attuned, described a girl in her class as follows: "Sophia exasperates me. She is so bright, so very sparkling in her thinking, such a delight to have in class. But she's in her own world half the time. She stares out the window and makes me feel as if I'm competing with falling acorns, lawnmowers, and squirrels. I end up having to repeat instructions to her. I have to tell her to look me in the eye while I'm explaining something important. Even then she might be picturing the lawnmower."

Children prone to visual distractibility are likely to be reading the white area of a page rather than the black letters. But there's a silver lining; often their parents comment, "One thing about my kid, she sure is observant. She notices things no one else would notice and she sees relationships between stuff out there that no one else would ever think of." Visual distractibility may even have some relationship to creativity. It may be that many highly imaginative graphic artists "suffer from" visual distractibility. They absorb diverse stimuli and see novel patterns that other people would deem irrelevant or unworthy of scrutiny. Nonetheless, poor visual selection control gets in the way when you're supposed to be learning.

Quite a few children appear to have leaky auditory filters, so they encounter trouble screening out distracting sounds. All the wrong sounds seem to undergo amplification in their minds. One little girl, Ina, came to my office and listened intently as I was describing some social perils of fourth grade. In spite of her long history of attentional dysfunction, Ina seemed genuinely absorbed in what I was expounding. But after seeming to listen for a couple of minutes, she abruptly interrupted me and, nodding her head, said, "Yes, but there's one thing I don't understand." I said, "What's that, Ina?" She said, "I hear an air conditioner in here, but I just can't see it anyplace." During the entire period I thought Ina was listening to me, she was intently tuned into the ductwork of my office. This is typical of kids with attentional difficulties that include auditory distractibility. They overhear better than they hear. Such individuals may someday have a vital role in the CIA. Ina's mother actually mentioned that her daughter was a remarkably perceptive eavesdropper. Unfortunately, auditory distractibility erodes day-to-day classroom functioning. Ina, the future spy, was not much of a listener in school.

Tactile distractibility is yet another errant pathway. Some kids can't resist anything that can be touched or handled, including, regrettably, their peers. Their hands are in a steady state of digital exploration; they keep going off on finger safaris, having to make frequent tactile contact and satisfy their need to touch, as they progress from rubbing their nose, to feeling the undersurface of their desk, to grabbing a classmate, or curling and twirling their hair.

Some students are too easily lured off track by their own memories. A teacher may say something that reminds Clark of something that occurred last summer. So he concentrates on last summer instead of what the teacher is saying. Finally, there are also those who are distracted by the future. I remember a mother commenting to me, "If only Michael would concentrate as much on what he needs to do today as he does on what he's going to do this weekend, he'd be in great shape, but he just can't stop looking ahead all the time." A kindergarten teacher painted a vivid portrait of one five-and-a-half-year-old who would arrive at school in the morning and ask, "When's lunch?" and then follow that with a succession of future-oriented inquiries throughout the day, such as "When are we going out?" when they were inside and "When can we go back inside?" when they were outside.

There's hope for all of them. Kids who are highly distractible need first of all to learn about their distractibility and be able to recognize moments when they are tuned in to the wrong programs. A parent can remind a child, "It looks as if you're getting off on distractions—let's head on back to the important stuff." Children themselves do better at controlling their own distractibility when they know what it is and when it's occurring.

As students with weak intake control grow older, they may manifest the second form of selection disruption: they often are at a loss when it comes to deciding what's important while they study or listen in class. They can't seem to distill out the highlights and downplay less central information in a chapter, a lecture, a word problem, or a diagram. As one boy once described to me in a doleful tone of voice, "This stuff just all runs together in my head—nothing stands out to me." You can't learn everything, you can't remember everything, and you can't use everything you try to learn and remember. Therefore, while listening or reading or viewing, it's important to know what's significant and what's irrelevant or maybe only a little relevant. If you can't screen for relative importance, it can be frustrating to summarize anything, difficult to take notes, and close to impossible to predict what will be on tomorrow's religion quiz (unless you benefit from some form of divine intervention).

When Felicia, a struggling, frustrated high school student, reported to me that she was suffering her most intense struggles in biology and history, I strongly suspected that she suffered from problems assigning importance to things. Biology and history can overload and overtake you with mountain-

ـ of information if you're not deciding what's truly salient and what ـ.ds like Felicia with intake control problems have their work cut out foـ ﻣem studying for tests, taking notes, summarizing information, highlighting as they read. All learning may cease when they need to retain the high points. More often than not, they come pretty close to including everything in a summary, like a monk copying verses from the Bible, because they don't prioritize among different levels of detail.

I recommended that Felicia get plenty of extra practice underlining, taking notes, and summarizing ideas—in other words, consciously judging the importance level of information. She had a tutor who helped her with this a few times by having Felicia read an article in the *Wall Street Journal* and then underlining the most important parts in the story. By the way, Felicia had a strong interest in business; it's always good practice to start strengthening a function in a subject area about which a child feels some passion. She had to defend why she underlined certain words, phrases, or sentences and not others. Before she did this, Felicia was totally unaware of the need to stop and think about what's most relevant while studying or reading. Practice gave her insight and made this step a part of her routine.

To tighten selection control among his entire class, one teacher I work with, John Reilly, gave students an article to read and asked them to summarize it in one hundred words or less. After they submitted their summaries he returned these and asked the kids to write a fifty-word summary of their summary. The following week they were asked to write a twenty-five-word summary of their fifty-word summary. All the while he emphasized the critical importance of determining relative degrees of importance in globs of information, a great academic lesson.

Throughout a child's education and on into adult life, there is a perpetual need to pick out the salient features of any object, place, message, or experience. Highlighting within your mind the most salient characteristics of a person's face allows you to remember that individual the next time you meet her. Knowing the most salient features of the word "laughter" enables a child to recognize that word immediately while reading. If selection control extracts unimportant or highly ambiguous features rather than significant and distinguishing ones, learning becomes a bit of a blur.

By the way, don't you think it's helpful in life to be able to walk away from any experience and know what was really significant about it? Yes, that's how we accumulate wisdom.

Depth and Detail Control

Once information is selected for intake by our minds, how deeply will it be thought about? How far into our consciousness will it be permitted to penetrate? We are all too familiar with the ancient parent complaint, "It went in one ear and out the other. He just doesn't listen. Sometimes it's as if he isn't even there." Somehow inflow led nonstop to outflow. That may mean that the absentminded little kid was scanning the information superficially, and not in enough depth to make a deep enough impression within his mind. Children like that may have trouble retaining new material in short-term memory. After all, what doesn't get in very far leaks out readily. Clark's teachers regularly complained, "We have to repeat things three times for him to hear them."

When information enters one ear and flees like a bandit from the other, affected children like our Clark tend to miss out on many essential details. If you are only superficially attentive, chances are you'll get the general idea or big picture of the content someone is teaching you or what you're ob-serving during a science demonstration, but specific details pass you right by. Clark could tell you a lot about a brewing Asian conflict that's been in the news, but he couldn't name any of the countries involved or their lead-ers. In fact, so many children I've seen who fail to take information in deeply enough appear exceptionally well equipped to see the big picture; maybe that's because they are not at all bogged down with the details. They view their universe through wide-angle lenses. Many become skillful at conceptualizing, generalizing, and extrapolating, but not nearly so capable when it comes to attending to details. Clark certainly was a big-picture kid. Recall that he had flagrant problems with fine details in mathematics despite his good grasp of the concepts. He didn't make such fine-grained distinc-tions as the difference between the numbers 46 and 64. Unfortunately, such attention control contributes to accuracy, a mathematical virtue. Clark im-proved when I got his parents to help him go back over his work a second time—"on a little-detail treasure hunt," we called it. His parents gave him points for every detail mistake he could find in math and also in his writing.

Incidentally, the exact opposite finding can also be a sign of attentional decontrol; that is, some students allow information to penetrate down into their minds too deeply. How does that happen? These are kids who work painfully slowly and seem so preoccupied with the details that they fail to see the big picture. As one teacher related following one of my talks, "I've had several students recently who have driven me crazy. They seem to do everything too slowly and painstakingly. They're kind of perfectionistic. They won't proceed until something is perfectly pondered by them. They keep going back over little details when they read or write to make sure they have every little thing just right. I feel tempted to give them a kick in the pants to get their minds moving along. They get lost in the minutiae and seldom see the proverbial forest for the trees. They keep on missing the big themes, the real issues, and the wider implications. I'm thinking of one little girl in particular who could tell you all the names and dates in a social studies chapter on the Civil War but then she would lose track of the serious human rights issues that made up the overall theme or purpose of the chapter." Such students need help learning to speed up, and stepping back enough to perceive the overall meaning of what they are pursuing rather than getting hopelessly entangled in the details.

There must be an optimal depth at which to plant and examine incoming information. Important data should be perused in reasonable depth but not so deeply that it slows you down and prevents you from getting the big picture, nor so superficially that you only pick up the broad outlines or general ideas of everything. Depth and detail control finds you the right mix at the right time. However, extremes persist; some people remain big-picture folks for their entire lives. They abhor detail and indulge the broad view, while others thrive on detail, tend to it, and may be unlikely to be great generalizers, conceptualizers, and visionaries. The adult world, its corporations, institutions, and organizations, needs both kinds of minds—collaborating! We can all cite examples of adults who are terrific detail people but are unlikely to generate very creative products and those who are innovative far-ranging thinkers who never want to be bothered with details—two kinds of minds.

Mind Activity Control

Is your child's mind active or is it passive? Does she keep connecting new ideas to what she already knows? Or does new information settle in her mind without ringing bells or causing any real excitement? Or could it be that her mind is too active so she keeps daydreaming, free-associating, taking thought trips? Just as soon as information is embossed in a child's thinking, it needs to send forth signals to various relevant brain sites. No sooner does an active mind take in information than it lets that new bit of knowledge ring bells, forming associations and linkages with preexisting knowledge or experience. A teacher mentions the dictator of an oppressed country, and an active learner starts thinking about totalitarian government and also about the country in question. He almost automatically thinks about what he already knows or believes concerning these topics and compares that with the newly processed information. An active mind is a vital aspect of attention control and a core ingredient of strong learning.

Students with active minds can get three to five mind bells to ring whenever they come in contact with new facts or insights. They are soldering new knowledge to several points of prior experience and learning, which, of course, makes the new inputs much more meaningful, more connected, and interesting than they otherwise would be. Referring to the students in her advanced placement biology class, a teacher pointed out, "I love to teach these kids, they are forever making connections. Whenever they read or hear about some new idea, automatically they fit it in with what they've learned in the past—like a piece in a puzzle. Also, they look for contradictions—how something they've just learned is different from what they thought before. And they can relate almost everything they learn to experiences they've had or things they've noticed on their own."

The opposite of a reasonably active mind is a mostly passive one, a common finding among some seemingly apathetic students with attention control problems. A teacher is describing a famous martyr, while Tiffany sits in class suffering from a bad case of malignant boredom. Her mind can't or won't attach that martyr to any other martyrs or to the country or times he lived in or even to his similarities to people she has known personally. Nothing binds to anything else. In her academic world, new information rings no bells whatsoever. The stuff just kind of bobs around on the brain's surface, sending out no offshoots, soldering no connections, resonating nowhere and with nothing. As Tiffany once confessed, "I'm bored to death in school in all my subjects, except, of course, lunch and recess and sometimes gym. I don't even know why we have to learn all that stuff; I'm never going to use any of it anyway. It's just a bunch of facts you have to remember. None if it fits with anything in my life." The curriculum isn't alluring if nothing resonates with anything else. Kids who are passive processors tend to reveal few or no academic interests, although it can be helpful to identify an area or topic that does kindle a little intellectual heat within their minds; such an affinity may be exploited to coax them to rev up their thought processes in school. While it is instinctive to most, these kids have to practice asking themselves, "What does this fit with? What does this change my mind about? What does this new stuff remind me of?"

Parents and teachers can encourage active processing by regularly asking learners to link new inputs with what they already know or have met up with in their lives. For example, "Now that you're learning about political parties in school, what do you think about the way your dad and I voted in the election last year? Would you have voted the same way?" or "It's great that you're learning all about fractions and decimals and percentages. Since you love reading about sports, let's see how this part of math helps you understand batting averages and other kinds of sports statistics better."

Parents and teachers beware! There are some zealous student thinkers who repeatedly overactivate their minds. Virtually every entering parcel of information or contribution from memory rings too many bells, triggers a burst of loose associations, and launches their minds into free flight. A teacher may mention something about a dog, and Clark is instantaneously reminded of his dog and how he and his friend Sal were at the beach with their dogs last summer. Beaches remind him of the ocean, and oceans are so cool because they have sharks in them. They have whales too. Wouldn't it be fun someday to go way out in the sea and try to see some mammoth whales? That would really be awesome. And you know you could also sail all the way to Africa and check out the elephants and rhinoceroses. That would be truly awesome. At any rate, Clark is on a safari while the rest of his class is discussing something else.

Such frequent-flier patterns of thought are common among kids with attention control problems. Their minds simply detonate and take off on extraterrestrial odysseys. These dreamers often enjoy wild and fertile fantasy lives. Many of them gravitate toward the rear of their classroom where they sketch surreal pictures of wind-powered space vehicles or solar-powered sixteen-wheel vehicles. These liberated thinkers and dreamers may be highly imaginative, but they tend to be spacey. Whenever you utter something to such a child, your words are likely to provoke a tangential comment, an obscure association, with only a marginal relevance to what you just asserted. Clark confessed to taking frequent mind trips during school. He once told me, "Dr. Levine, my mind really likes to travel. It goes way off into real cool places, especially during school, which makes my teacher real mad. She says I daydream too much. I guess she's right, but I can't help it; I have a traveling brain that likes to go on trips all the time." His parents echo Clark's perception. According to his father, "This kid is in his own world half the time. And he seems so happy there. He is the ultimate dreamer. And he is so inventive. Maybe that just goes with it. He really thinks up great things that he tells us about when he comes back to earth." Clark's vivid imaginative excursions needed to be scheduled for times other than the middle of math class. This is one thing I got his parents working on, giving Clark plenty of opportunities to engage in imaginative play and other creative exploits and then reminding him to cut off his free flights at moments when he needs to be attentive. With most attention control problems, I make no effort to erase a trait entirely (we probably can't anyway). Instead I try to help parents and teachers attempt to rechannel or, in this case, reschedule it.

Span Control

It has been common, perhaps even trite, to characterize many a child as having "a short attention span." But I think the problem is more complicated, since kids who don't concentrate long enough on certain inputs may focus too long on others. Then there are the children who seem to alternate unpredictably between focusing too briefly and tuning in for too long (a phenomenon technically captured by the vivid term "perseveration"). They seldom appear to stick with the right stimuli for just the right amount of time. As part of their control over thinking, children need to sustain attention long enough without overdoing it, without focusing for so long on a toy soldier that they neglect other information or demands.

Once they learn to regulate the span of their focus, it is possible for students to shift attention seamlessly. So, ten-year-old Rupert can transition from finishing supper to doing homework without any stormy emotional upheaval or verbal combativeness. That's because he is effective at starting, stopping, and redirecting his span of attention as needed.

The ability to divide a span of attention while sustaining it, to concentrate on more than one thing at a time for the right length of time, is yet another formidable challenge or threat to attention control. While at first glance keeping your attentional eye on several targets at once may seem foolhardy, there are frequent occasions during which divided concentration is mandatory. The best example is driving a car or riding a bicycle when simultaneously concentrating on where you're going and how to get there, on the complex skills such as steering needed to operate the vehicle, and on traffic. It shouldn't astonish us, therefore, that adolescents and young adults who have trouble with their attention controls have been found to be especially susceptible to causing serious automobile accidents. It may be that such teenagers should not be allowed to listen to the radio and drive at the same time, or talk on a cell phone. Also, it might not be a good idea for them to have a peer next to them, since the compulsion to show off while driving may be more than their attention controls can handle. The parents and driver education teachers of such students need to caution them on these specific hazards.

Work with a timer or stopwatch can be helpful for kids who seldom focus for the right length of time. They need some warning about how long something will take, and then they should be informed when they are halfway there. They should be encouraged to take periodic mind breaks, times when they stop and lean back and think about something other than what they are currently working on. Then they can get back and resume their attention. Such mental rest periods can help enormously with adjusting the amount of time given to a specific focus. In fact, I think all kids need to know when to stop and give their minds a refreshing break. Teachers should allow for this when engaged in an extended lesson or lecture. Nan Murphy, a teacher from San Diego, does this regularly in her eighth-grade math classes. She calls for a two- to three-minute "brain recess" at several strategic time points during her classes; as she puts it, "The kids come back from a mind break ready to roll; it replenishes their thought processes."

Satisfaction Control

Your kid makes up his mind about what to think about by quickly deciding what will satisfy him, what sort of information intake and use seems to meet a current need. He is likely to concentrate on something if it is entertaining, if it seems useful, or if it will yield tangible benefits in the future. So he can focus readily on his favorite comic, the directions on how to operate his new DVD player, or some advice on how to make a heap of money. If all is well, he can even focus on some information inflow that might not be instantly rewarding, gratifying, or entertaining but could have a big payoff later (such as a terrific report card). Unfortunately, quite a few children with attention control problems are accurately described as insatiable. That means they can only concentrate on stimuli that are exciting and immediately stimulating. It might be that a seventh-grade social studies class studying the early years of the Holy Roman Empire just doesn't do it for them. They are unable to delay gratification, to consider the possibility, for example, that succeeding in social studies will reap benefits down the line. Instead, they need to cash in and seek pleasure right away because they are so intensely insatiable. These perpetually restless children become bored and fidgety in a classroom as they yearn and burn for a more stimulating, immediately satisfying experience. As a first-grade teacher observed, "Jody simply craves excitement. He loves to stir things up. He gets bored and tremendously restless when things are calm in the classroom. He's a very sweet little boy, but he makes me angry when he causes trouble just for the sake of creating excitement. And that happens several times a day without fail." Jody himself put it pretty simply when he stated to me in my office, "Yeah, I just like to have fun. I don't like sitting and listening. I gotta have action or I start to squirm or I start fights and get into trouble with my teacher or something like that. It's kinda fun, but then I'm sorry."

Some kids have a special kind of insatiability that targets material acquisitions. That is, they constantly lust for more and ever more possessions. Clark's mom admitted, "Often I give in to him and let Clark have whatever he wants just to get him off my back. He won't let up until he gets what he's after, and then, a lot of times he loses interest in it and finds something else to go after. It can wear you down." Of course all children want things, but insatiable kids take such material longings to an exasperating extreme. Brothers and sisters usually resent the child's completely self-centered materialistic passions. Parents need not despair, as the trait is not all bad; material insatiability may evolve during adulthood into a virtue called ambition. Often having collections—of rocks, seashells, sports cards, dolls, moths, or whatever—helps these children. When their insatiability demands are getting out of control, they can be told to go add to their rock collection.

Insatiability for intense experience is a second type. Jody, the first grader mentioned above, exhibited this variety of insatiability. Children like him crave ultra-intense stimulation. When the local intensity level is set too low for them, they may see to it by turning up its volume, perhaps by becoming provocative, appearing to be troublemakers as they stir things up to appease their gnawing restlessness. At worst, in adult life, this form of insatiability can and sometimes does contribute to substance abuse, alcoholism, marital instability, and a reluctance to settle into any consistent career pathway. Whenever pursuing a long-term goal, such a person thinks about something else far more enticing and fulfilling he might be doing at the moment. On the other hand, experiential insatiability sometimes evolves into highly constructive risk taking; some children with experiential insatiability show signs of budding entrepreneurialism and ambition. As Clark's mother commented, "Clark is definitely a wheeler-dealer. I think he'd thrive in the business world. He's always scheming and talking about all the grandiose things he's going to do someday." Parents should kindle this drive by helping kids develop their own Web sites, subscription selling, or other enterprises. Also, these children need a constructive or at least harmless outlet for their insatiability. It may be Rollerblades or horseback riding or a team sport that satisfies them. But it is important not to let them go overboard and dedicate their lives exclusively to the pursuit of immediate intense gratification. Time limits for such activities clearly are in order.

✎ THE OUTPUT CONTROLS

Having control over your mind's output is as essential as controlling its intake. Parents can detect when a kid's mind lacks control over output. As one mom observed, "He just loses it, that's all, and then he does things without thinking them through." We have seen how with effective control over inflow, a child's mind can grapple efficiently with newly received information. Similarly, output control improves the quality of his products and actions. Of course, this productive output of a young mind is dependent on the control of inflow, since so often we base an output on incoming messages (e.g., doing what your mom tells you to do or tracking the arc of a fast approaching football and then catching it). So the two forms of attention control are often intertwined.

In taking control of output a child also relies to some degree on the control of mental energy. After all, it takes energy, in the form of mental effort, to rev up his mind's turbines and get his assembly line to operate. In fact, when and if output is efficient, he can actually conserve a good bit of his mental energy. It takes considerable energy to practice your French horn. But if you do so efficiently, it's not as exhausting, time consuming, and boring as it is when you waste a lot of time and don't concentrate on what you are doing.

To control her mind's output, a child has to monitor and regulate the quality of three main forms of such output—behavioral output, social output, and academic output. Children become planners of what they do rather than puppets dominated by their impulses. So Meyer stops and thinks about whether he should blurt out a profanity in church, and then decides that the utterance, hilarious as it is, would not be wise. So he censors himself in time to prevent social damage. In the same circumstance, Clark impulsively and in a loud voice lets it all out. That's because Clark often has little or no control over his output. His mother laments: "Clark is forever embarrassing us in public. When he thinks of something, he instantly says or does it, and we sometimes have to take the consequences."

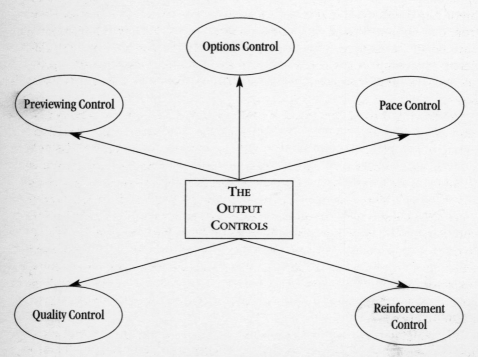

Figure 3-4.   The neurodevelopmental functions that regulate output.

Previewing Control

Prior to deciding how to act at a party or settling on a topic for your term paper, it makes good sense to look ahead and think about the most likely results of what is about to be done, said, or created. When he does so, your child semiautomatically addresses the all-important "What if I . . . ?" questions: "What if I say this? What will people think of me?" "What if I act like this? Will I get in trouble?" "What if I write a book report about *To Kill a Mockingbird*? What will that be like when it's finished?" "What if I solve this math problem? About what should the answer be?" Kids need to make continual use of preview scopes secured to the front walls of their brains. Those scopes allow them to look ahead, anticipate, plan, and make good predictions. By predicting or foreseeing an outcome, you can cancel a plan or modify an intention that's unlikely to have a happy ending. Sadly, there are some individuals who go through life operating like a photographer whose camera has no viewfinder. They keep snapping their shutters without having any sense at all of how their photos will turn out. They may get into trouble in school because they repeatedly act out or even lash out without ever gauging the likely consequences. They are also apt to say things that are unfit for publication because they state them without ever foreseeing or predicting their effects on others. Such students may need to be dissuaded from careers in the diplomatic corps! In tackling academic work, they may have no idea what their efforts are leading toward. As a result, they have difficulty estimating an answer in mathematics, foreseeing what shape a project will take, and envisioning what conclusions they will convey in a book report.

Previewing is so pivotal to the learning process that it needs to be taught explicitly in school. Whenever possible, kids ought to be engaged in coming up with a blueprint of what something will look like when it's finished. They should submit work plans and be evaluated on them. Such plans should include a description of what the final product will be like—much as a landscape designer would prepare a sketch of a proposed garden. Sometimes students should be required to write the last paragraph of a report first and then keep that paragraph up in front of them while writing the report. In other words, the final paragraph is their preview, the destination toward which they are navigating. In the middle of a story children should be given opportunities to predict how it will end. The students I know who read especially well are constantly previewing, predicting what's coming next while they read.

Many highly celebrated adults are "visionary," capable of looking ahead and previewing a product or a specific goal that would be invisible to lesser minds. A builder or an architect may inspect a vacant lot and imagine a shopping mall on that site. It is said that Mozart had very few corrections on the manuscripts of his piano concerti. Before he set about composing each movement, he had a clear view of what it would be like when it was finished. Howard Gardner offers the following statement from Mozart himself:

> All this fires my soul, and provided I am not disturbed, my subject enlarges itself, becomes methodized and defined, and the whole, though it be long, stands almost complete and finished in my mind, so that I can survey it, like a fine picture or a beautiful statue, at a glance. Nor do I hear in my imagination the parts *successively,* but I hear them, as it were, all at once. What a delight this is I cannot tell.

Gardner goes on to comment, "The claim to hear an entire piece of music—which may take twenty or thirty minutes to perform—in one's head at one moment in time when it has not even been composed seems incredible." That's world-class previewing.

Identifying an area in which a child is excellent at previewing can provide clues regarding what his or her mind is wired best for. I remember so well one adolescent named Sean, who was failing in ninth grade and was also a serious discipline problem. Sean's carpentry teacher commented about him, "He's the only kid in my class who knows exactly what a project is going to look like when it's finished before he even starts it." Sean is not a behavior problem in carpentry class. Following the carpentry teacher's observation, his English teacher commented, "This kid has no clue where it's headed when he tries to write a book report."

Options Control

Emily Dickinson often is quoted for her line "I dwell in possibilities." She's not the only one; we all do. In hiking through life, we come to endless branching trails, roads to be taken or not taken, things we could do, things we could say, things we might try, strategies worthy of consideration. Your English teacher asks you to make up an original story and you try to decide whether it should be about space invaders, elves, or gigantic man-eating toads. You think about the pros and cons of these topics and make a decision. This is what you do instead of simply writing about the first thing that comes to mind. From second to second, we have to make such choices between available options. Ideally, at each point in time we pick our best option while we inhibit or suppress less desirable possibilities.

Some children often omit this output selection step. In fact, at times we all do; we impulsively neglect a review of options and leap on the first thing that comes to mind. On the other hand, when a child weighs decisions, she is in a position to inhibit or at least slow down initial responses, inhibiting all her potentially ill-advised gut reactions and dangerous knee-jerk responses. She takes the time to think through her alternatives and then make use of a venerable process we call good judgment or wise decision making. One of his fellow school bus passengers once approached Clark at the bus stop and called him a decidedly unflattering four-letter word. Clark immediately thought of his first response to that provocation. Did he go for it? Or, alternatively, did he ponder his options and select the best one? He went for it instantaneously and pushed the younger boy into a snowdrift, caving in to his first and only response. Clark's mother told me, "That happens at least two or three times a day. If he would only think about it, he would realize there are other ways to react, other ways to save face."

It's not just behavior that's at stake here. Parents and teachers have to remind kids like Clark to review their options before they tackle a challenging school assignment. There is something to be said for asking yourself this question: "Let's see, what's the best way to make this painting look like early morning?" Often children with weak attention control and a failure to weigh options omit this query and therefore do too many things the hard way or very impulsively. A student who ponders options in decision making can survey a math problem and ask himself, "What's the best way to solve this one?" One who never thinks in terms of options just goes ahead and does the problem. In so doing, he may or may not come up with the most effective or optimal problem-solving strategy, often doing the problem the wrong way.

Throughout their education, kids should be taught about such decision making based on the conscious sifting through of options. At home, whenever a child gets into trouble, parents should spend time reviewing with her what her other options might have been. In school, students should have to think about multiple alternative endings for stories they read and then pick the best one. They should consider events in history and talk through the decision-making options that world leaders faced at different critical points. Students should acquire the experience that there is more than one option for handling every situation.

Pace Control

"I so often wish Clark would just slow down," lamented his teacher. "He's always in such a hurry. I keep telling him to slow down and cool it. He does things too quickly, and he invariably messes up. When I can get him to slow down, on the other hand, he produces fantastic work." Pace control regulates the *rate* at which activities are conducted. A child should not do things too slowly, nor would we want her to be frenetic and frantic with her output. There is obviously an optimal speed range for anything that we do.

Pacing can also be set at too slow a rate. I've seen some kids with output control problems who grind everything out too slowly. Some actually move around at a snail-like rate. Some clinicians refer to them as "hypoactive hyperactive kids." Their bodies move at a crawl, while their minds may flutter from one pursuit to the next. Interestingly, just about all the children I've known like this have been girls. I've heard other clinicians say the same thing. Boys with attention deficits are more predisposed to race their motors, while affected girls idle in low gear.

Pacing takes in synchronizing. A student faces numerous academic challenges in which multiple components have to operate in synchrony. Writing is the classic example. When a student writes, she or he has to synchronize letter formation (or keyboarding), spelling, punctuation, grammar, capitalization, prior knowledge, and vocabulary. All of these output tributaries have to flow into the main river at about the same rate. A budding young writer can't have the punctuation arriving eleven seconds after the capitalization. Difficulty achieving the required degree of synchronization is one reason many students with weak output controls find writing to be a form of cruel and unusual punishment. They balk at doing homework and may become visibly agitated and resistant when they have to transfer their thoughts to paper. We noted this frustration in our patient April, for whom writing was too massive an orchestra to conduct; she could never seem to get writing's players to play together. If a child has trouble conducting multiple functions at the same time, a parent might need to help her develop a plan for doing one thing at a time. These children can be helped by teaching them to do things in stages instead of all at once. They need well-thought-out work plans to facilitate this process. (All children need help to do things in steps rather than all at once.)

The output controls I have discussed thus far, namely previewing, weighing options, and adjusting pace, all serve to slow you down so you are a more reflective person. If you add together weak previewing plus the absence of options (i.e., doing the first thing that comes to mind), plus frenetic pacing, you come up with the well-known trait called impulsivity, the tendency that so sabotaged Clark's day-to-day behavior. In many respects the output controls have as their mission getting kids to slow down, to stop, listen, think, and look before they leap.

Quality Control

We need to watch how we're doing something and we should evaluate how well we did it right after we've done something. The process allows for regulation, for self-righting. Whether driving a car, solving a long division problem, or interacting with your friends, it's wise to sense how things are going. Are you on the right track? Should you modify your methods or strategies? Do you need to terminate this activity?

Children with output control problems tend to be oblivious of or insensitive to feedback. They may not notice when they're making fools of themselves. While explaining something in class they may fail to realize that no one is following what they are trying to say (that's called weak communication monitoring). They are not making sense to others. Sometimes when these kids don't understand something they're reading or listening to, they also may not realize that they don't understand because they're not monitoring their comprehension. The well-worn phrase "But I don't get it" is an indicator of excellent self-monitoring, super quality control over thinking.

Throughout the curriculum, teachers and parents should be emphasizing self-evaluation, the practice of gauging how you're doing during and after an activity. Kids should be encouraged to grade their own papers. They should use checklists to survey an assignment they might need to improve upon. For example, their parents can help students make use of a writing checklist that might include review of whether they have begun each sentence with a capital letter, varied their sentence structure, made use of topic sentences, and so on. Whenever a student submits a test to a teacher, he or she should insert in the upper-right-hand corner what grade he thinks he achieved. Kids should be rewarded with a few extra points if they are accurate at estimating their grade. The stress is always on knowing how you're doing or how you've done, the critical job of being self-critical. As one elementary school teacher commented after applying what she learned in our Schools Attuned teacher-training program, "In my class now, the students evaluate themselves way more than I evaluate them. And it's paid off. They are finding out that it's okay and safe to make mistakes as long as you catch them and learn from them. I see more kids making more use of their erasers and I praise them for it. They're really watching what they're doing."

Reinforcement Control

If something has worked well for your child in the past, it should be used over and over again. That's positive reinforcement. If, on the other hand, she behaved or performed an assignment in a way that led to failure or punishment, it would be best not to do it the same way again.

When previous experience seems to have no impact whatsoever on today's thinking, the results can be frustrating. Parents can tear their hair out when a child somehow treats every circumstance in life as if it is unique and unconnected to any of life's earlier episodes. He or she rarely seems to learn much from experience—positive or negative. Such a child may be immune to the effects of criticism, punishment, or even praise. As one despairing mother complained, "I keep telling him things like 'You had such a good way of doing that homework last week and you got such good grades. How come you're not just using the same tricks with tonight's work?'"

I encourage parents to work with children who have poor reinforcement control by helping them keep diaries of things that have happened to them, so that they can discuss the ways in which these events or incidents can or will affect future actions for them. One enlightened mother applied this technique especially diligently over several months. "This has worked quite well with my youngest son," she reported. "He actually makes bulleted lists of important 'news events of the day' in his life before he goes to bed each night. We go over his lists every few days and talk about what he did right and what he could have done better to make events go his way. When he does poorly on a quiz in school, we try to figure out what went wrong and then discuss how he could prepare differently in the future. And he does most of the talking. I try to be a good listener and avoid preaching to him. He comes up with his own advice to himself. I think he enjoys it. My husband did this with him recently, and they made believe they were a football team viewing videotapes of last Sunday's game to come up with strategies for their next game. The idea always is to learn how to learn from the past."

❧ THE IMPACTS OF THE ATTENTION CONTROLS

We have seen the many ways in which attention control impacts learning, behavior, and relationships with others. Well-calibrated attention control influences how a kid feels about himself and how his parents come to feel about their kid. It's really tough to be living with a sense that your mind is a bit out of control. And it's equally frustrating to be striving to raise a mind that's lacking self-control. It's hard for a student to be smart but not productive. Parents feel let down repeatedly. It's frightening to keep doing things impulsively and then regretting having done them. Parents wonder if they are punishing a child for actions that are beyond the child's control. Clark, by the way, beneath his charismatic surface, felt very sad. His mom reported that Clark often cried himself to sleep. April too went through dark periods of anguish, battling deeply felt feelings of inadequacy. Her mother kept wondering what they had done wrong, how they had let April down. "It's so hard to stand by and watch your child feel like a failure. There are times when you can almost see her self-esteem crumbling. And no matter what you say or do, she keeps saying she's the dumbest kid in her class. Then we begin to ask ourselves what we could have done differently, wondering how we contributed to her problems without knowing it. We can't stop thinking about April and how much she suffers every day in school, even though she puts up a pretty good front."

From a humane perspective, we are obligated to help children with weak attention controls and their parents realize that these are not bad minds, that their strengths will prevail in the end. We need to implant optimism and help these kids feel respected.

§➤ MINDS OVER TIME: KEEPING A WATCHFUL EYE ON THE ATTENTION CONTROLS AS CHILDREN AGE

Although they're unlikely to refer to these functions by name, all parents are constantly observing and often commenting on their children's attention controls. The controls play such a leading role in the scripts of everyday life that they hog the spotlight much of the time! Not only that, but the attention controls have to operate differently to meet the needs of different ages. Mental energy control develops most rapidly during infancy. That may be the reason why babies who have trouble sleeping at night are prone to develop attention problems when they reach school age. They never quite get programmed early on for the optimal balance between sleep and wakefulness.

During the earliest grades in school, you should expect to see fairly intact control over mental energy; your kids should have achieved a nice balance between sleep and wakefulness. Their alertness should be dependable, as should their slumber. They need to be able to mobilize mental energy at important intervals during the school day, such as when they must adjust to the seemingly unreasonable constraint of occupying a chair for extended periods. As one eight-year-old reported to me, "The worst part of school is all that sitting. It kills. My brain starts to hurt when I have to sit and listen and listen for a long time. I can stay in my seat, but sometimes I want to zoom off and run around the halls." By second grade you can anticipate that mental effort also is becoming well controlled, as kids learn to delay gratification and do some things they don't feel like doing but have to.

The intake controls display their steepest improvement while students are in elementary school. For example, there is a wide difference in how well a sixth grader can filter out distractions in a classroom when compared to a first grader or kindergartner. The latter are much more likely to be pulled off course by noises in the corridor or the fidgeting of a child at the same table.

In mid– to late elementary school, control over information inflow is expected to burgeon. A sixth grader is much more efficient at concentrating for an extended period and then shifting smoothly to a new relevant subject. A younger child may fail to sustain his focus or have trouble adjusting rapidly to transitions of attention. He is also more apt to tune out halfway through a story, especially if the plot fails to generate sufficient excitement.

As one teacher commented during a workshop on attention that I conducted, "Sometimes with my kindergarten kids, I feel like an entertainer. If something doesn't seem like fun, it's awfully hard to keep their attention. I used to teach sixth grade, and those kids still liked to be entertained, but they were much stronger at focusing on things that were important but not especially exciting. That allowed me to do more instructing without having to stand on my head to maintain their attention." Your older elementary school child should also be getting better at curbing or delaying appetites, so he is nowhere near as insatiable as he was in kindergarten.

Finally, the output controls ripen during and right after puberty. They come into their own as a key, but too often neglected, theme of adolescent development. Virtually all the functions I will be discussing in this book have to operate faster and faster as the child matures. However, as kids get older, output controls function slower and slower and slower. In other words, well-controlled output requires adolescent minds to work slowly, to be reflective rather than impulsive, to take their time and not do the first thing that comes to mind. This is ironic, of course, since our high schools force our kids to do everything as fast as possible. They have to write quickly, think fast, remember on the spot, sprint through timed tests, and meet tight deadlines. This frenzied pedagogical rhythm is totally contrary to what the students' brains are striving to become. The output controls are crying out, declaring that they exist to promote thoughtful, slowly executed work, which should be one of the principal missions of adolescence and the high school years. I think we should reward adolescents for taking as much time as they need to do a good job. Most tests should be untimed, or else students should be allowed to do as much as they can do well, perhaps finishing the rest at another time. The output controls are doing what they can to decelerate thinking, decision making, and output, to make kids thoughtful rather than impulsive. Secondary education, therefore, ought to incorporate as one of its principal objectives teaching kids how to work slowly. That's what their developing brains are trying to tell us.

A parent should monitor the extent to which an adolescent is able to slow down his mind, preview, think in terms of alternatives, and make use of previous experience to guide current output. I know one mother, a high school art teacher, who studied the attention controls, taught her daughter Joyce about them, and then made the controls a central theme whenever she assisted Joyce with her homework. As an example, when writing a report, Joyce first talked about what it would have in it when finished (previewing), then discussed her choices for topics to include or exclude (options), then worked out a timeline for completion of steps in writing the report (pacing). When finished, Joyce was helped to compare her report to her plan (quality), and along the way she listed facts and experiences she had in mind that could be added to the report (reinforcement—using prior knowledge). In this way Joyce's mother was fostering her fifteen-year-old's current mind development. The approach was successful, so she was also using it with her art students to guide them through projects.

The following table is an adaptation of the ANSER System, which is a parent questionnaire that we use at our Center for Development and Learning to define more specifically the controls that are affected in a child who has problems with attention. Parents can use such a grid to troubleshoot for various attention control breakdowns.

WEAK ATTENTION CONTROL:
A LIST OF TRAITS ADAPTED FROM THE ANSER SYSTEM,
A PARENT DIAGNOSTIC QUESTIONNAIRE

	Control	*Trait*
Mental Energy Control	Alertness	Has trouble staying alert
		Attention hard to attract
		Loses focus unless very interested
	Mental Effort	Has trouble finishing things
		Has difficulty starting homework
		Has a hard time doing work
	Sleep-Arousal	Has trouble falling/staying asleep
		Has trouble getting up in the morning
		Looks tired
	Consistency	Has unpredictable behavior/work
		Has excellent days and poor days
		Keeps "tuning in and out"
Intake Control	Selection	Is easily distracted by sounds
		Focuses on unimportant details
		Is easily distracted by visual things
	Depth and Detail	Forgets what he has just heard
		Focuses too deeply at times
		Misses important information

(continued on next page)

	Control	Trait
Intake Control	Mind Activity	Mind is not active while listening
		Has unusual ideas or thoughts
		Daydreams/free associates easily
	Span	Doesn't concentrate long enough
		Shows uneven concentration
		Has trouble shifting attention
	Satisfaction	Craves excitement
		Has trouble delaying gratification
		Gets bored easily
Output Control	Previewing	Doesn't think ahead before acting
		Has trouble planning work
		Is unprepared for what's coming next
	Options	Does the first thing that comes to mind
		Does not use strategies
		Does not stop and think through decisions
	Pace	Is overactive/fidgety
		Is disorganized with time
		Does many things too quickly
	Quality	Makes many careless errors
		Fails to notice when bothering others
		Has trouble knowing how she's doing
	Reinforcement	Punishment doesn't make a difference
		Seems not to learn from experience
		Keeps making same kinds of mistakes

✑ PRACTICAL CONSIDERATIONS

• All the attention controls are so basic in regulating what a child does and says that educators and parents need to have a clear understanding of how, when, and where they work. Schools and families should discuss and cultivate the fourteen controls of attention, which can be applied and strengthened in the teaching of virtually all subjects. If parents are familiar with the attention controls and how they sometimes fail to work, we will have far fewer kids with misunderstood minds. We will examine these issues in Chapters 12 and 13 when we design our model school and home.

• Children too should learn all about the attention controls and how they work. From time to time, teachers should talk about which specific attention controls need to be turned on to do a math problem or look at a statue or study for a geography test. We now have quite a few teachers who do this. Several have commented that they always have done this in a way but by being more explicit and teaching about and naming the controls, they can help their students concentrate better and think things through before they do them. Consciously thinking about the attention controls provides a structure for thinking and working, and many kids need that structure to succeed in school.

• Children are not all alike. Those with attention control problems are a heterogeneous group. Some are overactive and some are not. Some have behavior problems; others just have trouble concentrating or getting work completed. Some of them can't seem to sleep well, while others have no sleep difficulty. So let's avoid the current practice of lumping kids with attention control problems as "if you've seen one, you've seen them all." Actually, any combination of weak attention controls can be found in a kid; I've encountered endless variations on these themes. So parents and teachers need to think about each of these children and identify the specific controls that seem out of control as well as those that function well. Also, a child's attention controls may function nicely in some settings but not in others. Knowing where and when attention works well can help adults program times when children are more in control of their behavior and learning. They need those times for feeling good about themselves. So if a child concentrates well when playing a video game, listening to loud music, or riding a skateboard, such successful experiences on a regular basis may be good for their mental and intellectual health—in moderate amounts.

• When a child can't seem to control his behavior, there is a very real possibility that some of his attention controls may not be functioning as they should. That is to say, he is not evil, not a bad boy; he just needs to gain control. If you call someone bad long enough, he is apt to turn bad. Accounting for the behavior as a control issue and pinpointing the control(s) in need of repair can enable a child to determine what he has to do to stay out of trouble. I have seen children's behavior improve markedly when the adult world has stopped making their actions seem criminal. One child I know was helped by his teacher to rate his level of control at the end of each school day. He kept score of his attention controls and tried to improve them. He succeeded in doing so. He was far from perfect, but there was noticeable improvement when he no longer saw himself as a bad boy.

• In many respects the opposite of impulsivity is good problem-solving skills. Therefore a systematic approach to dealing with challenges and setbacks (as delineated on page 196) should be taught and actively practiced with all students, especially those who seem reluctant to plan and pace their output and decision making. Some children with chronic weaknesses of attention control may benefit from taking stimulant medication. These drugs are never the whole answer (see page 288), although they may be helpful in some cases.

• Parents and teachers should never lose sight of all the good things that come packaged with attention deficits like the extras you purchase with your new automobile. So many children with deficient attention controls reward their parents with such redeeming features as creativity, compassion, and perceptiveness. They may also shine as wheeler-dealers, entrepreneurs in their own right. Many possess specialized talents and rugged independence.

• Since the traits associated with attentional dysfunction can be impossible to erase, you should redirect these traits toward constructive pursuits instead of trying to eradicate them. For instance, we should recognize that kids with material insatiability can become great collectors, that distractibility is akin to creativity, and that the free flight of ideas can lead to some fantasy-filled artwork, unique, if far-out inventions, and strikingly original fiction or poetry. Go for it!

• It is rare to encounter a student who has trouble with attention unaccompanied by other kinds of dysfunction. Weak attention control is almost always one member of a little cluster of dysfunctions. Therefore, whenever a parent spots problems with attention control, he should always ask, "What else does she have?" A child may manifest gaps of attention plus deficits in language or attention plus memory or attention plus language plus social thinking. Little progress will be made in helping someone if these other issues are neglected and only the attention problem is managed. All too often, for example, kids get put on medication for their attention deficit, while a language or sequencing or social thinking problem is ignored. The medicine might help for a while, but it's like putting a Band-Aid over an infected wound without treating the injury itself. It looks better but is it really healed?

• Attention is as brittle as it is intricate. A child, therefore, can start to experience problems with attention control at any point. Many factors influence attention. If a student has trouble understanding in class, his attention is likely to deteriorate. If a child is anxious about something, the anxiety drains off attention. A variety of different physical ailments and mental conditions negatively affect the attention controls. Therefore, attention is a revealing bellwether. Surveillance of a child's attention controls is a critical way to monitor her overall well-being. Inattention is a distress signal, informing us that all is not well within that child or between her and her environment.

• "We know he can do the work when he wants to. In fact, when he can overcome his laziness and his attitude problems, he will succeed. Until then, it's up to him. We can't help him unless and until he helps himself." This was a terse report from the algebra teacher of a patient of mine. It is so typical of the kind of misunderstanding that causes children with attention deficits to shoulder all the guilt and blame for the way they are. When I explained to this boy that he was not to blame for the problems he was having, that he was an innocent victim of his wiring, he became radiant. There was hope. I gave him some articles to read about the attention controls, and he came back to see me with a lengthy list of questions. He was determined to get in control of himself. And by the way, his mom at a PTA meeting urged the school to get some training in neurodevelopmental function for the teachers. A lack of attention control may masquerade as laziness, a negative attitude, or just plain bad behavior. Yet these are struggling and confused students who want very much to succeed, to please themselves and win the respect of the adults in their lives. They need our sympathy and support at the same time that they need us to hold them accountable for working on their attention controls. When they sense that we're on their side and not accusing them of being bad or lazy, they often rise to the occasion and show steady improvement. Teachers, therefore, need to form strong alliances with these children rather than adversarial relationships. The same can be said for parents.

4

Remembering to Learn and Learning to Remember ✍

Our Memory System

> If any one faculty of our nature may be called more wonderful than the rest, I do think it is memory. There seems something more speakingly incomprehensible in the powers, the failures, the inequalities of memory, than in any other of our intelligences. The memory is sometimes so retentive, so serviceable, so obedient—and at others so bewildered and so weak—and at others again, so tyrannical, so beyond control!
>
> JANE AUSTEN, *Mansfield Park*

"Poor kid. He studies and studies and studies with hardly anything to show for it. A few nights ago he was up well after midnight getting ready for an exam. He must have gone over the material a hundred times. He was determined to ace the test. To make a long story short, he didn't. A couple of days after the test, his teacher posted the scores on the bulletin board where everyone could see them, and his was at the very bottom of his class. He felt bludgeoned, worthless. It broke my heart to see the expression on his face when he got home from soccer practice that afternoon. He went right to his bedroom and didn't say a word. I started to cry. I couldn't control myself. He is so motivated yet so totally frustrated by school. We try to help him study, but he doesn't want our help; he so much wants to succeed on his own, to impress us the way his brother and sister consistently do. The night he got that test grade back he was up going to the bathroom all night long; I'm sure it was the stress and disappointment that so upset his stomach. It's all gnawing away at him. I am so frightened—I just don't know what he's going to do to himself if he keeps on failing despite all that hard work and determination. He's such a wonderful kid, so kind and so interesting in the way he thinks. I just don't know how long he can take all this disappointment and frustration with himself." That was an impassioned e-mail I received from an understandably distressed mother of a fifteen-year-old I eventually evaluated. Our team discovered that this adolescent was up against some serious memory barriers.

Vastly more extensive and strenuous use of memory is required for school success than is needed in virtually any career you can name. Students must store and retrieve mounds of facts, skills, and concepts across unrelated subject areas and topics. Math procedures, spelling words, dates in history, foreign language vocabulary, and chemical symbols and valences all get crammed into a young mind's crowded storage silos. In creating this demand, education imposes an ever-growing burden on the neurodevelopmental functions that together make up memory capacity.

Memory is a complicated multidepartmental operation that does its work at many diverse brain sites, a lot of which have not even been located by neuroscientists. Nothing is ever learned without tapping into some component of memory. A child may be able to understand a fact, process, or concept as it is being explained or demonstrated; but without memory, none of it can be retrieved and applied. Without the collaboration of the proper memory functions, learning fails. A teacher explaining the steps in photosynthesis may make perfect sense to an attentive seventh grader, but if he can't properly store at least an overview of the information, the lesson loses much of its value. During your child's school years the pressure on memory intensifies across the curriculum without any letup. Plenty of students, who are astute in many other ways, just can't withstand the memory strains. So often I see a child with reduced memory capacity stigmatized as "dumb" or "slow" when, in reality, he or she possesses fine intellectual faculties but a flawed information filing system. As one fifth-grade girl confided, "Even when I think I know something, I don't know it on a test or when my teacher calls on me in class. The smart kids can answer Mrs. Evans's questions, but not me. Most of the time I can't remember or it takes me so long to remember stuff, I can't finish the test or I think of the answer when it's too late. A lot of times I wish I was as smart as my friends. They remember things better than I do."

Nobody has a perfect memory the way some people might have perfect pitch, nor, for that matter, is anyone shackled with a totally incompetent memory. We should always ask, "Memory for what?" Some people are uncanny when it comes to recognizing faces. Others have phenomenal musical memory; they can name that tune in a flash. Still others are revered as tour de force trivia retrievers. But no one, no one at all, has it all, a perfect memory across the board.

As children ascend through their school years, they keep coming up against encounters with new memory demands. In the earliest grades they have to remember which combinations of letters go to make which language sounds. Then they move on and have to recognize words on a page the instant they see them (their sight vocabulary). From there they proceed to filing in their memory banks thousands of spelling words and math facts. At each grade level, a tide of new memory demands engulf a child. Some students have enough storage capacity to succeed with distinction at a particular point in time or even throughout school, while others endure disheartening mismatches between the efficiency of their various memory facilities and the highly specific demands of the curriculum.

Our mind's storage depots can be divided conveniently into short-term memory, active working memory, and long-term memory as shown in Figure 4-1. By understanding something about these three major memory de-

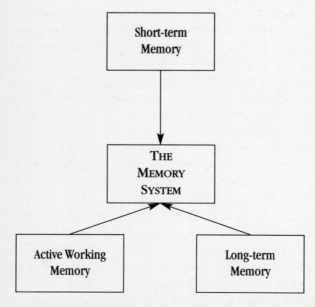

Figure 4-1.   The memory system.

partments, as a parent you can be alert for specific shortfalls that may at any point sabotage your child's learning.

Parents and teachers should keep in mind the well-accepted distinction between short-term memory and long-term memory. Short-term memory allows for the very brief retention (usually about two seconds) of new information, while long-term memory is the warehouse for more or less permanent knowledge; it's your hard drive. Long-term memory is where your child stores his name, address, and telephone number, to say nothing of common spelling words, math facts, and the all-important state capitals. Long-term memory makes use of an elaborate and intricate filing system.

Children also insert material into active working memory, which fits neatly between short-term and long-term memory. Information rests in active working memory for seconds to minutes to hours—not as briefly as short-term memory, nor as permanently as long-term memory. Active working memory is the memory you operate when you temporarily hold in mind all the different components of what you are trying to do right now. That way, a child can remember the instructions his coach gives while he is carrying them out. Active working memory would have failed him if, while striving to get a firm grip on the football, he forgot what the play was. For those readers who are familiar with computers, active working memory can be conceived of as one's random access memory, the memory needed for the program you are trying to run currently. This would include your immediate need to hold some meaning from the current sentence in active working memory limbo while reading the next few sentences on this page.

Parents are in a unique position to detect inadequate memory performance, especially if they are knowledgeable about the differences between short-term, active working, and long-term memory functioning, including how each operates and what the signs are that one or more of them is not keeping pace with demands. Teachers of course have a front-row seat when it comes to observing the day-to-day operations of a child's efforts to remember.

✎ SHORT-TERM MEMORY

Ira was a seven-year-old whose parents complained that he would never listen to them. His second-grade teacher was equally as stymied as she recounted the frequent instances when Ira would look as if he was paying attention and then completely ignore her verbal directions. She did observe that if she slowed down or gave shorter instructions, it sometimes helped, but she felt that wasn't fair to the rest of the class. (By the way, I deal with this issue of fairness all the time, but I believe fervently that to treat all children the same way is to treat them unequally. Different kids have different learning needs; they have a right to have their needs met. Besides, so many outstanding teachers I have met insist that it is possible to treat and teach students as individuals. That doesn't mean that a class of twenty-seven kids needs to have twenty-seven lesson plans, but it does mean teachers can be flexible in their methods of instruction and their ways of evaluating kids' learning.)

Anyway, getting back to Ira, both at home and in school, there were countless times when someone would go over and over a lesson, immediately after which Ira would act as if he had been absent. This was a regular occurrence during drilling on spelling or new reading words. Confusing the picture was the fact that Ira was not at all obstinate but a very well-behaved boy with a sizable collection of strengths and mostly strong attention controls. He was an outstanding athlete, an intuitive mathematician, a master joke teller, a nonstop, colorful speaker with an overgrown vocabulary, and a very popular kid. Everyone liked Ira and with good reason—he was a real people person. But his parents and his phenomenal older sister, Samantha, were forever trying to help Ira learn. His dad once told me: "Getting this kid to learn something new feels like trying to break into a bank vault, his mind's just locked shut. But I'll tell you one thing about Ira: once he knows something, he knows it forever. It's just getting him to pick it up in the first place, that's the killer. Recently we have asked him to repeat important instructions to us right after we say them. We obviously don't do that all the time, but when we do, it helps." Ira's father was describing a classic case of a child with short-term memory dysfunction.

Short-term memory is learning's front entrance. I tried to explain this to Ira. My explanation went something like this: "Ira, when you first hear or see something, it goes inside your brain and it stays there for a few seconds while you decide real fast how you will use it. It might be that you'll do something with it. So if your mind says, 'Ira, blow your nose,' you can remember what it said just long enough to do it or to decide it doesn't need blowing. That place in your mind where things stop off is called short-term memory because it holds things for such a short time. Some kids have a short-term memory that leaks. So they may forget things they've just heard or seen. I think that happens with you sometimes. You might forget what somebody just said to you."

Short-term memory also serves as one of our mind's relay stations. As chunks of data enter our minds, we can send them to long-term memory for later use, use them right away and then forget them, or make use of them and then save them for future use. Or, of course, we can simply forget the information and do nothing with it. Such options have to be exercised with

breakneck speed—in less than two seconds—unless, of course, you ap
for an extension. You can extend the life of data in short-term memory in
several ways: whisper it under your breath, form pictures in your mind's
eye, if it is visual you can put it into words, thereby lengthening the amount
of time that short-term memory plays host to the new inputs. These strategies, known as rehearsal strategies, can be beneficial for students. I asked
Ira's mother to teach him some of these tricks of the memory trade. They
seemed to help him significantly. Ira told me, "I especially like taking pictures with my mind camera. Like when my teacher's talking I sometimes
draw pictures in my brain. No, no, really it's like I'm making a video of what
she's talking about. And that helps me keep it all in my mind, you know, so
it doesn't leak out. Then when I want to remember the stuff, I can go rent
the video from my brain and watch and listen to it." I told you Ira was a colorful talker.

It's a good thing short-term memory is short. It needs to be short because
there is a constant torrent of new data competing for limited mind space.
Therefore, information has to enter and exit short-term memory swiftly. We
always need to make room for ever-arriving new information.

Short-term memory has a serious space crunch, and that creates its share
of grief for parents, teachers, and students. Do you know that short-term
memory can hold a mere seven numbers at a time? As part of psychological
testing, it is common practice to administer what's called a digit span—a
child is given a series of numbers and immediately has to repeat them in the
correct order. Most older children and adults can absorb and repeat about
seven numbers. A few can handle eight, but most early elementary school
kids can only cope with four or five. Regardless, the space in short-term
memory is absurdly tight, especially when you consider that long-term
memory seems to offer us seemingly limitless capacity. Think about it,
short-term memory can only maintain seven paltry numbers. What does this
imply for schoolchildren? For one thing, it means that just about everything
a teacher says in the classroom is way too big to fit into short-term memory!
As a result, almost every message entering short-term memory has to undergo a process called recoding. Recoding is a neurodevelopmental function that takes on the very crucial abbreviating or condensing role.
Incoming data get collapsed into a tighter format, so they can fit snugly
within short-term memory.

Recoding usually calls for paraphrasing, a method through which students shorten long statements—pretty much automatically, without even
being aware they're doing it. It's a well-kept secret, but kids are engaged in
such recoding throughout the school day. In fact, it is probably the case that
in any classroom the most competent students are the ones who are the

most proficient paraphrasers, master abbreviators of incoming information. If a teacher describes what you need to do for your homework tonight, there is no way you can remember verbatim what she has said. The input has to get recoded into a more manageable, tighter, compact chunk. So the abbreviating or recoding process becomes a critical part of short-term memory. A child may whisper to himself or else just think in words that condense his teacher's most recent announcement or pronouncement. A student may prefer a more visual form of recoding. This has been called a "visual scratch pad." He forms images in his mind of what the teacher is stating. Short-term memory comfortably accommodates such imagery.

I know of several teachers who have taken the time to explain to their class how paraphrasing or imaging works to help them remember things that are too long for them to store. In fact, in one class students took turns being "paraphraser of the day." At various points, the teacher would say something like, "Okay Luke, what I just said was pretty long-winded; why don't you shorten it, paraphrase it for us to make it easier to remember." The students got experience with paraphrasing at the same time that they were learning about learning. Just what the doctor ordered!

Some kids with short-term memory dysfunctions have difficulty recoding. Processes that are entirely natural, nearly instinctive for some children, have to be taught explicitly to others. Maybe we all have some functions that operate instinctively, and some we must be formally taught to operate. Remember Ira's teacher found that if she shortened information for him, he was more likely to capture it. I like to urge parents to help kids practice recoding by having them summarize instructions or even whole experiences they have fielded during the day. Ira told his teacher he could remember things better if he squeezed them down into a tiny ball.

In my experience not many teachers are tuned in to the paraphrasing virtuosity of their students. And how many kids even know what the word "paraphrase" means? Wow. Here we have a crucial neurodevelopmental function, one of the major ways of learning, and it is seldom if ever discussed or dealt with openly in the classroom. Ira was lucky.

We're not done yet with our investigation of short-term memory. Short-term memory function poses another obstacle. Ira and his classmates have to hold on to types of information that enter through specific sensory pathways and are arranged in different patterns. Sounds, smells, printed words, verbal utterances, and emotional experiences are among the varied media. There's information that comes into short-term memory all at once (like the features of someone's face), while other inputs are delivered to our minds in a particular order (like the digits in a telephone number). So short-term memory must be highly versatile in what it accepts for quick storage. And

here's where some significant differences between students become all ↲
apparent. Some of them may show superior visual short-term memory,
while others are great at retaining verbal communication but not so good in
capturing visual fragments. Some have problems grabbing any information
inflow that's arranged in a particular sequence, which can jam their brain
circuits when they need to follow directions. I've seen kids whose short-
term memory repels just one kind of information or else several different
kinds. In Ira's case there was short-term memory leakage across the board.
Data were lost whether they were visual, verbal, sequential, or anything
else we could test for. One girl's parents commented to me perceptively,
"She remembers things she's seen so much better than things she's heard.
She is terrifically observant. She remembers what you're wearing and the
expression on your face. She helps me find the car when we park in the
garage at the mall. But then she instantly forgets a telephone message."
What a potent observation! Kids need to make maximum use of their
strongest pathway of input whenever possible. A child whose visual-spatial
input is well received should try to do a lot of the kind of imaging, making
use of that visual scratch pad I mentioned in connection with recoding. Of
course many kids who get called visual learners do this spontaneously; others have to be taught and urged to visualize while listening or reading.

Short-term memory is beholden to the rate of incoming information.
Some students can enter material in short-term memory, but somehow are
unable to do so rapidly enough. They have a short-term memory rate limi-
tation. They are breathless trying to keep up with the rate of information inflow in a classroom. Their short-term memory can only absorb information
when it is presented at a slowish pace, at least significantly slower than that
used every day by the teacher, the rate of input that's compatible for most
other students. Ira's teacher obviously had made that discovery. She needed
to slow down for him. His parents arrived at the same conclusion: "We've
learned to slow down when we have something important to say to Ira," his
father reported. "That way he seems able to take it all in. When we talk at
our usual pace we run the risk of losing him. Recently Ira has started to remind us, 'Slow down so I can remember.' "

Before we move on to the two other major subdivisions of memory, let's
summarize with a few key questions that might guide a parent or a teacher
in inspecting a child's short-term memory:

- How effective is this student in recoding information? Can she paraphrase and summarize? Can she make pictures in her mind to help
  with remembering?
- Does this kid make use of strategies (such as forming associations,

visualizing things, or whispering under one's breath) to secure information in short-term memory a bit longer?

- Is this student able to handle various kinds of information in short-term memory? Or is there a notable difference between sequences, spatial information, or verbal material and perhaps other information formats?
- Does this child get confused when information gets presented at a rapid rate?

One further issue worth exploring is the intimate relationship between short-term memory and the attention controls. Needless to say, it's hard to remember something if you're not listening! Tuning out takes its toll on short-term memory. Likewise, a child who has trouble detecting what's important may continuously file the wrong information in short-term memory, and those with superficial attention may not imprint important details. Therefore, when a child isn't retaining in short-term memory, it is legitimate for a parent to wonder, "Is it attention or is it memory?" Generally, if most of the other attention controls are intact, it is likely that the child's "in one ear and out the other" problems represent a weakness in short-term memory.

Some potential short-term memory breakdown points are:

- Recoding: being able to shorten information chunks
- Registering in specific formats: visual, verbal, sequential
- Registering fast enough
- Using strategies
- Making attention and memory work together

Back to Ira once more: I can report that over the three years I have known him, Ira has made slow but steady progress. He has come to understand his short-term memory barriers, asks to sit close to the teacher, and is starting to use a lot of good memory tactics, such as whispering under his breath and storing things both visually and in words. During his last visit, I asked Ira how his short-term memory was doing. He responded, "Well, it's still not perfect." I assured him that no living person has perfect short-term memory. Ira added, "Mine's working a whole lot better. It doesn't leak as much as it used to. I guess I'm fixing all the little cracks in my memory and I'm really trying to store things my teacher says, but I have to think about it or I forget." We are seeing some significant progress in Ira, although he still sometimes glances around to see what others are doing when extended instructions are given. But this is occurring much less frequently.

✌ ACTIVE WORKING MEMORY

Amber was ten when she was presented to me at a conference in her school. Her teacher adored this child but was rightly concerned because she was hopelessly absentminded and forgetful. Additionally, she was way behind in reading, writing, and mathematics. But Amber, well liked by the other kids, thought up strikingly original poems and knew more about more things than anyone else in her class. This forgetful girl had an incredible memory for trivia and for little details associated with specific activities or incidents in her life. Her long-term memory was a real showstopper. It invariably astounded her parents. When called on in class for a specific question, Amber was unsurpassed. Her recall was fast and accurate. Her responses were elegantly packaged with clarity in complete, often complex sentences, and wrapped up in impressive vocabulary. Unfortunately, her writing was disorganized and difficult to follow. Amber herself confessed that she kept forgetting what she was going to say while she was writing. Most often she would even stray off the topic or question because she couldn't think about the subject at the same time she was spelling, punctuating, and forming the letters with a pen. As she once told her teacher: "There's no room for all that stuff inside my head. Every single time I try to write, I forget what I'm doing. If I think about one thing like spelling, then I forget all about something else, like punctuation, or else, when I have to think hard to figure out what I'm going to write, my handwriting gets really messy. . . . I just can't hold things together inside my mind when I write."

Amber was able to decode individual words during reading as well as anyone else in her class, but she had trouble describing anything she had read. When she pursued mathematics problems, she knew her facts and processes but seemed to lose track of what she was doing while she was doing it. Also, she made many careless mistakes because she insisted on racing through her work. When asked why she did math so fast, she responded, "I have to work fast or I'll forget what I'm doing." All this made Amber increasingly anxious in school. As she described it, "I get real nervous all the time in school, and then I can't concentrate and do my work well." Amber's mother reported that she frequently seemed exhausted when she got home from school: "She acts as if she has just returned from the battlefield. Often she wants to go right to sleep; either that or she wants to cry. It's like her ego's been badly injured during the battle to be successful in class." When questioned, Amber would admit that she felt dumb compared to other kids.

All of Amber's learning frustration stemmed from a mind that had trouble holding things together while using or thinking about them. In other words, this was a conscientious and bright little girl battling an active working memory dysfunction.

Active working memory is the memory that you use when you head for your closet to look for your tan shoes. En route, it is vitally important that you bear in mind the reason you had originally decided on your closet as a destination. If you arrive and you have no idea what you are doing there, you have experienced some humbling limitations of your active working memory. There are times when I telephone my wife, and by the time I reach her I forget what I wanted to ask her. Active working memory is the place where the multiple intentions or components of any activity are held in place long enough to complete that activity. As such, it plays a vital role in learning and in productivity in school.

Active working memory accomplishes four specific duties: 1) providing mind space for the combining or developing of ideas—so, for example, you can retain the beginning of an explanation while listening to the rest of it; 2) offering a mechanism for holding together the parts of a task while engaged in that task—so, for example, you can remember where you just put down the scissors while wrapping a birthday present; 3) making available a meeting place where short-term memory can get together with long-term memory—so, for example, you can remember the question you were just asked while trying to search memory for its answer; and 4) serving as a place to hold multiple immediate plans and intentions—so, for example, you can stop for gasoline on the way to the mall without forgetting that you were going to the mall to buy some T-shirts. Let's elaborate on each of these active working memory traits.

The role of active working memory in providing ideas with a place to gel is critical when it comes to how a student undertakes thinking, listening, or reading. Active working memory lets a child remember the stuff at the top of a page while reading the last few sentences of that page. One clever frustrated mother was ruing the fact that when her son read a whole chapter in a book, it seemed as if all the information was "going in one eye and out the other!" Active working memory is supposed to hold together within a kid's mind the fragments of a teacher's explanation while she is completing that explanation. Those who have trouble with active working memory may forget what they are reading while they are reading it. They may lose track of the beginning of an assignment while they are attending to the end of the instructions. In one example I heard about recently, a seventh-grade social studies teacher was comparing the industrial revolution in France and England. Betsy, one of her students, kept gazing blankly into space in distraught confusion because whenever Mrs. Daly described one particular aspect of France, Betsy would forget what had been said about that feature in England. In other words, she could not keep enough data on her screen at one time to form a cohesive picture of what was being compared. Parents have to encourage such children to write down as much as possible. These are also kids who need to underline important points while reading and then review these at the end of each page, perhaps even dictating them into a tape recorder.

Parents have frequently complained to me that their children keep losing their place in the middle of a math problem. (This was a huge problem for Amber.) While doing long division they may forget what it was they had already done and what it was they had intended still to do. This is typical of students who have trouble holding together the components of a task while they are striving to complete that task. The result is chaos and disorganization. If you are constructing a model rocket ship, and you put the glue down while you assemble several critical tail features, can you then remember where you put the glue that you soon need again? For some kids this requirement constitutes a terrible burden. They can't keep track of the different aspects of a task while engaging in it. Like Amber, they are often described as absentminded. In reality, they have a space problem in their memory. Kids like her should not use much mental arithmetic; they need to write down steps before a problem is solved. They also require very well-organized workspace (so that, for example, there is a definite place where glue tubes are put).

Another working memory challenge entails temporarily binding together different parts of memory. As mentioned, active working memory is the place where short-term memory and long-term memory work together. If a teacher asks a student a question, that inquiry enters active working memory via short-term memory. The student then needs to hold that question in place in active working memory while searching long-term memory and doing some reasoning to come up with a response. It would be frustrating if he forgot the question while looking for the answer. But we often see children who do forget the question when they are only partway through the task. They literally forget what they're doing.

Sometimes active working memory has to serve as a temporary holding site for multiple information bits streaming out of your child's long-term memory. If someone mentions the name of a person your child knows, he begins thinking about that individual by pulling up various fragments of personal knowledge filed in remote parts of long-term memory. You mention Aunt Rose to eight-year-old Phillip. He starts to think about the woman by retrieving her appearance, memories of the last time he was with her, thoughts about experiences they have shared, and various attributes of her personality. All of these Aunt Rose data are allowed to flow into and collect in Phillip's active working memory while he is assembling a reasonably comprehensive portrait of his beloved relative. In this way active working memory serves as the mind's easel, a place where the parts of a picture come together to form a whole picture.

The final active working memory activity allows a child's mind to bear multiple intentions or plans at once. A student with problems in this area might stop and think about where to put a comma in a sentence and in so doing forget what she was planning to communicate in the remainder of the sentence. Remember that this was a big issue for Amber. The critical placement of the comma is an immediate need or plan. The thoughts to be presented in the sentence are part of a longer range, more distant plan. Such disintegration plagued Amber whenever she wrote; as a result her written thoughts were often perceived as totally disorganized or incoherent. Ultimately, Amber's parents helped her by having her list the key ideas to be presented in each paragraph before she started writing and worrying about such matters as spelling and punctuation. The four roles of active working memory are:

1. Holding together parts of ideas/stories while they develop
2. Holding together different parts of a task or activity while doing it
3. Holding together short- and long-term parts of plans
4. Holding together short- and long-term memory

Other Factors Affecting Active Working Memory

If an ingredient of a task is easy and fully automatic for your child, so she doesn't even have to think about it, valuable extra space is freed up in active working memory. On the other hand, if an aspect of a task is too much of a struggle for a kid, that ingredient is likely to crowd out other components, causing them to lose space on the active working memory screen. For example, if keyboarding or letter formation is difficult for a student, the effort demanded could occupy too much space in active working memory with a resulting loss of spelling accuracy. I can recall many students who have been able to spell accurately during a spelling bee but then misspell some of the same words on a written quiz or homework assignment. They can spell when all they have to do is spell, but when they have to juggle spelling with several other processes (such as letter formation, punctuation, and good grammar) in active working memory, they have to put up with inevitable accusations of carelessness.

Rowena, a nine-year-old patient of mine, battled a common variation on this theme. She had to work and think much too hard to spell with accuracy. As a result, far too much of her active working memory space was used up with the effort to spell correctly, and that sabotaged her thought processes or original thinking during writing. The result was a skein of unexpectedly simplistic reports in eighth grade social studies submitted by a girl whose oral discussions of current events were nothing short of dazzling. Her teacher reported to me over the phone, "Rowena is so bright, so perceptive, so totally original in the way she views her world, but you'd never know it to look at her writing. It reads and looks like the work of a six-year-old. And I know Rowena, who always aims to please, feels ashamed of what she produces. You can see it on her face and hear it in her voice when she comes up to me to hand in an assignment. I'm careful not to be too critical of what she gets down on paper. I don't want to rub salt in those wounds, and, besides, I know if she doesn't get discouraged and inhibited, eventually her writing will become automatic enough to allow her to think brilliant thoughts and write at the same time."

Rowena was also burdened with serious problems learning to read. Because of gaps in her perception of language sounds, it was painfully hard for her to associate sounds with symbols. Her early efforts at breaking the reading code were nearly futile and exceeded the capacity of her active working memory. That's because in struggling to unravel a long word, by the time Rowena arrived at the word's last sound, she would have forgotten its initial sounds, so she was unable to blend those little sound units into whole words. As she improved her ability to attach sounds to groups of letters through intense practice (with generous rewards) at home, she could hold more sounds in active working memory and her reading of multisyllabic words improved dramatically. In a recent follow-up visit, Rowena explained: "My tutor kept giving me nonsense words to read, they weren't like real words and I had to figure out how to pronounce them right. So I had to remember the sounds the letters made and practice putting the sounds together to make the nonsense words. That helped me so much; now I can read real words better, even real long ones. Before I could never remember all the sounds long enough to put them together. I can now. It's real easy. Reading's starting to be fun."

Active working memory craves peace of mind. Anxiety infects it like a computer virus. If you're feeling sad and preoccupied, there may not be room for much else in your mind's working memory. If a young child feels seriously despondent because his parents are having major marital problems, his active working memory can fill up with worries and not leave much room for academic ingredients. That's one reason why some children decline in their school performance when there are serious family problems. Parents may want to shield children from some of their own personal problems so as to leave some room in a child's mind for learning.

Finally, attention control horns its way into the act; no doubt about it, tightly controlled attention expands active working memory space and weak attention diminishes it. When a student is not concentrating, ideas slide right off his mental counter space.

So when a kid appears to have a shortage of active working memory, parents and teachers need to check out the possible causes: Could it be attention? Could it be that she or he has to work so hard on one aspect of a task that other components are getting shortchanged in memory? Or could this be a child who is anxious or emotionally preoccupied? If none of these factors is playing a major role, then caring adults should recognize the strong likelihood of a basic dysfunction of active working memory.

One further nugget of diagnostic confusion: it is possible to have good active working memory in some subjects but not such good active working memory in others. Thus, we can see what we call content-specific active working memory weaknesses. A student may struggle over meeting the active working memory demands that come with using the quadratic equations but have no trouble holding multiple ideas in mind while reading *Huckleberry Finn*. So we always have to wonder whether an active working memory deficiency is localized or generalized. Some very heavy use of active working memory can be seen in many sports. A center in hockey, a football quarterback, and a basketball point guard all need to keep track of many different information sources all at once. Some individuals seem to have active working memory strengths that are specifically well suited or custom-fitted to sports or music or drama or engine repair work. You might say that this stems entirely from motivation or interest. It's easiest to concentrate on and store things you find exciting, but it is also the case that someone gets interested in things that come together in his brain most readily, making the most sense in his kind of mind.

§⃝ LONG-TERM MEMORY

Vance, at age seventeen, a seasoned saltwater fisherman, likened his learning in school to trying to catch baby minnows in a fishnet with three-inch openings designed to land gigantic tunas. As he put it, "I try to catch something, but I don't ever come up with much! It passes right out through the big holes in my memory." Feelings of emptiness and futility gnawed away at the self-esteem of this once highly motivated and idealistic teenager to the point that Vance dropped out of school midway through his second attempt at ninth grade. He still had unhealed wounds from two humiliating passes through seventh grade, following which he had convinced himself that he was "born to lose."

Vance's academic woes were most evident in his writing, in math, and in test taking in general. He was a superb and zealous reader. He read the Harry Potter books at least twice and also regularly devoured *Time* and *Newsweek*. He was a collector of far-out ideas, thorny issues, and puzzling concepts and paradoxes. He was a master problem solver when it came to discussions of current political issues. Vance also played the guitar and composed his own music and lyrics. He avoided sports and repeatedly spurned opportunities to join a clique or gang. Vance was very much a dreamer and loved nature. He often went fishing, hiking through the woods, or trekking up mountains all by himself and used these forays as times for meditation and creative thinking. He would sometimes compose one of his song lyrics while perched on a boulder or oak branch. His peers liked and admired him, even though they saw him as a little bit strange and considered him a loner. He was strikingly handsome and always personable and straightforward, with no hidden agendas, and seemingly no rancor toward anyone. But Vance was always hard on himself, exceedingly self-critical.

When I met Vance, a few months after he had dropped out of school, I administered the STRANDS (Survey of Teenage Readiness and Neurodevelopmental Status), which is a standardized interview we use with older adolescents to uncover their neurodevelopmental profiles as well as other matters connected with school. Vance was candid in his responses to my queries. He described how embarrassed he would feel when called on in class; he simply could not recall highly specific facts on demand. He would draw a blank during tests. He did best in subjects that emphasized reasoning, understanding, and creativity but inevitably underachieved or else failed when teachers or the subject matter called for heavy memorization.

While writing Vance was unable to remember spelling, punctuation, grammar, and facts; that was partly why he enjoyed synthesizing and writing poetry or music—much more creative and less drenched with precise memory. Although Vance had no trouble grasping the concepts in math, which he found fascinating, he had tremendous difficulty learning math facts (at age twelve he still was not on top of the multiplication tables) and would also forget math procedures. Everything pointed to challenges with long-term memory.

There were no detectable gaps in his short-term memory; Vance could accommodate recent inputs, regardless of whether they were spatial, verbal, or sequential. Nor was there evidence of difficulty suspending or juggling several priorities in active working memory. The trouble spots all had to do with the filing and finding of content in long-term storage. Paradoxically, when I reviewed this with Vance and his parents, they laughed and pointed out that they had always considered Vance to have the best memory of anybody in their family. They were really perplexed by their son. As his dad pointed out, "He can remember the tiniest, most insignificant details connected to things that happened when he was a very little kid." Vance added that he could still do that—more about this common phenomenon later.

Vance confessed to me that often he felt convinced that he was mentally retarded. During elementary school, his brothers and kids in the neighborhood seemed to verify his disconcerting hypothesis and frequently called him a retard. He believed them, especially after he was retained in seventh grade and not permitted to take algebra (which he had longed to pursue).

Long-term memory is a seemingly limitless repository for preserving knowledge, skills, and life experiences. Its massive storage vaults can be drawn upon throughout life. In fact, long-term memory is so enormously vast that there has been debate over whether information ever gets lost *from* long-term memory or whether, when we can't remember something, it is simply lost *in* long-term memory. There is plenty of evidence supporting the latter possibility. We are all familiar with the tip-of-the-tongue phenomenon, in which we are trying to remember a person's name and just can't come up with it. Then, three days later, while stopped in our car at a traffic light, the name suddenly spews forth. It was never actually lost from memory; it was lost in memory. It may be that we don't forget things, but that we forget where we put them. So it is that the great long-term memory challenge is to store information systematically, to put it where we are most likely to find it later. For that reason, long-term memory consists of two stages: filing and access. Filing is the act of systematically entering information into the long-term memory storage system, while access is the process through which we subsequently locate that information. We can look at these two stages separately.

Filing in Long-term Memory

The effort to remember what has been stored in long-term memory is rewarded richly if the item was filed or stored systematically in the first place. When a student fails a quiz because she has trouble remembering the anatomical parts of the sea urchin from *Introduction to Biology,* there's a strong likelihood she wasn't very systematic when she first entered this information in long-term memory. The act of filing such material for later use is called consolidation. And it turns out that students have available to them four principal filing systems or forms of consolidation. Information can be stored as pairs (names with faces), as procedures (how to tie a necktie), as categories (types of citrus fruits), or as rules and familiar patterns (where to put quotation marks in a sentence). And kids can have problems with any one, two, three, or even four of these forms of filing. Let's inspect these four common filing systems.

FILING AS PAIRS

We form memory pairs between words and their meanings, between melodies and their titles, and between events and the dates on which they occurred. Pairing occurs when two bits of information are wedded and stored in long-term memory together. Then when you come across one half of the pair, you will think of its partner. Children master and file hundreds of thousands of such pairs in school and in their daily lives. Of course, the process doesn't terminate during childhood; we form and activate specific paired data throughout our lifetimes.

I can recall Brent, a boy with discrete breakdowns in memory pairing. As a result of his long-term memory dysfunction, in social studies Brent strived in vain to associate countries with their capital cities. He also got mixed up when he had to learn which presidents were in office during which important wars in our history. Even though he studied these linkages repeatedly, he failed a fill-in-the-blanks quiz on the topic. But Brent was unbeatable when reciting the batting averages of every player on the San Francisco Giants. He could also view a car of any vintage and instantaneously tell you whether it was a Chevrolet, an Edsel, a BMW, or a Lexus. Car and sports associations cohered as if they were bound in cement. Again, we can raise the question: Is it easier for a child to form strong associations in areas that interest him or does he somehow become attracted to facts and ideas that resonate and endure readily in his kind of mind? Or is it a little of each?

Parents and teachers can detect vast differences between kids when it comes to the kinds of pairings that they create easily and the kinds of pairings that seem unwelcome in their memory files. Some individuals are excellent at encountering a familiar face and thinking of her name, while others have to struggle to pair any names with faces outside their immediate family (and even that may not be fully automatic!). Some students have no trouble mastering the gamut of pairings in geography but reveal sieve-like brains when pairing words with their definitions. So they find it tedious and even futile to go over vocabulary words. Others meet similar frustration with math facts.

Kids who have these highly specific pairing weaknesses need extra drills to master them. They also can benefit from trying to form a pairing in more than one way. For example, Brent could have linked presidents to wars by saying them out loud, writing them down, and making an interesting diagram of them on his computer. He might then practice by having someone name wars, after which he states the president and then vice versa. When-

ever it's possible parents should try to make a game of the effort to bring together reluctant pairings.

FILING PROCEDURES

The storage of procedures necessitates the use of another department
within long-term memory, the one that remembers how to do things. In
long-term memory we store a voluminous manual of motor and nonmotor
procedural blueprints, such as the ones for how to drive a car, how to operate word processing software, and how to affix a nozzle to a rubber hose.
Procedural memory plays an aggressive role all across academic as well as
nonacademic territories. It is especially important in mathematics; as such it
created serious obstacles for Vance, even though his understanding of the
subject matter was intact. Remembering how to do things is important in
virtually every subject throughout the curriculum from music to the arts to
the sciences. Procedural memory also stars in every athletic pursuit and in
the school orchestra. Therefore, when a child is struggling in school, it may
be that she is having difficulty with those aspects of her course work that require procedural storage and retrieval.

When a child is having trouble with procedural memory, a parent is
likely to encounter the following anguished refrain: "But I don't remember
how to do this." It may be observed that she forgets the processes in mathematics or can't remember how to carry out directions her modern dance
teacher conveyed earlier this week. She could do it during class but not
subsequently. Procedural memory enhancement requires that parents and
teachers give a child repeated exposure to the process that needs to get
filed in long-term memory. The child should talk through the steps in a procedure, even going so far as to make a tape recording explaining to others
how the procedure works. She could play back this recording just before
undertaking an activity or assignment demanding the procedure.

FILING WITHIN CATEGORIES

All students are engaged in compiling a brain-based encyclopedia for
facts. Factual memory is tapped brutally on examinations, and, like procedural memory, it's at the heart of many learning challenges. My patient
Vance obviously had great difficulty filing facts in long-term memory so that
he could find them later during a test in school or class discussion.

In general, the filing system for facts is organized into categories—not
just categories but categories within categories and categories within categories within those categories. The more information gets categorized and
subcategorized, the more readily you can find it when you need it. Consequently, we file together animals, and within the animal fact category, we

might subdivide into wild animals and pets, then within the pet folder we subcategorize into gerbils, parakeets, dogs, and cats. This system enables us to go back through the subcategories and find whatever fact we need as soon as we need it—if and only if long-term memory is functioning optimally.

Kids like Vance who have problems filing facts need to map out graphically the facts they are trying to learn; with the help of their parents they need to make diagrams such as the one in Figure 4-2 . Such diagrams help set up information in categories that comprise our memory folders.

FILING RULES AND FAMILIAR PATTERNS

Last but not least, information gets filed in long-term memory in patterns and rules, which include a wide range of experiences, information patterns, and other sets of data that we repeatedly meet up with in life. A pattern might

TREES OF THE SOUTHERN UNITED STATES

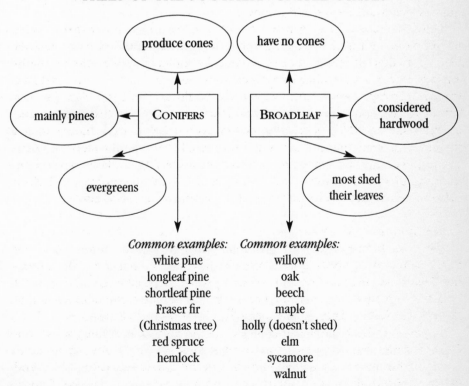

Figure 4-2.

be the arrangement of letters in a word or the shape of a right triangle or a particular social scenario (such as a disagreement with a friend) that keeps recurring in our lives. Closely associated with these patterns are various rules that help us predict patterns. For example, we might detect a pattern of a rectangle and associate that with the rule that rectangles have four right angles in them. I might have in mind a pattern or schema for an airport, so that even in an airport in which I have never been before, I have a sense of where the gates are and where I would need to go to collect my baggage. That is because I have filed airline terminal patterns in my mind. Throughout school, kids are exposed and reexposed to patterns in all subject areas. They become familiar with the patterns and they incorporate the rules associated with those patterns. Such consistent regulations as "i before e except after c" and "if this is the beginning of the sentence, then there needs to be a capital letter" represent the rules that you invoke when you come across a pattern, such as a word containing the consecutive letters "e" and "i."

Parents can help a child maintain a rulebook in any class where patterns and rules seem elusive. The rules are set up in two columns, one labeled "If," the other "Then." In the first column one might write, "If you see a rectangle with four equal sides"; in the adjacent column you write, "then it's a square." Also, children recognize patterns best when they've had practice making those patterns themselves (e.g., drawing squares while stating the rule).

Access to Long-term Memory

Finding what we know we know can be one of the most humiliating of memory assignments, a depressing occurrence all too familiar to those of us aging at an alarming rate! All kids struggle to recall. Some lose the struggle, some scrape by, and others are memory masters. We locate information in long-term memory through two primary channels: recall and recognition.

Recall

Recall is the process through which we excavate an entire chunk of knowledge or skill on demand. "Name the king of England at the start of World War I." "Who invented the cotton gin?" "What is the Fourth Amendment of the United States Constitution?" Over their years in school, kids have to become increasingly quick and accurate in such retrieval tours de force. Vance, however, lacked such speed and precision. When called on in class, a student has approximately three seconds to respond. If he takes longer than that, the academic atmospheric pressure rises steeply (along with his blood pressure). Vance lived in perpetual terror of being called on to provide a specific fact in a class discussion.

Students often have to engage in what we call convergent retrieval, the kind of memory called upon when there is only one possible correct answer, with no latitude whatsoever. Tragically for some, there exists only one capital of Nebraska, only one current prime minister of Great Britain. You either know the correct answer or you don't. This is in contrast to divergent retrieval, a kind of memory when there are multiple acceptable responses, such as "Can you give us some reasons why the United States economy is so strong?" Vance did much better when a question took this latter form and so could be answered correctly in more than one way.

I can remember a very discouraged student who kept coming up empty-handed when he had to rely on convergent retrieval memory. His father, an ophthalmologist in Boston, told me that nine-year-old Murray was "a leading authority" on the topic of prehistoric animals. This boy knew every prehistoric creature known to paleontologists. He was forever stunning the adult world with his encyclopedic repertoire of prehistoric animal taxonomy. Yet, when they studied prehistoric fauna in school, this boy actually flunked the quiz. Sure, he knew his prehistoric animals cold, but only when it was he selecting the one to talk about. When somebody else posed the question, and Murray had to find one specific denizen of a bygone eon, he failed. He could not converge in his long-term memory. This boy, much like Vance, was also having difficulty in other subjects that required such highly precise excavation of single data bits from long-term memory.

Recall breakdowns can be the hardest memory glitches to repair. Parents and teachers need to seek ways sometimes to bypass the requirements for rapid precise retrieval by allowing for more time on tests. Students need to take practice tests when studying for tests. They also need to be especially organized and thoughtful when they first file information in memory, discovering the right techniques to improve the filing system of long-term memory. In one of the schools we work closely with, the kids were discussing memory in a fifth-grade class. They described ways they can make it easier to file information. One girl said, "I have to get things in my mind in two ways. If it comes in words, I have to make pictures of it in my mind or even on a piece of paper. And if it comes in pictures I try to talk about it. That makes it much easier to remember." One of her classmates reported, "You know me, I like to talk all the time, so when I want to memorize things I just talk about them a lot, sometimes to my mom, sometimes to myself, sometimes to whoever will listen—even my guinea pig."

RECOGNITION

Recognition is a student's other essential information locator. This ability involves coming across some information or a particular pattern and knowing that you have encountered it before. School is teeming with recognition requirements. You have to recognize words when you read them. You have to recognize the operations that are called for within a word problem in mathematics. You have to recognize the personality traits of a character in a novel as that character emerges in one chapter after another.

Regrettably, although things keep making return appearances through the curriculum, they're not quite the same all the time. Kids have to recognize things they've heard or seen before although they're often obscured with differences on the surface. A word problem may concern a horse in frenzied pursuit of a fleeing goat. Greta, a struggling math student, has never before met up with horse and goat word problems, yet if she can penetrate the novelty of these animals in a math problem, there is an underlying challenge there (relative speed) that she has seen many times (perhaps it was a dog and a wild hare last time). Is she deceived by this superficial difference or can she peel it away to uncover a familiar pattern (a very frequent requirement in school)?

Greta studies the word problem and realizes that it will require setting up a simple equation. She then transfers over from her long-term memory the method of setting up such an equation. This is known as method transfer and is an active partner of recognition. Frequently, a student is expected to recognize familiarity (slightly obscured by superficial differences) and then transfer over from long-term memory the method that worked best in the past in the presence of that kind of information or that kind of demand. Recognition and method transfer is one of the major hurdles in mathematics. You have to see or hear something you have seen before and then use the methods that have done the trick in the past.

Familiarity somewhat clouded with superficial differences is reminiscent of themes and variations in musical composition. A composer may bring back a theme in a different key, a different tempo, or even turned upside down. A basic musical entity is somehow preserved, but in its reincarnations some surface differences can be heard. Incidentally, studies of experts from a wide range of fields have revealed that adults who are highly experienced at what they do are especially superb at digging out familiarity in the presence of superficial differences. A superior chess player observes a play evolving on the board. He has never seen that exact maneuver before, but he has encountered many other moves similar to it but with superficial differences. He will transfer over the method that has worked for him in the past, despite the fact that this time (and usually) there are some superficial differences. This is a critical key to successful learning, this awesome power to recognize familiar material in the presence of superficial differences.

Some children with long-term memory dysfunctions suffer from reduced recognition. Parents might fret over the fact that their son treats each math problem as if he's never seen anything like it before. These kids need lots of practice with recognition. For example, they might be given ten word problems in math and asked to identify which ones require subtraction, which division, which multiplication, and so forth. Then they should identify what was familiar in the problem that indicated what type it was.

Recognition yields another generous dividend; it makes learning more fun. School is boring and laborious if you fail to see the themes that keep coming back again in a biology class, in social studies, or in French. It is patterns, those regularly reappearing elements woven into a subject matter or discipline, that make learning interesting. Kids who fail to notice and appreciate recurring ideas and variations on those ideas may also fail to see the point of what they're asked to do and consequently become disengaged from the curriculum, one common cause of boredom in school.

Automatic Access (Automatization)

To succeed at writing essay questions on a test in high school, letter formation and most of the spelling of common words must be automatic. You can't stop to think about how to spell the word "entire" while having to write about contemporary Zambian government on a timed quiz. As children progress through school and life, access to much of what is stored in long-term memory is supposed to become increasingly swift and easy. This is known as progressive automatization. So much of what students are called upon to extract from long-term memory needs to be accessible instantly and available for use with virtually no expenditure of mental energy or effort. If a student must stop and think hard to remember basic math facts, it will take her far too long to solve her seventh-grade algebra equation. In fact, while struggling to recall the facts she risks forgetting the procedures. Vance's math career came to a halt because he was unable to achieve automaticity in his recall of facts and procedures.

Most reading comprehension difficulties in middle school stem from a lack of automatic decoding of individual words. If a sixth grader has to pause even briefly to sound out many of the words she meets in a paragraph, there is a strong likelihood she'll miss the point of much of the content. By early adolescence, word decoding should be pretty much automatic, thereby freeing up all of one's mental resources to interpret challenging ideas.

I can recall that when I was sixteen years old, my mother required me to take driver's education. I protested earnestly that if I underwent driver's education, she might have one fewer son, as I was never known for my motor coordination. Yet my mother stood fast (as usual). She responded bluntly:

"Look at all the dumb people who drive; even you can drive!" So, fortified with that encouragement, I made my ambivalent commitment to educated driving. It turned out that my initial estimates of my ineptitude were drastic underestimates! In fact, the shaken instructor considered a career change. One day when we were driving along (actually weaving along), he asked me to open the car window. I accommodated him by pulling over to the curb, turning off the ignition, putting on the emergency brake, and then rolling down the window. He looked at me, astonished, and said, "You don't have to do that." I answered, "What do you mean I don't have to do that?" He responded, "You don't have to park a car in order to roll down its window." In truth I had not yet sufficiently automatized the various motor subskills for driving to roll down a window while engaged in the act of driving. You could have one or the other but not both at once. I couldn't explain this phenomenon, since at the time I didn't fully understand it myself.

Parents can and must try to help students with delayed automatization. The only answer, I'm afraid, is plenty of drill on the basics. Whether it be math facts, spelling words, or keyboarding, nightly practice sessions are mandatory. Never was it truer that practice makes perfect. Kids whose lack of automatization has been ignored are going to feel overwhelmed in high school or even sooner. It's an absolute necessity for these kids. In general, schools do not have the resources to induce automaticity; whenever feasible it should be carried out at home, ideally with suggestions from the school. Ultimately, intense practice pays off.

✺ A Few More Memory Differences

Here are several more memory distinctions parents need to watch for. One of the most deceptive of these is the difference between voluntary memory and involuntary memory. Voluntary memory is the memory that you switch on intentionally, the kind of remembering that a student does when he studies for an examination or tries to warehouse a list of facts or concepts. Involuntary memory, on the other hand, is the memory that operates without turning on the ignition. Thus, if I ask you what you had for dinner last night, you might not recall it, having digested it without thinking about it. Voluntary memory is where all the academic action takes place. Students have to be adept at the intentional commitment to memory of generous servings of new information and skills.

Another important distinction separates episodic memory from semantic memory. Episodic memory is your memory for details having to do with events in your lifetime; it's your biographical storage. Semantic memory is your memory for formal learning; it's the storehouse of facts and ideas conveyed to you primarily in school. Vance's mother sighed as she voiced her bewilderment: "I have no idea why my Vance is failing in school. He has the best memory of anyone in our family." When I pursued this inviting clue and requested an example of Vance's remarkable memory, she replied: "Why, he's the only person in the family who can remember what color tie Uncle Marc wore on Thanksgiving three years ago. And five years ago we traveled to Florida on a vacation, and to this day Vance can tell you our hotel room number. We might go to a restaurant where we haven't been for several years. He remembers where we parked and can even recall what he ate and where the men's room was. But that kid can't ever remember his vocabulary or spelling words from last night." This paradox is typical of children who display an immense torrent of episodic memory amid a trickle of semantic memory. This contrast is so common that I wonder if these two memory capacities are somehow inversely related: the more you have of one, the less of the other. By the way, it is especially common to find phenomenal episodic memory among children with weak attention controls (see Chapter 3). As adults, they become impressive practitioners of Trivial Pursuit, having vacuumed up vast amounts of factual lint in their everyday lives. In the long run, strengths in episodic memory might even yield a constructive payoff. After all, in the adult world so much vital learning takes the form of on-the-job training, education through direct hands-on experience. In fact, these students often learn best through hands-on activities in which they are major players. Probably no one gets more out of a field trip than a kid with attentional dysfunction and a large-capacity episodic memory.

ᔧ THE OUTLOOK

It is common for students with memory difficulties to drop out of school, to write themselves off, or to just assume they are stupid. It is nothing short of alarming how many kids with excellent minds reveal memory deficiencies that they don't themselves know about. We have to reach these individuals before it's too late. Vance is a prime example. He is currently unwilling to go back to school, get a job, or think much about the future at all. He stays home, sleeps late, thumbs through magazines and newspapers, and watches soap operas and game shows on TV. As he puts it, "There's no use; whatever I touch goes bad on me. I've failed more than enough times in my life, and I'm not about to go through it all over again. No sir. No way." He still plays his guitar sometimes but has stopped writing music. He's clearly depressed and has been taking medication for this. But his antidepressant drug isn't helping him straighten out his life. When Vance and I discussed his memory problems, he felt redeemed, but he acted as if it were too late;

he had already given up on himself. What a shame, a scintillating mind going to waste. Vance felt as if he were so far behind in everything that there was no way to catch up. "It's like I'm buried and I just can't dig myself out." He's been frightened to venture into a career out of fear of more failure. We are still working with Vance. I think there is hope.

Many kids like Vance get involved with drugs and gangs. To his credit, Vance has resisted such escape routes. His parents and I continue to explore some safe pathways, ways in which Vance can use his toolshed of intellectual strengths and find a pathway toward productivity and gratification in life. If we can get him back on track, find him his niche, we can provide him with some ways of bypassing his memory weaknesses while also becoming more systematic in filing material in memory. I only wish that Vance could have understood himself sooner—before he had suffered such penetrating wounds to his self-concept. There are lots of misunderstood Vances out there.

Early detection of memory shortcomings can spare kids, their parents, and their teachers gallons of tears and hours of anguished sleep, to say nothing of arduous conflict.

✎ MINDS OVER TIME: KEEPING A WATCHFUL EYE ON MEMORY AS CHILDREN AGE

During early elementary school, keep an eye on pairing (attaching two pieces of information to each other and storing them together in long-term memory). This is a constant first and second grade need, as academic fledglings are challenged to link sounds with symbols, numbers with quantities, diverse objects with their names, and titles with songs and stories. Then as elementary school progresses, there is an increasing stress on recall, entailing the very exact remembering of a particular fact or skill on demand. As I have noted, so often there is only one correct answer that must be mined from long-term memory with unimaginable speed (three seconds during a typical class discussion). Writing is especially memory taxing from mid-elementary through middle school because that skill makes the heaviest demands on recall; as we have seen, students at that point have to remember spelling, punctuation, capitalization, grammar, prior knowledge, and their own ideas all at once. It is no wonder that many students who hate to write, write too little, or talk vastly better than they are able to write harbor underlying and memory inefficiencies that show up during middle childhood.

Recognition memory gets tested and retested throughout elementary and middle school. Students have to see the ideas or challenges that keep returning in mathematics, and whenever a pattern pops up, they need to recall the methods that have worked in the past when that pattern was present.

In middle school two other forms of memory merit observation, namely active working memory and automatization. As we have seen, active working memory, the brain's workspace, is vital for solving complex math problems, holding together all the parts of an essay you're writing, and remembering what you're reading while you're reading it. Middle school also is a showdown for automatization. Across the board, there is the prevailing assumption in seventh and eighth grades that basic skills in reading, writing, and mathematics are accessible by a student automatically, so that you can pile more difficult matter on top of them.

When students are in high school, all of the strains on memory become intensified, but no entirely new demands on memory are made. High school students, however, need to acquire insights into memory and its workings, so that they can become highly efficient and accurate in studying for tests. Such "metamemory" makes their learning lives vastly less stressful for them. They need to become proficient memory strategists; honor students play all sorts of remembering tricks. As an eleventh-grade straight A student let me know after a talk I gave at her school, "I love to think up remembering gimmicks. I make lists of things. I figure out fun ways to test myself before a test or I get in touch with my friend Jan, and we quiz each other over the phone or with instant messaging. I'm also big on making tables and diagrams of things and I've found out that by the time I finish making a diagram I know everything on it. It's kind of weird that I make a diagram to study from and then don't even need to study it." These strategies will serve her well in any career she tackles.

⮞ PRACTICAL CONSIDERATIONS

The following are some thoughts about management of the memory system during the school years:

• Kids operate their memory machinery in high gear day in and day out, yet we never teach them or their teachers how memory works. It is rather like driving a car without driver education or operating a DVD player without first decrypting its opaque multilingual operating manual. Students are driving in the dark with no headlights when it comes to operating memory and so too are many of their parents and their teachers. So parents and teachers must first learn more about memory and then impart their knowledge to their kids. I have developed something called the Memory Factory that we use to help kids understand memory.

• Writing, spelling, mathematics, and test taking are memory's biggest customers in school. Therefore, performance in these academic activities yields many clues regarding the memory workings of a student's mind. Also, continued practice in these skill areas can increase memory capacity.

• Students should realize that there's a big difference between being "stupid" and having trouble remembering certain kinds of things. Nobody's memory works with total accuracy.

• Studying for tests is a healthful exercise for mind development. Among other things it is a vivid lesson in getting prepared for or anticipating an upcoming critical event. Children have to realize that they will be taking such "tests" throughout their lives.

• In devising student examinations, teachers should strive for a good balance between understanding and remembering. Tests should not reward pure rote recall. In secondary school, in particular, students ought to be allowed to bring several pages of their own notes.

• Long-term filing works best if you go right to sleep. The minutes before bedtime are crucial. A student shouldn't study and then place a phone call to her best friend. Call your friend, then study, then go to sleep—in that sequence to foster optimal consolidation in memory.

• School policy makers should consider that long-term memory works best when there's sufficient time for consolidation. This does not occur when you partake of social studies for forty minutes followed by algebra for forty minutes, then English for forty minutes, and, immediately thereafter, physical education. Switching from one subject to another pretty much prevents the consolidation of the one that preceded it. Class periods should be longer, and there must be consolidation time—perhaps used by small groups of students who in the final twelve minutes of the session talk about what they've learned this period. Block scheduling (e.g., six weeks of nothing but chemistry) also merits consideration.

• Attention and memory are compatriots. When you're not concentrating it's hard to remember. Therefore measures used to improve attention will help memory function (see Chapter 3).

• Children need to be systematic in their use of memory. Studying for tests provides an opportunity to do so. They should be able to ask themselves, "How am I going to remember this?" and then come up with a deliberate plan for doing so. Before an examination, students should be told to submit their learning plans to the teacher. Such plans should include a timeline for studying the material, a description of the choice of material to study, a way of putting the information in an organized format that will make it easier to remember, and methods of self-testing. Schools should teach kids how to set up such a plan. In many respects, studying for tests in childhood is the same as preparing for an important career event when you are older (e.g., meeting with a major customer, going for a job interview, making a presentation to an influential audience). In all instances the key is proper preparation and anticipation.

• Students should master the tricks of remembering and include them in their learning plans. The best way to remember something is to change it, to transform the information in some manner. If it's visual, make it verbal, if it's verbal create a diagram or picture of it. Use plenty of lists, tables, graphics, and other devices so that you're not merely sponging up the subject matter intact as it was presented. Another way to alter the inputs is to elaborate on them, to connect new data to prior learning or experience and to file the new information in several categories of knowledge. The question "What does this stuff fit with or remind you of?" is key to remembering. The more richly you transform and connect knowledge, the more actively accessible it will be in memory.

• Students need to realize that recall and recognition work best when they work often. Practice makes perfect. If you seldom use certain skills or information, they'll be hidden away when you need them. If you only think about what you've learned between 8:30 A.M. and 3:00 P.M., it will be difficult to access.

• All learners should understand and then consciously activate and exercise active working memory. There are many ways to do so. Mental arithmetic is one such: How much is 21 times 11? Try doing this in your head. Children can practice with longer and longer numbers. The age-old game Simon Says stresses active working memory (i.e., can you remember the original instructions while listening to the more recent inputs?). It also calls for firm attention control.

• All kids can benefit from practice bolstering active working memory during reading. They can do so by underlining or highlighting and then going back and orally summarizing into a tape recorder.

5

Ways with Words ❧

Our Language System

It is . . . a serious drawback to me in writing, and still more in explaining myself, that I do not so easily think in words as otherwise. . . . I therefore waste a vast deal of time in seeking for appropriate words and phrases, and am conscious, when required to speak on a sudden, of being very obscure through mere verbal maladroitness, and not through want of clear perception. That is one of the small annoyances of my life.

FRANCIS GALTON, as quoted in Thomas G. West, *In the Mind's Eye*

If we went out on the street dressed the way we talk, we should be arrested for indecent exposure.

JAMES THURBER

Robert Frost, in commenting on his trade, once wrote, "A poem . . . begins as a lump in the throat, a sense of wrong, a homesickness, a lovesickness. . . . It finds the thought, and the thought finds the words." Frost was describing a miraculous and mysterious process, namely the constant back-and-forth exchange between words and thoughts. The establishing of this flow is one of school's most daunting demands. Students struggle endlessly to get their thoughts into words and just as often to use words to construct their thoughts. And their attempts to find thoughts within the words they hear or read can be just as taxing. That's where the language system comes in.

Parents should be aware that language is all-consuming in the everyday existence of their children. Obviously it is the medium for communication with friends, siblings, teachers, pets, and parents. It is as well an indispensable ingredient of reading, spelling, mathematics, and writing. Language is a close partner of memory; translating facts and ideas into words (especially their own words) helps kids retain information. Language is raw material from which vital concepts are shaped (such as the concepts of "racial harmony" or "ethical behavior"). Language even helps provide some internal control over your child's behavior; it is known that talking through conflicts or temptations, using inner voices, often prevents a child from being rash or lashing out. Also, effective language lubricates peer relationships by enabling a child to communicate with a classmate in a way that conveys positive feelings and is not antagonistic.

Children's language circuits handle heavy traffic throughout the school day. Language monopolizes English class, Latin, the social sciences, and many other wordy content areas. Verbal demands intrude on less obvious academic territories as well. For example, using words bolsters mathematical understanding, especially when combined with visualization. Describing and also picturing the difference between the radius and the diameter of a circle sharpens these distinctions in your child's mind. Language even gets into the game when it comes to sports—from understanding a coach's rapid-fire verbal commands to interpreting the pithy communications with teammates and adversaries.

Students who lack agility with words fall behind their wordsmith peer group. Nonverbal thinkers are beleaguered, often misinterpreted, and maligned. Children with neurodevelopmental dysfunctions that seem to limit their language capacities are missing some or all of the verbal tools needed to keep pace in classrooms. Our society unwittingly punishes and discriminates against these kids for the way they're wired.

❧ THE DIFFERENT LANGUAGES THAT MAKE UP LANGUAGE

Parents and teachers need to take note of the fact that kids are expected to be accurate with almost as many varieties of their own language as there are soft drinks to choose from. Some of these verbal options come in pairs, including automatic and literate language, concrete and abstract language, basic and higher language, and receptive and expressive language. Let's take a look at these varied communication codes.

Automatic Versus Literate Language

There are kids who sound like late-night-show emcees during informal chitchats yet are unable to deal with the language of formal learning.

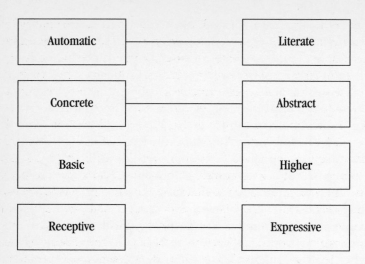

Figure 5-1.   Some languages that make up language.

There's a crucial distinction here, one that's mostly overlooked by parents and teachers, and that is the striking contrast between automatic language and literate language. Automatic English is the English spoken at the bus stop, in the lunchroom, and at the mall. "Hey, like, I'm not gonna touch that one; if she just wants to like chill out instead of goin' to the dance with him, like, that's her thing." It is the English of everyday banter and interpersonal dealings. The lingo tends to be concrete and calls for mostly very common words (so-called high-frequency vocabulary).

Literate language, on the other hand, includes sophisticated classroom talk as well as academic reading and writing; it's the verbal craftsmanship and showmanship that is exhibited when one is studying or expounding upon concepts like "due process" or "energy resources." Literate language is harder work. Often it is decontextualized, that is, removed from everyday familiar background settings, dealing, for example, with major differences between the last four Chinese dynasties rather than "what I most like to do on weekends." Literate English takes in technical terms (such as the workings of microcircuits) and relates to "the there and the then" rather than resting in the "the here and the now."

Arnold beautifully exemplified the enormous gulf that can separate literate from automatic versions of the English language. He was a twelve-year-old boy with undulating blond hair and blue eyes that glittered like opals. He dressed impeccably in cargo pants, red plaid bulky shirts, and silver Nike running shoes with laces untied. He was a charmer, always in high demand in the peer marketplace, and spontaneously witty. I invariably enjoyed my contacts with this jovial and ultra-cool if somewhat glib kid. He was a consummate talker, a verbal geyser, bantering intently and comfortably with adults as well as other profuse conversationalists of his own age. He had comments on everything and everyone he encountered. I was asked to see this middle schooler because of reading and writing problems; Arnold read too slowly and was always vague or incomplete in his comprehension. His writing was simplistic and brief with monotonous sentence structure and words confined to those used in everyday common speech. There was a sense that Arnold had to simplify his ideas to get them into language. When his thoughts couldn't find their words, he went for easier thoughts. There were also significant concerns about Arnold's attention; he was highly distractible, especially in a classroom setting. He had been taking Ritalin for this problem with only modest effects.

Arnold's academic frustrations were starting to take their toll on his sizable ego. He was rapidly losing interest in everything connected with school. There were nightly homework battles, and Arnold would have failed a lie detector test whenever he denied having homework to do. As if to vent all his pent-up academic anguish, Arnold was unconscionably cruel to his kid brother, an A student in third grade. Arnold tormented Steven incessantly, calling him a "dork" and a "fag," among other things. He spent extended periods on the phone and became obsessed with his video games, which he could have entertained himself with for at least twenty hours a day had he been permitted to do so. His parents were despondent and desperate. "He shows all these flashes of brilliance, absolute brilliance," his father commented. "But he doesn't seem cut out to accomplish much of anything in school." Arnold himself down deep felt the sharp pain that comes with being a disappointing kid.

When I first was introduced to Arnold, I chatted with him for a while and was struck by his fluent talking. I thought to myself with total confidence, "This kid surely doesn't have any language problems. What a terrific speaker!" Boy, did he have me fooled. Arnold had virtually no literate language ability despite being so articulate and fluent in his automatic language output. When we tested his understanding of language, Arnold showed clear evidence of very weak sentence comprehension. For example, when I read him the sentence "Linda's dog chased the kitten and ran away" and then asked him who ran away, Arnold responded, "The kitten." He gave that answer only because the noun "kitten" was closer to the verb "ran," a common kind of primitive distortion often found in kids with language dysfunctions. He committed plenty of other errors in his attempts to extract meanings from sentences. He also could not store chunks of language in short-term and active working memory; that is, in the midst of reading or listening, Arnold would simply lose his way and forget the content he was concentrating on. On a test of his ability to follow verbal instructions, I showed him a page filled with Xs, dots, circles, and squares and told him to "put a circle around the small X that is farthest away from the small square." He looked at me thoroughly confused and couldn't respond.

In the conveniently repetitive and predictable world of conversational English, Arnold could keep pace readily with language interchanges; his keen social sense helped him figure out and respond to what people were saying, even when he couldn't completely interpret their words and phrases. Arnold deceived his parents and teachers. They never suspected trouble with language in such an affable, talkative guy. Neither did I until we took a closer look at his writing and reading and directly checked his ability to comprehend. As an aside, Arnold demonstrated something we see all the time: kids with language problems who look as if they have attention deficits. In truth they are tuning out because it is so hard for them to understand. One of his teachers wrote on a questionnaire we sent her, "He's like two different kids. When studying English or social studies, Arnold is all over the place. He can't sit still. He has to poke, provoke, and cajole whoever is seated next to him. He stares into space and goes off into some dream world. Then when he has art class or when he studies maps in geography, that boy is riveted. He's as tuned in as you can get. It's as if his mind shuts off and goes off when he's immersed in words and sentences." Yes, Arnold's attention controls are turned off by language. This is not really an attention deficit. Rather his attention is not being rewarded with usable information, so understandably he tunes out. Attention needs to be nurtured. Kids like Arnold may improve a bit on medication, but not for very long. The drug is like a Band-Aid; it covers up the underlying language problem partially and often temporarily.

I meet up with many students like Arnold who impress you with their automatic English function and thus are colorful conversationalists, but they fall short on literate language capacity. Such discrepancies become increasingly conspicuous as they progress through the upper years of elementary school and into secondary education, but initially go undetected. Many pediatricians, for example, equate a child's personality (often revealed through conversation) with "intelligence." That can be highly misleading and may actually prevent personable kids with bona fide language dysfunctions from being understood and helped. One of my fellow pediatricians, in referring a child to me, reported: "This kid seems so damned bright in my office. He talks a blue streak and always has amusing and perceptive things to say. I've always thought of him as a genius, but it sure doesn't show up on his report cards or achievement tests. His parents and I need help sorting this guy out."

Concrete Versus Abstract Language

Parents and teachers should be alert for differences in a child's ability to handle concrete versus abstract language. Concrete language has meaning that comes directly from our senses. It portrays things we can picture, feel, smell, or hear. The words "cat," "perfume," "spiciness," and "noisy" are all concrete words. Abstract language, on the other hand, is language that can't be deciphered directly through a sensory pathway. It doesn't tap your sensory experience. It includes words like "elite," "irony," "symbolism," and "sportsmanship," terms resistant to instant visualization (unless you conjure up metaphors or analogies or personal experiences to illustrate them). As kids advance through school, an increasing share of the language inflow is abstract, disconnected from immediate sensory transmission. Learners like Arnold will experience increasingly severe academic stress as words and sentences become less concrete. In fact, the same teacher who commented on Arnold's attention pointed out, "He does pretty well when we're having a discussion in which kids share their own experiences, but when we talk about the world of ideas stemming from some book we've been reading, I know I'm going lose Arnold. He's very, very concrete."

Mounting levels of abstract terminology pervade the sciences, literature, and mathematics. That commonly leads to a decline in the grades of many students with language dysfunctions—unless, of course, they are highly aware of their problem, in which case they can keep a personal dictionary of the tough abstract terms and review it periodically. Parents and teachers can ask themselves: "Is this child incorporating some abstract words or is she totally bound to the concrete in the way she talks and in what she seems to understand?"

Basic Versus Higher Language

Another lofty hurdle separates what I call basic language from higher language. Basic language is the language of most of elementary or lower school. It is often quite literate English, but it tends to be practical and directly to the point. Higher language is more abstract and symbolic, more technical, more densely packed with ideas and information, more inferential (not saying all it's meant to imply), more likely to be ambiguous, more apt to reflect a particular point of view than absolute fact. Poems contain symbols, editorials express points of view, philosophical or political essays are drenched with implications that are never totally fleshed out for the reader. As kids progress toward secondary school, they have to ascend into these lofty realms of higher language, a slow elevator ride that enables them to attain new heights of sophisticated thinking, reading, and writing. Higher language clears a path for the pursuit of complicated ideas as well as the ability to talk about such things. Higher language capacity can make it much easier to learn a foreign language as well. The renowned speech and language pathologist Dr. Elizabeth Wiig characterizes the normal dramatic early adolescent transition to higher language as a student starting to use language as an instrument for learning. There is also evidence to show that the period from age nine to thirteen is a time of rapid growth in the language area of the human brain.

It is difficult to get through high school unscarred without having higher language as an instrument for learning. I was concerned about this when I saw Arnold and became worried about the pitfalls he was likely to encounter as a high school student. I needed to prepare Arnold for this looming trial by verbal fire.

More and more kids fit Arnold's description; they are underachieving and turning off their learning channels. As late as high school they remain verbally rigid, concrete, and vague when it comes to ferreting, figuring, and talking out complex ideas in science, history, and literature. Some, like Arnold, had problems earlier in their education, while others falter for the first time in ninth, tenth, or eleventh grade, as the demands of language complexity outpace and exhaust their language resources. Arnold's mother, a highly successful attorney, came to the conclusion when he was in tenth grade, "Arnold has gotten to the point where he doesn't seem to understand that he's not completely understanding, especially when he reads. He seems to skim the surface of meaning. When we can get him to study, all he does is memorize things, and half the time I think he doesn't know what he's memorizing. He simply aims to regurgitate it all on the test."

How do parents prevent this downfall? Kids from a young age need to keep reading and writing actively—that is, not just to complete an assignment or topic but to joust vigorously with the subject matter through words and sentences, verbal interchanges, rewordings, arguments, elaborations, summarizations. They have to stay in verbal shape. They need opportunities at the dinner table, in the car, and elsewhere to talk about intellectual issues at length. They need to read and discuss newspapers and magazines, along with their schoolbooks. Heavy doses of discussion at home can smooth the potentially turbulent and traumatic transition to higher language. There also may be a need to cut back on totally nonverbal and antiverbal activities, such as video games and some forms of television.

Receptive Versus Expressive Language

Some kids talk much better than they understand while some others understand much better than they talk. So our final distinction concerns the sharp difference between receptive language and expressive language. Receptive language comprises a child's understanding of verbal communication (spoken and/or written). This would include her ease at understanding the moral of the tale her kindergarten teacher is telling or the ability to get a friend's pun. Expressive language is language production, the means of translating thoughts into words, sentences, and more extended messages. This capacity is used when a student has a brilliant or at least a reasonable idea and has to put it into sharp words during a debate. Receptive language is the stuff of reading. Expressive language is writing's code. Arnold was experiencing the chronic pain that accompanies problems in both of these realms. But that's not always the case. Take Lenore, for instance.

Lenore was a shy girl I observed in a school in California. She loved to read poetry, and she and her mother raised prize orchids. Each day Lenore dressed carefully for school. In fact, she overdressed for school, as if she were attending a semiformal religious ceremony. Lenore was the lone dependable bassoon in her middle school orchestra. She was a conscientious early adolescent but one who put off her teachers by never saying much of anything in class. When called upon she would utter incomplete sound bite responses, manufacturing basically correct but subcompact answers encoded in highly condensed phrases. At times that made her sound almost hostile or, at the very least, blasé. But she excelled on tests, especially multiple choice and fill-in-the-blanks. In the classroom, she often appeared to be bored, but she never complained of boredom, and it was clear from her test scores that Lenore was absorbing and understanding more than most students.

Lenore was struggling with expressive language. Lenore's teacher, Mrs. Thompson, had been involved with our teacher-training program, Schools Attuned, and recognized the phenomenon. Mrs. Thompson provoked considerable faculty discussion with a great question: "Does Lenore have a problem? Or, are some people just meant to be highly competent strong silent types? Why do we feel that all of our students have to do everything well? Who decided that they must all be great orators?" I don't know, but no doubt as students move through the school years, their understanding of challenging ideas is helped by translating those ideas into their own words; that means that expressive language can strengthen the effectiveness of receptive language, a boost that may not be available to kids like Lenore. Also, this child needed more powerful language artillery to gain confidence, to relate well to others, and to cope with the inevitable stresses of life.

Talking through her worries with her parents actually worked better than the medication she was taking! I encouraged Lenore and her parents to "work out" verbally. I explained how important it was to help Lenore understand her language output dysfunction and then to begin "exercising her verbal muscles" whenever and wherever possible. She needed to immerse herself in class discussions, but her teachers were to alert her a day in advance regarding the topic, so she could think through how she would respond. I suggested to Mrs. Thompson that she could benefit from opportunities to give some lessons to younger children on the subject of raising orchids. Toward the end of that year, Mrs. Thompson felt that she had seen progress. She commented, "Lenore is definitely taking more risks in class. I've told her she needs to volunteer and say something at least once in every class discussion. Sometimes I inconspicuously tap her on the shoulder to let her know her comments are due. She responds well to this. I know her parents are also working on getting her to communicate more. Little by little, that verbal dike is opening." At home her mother and father were indeed coaxing Lenore to elaborate on her thoughts and talk in complete sentences. They encouraged her to keep a tape-recorded diary. Luckily during that same period Lenore discovered Janice, a best friend with whom she felt comfortable sharing her feelings and gabbing at length. The expressive language campaign was paying off.

In the past, we believed that if a person was keen in receptive language, he would be equally sharp when it came to expressive language. However, there is now evidence to prove that, as we saw in Lenore's case, wide differences between an individual's expressive and receptive language are very common. Kids who are better at talking than they are at understanding need to become more accurate listeners, and they need to be encouraged to read and engage in other language-soaked experiences to improve their reception. While young, they should listen to stories on tape. As they grow up, they ought to have limits placed on TV watching, which, in excess, may aggravate a dysfunction of receptive language by making the child too dependent on visual cues for meaning.

§• LANGUAGE LEVELS

Vigilant parents will notice when a child's language capacity is too limited to satisfy current learning requirements. In order to be keen detectors of language slowdowns, gaps, or delays in your kids, you need to know what I like to call the language levels, a kind of upside-down pyramid inside of which the verbal demands accumulate in larger and larger chunks (see Figure 5-2). The levels rise from the tiniest units, namely language sounds, up through important fragments of words (like prefixes, roots, and plurals), to entire words, to whole sentences, to lengthy chains of sentences, and finally to the process of not just thinking *in* language but thinking *about* language. Your child has his own degrees of ability at these specific levels of lan-

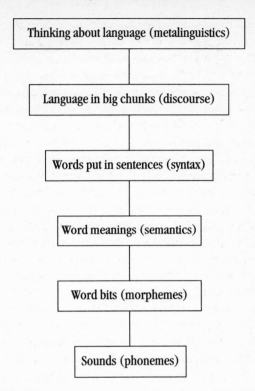

Figure 5-2.   The language levels.

guage. So a student may have no trouble acquiring a good vocabulary, but may struggle to pick up fine distinctions between language sounds (like "em" and "en"). Your child's performance at the six language levels is supposed to improve noticeably and become increasingly effortless over time. Whether he actually does so will critically influence his overall school performance.

Teachers and parents will discover that, over time, proficiency in these levels does not occur rigidly from bottom to top. In fact, elementary school-children grow in their understanding and formation of sentences (syntax) well before they have to contend with the proliferation of technical and abstract vocabulary that occurs in middle school and high school and college (semantics). Metalinguistics, the ability of your child to think about language and how it works, seems to grow at the same time as all the other levels, although such thinking usually accelerates in the upper grades of secondary school.

The Sounds in Words (Phonology)

Sounds within words comprise the most microscopic level of language. Words consist of arbitrary sounds called phonemes bound together in a wide variety of blends. There are somewhere around forty-four phonemes in English. Local dialects may introduce a few bonus and/or bogus sounds. A sampling of these language sounds is found in the following table.

A SAMPLING OF ENGLISH PHONEMES

Type of Language Sound	Sample Letters	Word Example
Short vowel	i	pig
Long vowel	o	throw
Consonant	m	macho
Beginning consonant blend	scr	screech
Ending consonant blend	nk	oink
Consonant digraph	ch	chalk
Vowel digraph	ea	each
Diphthong	ay	stay

It is useful to note that there is a substantial difference between a language sound and a syllable. Young children need plenty of practice becoming comfortable with the language sound system and coming to see phonemes for what they really are, word building blocks.

Children differ markedly in the extent to which they can discern subtle differences between the phonemes. For some the reception is excellent. They distinguish between sounds so cleanly that they have no trouble detecting the difference, say, between "boot" and "boat" without even benefiting from clues in a sentence (e.g., "He rowed the boat"). For some, language sound differences are blurry, their reception full of static. Certain sounds that ought to be distinctive are perceived by some minds as identical or nearly so, lacking the sharp audible borders needed for differentiation. As one thirteen-year-old boy, Pedro, said in looking back at his earlier language trouble, "When I was little, too many words sounded the same to me. So I had to listen real carefully when somebody was talking. Sometimes I had to guess what a word was from the words around it. And sometimes it was hard. Like if someone said, 'During that game he had a good team,' it might sound almost like 'During that game he had a good time,' so I'd have to try to figure out which one was right. But then I didn't have enough time because the person just kept on talking. So my listening had a lot of guessing in it."

Children who are poor sound sorters are said to have diminished phonological awareness. As they advance through school, like Pedro, they are apt to overutilize clues from sentences, engaging in a guessing game in which they gloss over some of the words due to their incomplete perceiving of the language sounds; they then strive to supply those missing words based on what would make sense. Such "betting on the meaning" is far too demanding and time consuming, and, as school content becomes increasingly removed from everyday contexts, the desperate guessing game gets harder to pull off. Children with reduced phonological awareness are at high risk for serious delays in reading, spelling, and writing. They also can start to have trouble with their attention controls, perhaps due to mental exhaustion.

Many of these kids suffer from impairments involving so-called phonemic awareness (as opposed to phonological awareness). The term "phonemic awareness" is used widely and signifies a child's level of insight that words consist of individual language sounds. That means she can divide a word into its language sounds and reblend the sounds to re-create a whole word. For instance, the word "magic" can be dissected into four English language sounds (phonemes): "m," "a," "gi," and "k," and then re-constituted into "magic." That taking apart and putting back together, commonly referred to as word segmentation and reblending, is a critical requisite for attaining reading decoding skill, the ability to identify words—words you are familiar with as well as words you have never seen before.

The phonological job of decoding a word is assisted by some visual analysis and visual memory for the appearance of that word. Once a child has analyzed and perhaps even vocalized the phonemes in a word, she can take that collection of sounds and compare it to words she has in her vocabulary, a process known as "lexical access." It's as if she is consulting an internal dictionary to see if the decoded word matches some word in her long-term memory. While all these processes are taking place, the student has to hold the various components of the decoding task in active working memory until the whole word is identified. Wouldn't it be a shame if in the process of sounding out the last phoneme in a word, the child forgot the first two? That happens all too often among unsuccessful readers. So a child's word decoding, like so many other learning endeavors, calls for a neurodevelopmental team effort. Reading problems may stem from dysfunctions of phonologic or phonemic awareness, deficient analysis or recognition of visual patterns, active working memory limitations, and/or reduced lexical access. The latter might be part of a much broader memory retrieval or language dysfunction.

There are data to suggest that at least 20 percent of the children in the United States have difficulty with these processes. It is thought that problems with phonological or phonemic awareness are the most common breakdowns. Early on, affected children demonstrate difficulty rhyming words. In first grade, when you ask them to break out the individual sounds in a word, they become confused, baffled by the request. As they get older it is hard for them to manipulate the sounds within words. For example, an eight-year-old with this form of dysfunction would be at a loss if you asked, "What word would you get if you took away the 'm' sound in moose and instead started it with the 'g' sound?" Such substitution exercises are commonly used to gauge phonemic awareness. These kids traditionally have been called "dyslexic" (another unhelpful label, in my opinion). They have serious problems breaking a word down into its sounds and then splicing it together again, a mandatory process for the deciphering of unknown words on paper. As they progress through the grades, they may make gains in their word decoding, but many of them continue to lag behind their classmates in reading. By middle school, they may be able decode far more words, but the process will demand way too much time and effort. They lack the automaticity we described in the previous chapter. As a result, so much effort goes into single-word decoding that they have few if any resources remaining to grasp the overall meaning of the paragraph and retain its important details.

Judy, a child with whom I'm currently working, is typical. At age nine and in third grade, she is reading only on a late kindergarten level. She has a very limited sight vocabulary (words you know as soon as you see them), so she has to stop and figure out too many words, including some of the most common and short ones. She becomes hopelessly confused when her reading tutor asks her to break a word down into its sounds. Judy can't spell at all and is aware that her classmates spell better than she. There is something glaringly conspicuous about spelling, something that inflicts harrowing shame on poor spellers. They take their misspellings as visible evidence of a defective mind. We adults can think of spelling as a rather trivial ability, one that has no bearing on a career; parents and children and some of their teachers take it seriously, often too seriously. That can needlessly wipe out the motivation and self-concept of a young child. Judy recently told her mother that she is "one of the dumbest kids in the class, even stupider than most of the boys." She sobs nearly every night at bedtime despite love and reassurance from her parents. They are at their wits' end because Judy loves to learn. She is most successful in mathematics, and her teacher reports that she reveals an abundance of knowledge about lots of different topics. She used to be enthusiastic about school; now she announces that she can't stand it. Every day is an excruciating confirmation of her inferiority to others.

Kids can't withstand that feeling for very long without suffering an alarming decline of self-esteem. This is especially true when they have no under-standing of the nature of their problem. Judy needed to find out that she was smart but having some trouble grappling with the language sounds. When I got a chance to explain this weakness to her, and her parents fol-lowed up with some booster doses of this demystifying information, Judy started to feel much better about herself; she came to see that she was not pervasively defective. Here's a condensed chunk of my explanation to her: "You know, Judy, there are loads of kids out there who are a lot like you. And they feel terrible about how they're doing in school. I sure can under-stand why. When it's hard for you to read and spell as well as other kids in your class, you feel really bad about yourself. You wonder what's wrong with you, and you think bad things about your brain. But it's not that you have a weak mind or anything like that. It's just that you have trouble figur-ing out the little sounds that go together in words. They don't come into your mind clearly enough. That makes it very hard for you to hear the sounds in word. It's not that you're hard of hearing or anything like that. It's just that your mind doesn't pick up the sounds clearly enough. So it's diffi-cult for you to do things with the sounds, like match up a sound with a lit-tle group of letters for reading or spelling. It's a really common problem, a problem that so many smart kids have, and we can all help you work on overcoming your language sound problem."

Our evaluation of Judy confirmed significant problems with phonemic awareness, a neurodevelopmental dysfunction impeding phonological awareness. When I asked her to name as many words as she could that rhyme with "lake," she included in her list "like," "leak," and "lock." On the other hand, Judy displayed clear strengths at other levels of language and across a wide spectrum of nonverbal neurodevelopmental functions, such as her spatial appreciation, her various memory functions, and her prob-lem-solving abilities. In the long run this is a positive sign. It means that when she breaks the reading code, Judy is likely to soar academically. How-ever, she requires intensive help right away to overcome her phonological dysfunction. She might still be left with some developmental scars in spelling and eventually she could experience trouble learning a foreign lan-guage. The latter is really a challenge when you have not completely inter-nalized the sound system of your first language.

Parents should realize that there are quite a few excellent curricula to help children like Judy. Kids can compensate for their fuzzy reception of language sounds by learning families of words (such as all those containing "-ight"), "feeling" letters with their fingers and pronouncing the sounds they make while doing so, learning rhymes that strengthen sound appreciation, and using pictures to reinforce word meanings. Often there is a need to get back to the basics and drill these children on the individual language sounds and the letter combinations that go with the sounds. Parents can provide a lot of help with this.

Like Judy, many children with even mild neurodevelopmental dysfunctions affecting phonology go on to become inaccurate spellers. Often their spelling errors directly reflect their lack of phonological sophistication. They may spell words in ways that look pretty close to the real thing but are unpronounceable or mispronounceable as spelled. For example, they might spell the word "bought" as "bohgt" (visually pretty close but phonologically unpronounceable). Spelling problems in students can be both disabling and shameful. As Judy informed us, "I hate it when the teacher lets other kids correct my papers and see all my horrible spelling mistakes. They must think I have no brains. So far no one has made fun of my spelling, but I'm always scared they will, like in front of everybody." Spelling errors are as hard to conceal as an outfielder dropping a pop fly during a baseball game, so conspicuous that they often make a kid give up on himself, particularly when it comes to handing in written assignments. Luckily, the same kinds of multisensory approaches described above to enhance reading in these students are also likely to lead to improved spelling.

The Smallest Bits of Meaning (Morphemes)

When I was in medical school, I had a ball making up words representing all sorts of diseases I had not yet heard of. I had been taught that "itis" at the end of a word signified some kind of inflammation and I was exposed to the insight that "gastr" was supposed to make you think about stomachs; so I creatively surmised (correctly) that the word "gastritis" might well relate to inflammation of the stomach. That was almost fun. Both "itis" and "gastr" are morphemes, the smallest fragments of meaning in language. They happen to be "bound morphemes," bits of meanings that have to be bound together to form words. These include prefixes, such as pre- or auto-, and suffixes, such as -ing, -tion, and -ism, that are meaningless on their own. They also take in various word roots that can appear anywhere in a word. Some morphemes are unbound. They can do double duty as whole words or parts of words. For example, "bird" becomes a morpheme when embedded in the word "bluebird." Articles, such as "a," "an," and "the," also qualify as unbound morphemes.

Why are morphemes important anyway? It's because we know that students with a strong morphological sense race ahead in amassing vocabulary, as they decrypt many meanings from the morphemes secluded within words—just as I was able to do in medical school. Morphological insights also provide generous clues to aid in accurate spelling. Morphologically unaware students, on the other hand, may be forced to overrely on rote memory to get on top of vocabulary and spelling. Words may not make a whole lot of sense to them when they are deprived of those meaningful hints gleaned from the parts of words. By the way, I believe that some kids who have dysfunctions in morphology in reality face a much broader problem with recognition memory (see Chapter 4). It's hard for them to recognize academic fragments that keep coming back in different disguises such as morphemes.

Although it's rarely done anywhere, all children need to be educated explicitly about morphemes and given exercises to make them consciously aware of how morphemes work in words. At home, parents can play word games in which children think up as many words as they can that, say, contain "auto-" and then talk about what all those words have in common. Kids can also be asked to make up some words that don't really exist but have sensible morphemes in them. For example, "Whenever I warm up in the bullpen, I'm preparing to pitch. When I get to the mound, I'm ready to 'postpare,' to use what I was preparing." A bit far-fetched, but this kind of exercise expands awareness of the morphemes.

Word Meanings (Semantics)

What are the differences between an equilateral triangle, an isosceles triangle, and an obtuse triangle? What is an adverb? What does refraction mean and how does it differ from reflection? What is plankton? Such questions reverberate from the walls of every classroom every day, as teachers pound away at the meanings of key words, which, in turn, provide access to critical knowledge. Semantics is the knowledge or study of word meanings. Over time students are expected to expand their vocabularies. Some of the heaviest sprays of new words occur during preschool—from ages two to five. Another major semantic downpour occurs in high school, and in college there is a torrent of new terminology of all kinds.

Academically successful students do not necessarily have larger vocabularies than their classmates. What really differentiates many top students is that they know the meanings of the words they know better than other kids know the meanings of the words they know. They might learn the word "altruism" and rather than simply memorizing its definition, they note that the word represents a form of kindness and that it is related to charity, helping, and caring for others, and self-sacrifice. They may also sense that altruism is the opposite of selfishness, miserliness, and insensitivity to others. That is, students who are semantic "athletes" boast profound knowledge of word meanings. They understand shades of meanings and they are adept at comparing words to other words, to words that are opposites, to words that are similar but not quite the same, to words that are synonyms. They also become agile at fitting words into semantic categories and subcategories, which makes words easier to consolidate (as we saw regarding long-term memory in Chapter 4). They file "altruism" within the category of very special positive personal traits, alongside heroism, courage, and compassion. Terms become cross-indexed, so that the word "accelerate" is thought of as a verb, as a concept in physics class, as what a student does when he takes advanced classes in school, as a synonym for speeding up, and as a term used to describe an important aspect of driving a car.

It is common to encounter neurodevelopmental dysfunctions that seem to blunt or stunt word meanings for certain students. Parents should be suspicious when an elementary school child uses only everyday high-frequency words and doesn't seem to be incorporating in her speech the kinds of vocabulary she is learning in school. They might also detect that such a child fails vocabulary tests and resists attempts to study words. As that child progresses, learning a foreign language may present serious problems, as trouble acquiring vocabulary in your first language portends even more difficulty trying to do so in a second tongue.

In helping kids expand their semantic capacities, parents should teach

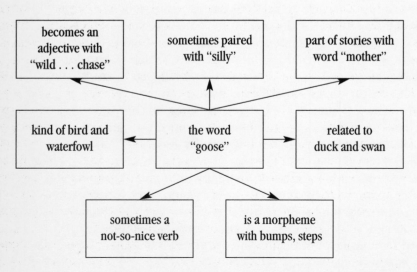

Figure 5-3.   A semantic map that extends and enriches the meaning of the word "goose."

them to learn words by comparing new terms to words they already know: "How does this word differ from some words you already have in your vocabulary? Which words are only somewhat like the new addition?" Some teachers will present students with a list of words and ask them to pick out any two on the list and describe the ways in which those two words are similar and the ways in which they differ. That activity helps to form a dense and accessible semantic network. Crossword puzzles and other word games can have a similar positive impact. Also, parents and teachers can have children make what are called semantic maps, diagrams of word meanings, such as the one illustrated in Figure 5-3. Computer graphic programs such as Inspiration Software help to make the activity easy and fun.

Students confront countless words that are decontextualized (detached from familiar surroundings and associations), abstract, and technical. The technical list includes a heavily loaded glossary of terms from mathematics and the sciences, hard words like "hypotenuse," "force," "mass," and "mitosis" that are not part of everyday parlance. These words became a serious threat to Arnold, our patient with good social language but lagging academic English. Like so many other kids with language dysfunctions, he was not forming much of a semantic network. He needed someone to teach him about such networks and to give him practice in mapping words. He could also benefit from making semantic maps and engaging in word games.

Word meanings become greatly enhanced when they are embedded in a context, especially a context governed by some predictable rules and regularities. That ushers in our next level of language, namely the sentence level, or syntax.

Language at the Sentence Level (Syntax)

There's an important difference in meaning between "That boy who shoved Mary went tumbling down the stairs" and "Mary, who was shoved by that boy, went tumbling down the stairs." The syntactic difference will determine which child will require an X ray. Syntax refers to the effects of word order on meaning. Word order, in turn, is governed by a complicated set of language laws, legislation we call grammar or grammatical construction. It turns out that some students are comfortable with language's syntactical rulebook, while others find it cumbersome and can never quite grasp its rationale and its diverse implications and applications.

As kids progress through school sentences gain weight steadily, acquiring what are called embedded clauses (such as "who was shoved by that boy" in the example above), and adding more and more confusing but meaning-loaded variations in word order. The table below describes some of the significant changes in sentence structure that kids have to be able to negotiate during their school years.

SOME EXAMPLES OF THE CHALLENGES TO SENTENCE UNDERSTANDING DURING ELEMENTARY AND MIDDLE SCHOOL

Challenge	Examples
The first noun in a sentence need not be the one who acts.	The Great Dane was chased by the Appaloosa.
The order of actions presented in a sentence need not match the order that is conveyed.	Call your friend when your homework is completed.
A noun may be the subject of both clauses and a clause may be located in the middle of a sentence.	The girl who borrowed that book showed it to her mother.
A noun may be the object of both clauses.	The teacher knew the boy who was punished by the principal.
A pronoun doesn't have to stand for someone in the same sentence.	Jim thinks he is a good cook.
A pronoun may be remote from the word it stands for.	Sandra was told to look for a crayon in the wooden box and then take it to her desk.
A noun closest to a verb doesn't have to be the one acting on that verb.	The man driving next to my sister skidded into the tree.
The meaning of questions depends a lot on the meaning of the first word.	Why is he visiting? Whom is he visiting? Where is he visiting? When will he be visiting? Where will he visit?
Sentences can have more than one possible meaning.	It is too hot to eat. She wondered how that fish smells.
Sentences can have figurative meaning.	She went out on a limb for him.
Sentences can be ironic.	You can really have a ball studying for chemistry quizzes.
Sentences may intend some meaning different from their literal interpretation.	Can you pass the marinara sauce? [Answering "Yes" is literally okay, but not the right response in a social context!]

Smug adults may examine these seemingly modest syntactic changes in this table and wonder what all the linguistic fuss is about. Yet, these acquisitions represent crucial language milestones (and sometimes millstones). Kids differ widely in their ability to surmount these linguistic hurdles. Imagine, for instance, what it must be like to be a kid who has trouble understanding different kinds of questions. He won't be able to respond to questions in science not because he doesn't know the answers but because he can't decipher the questions—a frequent, scary, misunderstood predicament.

Students are exposed to a seemingly arbitrary and threatening set of rules that teachers refer to as grammar. For some of them the rules turn out to be reasonably helpful, as they perfect their language usage by carrying out the formal linguistic laws they committed to memory. But then some children find the rules totally confusing; these are sometimes individuals with excellent grammatical sense that is entirely intuitive. A sentence simply sounds right to them. Other students, alas, have neither sentence structure intuition nor a very good grasp of the rules. They suffer a neurodevelopmental dysfunction at the sentence level of language. They founder in school as a result.

Over and above their need to decrypt the meanings of complex sentences, students have to formulate increasingly sophisticated sentences of their own. This entails a considerable construction challenge. A child needs to be able to think through a sentence prior to constructing it. An internal voice asks the speaker, "What's the best way to put this? How do I arrange the words in a sentence to have maximum impact, to convey as precisely as possible my feelings, my intentions, or the factual content I need to deliver?" Some students find verbal fluency a proverbial piece of cake. These are skillful sentence architects.

But some children have to deal with dysfunctions of sentence formulation. They may fumble, mumble, and show signs of frustration when they need to compose thoughts in a sentence format. A parent may note that a child seldom talks in sentences, preferring the use of phrases or perhaps just single-word utterances. When sentences are used, grammatical errors abound, tenses are wrong, there is poor agreement between subject and verb, and words are used in a misleading order ("I'm picking up the toys I put away" instead of "I'm putting away the toys I picked up"). Additionally, the child may show excessive hesitancy or overindulge in short, simple sentences when trying to express thoughts.

As students are expected to make use of higher language, the demands at the sentence level grow even more stringent. They have to draw inferences. That is, to extract enough meaning they have to supply missing information (that which is implied but not explicitly stated). They also meet up with sentences that are ironic, that express a particular point of view, or

that are susceptible to more than one possible interpretation. Higher order
sentences like these become a deflating ordeal for some individuals.

Robin was typical. At age ten this boy was under heavy accusatory artillery from his teachers and parents for "never listening." They alleged that
Robin ignored instructions and daydreamed in class when his teacher was
trying to teach. He had been put on a stimulant medication (called Adderall) by his family doctor because of his alleged distractibility. When I saw
him, I asked Robin if he had trouble concentrating. He said, "No, I just don't
get a lot of stuff." Our testing confirmed his frank self-appraisal. Indeed,
there was plenty of input he couldn't get, especially when it was packaged
in complex sentences.

I performed an examination on Robin to check out various functions
within the eight neurodevelopmental systems. Robin revealed advanced
motor capacities, superb spatial perception, and strengths in all tested components of memory. Furthermore, he demonstrated consistently clever
strategies, except during much of the language testing. I detected that his
mood changed, and he looked forlorn when tasks were primarily verbal. I
gave him a sentence comprehension test, the same one we used on Arnold,
during which I read a series of sentences and then asked questions about
them. To reduce contamination from expressive language all Robin had to
do was answer yes, no, or maybe to each of my questions. Here were some
of his responses:

DR. LEVINE: Jim thinks Tom is good at sports. Is Tom good at sports?
ROBIN: Yup. [should have answered maybe]
DR. LEVINE: It's usually safe to climb that mountain, although it's very dan-
gerous in the fog. Will it be safe to climb the mountain tomorrow?
ROBIN: Yeah. [correct answer: maybe]
DR. LEVINE: Maybe the band would have played last night if the drummer
hadn't quit. Did the band play last night?
ROBIN: Maybe. [No is the right answer]

I then gave Robin a different test to see if he could draw inferences from
sentences. One of the items went like this:

DR. LEVINE: Mary and Susie love to play with each other every day after
school. But each night just before they go to bed they keep arguing and
fighting. How do Mary and Susie know each other?
ROBIN: They play together. [actually, they're most likely sisters]

So we suspect that Robin has serious trouble interpreting sentence meaning. Conjunctions (such as "although") stump him, qualified statements

such as "thinks that" are understood as actuality, and inferences escape him entirely.

Robin also had trouble when I gave him several words and asked him to make a sentence using them. On one item, he had to construct his sentence from the words "walk," "road," and "until." After prolonged hesitation and several false starts, Robin produced the following: "Walk the road until I tell you to." Thus, both the interpretation and building of sentences were trouble for him. Interestingly, Robin didn't have any learning problems in first or second grade. He was in the top reading group. That's because he was so good with phonological awareness, visual memory, and most other critical functions needed for early elementary school. But when complex sentences were introduced, as invariably occurs in third and fourth grades, Robin was sunk—at least until he could surmount this verbal hurdle. He illustrated so vividly how a child can stumble at one part of language while succeeding at others. That also means that a language problem may emerge at any point along the way as the verbal demands intensify, and different language demands become accentuated in the curriculum. Moreover, Robin lets us witness once again how a receptive language weakness can masquerade as an attention deficit.

Robin was lucky enough to receive language therapy in school three times a week. There he experienced plenty of practice understanding complex sentences and formulating thoughts into grammatically correct syntax. His parents reinforced this therapy at home by giving him key words and asking him to make sentences from them. They also practiced by reading to him or having him read one- or two-sentence jokes, puns, riddles, and absurdities and then asking him to explain them. Recently, Robin has shown dramatic improvement in school. He is no longer taking medication.

Language in Big Chunks (Discourse)

From sitting in a circle listening to a Dr. Seuss story in kindergarten to attending a lecture on rococo painting in one's junior year in college, students are compelled to assimilate increasingly lengthy verbal discourses. Discourse takes in all language that goes beyond the boundaries of sentences. Its products include textbook paragraphs, biblical passages, magazine articles, novels, and encyclopedias. Discourse incorporates the four other language levels—phonology, morphology, semantics, and syntax, and it does so in abundance. Understanding discourse calls for active working memory as well as language capacity; readers and listeners need to remember what they are interpreting while in the process of reading or listening to it. They have to be able to extract meaning from a particular sentence without forgetting the information or events that led up to it. Episodes within a story, stanzas in a poem, and the fragments of an explanation have to be incubated together and allowed to ripen in active working memory. That way a listener or a reader is able to absorb the whole message, so as to tell it to someone else, apply the wisdom, or remember it for future display or use.

Discourse has its expressive side. Students should be capable of presenting information that goes beyond the dispersal of simple phrases or sentences while speaking or writing. That was problematic for Lenore, our teenager with language production weaknesses. Speakers make use of a kind of verbal organization as they sequence their ideas in the best possible order. They need to think about topic sentences, concluding sentences, and appropriate sequencing of their thinking.

Not surprisingly, students who harbor neurodevelopmental dysfunctions at the discourse level of language are unlikely ever to be caught reading for pleasure! They become bored and restless when expected to finish a novel or listen to a prolonged explanation in class. Yet these students can improve their appreciation of discourse largely through reading highly motivational content, which might include biographies of their favorite singers, sports magazines, or manuals on the latest video games. Discourse production and understanding are most readily developed in areas of high interest.

Thinking About Language (Metalinguistic Awareness)

If you think about how language works, you can understand the need for adverbs. If you never ponder how language works, you come to view an adverb as a word that ends in "-ly." The mouth-threatening term "metalinguistic awareness" refers to a person's ability not just to use language and memorize its conventions, not just to understand and communicate, but also to be able to pause and reflect on language and on how it works. Linguists are ardent fans of language. They feel a fascination, a genuine attraction to the melodic sounds of a language, to the intricate webs of semantics, and even to the clever rules that legislate sentence structure. Language is fun at the same time that it is amazing and amusing for them. Kids who are linguists are the ones most likely to savor Scrabble, puns, rhyming activities, and other modes of linguistic amusement. Because they are bound to language, they are apt to approach its interpretation and production with energy and gusto. They are able to access higher levels of understanding because they are so insightful with regard to the inner workings of the language system. Kids who have excellent metalinguistic awareness in English are in a strong position to acquire one or more additional languages.

There probably is no such thing as a pure, isolated dysfunction of metalinguistic awareness—at least I've never encountered such a phenomenon. It is more likely that a lack of language thinking or insight accompanies dysfunction at one or more of the other language levels. Some children have an intuitive feel for the workings of language, while others do not. I believe all kids need to learn about linguistics. They need to be aware of the levels of language as they have been articulated in this chapter.

❧ THE SPECIAL CHALLENGE OF LANGUAGE PRODUCTION

Language output is an especially elusive undertaking for some, and for that reason I would like to give it some further emphasis in this chapter. There was a time in our schools when every child was required on a regular basis to take a course called rhetoric. In contemporary culture, not as much attention is paid to oral language production, the ability to encode ideas into clear, cogent, and colorful semantics, syntax, and discourse. Verbal eloquence and fluency are dramatically less evident in many classrooms as a result. Effective oral language serves an abundance of purposes. For one thing, it correlates highly with writing skill. Quite understandably, "If you don't talk too good, it might be you'd not write too good neither."

Language production serves as a lubricant for memory. As pointed out in the previous chapter, verbal elaboration makes it easier to consolidate information and skill in long-term memory. We also make use of language as an implement for creative expression, as a wrench for tightening our grasp of concepts, and as an elixir for winning and keeping friends (see Chapter 9).

Expressive language plays a less obvious but powerful role in regulating behavior. Words and sentences can be peacemakers and problem solvers within a social milieu. We adjust our feelings and actions by talking to ourselves. Internal voices (normal ones, not hallucinations) enable people to self-coach, to verbalize internally, as they consider the likely consequences of various actions they are contemplating. They are also able to talk through, buffer, and modify their inner feelings.

When individuals lack expressive language ability, they may be susceptible to the development of aggressive behaviors and also depression or excessive anxiety. I participated in several research studies involving early adolescent juvenile delinquents. In these investigations we sought to uncover specific neurodevelopmental dysfunctions that were common among these kids. We were struck by how many teenagers in serious trouble with the law had signs of expressive language dysfunction as one of the risk factors that led to their downward spiral. In fact, it turns out that at two ages in particular, namely preschool and late adolescence, language production problems are strongly associated with acting-out, aggressive, and sometimes downright antisocial behaviors. So the stakes are sky-high when it comes to expressive language capacities.

Now here's the irony: we have described this crucial area of brain function. Even subtle weaknesses can have onerous repercussions. Yet it can be perilously tricky to uncover an expressive language dysfunction in a student. In many cases literate expressive language dysfunction is disguised under fairly good conversational skills—that is, the nice and fluent automatic English described at the start of this chapter. Additionally, the tests used by clinicians to diagnose language dysfunctions are weak at uncovering subtle expressive language problems, particularly in older kids. To make matters worse, the tests that are used often are culturally biased, and are hard to interpret. So, given the importance of expressive language and the need to diagnose kids who are having difficulties with it, how do we find out who is an expressive linguist and who is at an expressive disadvantage? There is only one way. We need to attune regular classroom teachers and parents to listen carefully to a child to determine whether there might be a breakdown in literate language production. Classroom teachers have the special advantage of having fellow students with whom to compare the student they are observing. That enabled Lenore's English teacher to suspect a problem with language production.

Kids with expressive language problems come up against communication barriers at home and in school. They need plenty of practice. I have told many of them over the years that they need to build up their "language muscles." They should be encouraged to tell a lot of stories and describe experiences, even if this is hard for them. In school they need opportunities to make oral presentations, especially on topics that excite them. In severe cases with significant word finding, articulation, or sentence-building weaknesses, students can benefit from the services of a trained language specialist in school or in the community.

§➤ LANGUAGE AND ITS AMBASSADORIAL FUNCTIONS

Language never operates in isolation. It is a constant collaborator with all the other neurodevelopmental systems. We have seen how language and memory get together to strengthen learning during discourse, how word retrieval is a language activity as well as a memory activity, and how verbal elaboration improves filing in memory.

Language also plays a significant role in motor function. During the early stages of building any motor skill, we are likely to talk our way through the steps involved. Language interacts with social thinking, as we shall see in a later chapter. We have to talk right to relate right. Language also interfaces with sequencing. When we tell a story or a joke, the sequence of our ideas is critical in presenting a message that is coherent.

Language sends compelling offshoots to spatial ordering and visual processing. The ability to form visual imagery while listening to a story or reading a text constitutes a vital visual and verbal linkage. Such linkages enrich language experience dramatically. They are in short supply among kids brought up on TV and without the advantage of storytelling sessions and radio dramas (both of which provide the sound while you conjure up the imagery). Language also has ties to higher order thinking and to attention.

Two Languages

A majority of the world's children are expected to become conversant in more than one language. For most, formal teaching or sustained exposure to two languages works well, as they have the language capacity to handle two or more different verbal codes without much stress. But there are many instances of students for whom acquiring a second language is a futile ordeal. Some may be kids from immigrant families trying to make it in English-speaking schools or they may be English speakers reckoning with a foreign tongue. Most often children who fare poorly with a second language harbor (knowingly or unknowingly) neurodevelopmental dysfunctions in their first language. A child who has never fully managed to absorb completely the phonology, semantics, or sentence structure in his native Spanish tongue is likely to encounter even more serious problems doing so in English. These children often need a very potent emphasis on the cultivation of the language levels in one language without totally giving up their exposure and experience in a second language. In many cases with bilingual children, it is best to stress English in school and work hard on the language levels while maintaining for at least a portion of each day the native language for everyday conversation at home. Also, as bilingual children go through high school and need to reach up for their higher English language functions, they may gain from some backup textbooks, crib sheets, or consultants in their native language.

English-speaking children with language dysfunctions should postpone foreign language learning until they show substantial progress in English. It is fair to say that you shouldn't be speaking a second language until you are reading and writing well in your first one. Some kids that I've seen need to have foreign language requirements postponed until tenth or eleventh grade. Incidentally, the myth abounds that very young children (such as preschoolers) pick up foreign languages faster than do middle or high school learners. This is not the case. In fact, several recent studies have shown that fourteen-year-olds learn foreign languages much faster and more effectively than do five- or six-year-olds. This is not to say we should stop teaching second languages to younger children, but it does mean we shouldn't justify it by asserting that younger kids learn languages better than their big brothers and sisters.

Because verbal abilities play such an aggressive role in education, their progress over time merits close monitoring by parents and teachers. At different age and grade levels, specific components of language seem to come to the fore and make their presence or absence plainly known. Let's grab a quick look at the most noticeable changes that occur.

✒ MINDS OVER TIME: KEEPING A WATCHFUL EYE (OR EAR) ON LANGUAGE AS CHILDREN AGE

From kindergarten through much of second grade, parents and teachers need to be aware that the name of the verbal game is phonology. Kids flex their phonological muscles as they show an interest in rhymes and start to pick up skills at word decoding in reading. Those with a keen sense of the sound system breeze through the reading and spelling experience, the ones who lack that sense are unable to break the code. From second through fifth grade, language function is reflected most vividly in how well a child can understand and construct sentences. As they pass through this critical period, children should reveal a growing capacity to follow directions, understand questions, and speak in complete sentences that vary in their syntax. When parents have to keep repeating directions, it may well be that the child is not being obstinate; instead, delayed sentence processing ability could be the hidden culprit. Kids who are accurate with the sound system and with sentences should be enjoying reading and they should be deriving substantial meaning from books. By fifth grade, students with good language skills become effective at reading to gather new information, a problem for those with language delays.

In middle school, individual sentences don't generally lengthen or become more complicated, but lectures, verbal explanations, reading passages, and books do. Discourse, all that language that goes beyond the boundaries of sentences, dominates the verbal terrain and demands that memory and language work in perfect or near perfect harmony.

Middle school and high school students experience a power surge of newly introduced vocabulary. Most of the new words are decontextualized; they are terms you never encounter at the breakfast table, in the barbershop, or on the school bus. Words like "factor," "stratosphere," "cosine," "iambic," and "monotheism" appear and must become part of an adolescent's mental glossary.

By high school kids should be actively applying their sharpened higher language functions, making use of verbal ability as a precision tool for making sense of abstract and technical concepts, for polishing off a second language, and for lucid and eloquent writing. By this age students should be adept at elaborating on ideas with words. Your adolescent should be able to talk about thorny issues in an extended, literate, reasonably thorough manner without revealing pained hesitation, overuse of stall words such as "like," and a lack of substance (called low ideational density).

In becoming aware of the challenging issues that confront a student at specific age levels, parents and teachers can detect language assets or deficits. Beware: a child can manifest a language meltdown for the first time at any developmental stage. On the positive side, language also can capriciously take a sudden turn for the better at any point.

✎ PRACTICAL CONSIDERATIONS

• Life at home should straddle the borders between automatic and literate English. Informal conversation helps grease the gears of family dynamics but should not be the exclusive style of family talk. With some regularity, parents should provide and partake of opportunities for the discussion of abstract ideas, contemporary issues, and other matters that are removed from direct practical family agendas (which of course also merit some dialogue). Here's a dinner table sample from a verbally instigating mom: "Well, kids, according to the news, they're doing experimental surgery on monkeys to find out more about how brain tumors grow. They actually cause the monkeys to get tumors and then try out different treatments on them. That might eventually help doctors treat people with brain tumors. Do you think that's fair to the monkeys?"

• Oral language needs to blossom progressively in all children, and we can help it along through rich verbal interactions. Kids should be encouraged to elaborate, avoiding conversational deterrents like "stuff," "thing," and "yeah." A firm home rule could stipulate: "In our family we only communicate in complete sentences." Opportunities for verbal enrichment are available especially at a meal table, at bedtime (horizontal kids are often more expressive and less distracted than vertical ones), and buckled up in the car. There might need to be a regulation banning radio playing for at least some of the duration of an extended auto ride.

• Parents should examine the extent to which a child's entertainment and recreational life is monopolized by visual-motor ecstasy, nonverbal activities where rapid (maybe even frenetic) movement is the primary attraction. Such intensely self-stimulating action relaxes children while helping them feel effective, but when there is an imbalance, when visual-motor ecstasy excessively entices their minds, it can be harmful and it certainly can stunt language growth. Skateboarding, Rollerblading, some other sports, and video games are examples of highly seductive fast moving conveyors of motor gratification that are also mostly mindless.

• Kids need to see their parents reading, and they need to be read to themselves as early as possible. Young school-aged children benefit from responsive reading of stories with their parents. Such literacy-nurturing activities have been shown repeatedly to foster optimal language development.

• Parents and schools should be especially vigilant in identifying students in early adolescence who are not on the upward slope that leads to higher language function. These girls and boys are very much in need of verbal enrichment at home and in school.

• Kids can benefit from language-oriented out-of-school entertainment, such as Scrabble, crossword puzzles, and other word games that can be played on a car trip. Keeping a diary is another desirable means of formal language application outside the classroom.

• All kids need to strengthen their summarization skills. Summarization lies smack at the junction between the functions of memory and language; as such, it binds understanding to remembering. Try this out: Father: "Well, George, I'll take you to the hockey game on Friday night if you are willing to come home and summarize it for us. You should do your summary on a cassette recorder, so you can listen and see how accurate you think it was." This verbal challenge can bolster summarization skills, although it runs the risk of reducing attendance at hockey games.

• Kids can best enhance their language skills by reading, writing, listening, and talking in their domains of personal affinity. A girl who loves sports needs to evolve into a prolific sports communicator. She should devour sports magazines, write about her favorite sports, teach sports to younger kids, and talk (with elaboration and complete sentences) sports talk.

• In second or third grade, kids should be given a formal course on linguistics. There they would learn how language works—such as what morphemes are and how word origins affect meaning. Kids should also have opportunities to manipulate and play games with the sounds of their language and to create their own poetry and rhyming musical lyrics. Word meanings, word orderings, and other parameters of language merit discussion and exercise.

• Students could also benefit from formal course work in rhetoric or public speaking as a way of correcting the current worldwide epidemic of impoverished oral language skills. This teaching should take place at several levels: one or two courses or units during elementary school, one in middle school, and twice in high school.

• Children should be creating lively verbal-visual associations in their minds. Having them listen to books on tape or attend storytelling sessions can facilitate this.

6

Making Arrangements ✌

Our Spatial and Sequential Ordering Systems

The sense of sight discerns the difference of shapes, wherever they are . . . without delay or interruption, employing careful calculations with almost incredible speed. . . . When the sense cannot see the object through its own mode of action, it recognizes it through the manifestation of other differences, sometimes perceiving truly and sometimes imagining incorrectly.

PTOLEMY, *Optics*

I felt a cleavage in my mind
As if my mind had split;
I tried to match it, seam by seam,
But could not make them fit.

The thought behind I strove to join
Unto the thought before,
But sequence ravelled out of reach
Like balls upon a floor.

EMILY DICKINSON

Is there a member of your family who is late for everything, who can never seem to handle a deadline or due date, and who gets confused when given more than two things in a row to accomplish? If so, that person may have trouble finding and creating order in the vast world of sequences, of information that has to be thought about or acted upon in a particular order. Do you live or work with someone who has a hopelessly misguided sense of direction, a person who is hesitant about the distinction between left and right, and who loses most worldly possessions most of the time? If so, that sometimes disoriented individual may be having trouble finding and creating order in the world of space, that hazy montage of dimensions and relationships beyond the borders of our bodies. This chapter encompasses two neurodevelopmental systems that help children set up and orient their learning, their thinking, their remembering, and their output—either in a usable sequence or in a cohesive spatial pattern.

Incoming and outgoing information is set up in a more or less orderly fashion. Most often the bits of data are arranged either spatially or in a set sequence or both (the frames of a movie are delivered to us in a sequence and within each frame there are spatial arrangements). Certain sets of data, such as the features of my face, are effectively set up as spatial patterns, assembled parts that occupy space and settle on the doorsteps of our minds all at once (my nose doesn't get to you before my lips show up). Other kinds of information are set up in sequences, such as the digits in a telephone number and the order of the months of the year. These serial tidbits gain admission to minds one bit at a time and in an order that's meant not to be missed.

Your child encounters the demands for sequential and spatial ordering throughout her day in school. Sequential ordering comes into play when a student recounts the steps in a science experiment, thinks through the stages of a planned art project, plays scales on the piano, or tracks the plot of a story. Spatial ordering comes forward when he discerns the difference between a "d" and a "b," studies the relative locations of Venus and Pluto, draws a map of South Korea, or pictures an octagon in his mind. Even when well equipped with strengths in attention, memory, and language, a student's learning would be chaotic were it not for the organizing jobs performed by these two ordering systems. They have their headquarters on opposite sides of our brain (sequential usually on the left side and spatial ordinarily on the right), and they are expected to grow in their capacities and efficiencies as kids make progress through school. Wide differences separate students; they vary in their effectiveness at interpreting, storing, or communicating information that is arranged either in a sequence or in a spatial pattern. So a logical question to pose about any developing young mind might be, "How well organized is he?" For parents to detect and deal with gaps in one or both ordering systems, they need to understand more about how these two systems assume their learning roles in thinking, in retaining information, and in the mobilization of efficient output.

Sequential and spatial ordering help our children learn on distinct levels that range from the most rudimentary sorting out of simple instructions to the most intricate ways of learning and performing, as shown in the following table. On that most basic level, a student has to interpret or perceive a spatial array (such as the shape of a country on a map) or sequential pattern (such as the order of beats in a musical rhythm), perhaps storing these key perceptions for later use (level 2). On the creating level (level 3), there are times when that student will need to manufacture his own sequences (such as while creating a melody on the piano) or spatial products (such as while shaping a ceramic pitcher). Often he will be expected to be well organized (level 4) with time (getting places promptly) and with space (remembering where he left his keys) and (level 5) to be able to reason, conceptualize, and problem-solve using sequences (by thinking through a math problem in a logical order) or mental imagery (picturing electricity flowing through a wire).

SPATIAL AND SEQUENTIAL ORDERING: THEIR LEVELS OF OPERATION

Ordering Level	Description
1 Perceiving	Figuring out the important characteristics and relationships inside a sequence or pattern.
2 Remembering	Retaining the serial order or spatial relationship that you have perceived for later use.
3 Creating	Putting out products that are arranged in a useful and/or aesthetically pleasing sequence or spatial pattern.
4 Organizing	Being good at time management (sequential) and materials management (spatial)
5 Thinking on a higher plane	Using sophisticated reasoning, problem solving, and concept formation through spatial and sequential ordering.

Anything is possible. Your child may be strong or weak at any or all of these levels in sequential or spatial ordering systems (or in both systems). And you may find that one or both of his parents may also struggle with time or space—or perhaps a little of each. These strengths and weaknesses are in plain view in school and at home. I will be describing the effects of strength and weakness in these ordering systems regarding school performance as well as some of the other disturbing and too often misunderstood setbacks that occur when an unsuspecting kid encounters difficulty with respect to order.

First we'll examine sequential ordering, then spatial ordering.

✥ SEQUENTIAL ORDERING

"Why is it that my Carol seems to do everything the hard way? And how come she does most things in the wrong order?" Parents may be perplexed by the realization that their child's life is somehow "out of order"—from getting herself dressed to reciting the alphabet. She meets havoc throughout the school day, bewildered by teachers' rapid volleys of multistep directions and expectations for efficient sequential output. She may find it hard to organize her thoughts to present them orally in coherent steps. She most likely feels defective and markedly inferior to peers. Here's a typical brief biography of such a needlessly suffering ego:

Joann's parents arrived at the indisputable conclusion that this gusher of pure charm didn't know the meaning of the word "time." When I first saw Joann in my office, she was eleven, a very anxious and withdrawn student from northern New Jersey. She was always out of time and never known to be on time or even close to functioning in step with time. To Joann, schedules of any sort were cloudy notions, and deadlines were vague and forgettable goals at best. She was in a perpetual time warp, inevitably unaware of when she was running behind or getting ahead (the latter a most rare occurrence). Interestingly and not at all unusual, her father had a similar lack of orientation in time. Joann's mother said the two of them made her tear out her hair when the family needed to go someplace; Dad and daughter were never in a state of readiness. In fact, I'm pretty sure the problem caused Joann's father, a furniture designer, to lose two jobs and to be passed over for promotion once. He confessed that he did everything at the last minute and often missed important deadlines. He had a reputation for being unreliable at work, even though the drawings he ultimately produced were quite good. Too bad this man never knew he had a lifelong sequencing problem—that is, until we discussed Joann's glitches. He could have worked on them and saved himself a lot of agony. That happens all too often in my office. I discuss a child's dysfunctions, and one or both parents recognize themselves in what I'm saying.

Reliably late for all dates and appointments, to this day Joann remains unsure about the order of the months of the year and often gets mixed up when given three or four things in a row to do in school or at home. As a preschooler and well into early elementary school, Joann had trouble reckoning with the order of days of the week and sequences of steps in various math procedures. This child was noticeably late learning to tell time and is still hesitant in doing so (her digital watch has been a lifesaver). Throughout elementary school, Joann was told over and over again that she wasn't really trying. She was made to feel that her tardiness and disorganization were her fault, that she had a bad attitude. On frequent occasions she told her mother that she didn't much like herself.

In kindergarten and first grade, Joann became disoriented when sentences contained temporal prepositions, such as "before" and "after." For instance, she once told her dad, "I hope you get home late tonight so we can play together outside before it gets dark." Joann has always excelled in science. She currently loves her physics class and has gotten As in all her science courses. She wants to be either a geophysicist or an anthropologist. She is universally popular. A deft athlete, she also has a passionate interest and high skill level in Scottish Highlands dancing. But in school Joann struggles with anything requiring sequencing, a fact no one has observed. In third grade and fifth grade she was evaluated for possible learning disabilities but, because there was no significant difference between her IQ and her achievement test scores, she was deemed ineligible for any services and determined not to be learning disabled. But no one ever said what she was!

The way we test for learning disabilities is especially irrational, since there has never been much agreement regarding what learning disability is. This kind of nonsense goes on all the time, as all sorts of invalid formulas are used to determine who has a genuine right to be helped and who does not. Joann was victimized by her school's special formula. Her parents were totally confused. After all, if she's not LD, then she must be stupid or hopelessly lazy. What else is there?

I met Joann shortly after her second school evaluation, after which her mother declared, "Nobody understands this girl. I know there's something going on here, and it's being dreadfully overlooked." Our team tested Joann. From her history I suspected she might be struggling with sequencing. This was soon confirmed. When I showed Joann a series of different shapes and pointed to each of these in a particular order, she was unable to remember and re-create the order. She could only retain a sequence of three objects but she should have been able to remember five or six. She also had trouble repeating numbers in the correct order. By the time we were nearly finished with our various sequential ordering tasks, I could see tears welling up in Joann's eyes. It's amazing how often a child's sad moods and feelings come forth and become amplified when confronting a specific area of weakness. So, out of compassion, I promptly quit this pursuit and switched to something she could do well. Joann bounced back.

Once we pinpointed Joann's troubles with sequential ordering, we were able to make recommendations. The first was to help her understand the nature of her sequencing trouble. Ann Hobgood, our educational diagnostician, met with Joann several times and talked to her over the telephone regularly. Joann was encouraged to be especially alert in the presence of sequences, to visualize while people were talking to her in sequences, and to whisper under her breath. She also was taught to make flow diagrams to help her think about different sequential processes in math and science. Because of her past lack of progress, Joann was taken out of school, and her mother home-schooled her for two years, during which time she made dramatic gains in her overall academic performance, her sequencing strategies, and her organizational practices. Back in a regular school program in eighth grade, she continued to thrive academically.

Now nearly seventeen, Joann has learned to apply computer graphics effectively; she creates flow charts, timelines, and other such diagrammatic representations to help her learn and remember processes or events that take place in a specific serial order. Her parents, after coming to understand the nature of their daughter's neurodevelopmental dysfunction, encouraged her to exploit her keen spatial abilities to compensate for her unreliable sequencing. Joann made that discovery herself. After years of struggling at the bottom of her class, Joann's stock is starting to rise. Much of this acceleration resulted when one perceptive teacher finally sat down and reviewed with Joann the fact that she had all the abilities she needed to succeed in life but that she was being hampered by problems with sequential ordering. Joann felt redeemed; her motivation was restored and she was able to make much better use of her admirable assets.

Sequential Perception

A four- or five-year-old needs to perceive that Tuesday predictably precedes Wednesday (every week, without fail) and summer occurs before autumn (year after year). A student's mind must appreciate such stable internal order within all manner of sequences. Early on, when exposed to the letters of the alphabet, does this kindergartener really and truly see their order? How deep an impression in consciousness is made by the order of the twelve months of the year? When a teacher is describing the procedure for accomplishing long division, does a student thoroughly interpret the *order* of steps needed to arrive at the correct answer? Each of these questions would have been answered "not that much" in Joann's case as it would be for so many others like her. Some students are astute, highly sensitive detectors of serial order, while others like her are comparatively oblivious.

Early on, parents may wonder why the months of the year never were fully mastered by their kid, why that same son or daughter may have had difficulty learning letters of the alphabet in the correct order as well as why he or she has problems with everyday sequencing hurdles such as combination locks, telephone numbers, and the interpretation of multistep commands or instructions. When they suspect a possible dysfunction, parents can teach their child rhymes for the sequences, make use of comic strip stories to combine sequencing with visual imagery, and even have the child try a musical instrument that stresses serial order without being too oppressively sequentially complex (trombones, percussion, double basses, and drums are relatively user-friendly candidates). Rhythmic dance might also be helpful in reinforcing sequential ordering.

Sequential Memory

Remembering how to tie your shoelaces or, later on, your necktie requires the ability to consolidate in memory and later retrieve motor sequences. The recall of birthdays, the remembering of a recipe for apricot mousse, and the recall of a rather long joke also enlist the ability to remember things in the right order. Four different forms of sequential memory challenge students in school. The first calls for briefly holding a sequence in short-term memory, while the other three involve more or less permanent storage in long-term memory.

As we saw in Chapter 4, there is a never-ending requirement to secure sequences in short-term memory. While receiving directions to our destination at a service station, we need to hold the new information in short-term memory at least long enough to begin navigating toward the sought destination. When somebody provides you with a telephone number so you can order a pepperoni pizza, your appetite will be satisfied if and only if you are able to retain that digital sequence in short-term memory—at least long enough to place the call.

Our lives are strewn with short-term sequential memory necessities. For the most part, they are a breeze, but not so for my patient James. At age eight, in second grade, James would hear his teacher give her instructions in class: "Now, students, I want you to open your books to page fourteen and copy down those new words. Then turn to the end of the chapter and answer the first three questions. After that, I would like you to close up your books, set down your pencils, and sit up straight so I will know you are finished." James would process something about a pencil. He was unable to register multistep verbal sequential inputs in short-term memory. It was catch-as-catch-can when it came to the internal stabilization of serially arranged linked commands. These wordy trains of thought were forever uncoupling in James's mind. Incidentally, at home, his parents picked up on the same phenomenon, as they would direct him, "James, why don't you put out the trash and then come back and put your pajamas on and pour yourself a glass of milk. Then come and watch TV with us." Twenty-five minutes later: "Where's James? Whatever happened to James?" His dad would proceed to the kitchen to find his boy wandering about half-naked with a concerned and dedicated miniature schnauzer in loyal pursuit, both visibly disoriented. In general, canines do better processing smells than sequences! James, rather like Joann, was having some problems preserving sequential directions.

A mind may not be set up very well for the short-term storage of sequential inputs. Rapidly disintegrating sequential data might be visual (a coach showing you how to slide into home plate), verbal (your mom going over plans for this Saturday), or both (watching a science class demonstration on spontaneous combustion).

In addition to short-term memory, three components of long-term memory involve heavy-duty sequencing. The first two of these entail procedural memory as introduced in Chapter 4. The first, motor procedural memory, consists of your ability to file away and later recall the steps for accomplishing recurring tasks in and out of school. It includes the "formulas" for tying your shoelaces, using cursive writing, remembering how to serve in tennis, and recalling the steps needed to do "The Wabash Cannonball" at a square dance. All of these examples constitute motor procedural memory because they are all primarily muscular activities adhering to a sequential blueprint.

Nonmotor procedural memory is our second form of sequential long-term storage. Nonmotor procedural memory includes a vast array of processes that do not primarily involve muscular output yet still represent ways of doing things. The potentially puzzling procedure for reducing a fraction, the daily routines of a classroom, as well as the steps involved in reporting the results of a science experiment are kept on file for quick access in nonmotor procedural memory.

Factual sequences are the third component in long-term sequential memory. Included here are some items I have already mentioned, including the days of the week, the months of the year, alphabetical order, telephone numbers, and many mathematical facts. It is noteworthy that so many children who have trouble filing factual sequences have a hard time remembering the multiplication tables. There's a convincing correlation between the ability to deposit and recall this kind of mathematical information and the storing of other factual sequences. So often when parents find that a child can't seem to learn math facts, the neurodevelopmental culprit seems to reside in sequential memory. Affected kids need extra drill and also benefit from the various tricks of the trade that many math teachers know that serve to make multiplication facts more logical and less dependent on rote recall. (Check with your local math guru for advice.)

So it is that there are four kinds of sequential memory functions: short-term sequential memory, motor procedural memory, nonmotor procedural memory, and factual sequential memory. All four of these systems should operate smoothly during one's school career and beyond. In Joann's case they did not. But some students may have problems with only one or two of these filing systems; that's why parents and teachers need to be keenly aware of all four.

Sequential Output

Kids with sequential output problems are likely to leak the punch line first when they tell a joke! Or else, in relating a personal experience, they are apt to communicate the chain of events chaotically out of order. Many forms of output have to be arranged in a logical sequence. For some individuals, sequential output is a struggle. Despite Joann's good language skills, people often misunderstood her when she attempted to narrate personal experiences. She just could not impose sequential structure over her very good expressive language capacity. Here's how she once described her family's excursion to the state fair: "They had all these huge bulls and cows there. We got to the fair on a shuttle bus. So you couldn't park our van right near the fairgrounds. They had a rodeo there too that we didn't go to. That came before we got there. And two of the biggest steers in the show won blue ribbons." With awareness and practice arranging ideas in the best order (using bulleted lists), ultimately she improved and actually got to be quite a good storyteller.

Students with a neurodevelopmental dysfunction thwarting sequential output become frustrated in arranging things sequentially or performing tasks in the best order. As the parent of a first grader you might witness your child getting dressed in the morning and find that there is absolutely no rationale for the order in which she puts on her clothing. First, she puts on a sock, then an undershirt, followed swiftly by another sock, and next some other randomly plucked fragment of attire. This dearth of sequential ordering might be an early warning signal in a child destined for academic sequencing chaos.

Sequential Organization—Time Management

"Whenever we have to go anywhere, someone asks, 'Where's Joann?' She's dependably the last one out of the house. She makes us late to church with alarming regularity, and when we're all in a state of imminent starvation, we have to plead with her to be ready to leave for the restaurant. It's led us to do more takeout. It's just not worth the combat involved in getting her ready to go somewhere." Time is our most pervasive and potentially perverse sequence. As we saw in Joann's case, children with weaknesses of sequential ordering can aggravate and provoke well-intentioned parents with their exasperating time vacuums. Being organized in time rallies the ability to allocate time, to estimate time, and to be aware of the passage of time. It enables your child to gauge when he is running ahead or running behind, and it helps him meet deadlines and cope with transitions (such as leaving home to go to a movie). A modicum of time management savvy is needed for a student to realize that if he has a book report due on Tuesday, there exist some very undeniable implications regarding when he needs to read the book!

For some students, including Joann, the planning and plotting of time make no sense. They are like stowaways on a timeless raft. These perpetual laggards and drifters have trouble thinking about time, using time efficiently, and organizing themselves within any kind of time frame. The meeting of deadlines consequently seems like an arbitrary imposition, and they are loath to estimate how long it will take them to accomplish something, which, in turn, makes it hard to allocate the time to do whatever it is that needs doing. Such seemingly lackadaisical behavior can infuriate a nonunderstanding parent or a demanding, compulsive teacher, especially when these supervisory adults are paragons of punctuality themselves. Very often vociferous bullets of moral accusation are aimed at the out-of-step student.

These kids need a lot of help from their parents in planning a schedule for the week ahead, making explicit plans for meeting deadlines, deciding what will get done when. It's helpful for them to keep lists of things that need to be accomplished during the day and evening, checking off each as it is achieved.

Higher Sequential Thinking

"If Tom gets home earlier than Jack and Sue always arrives after Tom but before Jack, who gets home first, who gets home second, and who gets home last?" To solve this provocative problem, a young child must tackle the challenge of reasoning with sequences. Many aptitude tests include items like "Read the following list of numbers and decide what number comes next: 2 6 18 54 ___." These activities require some high-potency sequential thought processes. The ultimate in sequential ordering is performed on this stratospheric plane, which takes in the ability to make good use of deductive and inductive logic and to reason and problem-solve in a systematic sequential manner. Well-worked-out geometric proofs are likely to be among the most dazzling exhibitions of higher order sequential thinking, as they stress steps in the best order to prove a point.

Higher sequential thinking fosters "step-wisdom," which is simply the much needed realization that in order to accomplish anything substantial or complex, the activity must be broken down into a series of incremental, bite-size, manageable sequential steps. Some students are devoid of any awareness of the virtues and advantages of step-wisdom. A parent may observe, "When this kid finally settles down to do homework he has absolutely no idea of where or how to begin." These children are overwhelmed because they lack a sense of how to break down a task into a series of achievable sequential stages. If you don't know what to do first, second, and third, how do you begin? You get stymied before you even start. The solution is straightforward: parents have to give such children a jump start. They have to help the student get started and also get him to talk through the different steps he intends to go through to get the job done.

✎ SPATIAL ORDERING

Getting oriented and organized in space is yet another challenge faced by growing minds. Knowing left from right, working within the margins on a page, picturing characters while reading, and remembering where you put down the other sock are formidable developmental hurdles that are effortlessly managed by some kids but not others. Alvin is an example of a kid who was always out of space, if not rather spacey.

Alvin at age six was stressed out in first grade. This rather withdrawn and passive child, the tallest and stockiest kid in his class, had problems telling left from right, tying his shoelaces, and copying from the board. When engaged in any kind of arts and crafts activity Alvin could be seen leaning over his sloppy work, trying furtively to conceal it from public view with his chunky forearms. To make matters worse, he kept losing things; he was on a perpetual pencil search. The interior of his desk was a crumpled paper haven with loose crayons, rubber bands, and heaps of other refuse. At home Alvin's parents complained that he didn't know where to put or find anything. When getting dressed he regularly put shirts and underwear on backward. Alvin could be a friendly guy at times despite his passivity, but his interactions with other children were limited by a lack of confidence in his ability to keep up in sports. Alvin could neither catch nor throw a ball, although he was good at swimming and running. Any athletic pursuit that required precise spatial judgment eluded him.

This boy had a delightfully crazy fantasy life and adored imaginary play.

He made liberal use of his impressive vocabulary and sustained a strong interest in outer space exploration. He was reading at a third-grade level, displaying good spelling skills, and writing fanciful stories in complete sentences. On the other hand, Alvin was failing to assimilate key concepts in arithmetic that are best grasped through imagery. He couldn't quite picture what was happening when a child in a word problem gave away three of his six pieces of chocolate. This child was succeeding in life in all areas except those that demanded spatial ordering.

Spatial ordering contrasts with sequential ordering. In the latter, as we have seen, information is or becomes coded in a particular serial order, and that serial order dictates much of the meaning, storage format, and application of that information. In spatial ordering, very different arrangements prevail. Data arrive or depart from the brain simultaneously or nearly so, as a whole or in configurations. Thus, a painting by Mondrian, the shape of a flask, and the spiraling petals of a flower all comprise simultaneous arrays of data. Our minds are expected to deal with the contained stimuli and their interrelationships virtually all at once. If, for some reason, we decide only to process one internal feature at a time, it will not be helpful in our appreciating the overall pattern.

Spatial Perception

"How many rabbits are hidden in this picture?" "Which of these figures has a right angle in it?" "Touch your left shoulder with your right hand." All these demands trigger our perceptions of objects in space. Spatial perception has always intrigued scholars ranging from philosophers to cognitive scientists. The various features and relationships within a display of simultaneous information together represent its perceptual content. Highly specific features come together to form a complete image or a pattern. They include such vivid variables as the relative sizes and locations of component parts, an awareness of what's in the foreground and what's in the background, three-dimensionality, symmetry versus asymmetry, and left versus right. Another feature of spatial perception is known as whole-part relationship. What goes with what? How does the whole relate to its constituent pieces? So, in gazing meaningfully at a portrait or scanning a bus map, one surveys its parts and their relative positions, almost at the same time discerning which of the parts connect through various linkages with other points in space. When perusing a map of Alabama, we observe that certain towns are part of a particular county and that a group of counties comprise the whole state map. We have discovered an essential whole-part relationship. Interestingly, there are some young children who become confused by these whole-part determinations; they seem to have a weak sense of such crucial relationships. As a result, when they write there may be as much space between letters as there is between words. They are bewildered by what goes with what within a spatial package.

Every single one of these perceptual issues was problematic for Alvin and took its toll on everything from artwork to copying from the board. As he ventures into young adulthood, Alvin might discover that his sense of direction is a problem. He may find himself getting lost frequently when he drives a car. He may turn out much like the author, who has the incompatible liabilities of a totally inadequate sense of direction combined with unwavering complete confidence in his sense of direction!

Alvin's parents have become aware of his plight. They are wisely using his good language abilities to reinforce spatial perception. He is practicing talking about what he sees in a kaleidoscope and spends some time talking about various swimming patterns he observes in his beloved guppy tank. He's using language to reinforce his perceptions of space. His parents also realize (correctly) that there are many children and adults with deficiencies of spatial perception who nonetheless do extremely well in school and in their careers. Being great at spatial perception seems not to be a graduation requirement. So we may elect to do nothing about a shortcoming in this neurodevelopmental function. After all, we don't need to fix everything!

Spatial Memory

It's helpful to remember the size and shape of a quarter and how that differs from a nickel. It's convenient to remember exactly what your aunt looks like so you will know which sixty-year-old woman with red hair she is. It's necessary to store some important spatial information in memory. Often this form of long-term memory is considered to be "visual memory" because so much of what we retain from spatial experience passes initially through the visual pathways in our brains. However, we also harvest abundant spatial cues with our probing fingers and by moving our bodies through all sorts of spatial pathways. You put your hand in your pocket and discover a paper clip; you can identify it without removing it because touch sensation has its own spatial memory facility. Spatial data is a multisensory venture; no one pathway monopolizes it. Nevertheless, it is fair to say that in school, the eyes have it. Visual memory predominates in telling a Pablo Picasso from a Norman Rockwell, in remembering the difference between a flask and a beaker, in recalling how a small "g" and a small "q" differ, and in knowing a semicolon every time you spot one.

Spelling is sometimes considered a triumph of visual memory, since it seems to require recalling the appearance of a word. We now know that this is not at all the case; most spelling occurs through one's knowledge of how language works. You might recall that despite his spatial woes, Alvin was learning to spell well. However, there is evidence to suggest that visual memory is actually our built-in spell checker. You write down a word, then glance at it, and realize it does or does not look quite right. If it doesn't look familiar, you make some modifications. Thus, the visual feedback that you receive comparing a word on paper to your memory of how the word looks provides a second chance and thereby ensures accuracy—if it works.

Alvin's spatial memory weaknesses will create some roadblocks for him as he steers his way through school. The problem could be especially acute if he, his parents, and his teachers remain unaware of the bothersome effect of his spatial breakdowns. For example, he is susceptible to problems in certain heavily spatial parts of mathematics, social studies, and science. Alvin may find it hard to remember the appearance of a parallelogram, the chemical symbol for tin, or the shape of a cumulus cloud. While these learning tasks will not be insurmountable educational barriers, they have the potential to vex a child's education. With strong verbal capacity, intact memory functions, along with strong sequencing and attention, Alvin may well withstand the negative effects of some spatial deficiencies. Parents and teachers should encourage their kids with leaky spatial memory to transfer as much visual learning as possible to verbal memory. Alvin needed to talk through the strokes needed to make each letter when he was starting to write: "Hmm, let's see, first I go up and then turn right and then come halfway down . . ."

Spatial Output

Arranging flower stems in a vase, straightening pictures on a wall, and conquering a 1,500-piece jigsaw puzzle may not be passkeys to stellar success in our society, but they do provide gratification and a nice way to feel effective. Spatial output may allow a striving child to take credit for things that are useful and/or attractive. Many creative arts, such as sculpture, painting, and interior design, represent worthy conquests over space. Strong spatial output teams up with creativity and excellent motor ability to generate oil portraits or fantastic Lego creations. As one mother informed me, "Gerald is in complete command when it comes to the world of objects, of hands-on work. He is our Mr. Fix-it and also Mr. Build-it. From constructing his gigantic tree fort to building moving dinosaurs with his Legos, to fixing our computer printer, he's Gerald with the magic touch. His whole body and soul get involved when he is building or fixing some contrivance. And, boy, can he concentrate when he's involved in that kind of thing. That's so obviously what his mind was designed for."

The Geralds of our world are prodigies when it comes to creating praiseworthy spatial products. I have met innumerable children and teenagers with serious problems writing reports, understanding what they read, controlling their attention, or completing math homework, who succeed with flying colors when they are using their hands to conquer space, to create attractive and/or effective spatial output. It becomes their redemption; an art class may be the only venue in which a student feels good about himself in school. A hunk of clay, assorted acrylic paints, or an opportunity to design T-shirts may bring forth strengths in individuals who have been unable to display special ability in other academic domains. Indeed, spatial output is too often an untapped natural resource of many underachieving students. These students would have little trouble designing Web sites as adults. One could do worse!

On the other hand, there exists no shortage of kids like Alvin who fall flat on their face when it comes to making use of any spatial plan or connecting spatial intentions with various forms of motor output. A parent or teacher may feel a sense of annoyance at a kid who seems to do such shoddy work. Spatial incompetence may come across as a lackadaisical attitude. Such a child may feel ashamed and believe he is totally inept. He may struggle to divert classmates from seeing his work, especially in the early grades. Over time, such conspicuous challenges as hammering a nail in straight, inserting a key into a lock right side up, operating a pair of scissors, drawing a straight line, and penciling a realistic sketch damage the self-esteem of a child with sloppy spatial output. Parents need to reassure a child like Alvin that his spatial defeats are not a cause for great worry in the long run, that many of the world's most successful adults have had trouble succeeding in the worlds of arts and crafts and manual repair. It is especially important to emphasize the strengths of such a kid, since his dearth of spatial mastery is so visible to the world at large that it may obscure less obvious abilities, such as creativity, strong problem solving, or excellent receptive language. It is also possible to make use of technology to allow a child to savor the satisfaction that comes with spatial accomplishment. Computer graphics is likely to do the trick; teachers should encourage its widespread use among those with spatial output impairments. Using such graphics, these students derive some pleasure from producing attractive imagery and layouts.

Some division of labor can also help. Alvin's sensitive teacher had him think up a skit for the school revue while one of his more spatially productive (and less verbal) peers designed the lighting and the scenery. Show business takes all kinds of minds.

Spatial Organization—Material Management

Does you child keep losing gloves, pens, sweaters, homework assignments, and lunch money? Does he forget to take the field trip permission slip to school? Are all the tattered pages falling out of his bulging loose-leaf binder? Does he have trouble finding a place to write his book report because of the heaps of socks and underwear occupying his desktop? Does he forget to remove one of his socks when he takes a bath? If the answer to any of these questions is yes, then your son or daughter may be suffering from a material management dysfunction, a chronic condition that at once borders on the ludicrous at the same time that it incites flagrant bouts of anguish and anger on the part of well-meaning parents. Just as time management is the organizational by-product of sequential ordering, material management helps your child organize her physical world. Some individuals are brilliantly organized in space. They know where everything is. They can locate whatever they need whenever they need it. Others, like our first grader Alvin as well as the author of this book, are under the steady stultifying spell of spatial disarray. We materially disorganized martyrs spend much of each day in vain quests for lost objects.

Children with spatial disorganization often have trouble managing a notebook. They seem to lose important papers on the way to or from school. For these materially challenged kids, everyday life is an endless chain of visual-spatial defeats.

There's hope; parents can help a child organize a home office with labeled drawers, shelves, and boxes. Notebooks can undergo periodic refurbishment under parental guidance. Sometimes parents need to take over entirely the chore of keeping a kid's workspace neat so he can acquire a taste for material order. This tactic may or may not work. Mothers and fathers at the very least can take solace in the fact that many an absentminded professor has a disastrous office and an endless paper trail.

Higher Spatial Thinking

Determining why your skateboard or bicycle isn't working right demands high-level spatial problem solving. You look things over and try to figure out where the mechanical glitch may be and what you need to do about it. Understanding how the airflow created by a jet plane affects its altitude and forward thrust takes higher spatial thinking. Conceptualizing a partial eclipse of the moon likewise demands a reach into this lofty realm of thought.

Observe your child problem-solve and strategize like a five-star general overseeing the field of battle as he conquers the latest esoteric computer game. You will have encountered scintillating glimmers of higher spatial thinking, a set of mind operations that enables kids to think about and move around within their minds impressively complicated images and spatial relationships.

I've mentioned how language-loaded school tends to be. Higher spatial thinking offers some relief from the verbal aches and pains of the standard curriculum. It lets students work around, back up, or minimize the use of words and sentences in understanding. Good use of mental imagery relieves the need to put every single idea or skill you learn in school into words and sentences. And there are subjects in which higher spatial thinking is generously rewarded. Certain scientific mechanisms and mathematical concepts (such as place value, equations, and resistance in a wire) are optimally thought about without the exclusive use of language—simply by shifting into the higher spatial thinking gear.

There are students who enjoy spatial ordering, and they tend to be virtuosi at depicting imagery to capture many an otherwise hard-to-grasp idea or explanation. Kids like Alvin have to put almost everything into words if they are to understand. Alvin and I, we word-bound thinkers, are similar in that regard. If there is something I can't explain to you in words and sentences, you can be sure I don't really understand it.

It would be hard and mostly unnecessary to concoct vigorous interventions to help kids improve their higher spatial thinking. Instead they should be aware of this weakness and seek verbal and/or sequential or even hands-on ways of problem-solving and conceptualization.

§➊ SPATIAL VERSUS SEQUENTIAL ORDERING: WHICH WOULD YOU RATHER BE GOOD AT?

If you are ever reincarnated and are offered an opportunity to choose whether to be especially strong in spatial ordering or sequential ordering (assuming, of course, you want to succeed in school), I recommend you opt for sequential ordering. School is a tangle of sequential chains that threatens to shackle our students. Many children are like hikers in the dark when it comes to spatial ordering yet they take home report cards spangled with As. So Alvin may grace his school's honor roll sooner or later. Of course, there are scholastic moments when spatial ordering asserts itself heavily, especially in mathematics, art, and many facets of science. It is ideal, then, to have both, but many students are strongly oriented or specialized in one of the two ordering systems.

Understanding which system of ordering works best for a child could have a bearing on her future learning and academic productivity. Parents, teachers, and students themselves should seize this opportunity for understanding a mind's preferred pathways. You have the option of deciding whether to strengthen one or more weak levels of an ordering system (such as trying to build up sequential short-term memory), to work around a weakness (such as bypassing poor visualization through verbalization), or to go about vigorously strengthening an existing strength (such as providing lots of studio art experience for a girl with remarkable spatial output). These options are not mutually exclusive; it's possible to attempt all of the above. We always have the opportunity to strengthen strengths at the same time we are working on weaknesses.

§➤ MINDS OVER TIME: KEEPING A WATCHFUL EYE ON SEQUENTIAL AND SPATIAL ORDERING AS CHILDREN AGE

Parents and teachers can see that during the earliest grades, kids are introduced to the world of time and sequence at a pretty sophisticated level. Discerning the order of letters in the alphabet, figuring out which numbers are greater than which others, and telling time represent sequencing milestones for five- to seven-year-olds, who also are expected to mop up time-soaked vocabulary, words such as "before," "after," "until," and "when." Their ability to comprehend and use these terms depends in part upon their inner sense of time and sequence. By the middle of elementary school, students must comply daily with multistep instructions: "Now go find your workbooks, then open to the exercise on farm animals, the one we were doing yesterday, then answer the third and fourth questions before you read what I've put on the board." Time and sequence together are infrastructure for a sizable proportion of a classroom teacher's instructional outflow.

By the middle of elementary school, sequencing is a dominant force in mathematics. Multistep processes and multiplication facts, among other things, are strenuous exercises in sequential ordering. Meanwhile, kids are expected to tell stories, relate incidents, and construct written paragraphs using logical sequences to guide the flow of their thoughts.

The demands for accurate and fast sequential ordering don't diminish in secondary school. As the workload burgeons, middle schoolers need to demonstrate time management skills. They are supposed to meet deadlines and complete long-range tasks in a logical sequence of steps. They need to be aware of time's passage when they take tests and quizzes in class, so they won't run out of time or rush through items they could have tackled more accurately at an easier pace. They have to experiment with this kind of speed-quality trading off. The time management mandate is emphasized repeatedly in high school, although many adolescents don't quite hear or answer that call. Sequential ordering becomes even more important in college.

In high school children are required to achieve ever more challenging logical sequential thinking, especially in mathematics and in scientific experimentation and reasoning. As we have noted, geometric proofs are notorious for their drain on higher order sequential thinking. History classes presume to cultivate one's taste for chronological relationships. Sequential processing helps students ferret out what caused what, enabling them to discover how the Boston Tea Party contributed to the igniting of the Revolutionary War and how oxygen contributes to the igniting of flames in the atmosphere.

As I have noted, spatial ordering tends to fade somewhat as a higher level academic necessity. It is most important during the earliest grades as children are assimilating the shapes of numbers and letter symbols and engaging in such tasks as pasting, tracing, cutting out, and so on. While listening to stories, elementary school minds synthesize mental imagery as they create internal pictures or verbal-visual associations, thereby enriching the content of the tales they hear.

As kids get older, spatial abilities enhance performance in many sports. Problems with material organization (a form of spatial ordering) may erupt at any age, but they seem most pronounced in secondary school when students face a mountain of academic props.

৯ PRACTICAL CONSIDERATIONS

• All kids (and lots of adults) need help with time management. Your children can get a handle on time management by setting itineraries and timelines for errands and vacations. Children and teenagers should wear analog, not digital, watches; they need to observe the sweeping second hand and program themselves for the passage of time in continuous intervals. Every class in school should stress time management, having kids devise schedules, complete projects in stages, and demonstrate work in progress.

• Teachers and parents need to be alert to kids who become disoriented, inattentive, or possibly even disruptive when faced with multistep instructions. They may be battling inadequate sequential memory. Teachers should repeat directions and encourage these students to check with classmates regarding what is expected. These students may also gain from receiving written or graphic directions. Also, these children need to be aware that their minds are not hospitable to newly arriving sequences.

• Rhythmic games and songs early in life can help reinforce sequential ordering. Songs and rhymes about the alphabet, the months of the year, and other practical sequences are particularly effective. Music, in general, can be a forceful promoter of sequential ordering.

• Help with material management may be scholastic chemotherapy for some individuals. As I have suggested, a well-organized workspace at home is especially curative. Parents should be accommodating in helping a materially confused child get organized. In this context parents should not say, "You know, Johnny, I'm not going to be around all your life. Someday you'll have to be independent and do all this on your own." This is generally a waste of breath and a needless put-down. I recently advised a young boy who had been overdosed with this all too familiar maternal refrain to say that he has every intention of marrying a woman just like his mother.

• Kids who appear to be at war with the spatial realm should become accustomed to verbalizing spatial phenomena. They should talk through where they left something, whispering under their breath, "I put it in the bottom drawer." They should translate geometric shapes, planetary movements, and chemical structures into linguistic form as far as possible. For example, instead of picturing a pentagon, a child linguist can readily sop up the fact that "penta" usually means five, so a pentagon must have five sides. She can compose a verbal mnemonic about the planets and their relative distances from the sun, and she can revel in the realization that carbon tetrachloride is linguistically required to contain four chloride ions.

• Children who have either spatial or sequential strengths should exploit these capacities through art, dance, music, and opportunities to work with their hands. Their ordering strengths are likely to be longing for cultivation.

7

Mind over Muscle ꟾ

Our Motor System

> Nine boys to a side, four already chosen, ten positions left, and the captains look us over.
> They choose the popular ones fast . . . and now the choice is hard because we're all so
> much the same, not so hot—and then they are down to their last grudging choices, a
> slow kid for catcher and someone to stick out in right field where nobody hits it. . . . Just
> once I'd like Daryl to pick me first. . . . But I've never been chosen with any enthusiasm.
>
> GARRISON KEILLOR, Lake Wobegon Days

RETURNING a Ping-Pong serve, threading a needle, making a graph, and
playing scales on a fife all have in common the need for extensive highways
of branching nerve cells that communicate with diverse groups of muscles
situated throughout our bodies. These intricate motor pathways enable us
to perform pursuits that range from surfboarding to keyboarding. During
the school years, successful motor function contributes generously to a
child's self-esteem while opening doors to a range of recreational activities
and opportunities to be productive with schoolwork.

Most children are eager to show off some grandiose display of motor
magnificence, as we can witness in the following familiar scenarios:

"Watch me, Daddy, watch me," Julie pleads vehemently as she proudly
plunges from the diving board like a plump sack of Florida pink grapefruit.
Her parents affectionately react to this dubious splash of motor distinction
with contrived awe.

Andy, an eager six-year-old, arrives home proudly unfurling his tattered masterpiece, a richly textured, unintentionally abstract work of art whose provocative pigmentation resembles a montage of chunky peanut butter and lumpy marinara sauce. He exudes pride in his art and requests prime space on the refrigerator door.

Louise and Rhonda are spending hours upon hours mastering their almost ceremonial jump rope routines, striving to integrate their rhythmic chants with the synchronized gyrations of the rope. As they improve, they grow almost ecstatic at their success.

Walter and his father seem to have bonded permanently, as this self-sacrificing dad proudly serves as the assistant coach of his son's soccer team. The two talk as seriously about the most recent soccer game as if they were reviewing military tactics. Their weighty soccer dialogue glows with incandescent intimacy, a special form of love.

These vignettes highlight the dedicated seriousness with which children and teenagers relish motor achievement. Muscular mastery is like an ego-sustaining vitamin; an optimal level nourishes personal pride and self-concept when you are a kid—it works in some adults as well. By excelling in a sport or craft, a child is able to display and savor a fundamental sense of mastery.

Children view one another's motor displays as open windows revealing their overall competency, bodily effectiveness, "boyishness" and "girlishness," along with their courage for handling rivalry and adversity. Motor output provides a socially acceptable way of channeling intensely felt competitive drives as well as a chance to reveal grace under pressure (sometimes referred to as "coolness"). And children make liberal use of their motor exploits to compare themselves with peers. The thirst for competitive advantage can be nearly unquenchable during childhood; athletic skills are a convenient and highly visible way of satisfying this drive.

Obviously, the motor system involves more than just ego inflation, although it certainly allows kids to feel very good about themselves and helps some to establish a satisfying level of equality or even superiority over their peers. Motor activity fosters physical conditioning and permits the acquisition of a wide repertoire of self-help skills, ranging from clipping fingernails without bloodletting, to repairing a bicycle chain, to sewing a hem. At its best it can also encourage collaboration, planning, self-monitoring, and high moral standards (i.e., good sportsmanship).

Efficient motor output also helps accomplish some important academic skills. Most obviously, some of the most complex muscular manipulations are demanded for writing. As we shall see, there are countless students with good ideas whose fingers just can't keep pace with their thinking, as a result of which they come to despise and avoid writing.

Well-coordinated muscular output also works its wonders in some less obvious ways. When operating well, motor actions reinforce memory and learning. Direct hands-on experience, manipulating materials in a science experiment, or engaging in athletic pursuits can actually improve various neurodevelopmental functions, such as active working memory and problem solving. Clearly, a student engineering a crucial basketball play and responding to the hard-to-anticipate moves of other players is exercising not only his muscles but also some problem-solving and reasoning faculties. Motor engagements enable kids to learn by doing. This can be one of the most meaningful ways of learning.

§➥ FORMS OF MOTOR FUNCTION

Five distinct forms of motor function dominate work and play and together comprise the major components of the motor system. They include: gross motor function, fine motor function, graphomotor function, musical motor function, and oromotor function.

Gross motor function involves the activity of large muscles, making possible all the actions needed to serve a tennis ball, engage in a strenuous workout, pedal a tricycle, or toss a bale of hay.

Small muscles, principally those in our hands and fingers, dedicate them-

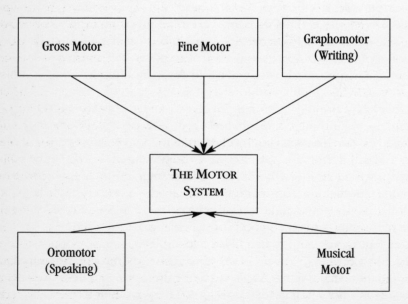

Figure 7-1.   The motor system.

selves to fine motor function, manual dexterity. The nearly synonymous term "eye-hand coordination" reminds us that the purposeful movements of our fingers need visual supervision. Your work's cut out for you if you try trimming your toenails, pounding in a nail, or creating origami figures with your eyes closed!

Fine motor and graphomotor function are quite different. Graphomotor function is the highly specialized motor output used in writing. Many students boast superb fine motor abilities and unacceptable graphomotor function. Such was the case with Raoul, who, in his final month in third grade, was battling major obstacles to letter formation. Deciphering his hieroglyphic handwriting was a daunting challenge for any adult; Raoul himself often couldn't read what he had written. He was downright ashamed of the appearance of his written work. Raoul always was more than willing to engage his magnificent verbal fluency to tell jokes and outlandish stories but could get none of this down on paper. But what mystified everyone was the fact that he was a born graphic artist. From the age of two Raoul loved to draw. At nine his cartoon creations displayed precise fine motor control. But somehow Raoul could not engage in the rapid assignment and activation of his finger muscles required for letter formation, a classic example of strong fine motor function accompanied by a stubborn graphomotor dysfunction. Raoul is starting to use a keyboard, and it's helping somewhat.

Musical motor output has to be one of the more obscure brain operations. A wide range of muscular responses and sensory inputs achieve their special harmonies. Playing the harp, square dancing, appreciating and mimicking rock rhythms all draw upon an individual's musical motor coordination—yielding varying degrees of triumph or despair.

Oromotor function is yet another manifestation of controlled muscular activity. Our cheeks are stuffed with some of our busiest muscle groups, which carry out the incompatible roles of pulverizing food and generating speech. Obviously, such activity plays a critical role across the gamut of oral communication from complaining to yodeling. Oromotor fluency facilitates participation in class discussions. Interestingly, many of the same kids who have trouble with oromotor function experience difficulty with graphomotor function. In fact, a great many preschoolers who receive language therapy for speech articulation end up having writing difficulty in the early grades in school. In all likelihood, this is because both oromotor and graphomotor function involve rapid motor sequencing. Everyday eye-hand coordination activities, such as connecting the dots in a puzzle and buttoning a blouse, are not executed with nearly the speed and complicated sequential flow that drives written output and talking.

Gross Motor Function

I don't think anyone has ever brought a child to see me just because he was inept at sports. Yet a segment of the children I am asked to evaluate for their learning differences are also enduring poor large muscle coordination. Humiliating performance in sports deflates self-esteem the way a sharp nail in your driveway leads to a flat tire, especially in a kid whose report card also leaves a whole lot to be desired.

It turns out that a child's proficiency in sports offers one of the most transparent views of certain brain connections. As a parent you may note the ease or awkwardness with which your daughter runs, hops, skips, and catches or hurls a ball. As you witness these motor exploits you are observing the circuits that link many varied neurodevelopmental functions. Watching a child swim, for example, offers insight into her ability to locate her body in space, her capacity to coordinate the activity of several limbs at once, her muscle stamina, and her motor sequencing abilities.

Athletic prowess (or its embarrassing absence) is a highly revealing gauge of gross motor performance during childhood. Boys and girls succeed or fail at one or another sport according to the effectiveness of specific brain-to-large-muscle connections that allow a kid to be well coordinated.

No matter which sport a kid partakes of, his or her interpretation and use of sensory data are crucial, although the exact modes of sensory intake differ from sport to sport. Your budding young baseball or tennis starlet boasts very precise perception of outer spatial data—all those balls traveling to or from her in all manner of trajectories! An outfielder must gauge and predict accurately and with lightning speed the trajectory of an approaching ball. The child fielder estimates the ball's velocity and vector, and then navigates her own body toward the projected landing point. Imagine the spatial judgment required to pull this off. There are wide individual differences in the ability to do so: some kids make it look easy; others can't do it at all. As one thwarted nine-year-old left fielder confessed to me, "By the time I figure out where the ball is going, it's already landed on the ground somewhere. Then I go chase it and by mistake I kick it away with my foot. Then I have to chase it again. Then finally I pick it up and start to throw it, and I drop the ball. While all this is happening everyone's yelling at me or calling me real bad names. I guess you can see why I hate baseball."

Because some kids find this high level of rapid spatial processing unmanageable, they wisely avoid ball sports. Luckily, some athletic exploits require virtually no outer spatial perception but instead rely upon information communicated to your child's brain from his own joints and muscles. Gymnastics, many track and field events, ballet, swimming, and skating are prime examples of this alternative routing of information. Ted, the frustrated left fielder, was surprisingly aware of the difference: "You know, I can swim good. I'm a real fast runner too. I can be good at sports where you don't have to keep using your eyes over and over again to decide what to do or where to go. I mean I could swim with my eyes closed. I could even run fast without looking—oops, maybe not, I might hit a tree."

A few years ago I visited a high school on a hot and humid North Carolina spring afternoon. I stepped outside to talk with a coach who I knew was very interested in the ways kids vary in their motor performance. (By the way, coaches have the potential to be some of the most astute observers of how kids function.) This coach, Rod Benson, pointed to a trim, attractive senior girl who was having a dreadful time coping with the back-and-forth arching intricacies of big-time high school volleyball. Kimberly kept missing the ball with agonizing regularity, bringing out the vocal abuse of her teammates. Nor was she any better at serving the ball when her turn came. As we witnessed her frustration, Mr. Benson mentioned that Kimberly had just received a full scholarship to a noted college. He informed me that one reason for this honor was that Kimberly was "the best modern dancer in the state." She had received widespread recognition for her phenomenal performances at recitals over the last several years and she toured with a professional troupe during the last two summers. Kimberly clearly displayed very specialized gross motor abilities that went into hiding during volleyball tournaments.

You wouldn't think that while playing hockey your child is straining his memory as much as he's depleting his physical energy. But he is. Not only does he have do things in hockey, he has to keep remembering how to do things. Some of the most complicated and strenuous remembering feats are accomplished by muscles, as the mind of a young athlete uploads and downloads the programs for how to ride a bicycle, at what point to release a bowling ball, or which muscles are to be recruited to manage cartwheels in gymnastics. The blueprints for these tasks are stored in motor procedural memory. You can have three kids in your family who differ dramatically in the ease and accuracy with which they are able to put into storage and eventually call up these highly specific motor plans. Over the years I've been aware that sports with especially complex memory blueprints, such as gymnastics and diving, frustrate some of my patients while being wellsprings of uplifting gratification for others. As with all memory, the more a child employs his stored skills, the easier it becomes to access them in a pinch. So practice makes perfect in sports (as in other matters), but some children will require substantially more practice than others. Individuals vary in the extent to which they need to practice in order to perfect a particular form of motor ability and agility. Highly talented athletes require less practice.

Regrettably, because gross motor function is so visible to the outside world, many children are reluctant to practice a particular subskill, like throwing or kicking a ball. Therefore, they actually end up with less practice than their peers, and so their skills never reach competency. I guess the conclusion is obvious: parents should provide students with gross motor dysfunctions sufficient privacy during their awkward practice sessions. They must not feel exposed to the critical gazes of their peers. And we adults have to let them decide whether the practice is even worth the trouble—and then support their decision!

It may not be immediately apparent, but your child actually uses some powerful language functions in mastering certain sports. Fascinating dialogues occur between language and gross motor function. During the early stages of attaining a gross motor skill kids use verbal self-coaching. They actually talk their way through an emerging skill. "Let's see, I'd better keep my bat off my right shoulder and then I have to remember to step into the ball after he throws and then I have to swing level, and I need to follow through after I swing." Over time, as motor procedures become more or less automatic, talking to yourself plays a dwindling role.

Intense communication passes back and forth between a coach or physical education teacher and her players. Kids differ in their ability to process language that describes or regulates motor function. Some very good linguists in all other areas of school have trouble interpreting the words of coaches! They simply cannot decipher language that imparts motor instruction. One child I knew, Janine, was getting all As in seventh grade, having no difficulty whatsoever understanding teachers in social studies, math, and Spanish, but she had no clue when it came to what her physical education teacher was trying to communicate. When I conversed with her (in motor-free English), it was clear that this girl was a proficient linguist—both receptively and expressively. Her mom reported that Janine was a beautifully coordinated child, surefooted, and a budding ballerina. However, when she submitted to dance lessons, Janine was perpetually confused, and quit the class after seven humiliating sessions. She experienced similar futility in physical education class. When Janine and I chatted, she confessed with a broad smile: "I could never understand my dancing teacher; they all talk too much and too fast, trying to explain things all the time." Then she sighed and reported, "You know, I was thinking about it; I'm pretty sure I've never had a coach I could understand either. In PE all I do is watch what my friends do." Janine had a hard time interpreting language that referred to movement and space. In my unending celebration of neurodevelopmental variation, I am pleased to note that the opposite also occurs; quite a few students I've met over the years have had trouble interpreting language in school *unless* the words refer to space and movement. These athletes are at their verbal and motor best when handling the language of one another and their coaches.

Heavy-duty oral banter punctuates many games. Often kids with pervasive language difficulties throughout the curriculum have trouble engaging in sports that feature such steady oral exchanges. They shy away from team sports like baseball because of the inevitable fast talk among players. I remember one nine-year-old Little League rookie who was a whiz at batting and at playing second base but quit the team early in his first season. He told his mom, "I get all mixed up—everyone keeps telling me what to do, where to go or where to stand and stuff, and then they yell at me if I go to the wrong place. I hate that." This boy was also facing language difficulties in the classroom and was still reading at a late-first-grade level. A student so affected may excel at a sport like golf or an activity like the broad jump where talk between players and coaches never reaches the level found during team play.

Attention is a starting player in most gross motor performance. The planning and previewing of an athletic move demands tight control of attention. Impulsive play can be disastrous. And needless to say, if you're a soccer goalie and you get distracted by chatter on the field or the sound of a distant freight train, your team's defense is seriously at risk! A basketball player preparing to make a foul shot is planning his trajectory, picturing the ball in the air headed toward the hoop. On a more unconscious level, he is pondering which muscles to use and with how much force. He is concentrating intently. He has the attention control it takes to be a good athlete.

When your child plays a sport not only may he be part of a team of players but within his body there needs to be some incredible teamwork between various muscle groups and his brain and also among all the diverse mind functions that play the game. When one or more of these inside players isn't playing, your child might find himself being perpetually thought of as klutzy.

Fine Motor Function

The extra long cables that connect your child's fingers to her brain carry loads of signals all day long, but the heaviest transmission occurs during the school day. As their fingers do the walking, kids demonstrate what they know on tests and what they can do through all kinds of tangible projects and products. Fine motor function follows many of the same pathways as gross motor output—with a heavy dose of memory as well as eye-hand co-ordination (your visual pathways and your fingers coordinate closely). A hefty load of language input, such as your daughter's art teacher's verbal di-rections, delivers the marching orders directing a fine motor maneuver. Some of the same students who have trouble understanding motor direc-tions in a physical education class become confused when a ceramics or woodworking teacher issues instructions for a project.

I personally have long felt that my own fingers are only attached to my upper limbs for cosmetic purposes. I willingly confess to being a fine motor klutz. As a child I remember feeling very self-conscious about this, espe-cially at certain points during the school day. Once, while I was a student at Oxford, one of my friends at breakfast earnestly inquired, "Mel, how come you're buttering your finger and not the toast?" At that time I was unaware of this handicap, but over the ensuing decades, it has become clear that my eyes and my fingers function totally independent of one another! That au-tonomy has taken its toll in the form of hundreds of stained neckties, more than my share of broken dishes and glasses, coffee stains on my desk blot-ter, and other assorted fine motor calamities.

For better or worse, children during preschool and elementary school, in particular, are apt to be sensitive about their fine motor performance. It is possible to become an honor student despite fine motor dysfunctions (as occurred in my case), but noticing that your classmates accomplish great things with their fingers while your own digits strike out repeatedly can do much to make you feel inferior. If you're the parent of such a child, you need to offer him some reassurance and then decide whether to work hard with him to blaze some sort of fine motor trail to gratification. Obviously, if your son or daughter is receiving plenty of rewards in other parts of life, fine motor success may not be all that important and his shortcomings can be chalked up to the "nobody's perfect" reality.

If you have several children, the chances are that at least one is a fine motor achiever. Such a child is apt to be good at slowing down and think-ing through her finger works. Happily, most fine motor activities are not pursued at the breakneck speed common in so many gross motor feats. As a result there is much more time for planning, for previewing, for monitor-ing, for pacing. The great sculptor Henry Moore was not in as much of a hurry as the great hockey defenseman Bobby Orr. But there are at least two big exceptions to the slower fine motor control: one is computer games, which often demand speed combined with eye-hand coordination, and the other is musical performance, which requires some diligent control over speed—more about that later in this chapter.

Because so much of fine motor output is kept on course through visual inputs, you are apt to notice a strong correlation between your child's effectiveness in spatial ordering and his or her fine motor dexterity. Although it is not always the case, students endowed with a superior sense of spatial arrangement, those with strong spatial perception and memory, often generate the most impressive fine motor displays. Their command of space may be apparent in their art- or craftwork, in their ability to fix broken objects (likely to have been damaged by a sibling with fine motor dysfunction), and in the ease with which they pick up new manual skills. One teacher, commenting on a student in her fifth-grade class, related, "It's almost as if he has brains in his hands. His fingers can solve problems, be creative, and even remember how to do things they've only done once before. He's a virtual fine motor genius. If only he could read up to par . . ." Here's yet another example of a highly specialized young mind.

As we noted in the last chapter, an art class may become an academic oasis, a magnificent blessing for students with language-based learning difficulties. Art teachers in elementary and secondary schools keep reminding me that a sizable number of kids who thrive and distinguish themselves at an easel or with a lump of clay live with humbling delays in reading, spelling, or mathematics. Art sometimes is the sole way a student feels effective. Other fine motor redeeming opportunities include fixing cars, building bookshelves, and cooking. If you know a child with significant academic woes (and who doesn't), investigate possible fine motor opportunities for the restoration of self-esteem. If you are the parent or the teacher of a struggling student, seek whatever opportunities you can to exploit a fine motor pathway that seems to work and heap plenty of praise on the resulting efforts. Fine motor pride can keep your child going.

Graphomotor Function and Keyboarding

As I have mentioned, it is possible and even common to be impressively dexterous at fine motor function while harboring disabling and disturbing graphomotor dysfunction. Quite a few students, like my patient Raoul at the start of this chapter, have probing and insightful ideas each day in class discussions but can't transcribe those ideas. Graphomotor dysfunctions are one of the most common reasons a child is referred to me. Parents and teachers are often baffled by a bright kid who can't or won't write. There can be many reasons for this kind of output failure, but graphomotor dysfunction is often the cause.

We might discover that your child hates to write because of feeble connections between his memory and his fingers. Motor memory guides writing as it does the moves in sports. A very heavy flow from memory takes place when your child sets out to put things down on paper. To begin with, that child needs to be able to recall letter shapes and the chain of tiny muscle movements he needs to execute them. It sounds easy, but it isn't. The Russian neuropsychologist Alexander Luria described what he called "kinetic melodies," the highly precise sequences of finger muscle movements required to form letters during writing. Each letter encrypts its own unique kinetic melody, its coded sequence of muscle motions for forming that letter. Kinetic melodies (also called "motor engrams") are filed in motor procedural long-term memory. Students vary in how rapidly and accurately they can recover from memory these elusive motor sequences. As one second-grade boy told me, "A lot of times when I want to make a 'd,' my brain tells my fingers to make a 'b.' Then I notice it later and have to fix it."

Interestingly, students who have trouble recalling the motor sequences as well as those who have trouble visualizing the letters seem to arrive at one very consistent conclusion: they discover and insist that they prefer printing to cursive writing. The inclination is entirely understandable, since in printing you have only twenty-six discrete patterns to visualize and execute. Cursive writing, on the other hand, involves the mastery of an unending flow of lengthy visual sequences. So, if and when a child insists he can print better and faster than he can do cursive, please invite him to use printing for the rest of his writing life!

Assigning just the right muscles to letter-making responsibilities is another graphomotor hurdle that may undermine your child's quest for legibility. Certain muscles are brought into play to grasp a pen or pencil with reasonable firmness, while other finger muscles are supposed to keep it moving in the desired direction. Some muscle groups accept assignments to vertical movement, others specialize in horizontal movement, and still others handle rotary movement. For some children this very precise assignment and mobilization of specific muscle groups on demand is all but impossible. Most often, they come to detest writing, and, like Raoul, they talk so much better than they write. These students have motor implementation problems. As a parent of such a child you may have noted his awkward pencil grips. He may exert far too much pressure, write with a fistlike grasp, or maintain his pen perpendicular to the writing surface. Every muscle might seem to have put in for stabilization duty, and none remain to move the pencil through letters. A student like that seems to be writing with his elbows rather than his fingers. Writing becomes painfully slow and labored. As one teacher put it, "I hate to watch him write. It's painful for both of us. He bears down so hard it hurts him after a while. And his hands can never keep up with his ideas. I guess that's why he so despises writing." Too often the effort required is so great that the quality of ideas and spelling accuracy are eclipsed.

In observing your child during the act of writing, notice whether he keeps his eyes too close to the page. If so, he's trying to get some feedback on his letter formation, but he's doing it the hard way. The need for feedback during writing never slackens. You have to know just where your pen or pencil is at all moments while you're etching those letters. Some students harbor a condition we call "finger agnosia." Believe it or not, they lose track of where their fingers are. When still quite young, they keep their eyes close to the page watching those digits diligently, substituting visual feedback for data that should be coming from the joints and muscles of the fingers themselves. Often I find that these kids use their wrist muscles instead of their finger muscles, and since wrist muscles move so much more the feedback may be easier for them to pick up. Regrettably, it is hard to write with your wrists.

Different breakdowns in graphomotor function can dishearten your otherwise highly competent child, rendering him underproductive when it comes to homework completion, test taking, and all written output in general. For many the answer to this problem rests on a keyboard. Making use of a computer's word processing program, they may evolve into respectable writers despite their graphomotor dysfunction. One cautionary note, however: many of the same students who have difficulties with graphomotor function experience trouble with keyboarding. This is because keyboarding, like ordinary writing, involves rapid motor sequencing. Yet, a computer keyboard offers a child a definite advantage: the results are likely to be much more aesthetically pleasing. Your child, even when she attains reasonable graphomotor efficiency, may be left with unattractive and perhaps borderline legible handwriting. Such scrawl may make her reluctant to submit work. One girl who was initially hesitant to use her laptop told me: "Now that I'm pretty good on the keyboard, I really like writing. Before I couldn't stand it. And I'm starting to be able to think while I'm typing. Before I could either type or think but not both. It's real cool. I just got an A– on my social studies report, and it looked real nice. That never used to happen. The computer has saved my life in school."

Other Forms of Motor Function

At the start of this chapter, I mentioned oromotor and musical motor function as two important outflows. However, I will not elaborate very much on these modalities. There are indeed some kids with impediments of oromotor fluency. They may stutter or endure other speech articulation difficulties. It can be frustrating when your mouth can't keep pace with your flow of ideas, although this state may be preferable to having a mouth that's moving all the time despite a lack of ideas. Many kids with oromotor dysfunctions write better than they can talk. In cases where the motor aspects of talking seriously constrain classroom participation, affected students benefit from speech therapy.

As a parent, you should be exploring musical options for your kid. Much like fine motor function, highly attuned musical motor function can do much to bolster the self-esteem of children. A student's motor outlet for music might be vocal, manual, or gross motor. Gross motor musical performance includes dancing and marching. Some children are gifted when it comes to the linkage of gross motor function to music. Most of them possess a keen sense of rhythm and cadence along with crystal-clear reception of musical tones. Parents should look for and exploit those sometimes hidden capabilities.

Selecting the optimal musical instrument for your child can be difficult. Musical instruments differ in the highly specific demands they make on your neurodevelopmental function. Rapid motor sequencing is essential for keyboard instruments and for the guitar, whereas some forms of tympani (cymbals and kettledrum) are less demanding with regard to the rate of sequential flow. A trombone stresses the use of large limb muscles, while a clarinet demands more fine motor function. If you analyze a particular student's neurodevelopmental profile and understand the unique demands of individual instruments, you should be able to match kids to musical instruments that are likely to succeed. One student I know was frustrated by the piano because the rapid sequencing of his fingers seemed beyond him, but he thrived musically when he switched to the bass drum in the marching band; he seemed to have much better control of the muscles that were larger and closer to his brain.

In Search of Motor Gratification

Byron was a second grader who at age eight already was in line to become a motor function dropout. His disheveled appearance included shirt-buttoning arrangements highly suggestive of fine motor neglect. From his earliest days, his parents regarded Byron as having "two left feet." When Byron was four, his dad, once a letterman in three college sports, spent countless hours trying to get Byron to pass and kick a football. But Byron lacked whatever it took to make his hands available at the right time and in the right spot to catch the ball. His throwing was no better.

Byron also struggled in vain with fine motor activities. His drawings in kindergarten and first grade subjected him to ridicule from even his most benevolent peers. This southpaw had trouble using a scissors, tracing, and even tying his shoelaces. He owed a profound debt to the inventor of Velcro. As a preschooler Byron had been enrolled in violin class. In an unprecedented admission of defeat, his teacher suggested Byron discontinue his lessons. (Byron was thrilled.)

In spite of his motor success deprivation, Byron was an upbeat person and a marvelous student. His reading was two years above grade level. He loved mathematics, in which he was a brilliant problem solver. Byron consumed knowledge in science and in current events as if it were cotton candy. At home he related with intimacy and affection to his pet scorpions and hermit crabs. He was a collector of anything he could possibly afford and hoard.

Byron enjoyed his fellow children, and they liked him in part because he was a leader in totally preposterous forms of imaginary play and partly because he was just plain hilarious (at least according to second graders). Yet Byron would withdraw surreptitiously and flee to the safety net of home when it looked as if other kids were about to engage in a gross motor activity. Byron's parents kept trying to entice him to participate in art, music, or sports, but he became increasingly stubborn in his resistance. His parents wondered how much pressure they should exert on Byron, so that he might taste the joys of motor pleasure that other family members so relished. I told them to ease off. There are many other forms of gratification, and this boy had already discovered some of the best ones. From time to time and with some protection from humiliation, he might give a motor activity a try, but he and his parents needed to accept the fact that there are all kinds of minds and not all of them need motor success.

Over the years I have encountered too many parents who exert excessive motor pressure. Such overemphasis on sports or other motor pursuits can either dishearten a child or overinflate his ego. A father or mother may experience vicarious pleasure from watching a child triumph in a sport. But is this in the best interests of the child? Sometimes it isn't. I've seen some casualties, especially in young adulthood, when a former star athlete no longer has much to show for all of his motor exploits. I've also met younger children who are buckling under unbearable pressure from parents and/or overly zealous coaches who have forgotten that games are just games. Their own adult egos sometimes take advantage of both good and not so good athletes, overgratifying the former and humiliating the latter. I have seen quite a few pretty depressed kids who are victims of adult overinvolvement in sports.

Please don't allow your children to overdose themselves with motor satisfaction. I call this condition "motor intoxication." Affected individuals are kids or young adults who have been revered as a result of a succession of athletic feats or related motor victories. They develop so much confidence in their own bodies that little else seems important to them. I have seen cases where such students have become very depressed and unhappy as young adults because they invested too much of their identity and drive in the motor domain and began to feel inadequate when they arrived at a period in life when their motor abilities became hard to market. One college student said, "I got to love my own body so much that nothing else was important to me. I was always good looking and a fantastic jock. I thought the show could go on forever. Then in college my professors didn't care how I looked; they didn't even know how I looked. And I wasn't even as good an athlete as I thought I was. So I had a body that wasn't getting me far and a mind that had gone to waste. My huge ego came crashing down. My high school teachers used to worship me. Anyway, you know I dropped out in my sophomore year. Now I'm trying to put my life back together."

ᔑ⬤ MINDS OVER TIME: KEEPING A WATCHFUL EYE ON MOTOR FUNCTION AS CHILDREN AGE

Children vary widely in their interest in motor activities. Parents can observe the emergence of motor preferences and abilities. In the earliest grades, arts and crafts pursuits take on special significance as manual mastery is valued and respected by both teachers and classmates. Based on his early motor track record, your child is more willing or less willing to take risks with his hands. Developmentally, children from kindergarten through second grade are especially vulnerable to deep feelings of shame when they can't color, trace, or paste with the best of them. They need reassurance from their parents, so that they don't overreact to these weaknesses. Prowess on the playground also becomes conspicuous as kids display for all to see either their motor awkwardness or the graceful flow of their musculoskeletal systems. Trampolines, jungle gyms, and ball sports are some early challenges to gross motor function.

Graphomotor function is even more conspicuous and a potential delicate issue. Rapid and precise letter formation, as I have described in this chapter, can start to be a problem in kindergarten and persist stubbornly for years. Often kids who can't write won't write. They can lose even more ground at this age due to a serious shortage of practice.

By the middle years of elementary school, your child's athletic indulgence or abstinence may rise to the surface. Once again you are likely to find that competition actively asserts itself, so a child feels compelled to compare his own running speed, coordination, and balance to that of his peers. Parents and teachers observe and often comment upon a child's competence or ineptitude at sports (mostly catching and throwing a ball). Rapid and automatic motor sequencing figure prominently in such highly charged events as swimming, hopping, and skipping.

In secondary school, sports become serious. The pretty good athletes are bypassed for the great athletes, a tragic phenomenon known as "elitist sports." Overly zealous secondary school coaches acting out some personal fantasy may perpetrate this elitism, damaging the self-images of too many kids.

By high school kids should have found one or more motor niches from which they can absorb ample personal satisfaction and remain in decent physical condition. In one of the schools I have worked with, there is a remarkable coach from whom I have learned so much about kids. Marty once told me during one of my visits to his middle school, "Mel, it's a challenge to find a way for any kid to take real pride in what his body and mind are capable of when they work well together. I love finding those ways for all my students. And I never let them forget that it's a game; it's supposed to be fun more than anything else—whether you win or lose, hit a home run or strike out. And I have a zero tolerance policy for any student who ridicules another player for making a mistake or looking bad." By the way, Marty is a superb mentor for many kids, both athletes and nonathletes. Like so many other coaches he has a keen insight into their needs. Kids come back to see Marty long after they graduate.

℘ PRACTICAL CONSIDERATIONS

• Not every kid should be expected to throw a sharp-breaking curveball, become a guitar-strumming sensation, or emerge as a widely esteemed painter. Indeed some children may derive ample gratification through nonmotor activities. They may be entitled to relief from motor pressure. However, one or another motor success provides solid scaffolding for a kid's self-concept.

• Art teachers, music teachers, and coaches are among the most perceptive observers of neurodevelopmental function in any school setting. They are in a position to understand a kid's motor output as it connects to other brain functions. As a band leader at a high school reported about one of my patients, "She has this incredible musical memory; after hearing a piece just once she can play it on her flute with amazing accuracy. Her sense of rhythm is evident through her whole body while she plays. I think she has a natural talent for anything that comes in melodious sequences." A second grader's art teacher voiced, "He has this terrific vision. He seems to be able to visualize what he's drawing before he ever picks up his crayon. When he's finished he looks over his work and insists on improving it. His concentration is something to behold. He doesn't even hear you when he's at work on one of his little masterpieces. And it shows up in all the little details he inserts." When a student is experiencing academic stress and failure, art, music, mechanical pursuits, or sports may serve as venues in which he feels successful and can obtain longed-for positive recognition.

• Motor ineptitude causes many kids to feel worthless, and sometimes it brings with it social rejection and repeated public humiliation. Some children live in fear of being yelled at during a game. Some egos ache when classmates correct their papers and make highly audible comments about their messy handwriting. Conspicuously "babyish" motor output on paper, on the playground, in an art class, or in the gymnasium can make a young child feel terrible and want to withdraw. Our society has to be careful to protect these children. If a girl weighs 240 pounds and is clumsy, she should not be asked to climb ropes in a gym class while her fellow students are pointing, giggling, and jeering in amusement.

• Kids with gross motor dysfunctions, who have trouble catching or throwing a ball or running or balancing, should concentrate on just one sport and get as good as possible at that (unless of course they opt for total athletic avoidance—which is their right, I believe).

• As I have stated, computers offer students a convenient opportunity to savor motor effectiveness. Those with handwriting problems can produce attractive-looking text. Those whose artistic endeavors have met with defeat can become computer graphics Renoirs. If you know such a child, launch her with computer skill building in the earliest grades. Sometimes the students who need this the most are the most resistant to it. Cajole them, bribe them, and if need be lash them to the monitor; it's no longer a luxury—especially if you're on a collision course with the writing parts of schoolwork.

• Parents and teachers should be alert for fingers that seem unable to move on paper as quickly and readily as language and ideas require. As noted above, kids with such output problems had better start using word processing programs as soon as practical, but they also need consistent practice forming letters. Many require help developing a more workable way of holding a pen or pencil. Other methods for unleashing restrained writing are covered in my book *The Myth of Laziness*.

• Some kids benefit from the services of an occupational therapist or from participation in a remedial gym class to work on their motor skills. Such intervention should be made with sufficient sensitivity and privacy and without setting expectations too high.

• Coaches and parents sometimes need to be reminded that their players are actually children. Excessively high-octane coaches can inflict mental and emotional damage on students or else create pseudo-heroes of their best athletes, who eventually come crashing down off these pedestals. It's all just a game.

8

Some Peeks at a Mind's Peaks ᕫ

Our Higher Thinking System

Grown-ups never understand anything for themselves, and it is tiresome for children to be always and forever explaining things to them.

ANTOINE DE SAINT-EXUPÉRY, *The Little Prince*

THE following is from a letter I received from a teacher:

Re: Austin Brown

Dear Dr. Levine:

I write to give you some indication of Austin's progress as we approach the end of sixth grade. I am very pleased to report that he has made great progress in his reading comprehension and spelling. He is starting to write with more sophisticated language and ideas, although he still can't apply rules of punctuation. It's as if such rules don't make much sense to him.

Austin has met with some success in social studies. He likes to memorize dates and events and shows good recall of such things. He is also quick and accurate at locating answers in a text or reference book or on the Internet. He has some difficulty, however, when he has to be critical or form his own opinion of what he is reading about. Austin has a tendency to take too many things at face value.

In English Austin gets introduced to concepts but then can't seem to apply any of them while reading or in discussions. He recently participated in a class discussion on the concept of "heroism," and he could not describe what it was that made a character in a story we were reading a hero. He also experiences frustration in coming up with his own ideas and usually wants me to tell him what to include in his writing.

Math has been Austin's area of real blight. He has managed to memorize his facts extremely well and can carry out most procedures by rote. However, he can't grasp the concept of place value and is also confused about money. Often he can seem to grasp a concept or a rule, but then he fails to apply it during problem solving. He doesn't generalize or somehow use what he has learned. Also, he gives up far too easily in the middle of a math problem; the slightest impasse causes him to shut down completely.

Overall, I can say that he has made great gains in his basic skills but somehow hasn't come close to reaching into that higher plane of thinking that starts to become so crucial at this grade level.

Thanks for your continuing interest and help.

> Sincerely,
> Lonnie Gordon
> Sixth-Grade Teacher

Your child's higher thinking system activates whenever he or she meets up with information or challenges whose meanings or solutions are not immediately obvious. If his bicycle is making a mysterious screeching sound, if he's trying to understand what is meant by the term "parity," if he has to write a civics report and can't conjure up a decent topic, it's time for his mind to shift into higher thinking.

Five forms of higher thinking are especially germane when it comes to school performance. In different children, each of these forms of higher thinking may constitute an area of dysfunction or strength. They follow, with an example of each: 1) thinking with concepts (important when comparing socialism with capitalism); 2) problem solving thinking (applied when figuring out how best to settle a dispute with your older sister); 3) thinking critically (mobilized when deciding whether you support drilling oil wells in Alaskan wildlife reserves); 4) thinking with rules (brought to bear when changing a verb to the past tense); and 5) thinking creatively (in operation while composing a poem about a beaver with a fever). For some kids, the use of these, the most sophisticated and complex brain functions, makes learning a far more stimulating experience; for others their efforts yield few dividends.

Children deficient in one or more of these five key higher order thinking functions may be forced to overrely on rote memory and the mimicking of procedures instead of engaging in in-depth learning. As one adolescent with problems forming concepts confessed to me, "When I sit there in chemistry, I keep wondering what the hell I'm doing here. I mean I can learn the stuff, I guess, but I don't really know what's going on."

How well our five forms of higher thinking operate depends a lot upon what an individual is thinking about and who that individual doing the thinking happens to be. Your son or daughter may have awesome problem-solving thinking when fixing a car but not when settling a dispute with a classmate. Your kid may be highly creative in music but not in writing. A student may be intuitive about human relationships but not at all intuitive when it comes to working with computers. Such inconsistency in thinking has powerful implications for parents, who should be watching both for areas in which a child reveals higher thinking as well as for important parts of life (in school or out) in which your child's higher thinking just isn't high enough. Parents should realize that higher thinking abilities often are highly specialized. Here are a few examples of the uneven, eccentric nature of

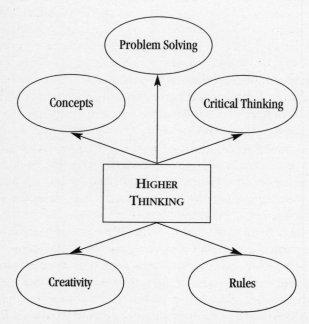

Figure 8-1.   Higher thinking.

higher thinking. In reading these little vignettes, think about how you might describe your own children in terms of higher order thinking preferences.

Rebecca is an inventor. Her parents are justifiably thrilled by her accomplishments when it comes to hands-on projects that she initiates. She recently designed and assembled a doll endowed with interchangeable, contrasting-colored see-through eyes. Each hue reflects a different mood. There are contented eyes, forlorn eyes, funny eyes, and hopeful eyes. Rebecca is currently working on a new version with different kinds of ears, ears that can hear different kinds of messages. It all borders on the bizarre, but Rebecca loves coming up with her own original contrivances. She seems happiest when she is doing her own thing in her own way. Rebecca has no real close friends, and her grades are below average. Her English teacher has been especially disappointed with Rebecca's attempts at creative writing. Her teachers are unanimous, however, that when it comes to her personal brand of creativity, expressed through handicrafts, Rebecca's a winner.

Marvin, at age eleven, is a precocious theoretical thinker and futurist. He is a concept addict. He can talk authoritatively about energy conservation, freedom of speech, and human rights, offering acutely perceptive, probing commentaries and predictions. He may lack or misrepresent critical supporting details, but his overviews of issues convey an aura of expertise and profundity. This boy has always preferred ideas to hard facts. Also, Marvin will gladly tell you how much he loathes math and science. He is good at conceptual thinking when the content is highly verbal. When he has to conceptualize without words, his screen goes blank and he's bored. He still doesn't understand what a fraction is or what it does; he can't picture this entity in his mind. He is a born highly specialized verbal conceptualizer.

Faith is a child everybody likes and respects. She is conscientious, thorough in whatever she undertakes, and is she ever organized. She is a first-rate conceptualizer and problem solver. But her parents note that Faith seems to take everything at face value. She has a positive view of the universe but one that is totally naive. At age twelve she accepts in toto every inflated claim on television commercials and is unable to grasp the notion that people can have ulterior motives, that they don't always mean what they say. She seems unable to do critical thinking.

Serena, a solid writer and reader, is doing adequate work in most of her academic subjects. She has gotten honor grades in social studies, where she savors the concepts and enjoys wrestling with (i.e., problem solving) various historical dilemmas that have plagued world leaders. She receives average grades in mathematics. But Serena has sustained mortal ego wounds in trying to pass French II in tenth grade. She also seemed to suffocate intellectually during a long unit on grammatical construction in her English class. Serena experiences frustration when it comes to the understanding, retention, and application of rules—spelling rules, grammatical rules, science rules, and mathematical rules. Rule-based thinking completely escapes her. Interestingly, however, she has never had trouble understanding and following rules in sports.

All four of these students are deficient when it comes to one or another specific aspect of higher thinking. In fact, all of us and every single one of our children have been dealt hands of unevenly distributed strengths and weaknesses in higher thinking. This is a major way in which children (and their parents and teachers) have their own kinds of minds.

As a clinician who specializes in children with learning difficulties, I run into endless variations on the themes of higher thinking. Often higher thinking issues arise in a high school student who is referred to me with trouble in one specific subject area, such as history or chemistry. She may be having problems forming the kinds of concepts or undertaking specific kinds of critical-thinking or problem-solving challenges in a subject. Sometimes an educator or a parent refers a child who is overly concrete, unable to deal with abstract concepts. Sometimes it's a student whose teachers say he seems able to learn concepts and ideas but then has trouble knowing how and when to apply them. These are common clinical mysteries in my experience, and often the answer lies in some subtle and often hidden gaps in one or another facet of higher thinking. Such dysfunctions may not be evident in traditional psychological testing but will be fairly transparent when I talk to the student, hear from his teacher, and inspect samples of his schoolwork. If a parent, teacher, or clinician is to uncover a higher cognitive weakness, that adult must be knowledgeable about the possible breakdown in this kind of thinking.

In so many ways fertile higher thinking is the ultimate educational harvest. For that reason, parents and schools should aim at our five forms of higher thinking and do all they can to cultivate them from an early age and throughout a child's education. Schools should carefully inspect how they teach to determine whether they are fostering the growth of these lofty neurodevelopmental functions.

§⌐ CONCEPTUAL THINKING

Concepts abound. In math there are concepts like place value, proportion, and equation. In literature kids encounter concepts like irony and tragicomedy. In science they come across osmosis and survival of the fittest. In their study of religion, they face concepts like fundamentalism and spirituality. Students constantly absorb from their teachers the monotonous refrain,

"This is an important concept. This is key. You guys really have to grasp this concept because so much that we are going to learn is based on it."

A concept is a collection of features that often go together to create an idea or category of ideas. Additionally, each concept has a name, such as the concept of furniture, the concept of capitalism, or the concept of endangered species. Concepts keep getting built upon, so if you don't grasp them too well initially, they have a way of haunting you. In the case of endangered species, the critical features might include that it is likely to be a living thing, a plant or animal, that it is diminishing in its numbers, that it is in danger of becoming extinct, and that it represents a distinct, highly specific group of living things. Presumably you have a good understanding of the concept of endangered species if you can delineate the critical features of which it is composed. It is also important to be able to offer examples or so-called conceptual prototypes. Additionally, it is helpful to think about related concepts and opposite concepts. The concept of extinction is related to endangered species, while the notion that a living thing is abundant is conceptually opposite. Identifying critical features and providing examples would help delineate any concept in science, in social studies, in mathematics, or in English class. Concepts also abound outside school. Sales tax, sales pitch, and sale item are relevant shopping concepts.

Concepts make reasoning far less strenuous. They allow your child to compare big ideas, such as the difference between liberalism and conservatism. If a student understands what democracy is and she's told that Belgium is a democratic country, she has a way to compare it to other nations, such as Iraq, China, and Libya. Among their other intellectually philanthropic activities, concepts spare memory. Conceptualizing reduces memorizing by allowing you to infer things. If you know the concept of despotism and someone tells you that a certain nation has a despotic government, you don't have to remember whether or not they hold presidential elections there. On the other hand, if it's a democracy, you can assume they do.

Concepts come packaged in varied formats. For example, there are abstract concepts and there are concrete concepts. A concrete concept is one that has direct appeal to one or more of the five senses; it is a concept you can touch or feel or smell or hear. Examples would be furniture, dessert, and globalization. Such tangible concepts contrast with the far more abstract ones, terms such as naive, agnosticism, factoring, and impressionism. As students move up in their educational careers, abstract concepts assume greater and greater importance in the curriculum. Some struggling students in high school lag behind because they remain at a very concrete level of conceptualization.

Process concepts form a third packaging type. Not surprisingly, process concepts deal with processes, such as kinetic energy, internal combustion, photosynthesis, and sautéing. In each case, the critical features of the concept are the steps that take place as the process occurs.

Some concepts are predominantly verbal, others nonverbal. You may recall that Marvin could only form concepts through language. Verbal concepts are readily taught and learned in words and sentences. The concept of a conservative politician can be thought about and communicated linguistically. Nonverbal concepts are those in which a degree of visualization is necessary to solidify understanding. The concepts of proportion, planetary orbit, and molecules in many respects are better visualized than verbalized. Some children are highly effective when it comes to the mastery of verbal concepts, while others orient toward nonverbal conceptualization. This orientation may be a major factor in the extent to which kids savor language arts classes rather than science and mathematics. In math and science there is much greater opportunity to conceptualize without words. Of course, it is most desirable to be able to move back and forth from verbal to nonverbal conceptualization and sometimes to form a concept both ways—by verbalizing it and also creating a mental image.

Different kids vary in the extent to which they master concepts. Some have virtually no grasp of important concepts, and are not able to identify any of a concept's critical features. Others have chronically tenuous conceptual grasps, in which case they may be able to name only one or two critical features of a concept while missing the rest. Some children merely repeat the meaning of a concept the way the teacher said it, while others imitate the use of concepts without really understanding them. The latter is a common pitfall in mathematics. There are students who can compute percentages without knowing what they are or how percentage relates to the concept of a decimal. Ultimately, a tenuous grasp of concepts catches up with a student and makes her feel overwhelmed as the subject matter becomes more complex and incorporates new concepts that are based in part on previous concepts. It's hard to master fractions if you never really grasped the concept of a denominator and, instead, thought of a denominator as nothing more than the number on the bottom.

A patient of mine named Garth was a tenuous (at best) grasper of many key concepts in school. Garth, a boy from New York City, was a generally upbeat kid who loved life as much he detested school. This boy was a stellar performer when it came to locking down basic academic skills. During elementary school he was dependable, securely perched in the highest reading group, by far the most valuable participant during a spelling bee, and he could hold his own readily in mathematics. Garth also was a phenomenal soccer player, his legs and his feet in clear communication with the motor command centers of his brain. Garth was also a very nice guy—described by his parents as well mannered, cheerful, affectionate, and helpful.

Garth first came to see me in tenth grade because he was failing history and English, while barely surviving in biology. His educational course had been steadily downhill since seventh grade, and he had lost all interest in the academic side of school (while still clinging to his infatuation with physical education and lunch hour). He complained to me that school was boring, all memory work, and that it didn't seem to relate to anything that mattered to him. He was clearly sad; this boy who always wanted so much to please his parents felt terrible and yet helpless, letting them down with his current school performance. When I talked to Garth about his school difficulties, he kept providing me with glaring instances of tenuous concept formation. At one point he commented, "Take my history class; it just makes no sense at all." I asked what it was that made no sense. "All those '-isms,' they have no meaning to me. The teacher, he was talking about how liberalism was developing in this country over the years. I couldn't figure out what liberalism was, and this guy was telling us how it was changing."

Garth had been put in this advanced placement history class because he scored so well on a reading achievement test. I asked him if he knew what a concept was and how you can form them in your mind. He had no idea what I was talking about. Garth was doing best in mathematics; the concepts in that subject were somehow accessible to him. But he was drowning in the highly verbal and abstract concepts in his other classes. He was exactly the opposite of my patient Marvin, the verbal conceptualizer. They'd make terrific lab partners! I took the time to demystify Garth about concepts and concept formation. We talked about his inability to grasp concepts and how that was causing him to be too much of a memorizer rather than a comprehender. We also agreed that weak concept formation was making his schoolwork abysmally uninteresting. Garth rose to the challenge and started to keep a record of key concepts and their meaning, which helped him understand these concepts better when they reappeared in his course work.

Garth was helped dramatically using a technique called conceptual mapping, which I have applied widely. In fact, it would be desirable in any class for kids to keep an atlas of concept maps, diagrams of the most important concepts underlying a particular subject area or course in school. One example of a concept map is seen in Figure 8-2. I showed this to Garth, and he seemed to understand it, even to conceptualize the map totally. I knew then that we were on our way to conquering his weakness.

As a parent you can serve as a sensitive barometer in gauging how well your child is mastering the critical mission of thinking conceptually. If your son or daughter begins feeling disoriented or disillusioned with a body of subject matter, ask yourself, "Is my kid grasping the concepts? Or is he using memory at the expense of true understanding?" The easiest way to find out is to look over a recently covered chapter or unit in your child's textbook or notebook, pick out a few key concepts, and have him tell you about them either orally or by drawing pictures or diagrams. It will be readily apparent if he has no sense of the features of the concepts. Parents can help children by discussing the concepts with them, assisting them to find good examples of these concepts and also of concepts that are opposite those under consideration. Parents can assist a child in mapping important concepts and maintaining that atlas of key concepts throughout the school year. Both parents and teachers need to ascertain that a child knows what a concept is. After all, how can you think conceptually if you've never thought conceptually about a concept?

&✎ PROBLEM-SOLVING THINKING

A war has broken out in a remote, underdeveloped country in southwest Africa. Widespread famine prevails and suffering abounds in the face of government corruption and avarice. Brutal killings are said to be common. Our secretary of state is trying to decide what should be done there and the extent to which our country ought to intervene. It would be our hope that this decision would be made with care, consciously taking into considera-

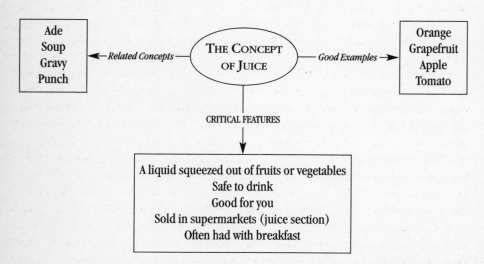

Figure 8-2.   Concept mapping.

tion a wide range of issues and possible actions. We are demanding high-level problem-solving capabilities.

Over the years, I have known lots of students who seem to lack systematic ways of solving problems. Often they are referred to our center because they are said to be impulsive, only capable of doing the first thing that comes to mind rather than thinking in a logical, sequential fashion when confronting a challenge. I have come to realize that this is a specific kind of deficit that plagues some children and most often goes undetected and untreated. Unfortunately, many of these kids get thrown by clinicians into the vast ADD heap and never receive the highly specific assistance they desperately need to emerge as problem solvers in a world that has no shortage of problems for individuals to solve. Affected children can't even problem-solve well when they are concentrating, although many of them become impulsive and look as if they have attention deficits because they can't seem to access this higher thinking process.

Problem solving is not an ability you can measure with confidence on an IQ or end-of-grade achievement test, yet it may be so much more relevant in life than a standardized score in spelling accuracy or an intelligence test component that requires a child to repeat numbers in the correct order. Effective problem solving is a systematic, logical, well-paced, and planned step-by-step process. It is the direct opposite of doing the first thing that comes to mind. Instead it represents excellent judgment, well-founded decision making, and the use of logical thought processes. In school and in everyday life we can be sharing and modeling meticulous problem solving in nurturing the developing minds of kids. I think parents and schools should be preparing students for those many critical moments in life when they will need to shift into a sophisticated and systematic problem-solving mode.

Jenny was one of the juvenile world's foremost non–problem solvers. Among the concerns her parents voiced when she was referred to me by her third-grade teacher in St. Louis was the fact that whenever she faced an obstacle in school or even in her home life, she just gave up. Her teacher commented, "At least six or eight times a day, I hear Jenny say, 'I can't do this.' But I know she can if she would only slow down and think it through. She can't seem to shift into that gear on her own." Meanwhile, Jenny offered the world an abundance of positive attributes. This eight-year-old lover of the printed word exhibited penetrating concentration while reading and listening. She displayed the language facility of a preacher. An impish and coy child who sat on her heels every time I met with her, this charmer bubbled over with surplus social energy and was said to be a gale-force runner and a swift swimmer.

But Jenny presented her parents and teacher with some paradoxical academic quirks. Her work in math could only be described as shoddy. She seemed to grasp the concepts and she could recall the needed facts and procedures, yet she rushed through calculations and simple word problems without stopping to ponder what was being asked and what methods were available to get to the correct answer. She left a trail of senseless, careless errors. Often the instant she would meet up with a problem, Jenny would leap to conclusions regarding its solution; for the most part, she was far off base. Here's one example from a math worksheet I have in her folder: "Susan and Jack went picking peaches. They filled their basket with 18 of them. They then divided them evenly. How many did each child receive?" Jenny quickly and proudly offered 36. On other occasions, as her teacher, Mrs. Bates, noted, Jenny would just decline the challenge and plead incompetence.

Mrs. Bates told me that Jenny had no ability to handle stress. The least social or domestic setback would ignite a fiery temper tantrum. Whenever Jenny went shopping with her mother, she would want the first thing she saw and then she was inflexible, unwilling or perhaps unable to shift her mind-set—no matter how preposterous the selection. Jenny's mother captured it succinctly when she pointed out, "Jenny hates to have to stop and think about anything." In watching Jenny tackle some word problems and other academic hurdles, I've came to the conclusion that Jenny doesn't seem to know how to stop and think or what to do when we tell her to stop and think. In other words, she lacked problem solving, the stopping-and-thinking ability, the consideration of options that leads to sound decision making.

To understand how problem-solving thinking operates when it's operating the way it should, we need to examine ten steps that readily fall into place for many children.

Step One—Knowing a Problem's a Problem When You Meet One.   If your child is a good problem solver, he has a broad sense of the word "problem," one that incorporates any reasonably important decision-making activity or output demand. Resolving a conflict with your friend, deciding on a topic for your science essay, preparing for a driving test, figuring out what to include in your book report on *Little Women,* repairing your bicycle, and combating a software glitch are all instances where an internal voice is supposed to pop up and say, "This is a problem. I need to slow down and think it through." That voice seems to be mute in Jenny's case. As a parent it can be instructive for you to note whether your child merely glosses over problems or is capable of thoughtful hesitation.

Step Two—Previewing the Outcome. To solve a problem, it helps to look ahead and preview or estimate the outcome of the problem-solving act. I mentioned this in the chapter on attention control, where previewing was noted to be one essential component of production or output. Previewing is also important to problem solving. In mathematics problem solving previewing provides an estimate of the answer. In everyday life, it might conjure up a lucid vision of a desired result. In negotiating a treaty between two battling nations, a mediator might preview the outcome that when the problems are solved, the countries will live in peace, respect each other's borders, engage in commerce, and exchange cultural resources. It's hard to solve a problem without a fairly clear sense of what the solution will look like.

Step Three—Assessing the Feasibility. You may find your child seems to come apart at the seams when trying to estimate how difficult a task is going to be. Daily challenges either look like too much of a cinch or else they seem forever out of reach. In accessing feasibility, a proficient problem solver undergoes a bit of a reality check: "Can I solve this problem? Do I need outside help to do so? If so, from whom or from where? How long will it take? How difficult will this be?" Teachers take note: this can be gist for a worthwhile class discussion before students tackle long-term projects, say in social studies or science. Feasibility also entails looking at the costs and the benefits of solving the problem. Is it worth the effort? What will happen if I try to solve it? Why not just forget it? Should I go to the trouble of writing this book report? What will happen if I don't write it? What if I write it and get a bad grade? Is that better than not writing it at all? Such cost-benefit analyses are an integral part of problem solving (although they can also justify some outlandish rationalizations for inaction or apathy).

Step Four—Mobilizing Resources. How resourceful is your child? Does he know what he needs to get a job done? In helping your child complete a complicated assignment or in collaborating on a home-based venture (such as planning a trip), parents can work through and talk through what will be required in order to accomplish specific aims. Making lists can help. Additionally, this step involves pulling together whatever it takes to get at the problem and its answer. That could entail the child soliciting help from Mom, use of the Internet, a review of class notes, and a search of her own personal experience. The latter involves recognition memory (see Chapter 4), namely, "Have I seen this kind of problem in the past, and, if so, what have I done before that's worked well?"

Step Five—Thinking Logically.   As a parent or teacher, you would like to think that a child is reasonably rational, at least much of the time. That is, she or he makes use of logical thinking during problem solving. So it is unreasonable to separate reasoning from problem solving; they pursue the same missions. Good reasoning or logical thinking permits a problem solver to think in neat propositions, such as, "If I do this, then . . ." or "If it is true that, then it must be the case that I can . . ." Logical thinking also includes using analogies to solve problems. "Mango juice is a liquid like water, and if you put water in the freezer it turns to ice, so I can make mango Popsicles by freezing mango juice." Both teachers and parents should question and prompt a child's use of logic. Such cognitive coercion can make for rich dinner table and car talk, namely: "How did you come to that conclusion? Can you think of any good analogies that would help explain what you did or how you solved that problem?"

Step Six—Considering Different Strategies and Picking the Best One. Your kids need to learn to think strategically. This is the stage of problem solving during which an individual reviews possible methods that could facilitate the process. Good problem solvers think in options; they consider more than one approach. This should remind you of our discussion of having alternatives when I described the production controls of attention (see Chapter 3). Example: "Let's see, I could learn these words by making flash cards. Or I could try using each one in a sentence, or I can practice them with Emily, or I might make a semantic map of each one. Let's see, I think I'll use flash cards this time; that worked real well on the last quiz." The review of alternative strategies was never a part of Jenny's academic repertoire. This also related to her inability to deal with stress. She couldn't cope because she couldn't think through her alternatives—having choices provides some insulation against adversity. She should be helped to say to herself, "Why don't I try doing this, and if that doesn't work I can always try that other approach or the one I just thought of." Having such alternatives eases stress considerably. I think whenever a child makes an incorrect decision, parents and teachers should seize the opportunity to discuss what other alternatives might have worked better and might be feasible for future use. Children need to learn from their mistakes.

Step Seven—Starting and Pacing.   This is where time management merges with problem solving. A proficient problem solver has a sense of time and timing, sensing when and how to get going, knowing when the process is speeding up excessively or when it is getting bogged down and needs to be moved along. Children like Jenny race through challenges, revealing poor pacing. Her parents, by the way, are now stating when necessary, "Jenny, let's slow down our thinking and figure all this out logically— step by step." These little reminders, served up with good humor and devoid of any accusatory or moral overtones, have been of some benefit to Jenny. Now she even tells her parents to cool it and think more slowly before they make decisions affecting her and her sister.

Step Eight—Self-Monitoring.   As your child's problem-solving gears grind away he's supposed to keep an eye on what they're doing. "Am I getting anywhere with this? Am I on the right track? How is it coming along?" Such quality control inspections help with pacing and with the ongoing surveillance of the chosen strategies. Self-monitoring also comes up as a final check on a problem's solution. "Is this the right or best answer? Does my answer make sense? Have I done a good enough job with this?" Self-monitoring allows for self-regulation or what is sometimes called self-righting. I have dealt with an awful lot of students who barely seem aware of how they're doing or how they've done. Their dismal report cards come as a total surprise to them. Also, they are apt to turn in shoddy work without checking it over and making even the most basic non-time-consuming corrections. Kids have to be encouraged to lean back amid problem-solving tasks and say to themselves, "Okay, now it's time for some of that quality control stuff." A student always has the option of reversing gears and going back over and tweaking or making adjustments to a solution or end product. First-rate problem solvers exercise this option. Parents and teachers can prompt self-monitoring by asking, "How do you think you could make this better?"

Step Nine—Dealing with Impasses.   This step entails knowing how to respond when problem solving encounters an obstacle (as it often does). Or, it may happen that the selected strategy has stopped working. That impasse may require the resilient problem solver to go back and make use of an alternative or backup strategy. Is your child that flexible? Or does he give up or retreat when he meets with frustration? I think parents and teachers need to serve as impasse consultants. "Let me know if you have a problem with this. That's what I'm here for. Call me if you get stuck. I'll never criticize you for asking for help." We want to be sure we don't create kids who are quitters when the going gets tough.

Step Ten—Arriving at the Solution.   The problem has been solved, although in the case of some problems it can be hard to know when you've finished, when you have the right or final answer. Hopefully, a student can do better than a well-known abstract painter, who when asked how he knows when he's finished with a work responded, "I can tell I'm finished when I'm sick of it." I've met more than a few students who might echo those sentiments, as a result of which they tend to finish when they're not really finished.

Once a problem has been solved, your triumphant child should think back over the process, largely to determine explicitly what he has learned and how it might be applied in the future. This kind of reflection is often omitted and should certainly be integrated with all teaching and learning. Teachers, in particular, should get into the habit of asking kids after a test or at the conclusion of a class discussion: "Let's think of the different times and places where this kind of problem solving can be used again to create something or to help you out of a brain jam of some sort."

When a parent sees a child frequently stymied by certain kinds of academic problems, a problem-solving opportunity may exist. The steps described above can be easily translated into some questions worth thinking about: When Abe tackles these word problems in math, does he pace himself or rush through them? Does he seem to have strategies or does he do the first thing that comes to mind? Does he preview or does he have no way of estimating the answer? When all arrows point to weak problem-solving thinking (either generally or just in math), someone needs to model the problem-solving steps for the child. One math teacher I had lunch with at a workshop I gave told me, "My biggest challenge is getting my students to slow down and really think about what they're doing rather than just getting it over with. To encourage good problem solving, these days I'm asking my students to do fewer homework problems but then be prepared to come in and describe or demonstrate the problem-solving steps that they used. I'm trying to stress that the process they use is more important than getting the right answer." I agree. Let's keep asking, "How'd you do that?"

Often kids can benefit from using a list of problem-solving steps or a self-assessment that they fill out after solving a problem (with questions such as "Did I rush through this?" "Did I use any strategies?" "Did I estimate or preview my answer or product?"). All children would benefit from help in becoming more conscious and systematic in their problem-solving activities. One teacher who did so reported: "My students now talk about problem solving as if it were some kind of sport. Also they've come to realize that problem solving enters into so much of what they do in their lives, including writing a book report, deciding what to do with their birthday money, and figuring out whom to pick as a friend. We talk about these processes a lot in my sixth grade class. The kids really get into it."

At home and in school, children need plenty of practice solving different moral problems, trying to resolve political issues, and tackling personal problems by going through the steps I have outlined. Typical topics might include: "Do you think violent children should be tried as adults for serious crimes? If so, at what age would you start and why?" "What can be done to solve an energy shortage?" "How can we put an end to bullying in schools?" This kind of activity should be accomplished in writing or with a computer template. Also, step-by-step problem solving is facilitated when kids talk (or whisper) their way through the steps. Self-coaching helps organize and strengthen the sequential progress of problem solving. Eventually, the process can become more or less automatic or unconscious.

ᔔ CRITICAL THINKING

A probation officer in New York City was talking to me about a boy I had met a few months earlier in a middle school. With obvious compassion the officer explained, "I think Anthony is basically a good kid, well intentioned, well meaning. To me his real problem is that he takes everything literally. He doesn't know what's real and what's fake—so he gets sucked in all the time. Someone comes to him with some kind of crazy proposition, and he believes every word the guy says. That's why he's in detention now. That's why he ran drugs. The kid just can't seem to look beneath the surface and see the reality of things. He'd believe anyone." All kids, like Anthony, need to become astute evaluators, learning how to judge products, statements made by others, and even pausing to evaluate themselves from time to time.

Your children probably were not born with razor-sharp critical thinking. Growing up they require plenty of experience and direct exposure to this higher thinking process. They should hear their parents and teachers assessing the validity and quality of ideas, people, and things.

Critical thinking functions represent a triumph over naïveté as they equip kids to resist deception and to become more perceptive evaluators. Noncritical thinkers accept far too much at face value. They may be more concrete and have trouble looking beneath the surface, analyzing and evaluating that which is more than what meets the eye. Others, of course, go too far and become out-and-out cynics. They detect fault wherever they look and are willing to accept nothing without questioning. Quite obviously there are certain ages in which this kind of evaluative cynicism (often caustically conveyed through sarcasm) becomes a way of life (eighth grade more or less being the watershed), a seeming-to-know-it-all attitude, in which kids are reluctant to accept what they encounter—especially when conveyed by parents!

As with problem solving, parents and teachers can walk kids through a step-by-step approach to critical thinking:

Step 1—Enumerating the Facts.   You might say to a child, "Let's start out and describe the video you watched; later on we'll decide if it was any good." In other words, whatever it is your child is to evaluate should first be described objectively; just report the facts. For example, in writing a book report your daughter first recounts details of the plot if it's a novel or summarizes the content of a nonfiction work. After all, she can't evaluate something if she hasn't focused on its important details.

Step 2—Uncovering the Author's or Creator's Point of View.   A student should practice some serious detective work at this step. You can prompt your child to expose and describe any point of view, intention, or motive she can uncover in the work. For example, "This ad is trying to sell Toyotas" or "I think the person who wrote this article wants us to vote for a Democratic candidate."

Step 3—Establishing What the Child Thinks.   The child asks herself, "How do I feel about that? What's my opinion or point of view?" As a parent or teacher, you can ask, "How do you think your feelings about this are going to affect your critical thinking in this case?" So a child, with you as a guide, identifies her own point of view or personal biases. I remember a mother once proclaiming that her son "always has his mind made up before he ever sees or does anything." She added, "When he was very young he told us he hated vegetables. I tried to help him see that not all vegetables are created equal, that you need to give each one a chance. But he had such a powerful anti-vegetable bias that he couldn't check out the goodness of any bean or pod. To this day, he's like that about a lot of things in his life. I guess that about calls a halt to any fair critical thinking on his part. And, wouldn't you know it, my husband's the same way."

Step 4—Searching for Errors and Exaggerations.   Look for and describe any errors, distortions, false claims, or exaggerations in what is being evaluated. If you are evaluating a person, is that individual honest, the genuine item, or a phony in some respects? Included in this step is what is called appearance versus reality, namely, what's on the surface and what's authentic? You can practice this step with a child by jointly critiquing ads in a magazine or on TV. On the surface the soup they're advertising appears delicious and nutritious; in reality, we once tried it, and it was gross—

watery and loaded with preservatives and artificial food coloring, and it tasted like diluted cough syrup.

Step 5—Getting Outside Help. Parents and teachers need to alert kids to the fact that you don't have to go it alone. There are lots of resources around to help you with your critical thinking. This step might include gathering other people's opinions, checking out *Consumer Reports,* or downloading relevant information from an expert Web site. There are many ways of combining research with critical thinking. A student might read a book or see a movie and then read one or more reviews of the work. In his critical appraisal, he might quote from a reviewer. He can even do some critical thinking about that critical thinker.

Step 6—Weighing the Evidence. During this step your son or daughter or student pulls together all of the above steps to produce his own well-informed opinion. This entails separating and considering the objective findings, your own biases, the intent, motives, or point of view of the subject, and the information you have gathered from various sources. And then through some mysterious, possibly quite subjective formula, a child develops a critical view that he can defend.

Step 7—Communicating. The task is not over yet; once an evaluation is complete, a child needs to exercise his communication skills to share his critical thinking with the outside world. This needs to be accomplished in a reasonably cohesive and convincing manner. It would be a shame if excellent points were obscured by deficient or unclear communication. Effective expressive language therefore dramatically enhances the end products of critical thinking. Kids with language difficulties are at a disadvantage when it comes to critical thinking. In fact, it has been shown that many of them are handicapped by a chronic inability to formulate opinions using words. And when you can't shape an opinion, you are left with biases, prejudices, and gut reactions, any or all of which can get you into trouble—which happens all the time. As one teacher pointed out, "The toughest question I can ever ask Suzanne is, 'Well, what's your opinion? What do you think about this?' That girl has so much trouble telling you what she thinks that she's stopped thinking! Instead, she just memorizes what's in an editorial and tries to reproduce it nearly verbatim on a test or homework assignment."

The above steps can be used to help your child evaluate products, decide whether a television commercial for breakfast cereal is providing accurate information, or expose the manner in which that commercial is biased and making false or exaggerated claims. The critical thinking sequence also can be used to evaluate ideas. Kids can practice this by reading editorials, identifying the writer's point of view, comparing it to their own, and bringing to bear outside objective information. They can also practice evaluating people. They can pick a particular trait or value, such as altruism, and analyze individuals in terms of the extent to which they exhibit this positive attribute. Finally, students should learn to be self-critical, to step outside themselves long enough to evaluate their own output, character, values, or social patterns using a similar systematic, step-by-step approach.

You don't want your child to be victimized or taken in by any person, product, or set of ideas. The procedures and habits for critical thinking can keep a kid out of trouble and intellectually sharp. Critical thinking is also a lot of fun. Kids display wide variation in their critical thinking across areas of content. Some may be astute sports analysts (junior Monday morning quarterbacks), while others are precocious literary critics and still others are master appraisers of character within the local social panorama. As with other areas of higher thinking, we should teach explicit critical thinking skills starting out in the realms toward which a child has a natural interest and then transferring these thinking skills into other areas. I saw this accomplished masterfully by a fourth-grade teacher in Texas who devoted some time to teaching kids the meaning of critical thinking. Then each student was told to pick a subject or activity that he or she really enjoyed and write something critical about it (using a watered-down version of the format I outlined above). While I was visiting the classroom one child critically evaluated his latest computer game (giving it mixed reviews), another assessed the Texas Rangers (giving them mostly positive reviews), and a ten-year-old aspiring gourmet put forth an informed opinion regarding the cuisine in her school's lunchroom (highly negative). The kids were having a terrific time while exercising and incorporating a vital higher order thinking capacity.

A boy named Jefferson, from rural Alabama, is my favorite example of uneven or perhaps highly specialized critical thinking. By the time he was fifteen, Jefferson was the consummate connoisseur of new and used pickup truck data. He had always loved such vehicles and had teamed up with his dad to restore several physically abused early models. Jefferson subscribed to truck magazines and knew the specifications for all current and recent models. But his most distinguishing persona was that of Jefferson, the self-appointed under-the-hood critic. You'd think General Motors or Ford had hired him as a troubleshooter. He loved explaining the pros and cons of various engine mounts or carburetors. When I requested some advice from him regarding a truck for use on my farm, he proceeded to describe my options, all punctuated with fascinating critical comments, such as "They've put a lot of torque in that engine, but she burns oil and guzzles gas like my brother drinks Mountain Dew. The 410 is a lot more efficient and uses less gas, but driving that truck is about as excitin' as watchin' grass grow."

It was plain that Jefferson had done his truck homework. But he was a boy with some learning problems. One of his teachers' complaints was that he was devoid of critical thinking, accepting everything he read at face value. When asked to critique a Civil War newspaper cartoon, Jefferson simply described it in some detail without any comment; his book reports were likewise boiled down summaries of plots. When prodded to provide his views on what he read, Jefferson would shrug his shoulders and admit, "I haven't given it much thought, I guess." He never did. Fortunately, Jefferson was helped a lot when his reading tutor reviewed one of his truck magazines with him and helped him understand the ways he was already using strong critical thinking when he read about pickups. Together they made a template of the process described earlier in this chapter. Jefferson was then helped to apply this template to criticizing a column written by a sportswriter (sports were another interest of his) and then finally to evaluating a political editorial (a domain of absolutely no attraction for him). Jefferson felt this was a "good and fun" approach, and his English teacher noted a significant improvement in his book reports.

ᗌ RULE-GUIDED THINKING

School is saturated with rules. There are rules wherever you look. They govern behavior or decorum in the corridors, the boys' room, and the lunchroom. Tightly regulated procedures cover obtaining permission to urinate as well as the proper certification when you need to depart early or arrive late due to a dental appointment. Violations such as gum chewing lead to punitive action. There is also a collection of formal academic rules, which include spelling rules, phonetic rules, scientific rules, and mathematical rules (sometimes called formulas).

Rules generally take the form of "if . . . then," such as: "If this is the beginning of a sentence, then there needs to be a capital letter" or "If you are adding fractions, do so with the numerator, not the denominator, if the denominators are the same" or "If you use the word 'although' in a sentence, then the two clauses have to contradict each other." The ubiquitous "if . . . thens" infiltrate all subject areas, and some kids are more able than others to cope with the rules they need to learn and can even think up some handy rules of their own.

Serena's a prime victim of what I call rule aversion (and evasion). An average student at an elite independent boarding school in Massachusetts, she could have been achieving more and feeling better about school were it not for the fact that she was faltering badly in all of the subjects that were based heavily on the understanding and use of rules. This girl, mentioned at the beginning of the chapter, was a stellar performer when she could sidestep rules and do her thinking in her own liberated, spontaneous style. That's because she had trouble comprehending and retaining rules, be they rules of grammar, rules of the French language, rules in mathematics, or rules in other domains. Also, she could use good grammar without grasping its rules (i.e., she knew what sounded right). Unfortunately, this approach fell short when it came to mastering the conjugation of French verbs.

Serena was compliant, however, with behavior expectations in school and at home. It was the more cognitively based rule regulation that confused her no end. English class was most revealing. Mrs. Madigan described Serena as her top creative writer and a very penetrating reader. Her interpretations of text material and fiction were like successful mining expeditions—she always hit literary pay dirt. She had the analytical skills of a budding book reviewer for *The New Yorker* magazine. On the other hand, when the class studied English grammar, she became hopelessly confused and anxious. Mathematics rules likewise stumped Serena; fortunately she benefited from helpful intuition in that subject as well as in grammar.

As a parent you may find that your child has his greatest difficulty in subjects that contain and depend the most on rules. Studying grammar, learning a foreign language, and succeeding in mathematics and physics may be thwarted as a result.

Children who are having trouble using rules to guide their thinking should maintain a rulebook in school. They should receive specific coaching in the interpretation and use of rules. They need to recite rules, translate them into their own words, and offer examples of the rules at work as well as examples of exceptions to the rules.

One reason for having your child understand and make liberal use of rules is that they enable kids to deal smoothly with situations that occur predictably on a regular basis (such as the need to punctuate a sentence). But, in addition to fostering a strong sense of regularity, rules also set the stage for recognizing irregularity, for noticing the exceptions to the rule. If you don't have a profound grasp of rules, you may be insensitive to the irregularities that erupt within any body of subject matter or skill. Thus, by understanding spelling rules, a student often can predict the spelling of a new word, and this can sensitize a kid to words that are illegal, i.e., irregular words that violate those venerable spelling rules. The English language has more than its share of these notorious violators!

✎ CREATIVE THINKING

Every child has within him a creative voice crying out for discovery. In some girls and boys the cry is quite loud; in others it's a soft murmur. Parents and teachers need to remain watchful for little creative sparks awaiting ignition. Creative opportunities liberate a child's mind to cross into personal zones of higher thinking. In being creative, kids unshackle their minds and discover novel possibilities for self-expression and mental free play. Sadly, kids differ in the opportunities they are given to become creative thinkers and doers, but when given the chance most kids can discover and enjoy a personal channel for original thinking.

Highly creative kids and adults share some basic neurodevelopmental qualities. In my own work with children who have learning problems, I have been struck repeatedly by how many struggling students display creative tendencies as they engage in imaginative ventures. Creative thinking boils down to an amalgam of behaviors and traits that promote originality. The pages that follow detail these behaviors, a number of which I gleaned from Dr. Howard Gardner's superb (and highly creative) book *Creating Minds*.

Divergent Thinking. A willingness and ability to free-associate, to emancipate your mind to go off on interesting and original tangents, often not knowing where exactly you're likely to end up. Divergent thinking is the opposite of convergent thinking. In the latter, thoughts are highly specific and directed at finding a narrowly defined fact or solution to a problem.

Top-Down Processing. A willingness to sprinkle liberally your own personal associations, values, and perspectives over much of what you come across. Top-down processing makes you highly subjective in reacting to information and experience. For example, some students are described as top-down readers. When they read a short story, they relate it to people, places, and experiences in their own personal lives. They often impose over their reading their own unique and characteristically personalized interpretations and ideas (even though this may not be what the author had in mind). They dislike having to stick to the facts as provided in an article or textbook. When given an assignment, a top-down student is likely to try to improve upon it, somehow modifying the expectations to allow her creative machinery to operate without restriction. Some teachers encourage this form of thinking; others punish or ban it.

Return to Naïveté. A willingness to return to a state of ignorance, to make few if any assumptions about anything, to be willing to take a fresh look or assume a totally new point of view. This requires that a creator wipe the slate clean and try not to be burdened with too many assumptions or too much knowledge. Some uncreative individuals are so devoted to what is already known that they come to feel there is little new that can be created.

Risk Taking.   A willingness to risk being wrong, to risk creating something others will denigrate, mock, or otherwise react to disapprovingly. Creative kids and adults have to resign themselves to being controversial; they may even come to enjoy that status. My own boss at Harvard Medical School once warned me at the start of my career: "Mel, if you're not controversial, it means you're not being very creative." I guess that means I'm creative.

The Integration of Technical Skill with Originality.   A willingness to combine some rigorous technical discipline with innovative thinking or output. A poet may infuse personal and original insights within the rigorous structure of a particular poetic meter. A future composer should try to take his piano lessons seriously.

Autonomy from Peer Pressures and Standards.   A willingness to think and produce in a manner that runs the risk of deviating from accepted norms among your own peer group. A highly creative person is likely to be unwilling to alter his work substantially just to please his audience or his colleagues. I have seen too many teenagers whose creativity is stifled because they are so anxious to please their friends. I remember one boy who at age eleven was writing original solo music for the viola. He had a passion for the instrument. Then in eighth grade hormonal geysers erupted, and other kids became all important in his life. On multiple occasions he was accused of being a "dork" for playing the viola. He stopped taking viola lessons and ceased to compose his own sonatas. He opted for being cool rather than creative. There's enormous pressure on kids to make this awful choice. His parents and I tried to explain that a person could be cool and popular *and* play the viola. I also informed him that when you grow up playing the viola is considered very cool, and going to the mall with your friends is pretty close to the bottom of the coolness scale. He couldn't seem to hear any of this because he was so hopelessly infatuated with his peers. His friends had siphoned all his creativity.

Suspension of Self-Evaluation.   A willingness to resist being too critical of yourself while you're trying to be creative. An artist can be paralyzed if he is constantly trying to decide if he's any good amid the process of creating.

Discovery and Pursuit of the Right Medium.   A willingness to search and come up with a channel for one's creative drives. That may be sculpture, dance, musical composition, comedy, or any number of other possible pathways. Parents and teachers have an obligation to chaperone kids on such creative opportunity-shopping expeditions through their school years. Many years ago, the headmaster of a New England vocational high school was showing me around his building. During the visit he stopped to talk with one of his faculty members, a man who ran auto body classes, and he asked how Francis was doing. The auto body teacher said, "Great, that kid's on a roll. I have no trouble with him, and he's really picked up in his academic subjects. He's like a new kid, completely refurbished." As we walked away I asked the headmaster who Francis was. He replied that Francis was a totally incorrigible sixteen-year-old who was a serious behavioral threat in the school and was doing no work whatsoever in any of his classes. He was failing in his chosen field of heating and air-conditioning, and the faculty pretty much agreed there was no point in keeping him on. Then the headmaster decided to give Francis one last chance for survival, pinning his hopes on the auto body teacher I'd just met. Over the years that teacher had turned around countless kids that others had called losers. Anyway, when Francis reported for auto body, Jack, the teacher, knowing the boy was pretty good at drawing, told him he wanted him to try to specialize in detail painting on vans and minivans. The teacher said that he didn't have anyone who could do this right now and he needed someone he could rely on for this kind of work. Those words made Francis feel important, and he agreed to give it a try.

Jack encouraged him, helped him draft practice designs on paper and then apply them to the vehicles. Within six weeks, Francis savored the sweet taste of success for the first time in his life. Other kids would gather around to watch him detail a van. He had found a niche, an authentic outlet for his creativity. His whole outlook on life and school changed overnight. Then the headmaster said, "To tell you the truth, I can't think of anything at all that makes being an educator more worthwhile than our experience with Francis." I agree. Jack represents educational heroisms in my view; he helped Francis discover a viable creative medium.

Stylistic Distinctiveness.   A willingness to be unusual, to develop a unique voice, niche, or personal style and then imbue this distinctiveness within your work. Your child can begin to do this during his school years. Great artists become distinctive rather than imitative. That's how we recognize that a painting is a Picasso, even though we've never before viewed that particular canvas. A person may be creative at making unusual satirical steel sculptures of animals or finding a niche as a composer of modern-day madrigals.

These traits I have described seldom represent conscious policy decisions on the part of creators. Rather they are most often unconscious behaviors even during childhood. There are kids who are spontaneously creative; they do all or most of the above without any adult coercion. At home and in school it's helpful to foster a climate and the right opportunities, so that creative tendencies are stimulated and cultivated over time.

No one has ever sought to refer a kid to me because of some kind of creativity deficit disorder. But I have been asked to see children and teenagers who get no pleasure from learning, who are somehow unable to take pride in anything they produce. Many have retreated into the passive chasms of television viewing, Web surfing, and just hanging out with friends. All too often I have found such students to be lacking any satisfying pathways to creative achievement of any sort. Close examination of the different manifestations of creativity may reveal why some students exhibit no creativity whatsoever. When a parent encounters a child who is missing out on the pleasures of being creative, she or he can ask diagnostic questions based upon the above list: Is she too fearful of taking risks? Has she been unable to find a medium? Is she overly convergent in her thinking? Do her peers suppress her? Has she not felt that it's okay to be top-down, to put one's own subjective slant on things? A sizable portion of the impetus for creative activity must come from a child's environment, from peer and adult role models, and from opportunities that are intentionally provided at home and in school.

Brainstorming is a subsidiary of creativity, an activity that entails starting with little or nothing and generating a product or innovative collection of insights, often making liberal use of creative thinking. Creativity and brainstorming are such compatible brain allies that I link them tightly in discussions. Some students will grab any chance they get to engage in freewheeling brainstorming, while others stubbornly resist the challenge. They'd much rather have their teacher give them a topic to write about and tell them how wide the margins need to be than come up with their own ideas and formats.

Alisha from Phoenix, Arizona, at age twelve, was a member of the brainstorming resistance. She was a very tall, dark-haired girl with tightly woven long braids and equally taut braces. She dressed impeccably like a modern-day Saturday night cowgirl. An A and B student, she was near the top of the curve on examinations in every one of her subjects. Alisha was a totally reliable worker, a capable basketball forward, an agile equestrian, and an esteemed citizen within the highly judgmental society of her peers. Adults admired her too. But some peculiar shortcomings were consistently observed. When her English teacher asked the class to write a story on a topic of their choice, Alisha requested that Miss Mattioli assign a topic to her; she dreaded the prospect of having to brainstorm and come up with a selection of her own. When she wrote reports for social studies, they were cut-and-dry semiplagiarized hybrids of downloads from the Internet. They reflected no creative input from Alisha herself. All of her writing was impeccable when it came to spelling, grammar, and punctuation but sterile with regard to personal thought. This girl could not have been more conscientious and less original in her academic work. I met Alisha in her school when I was invited there to conduct a seminar on the topic of higher thinking for the teachers and administrators. Several faculty members wanted me to interview Alisha and got permission from her parents for me to do so. I asked this girl if she knew what the word "brainstorming" meant. She did not. In fact she told me she liked school best when her teachers were very specific in describing what they expected from her. Unlike for Alisha, brainstorming is a natural inclination for many other kids. I've encountered quite a few students with serious learning problems who are at their best when brainstorming. They would much rather think up a topic than be given one. For others, like Alisha, the process has to be taught and practiced. They need practice coming up with topics, sitting down with a blank pad of paper and manufacturing high-quality personal thoughts and reactions to things.

Opportunities to be creative and to brainstorm can be the salvation of children who are having a hard time succeeding academically. Art classes, music classes, and creative writing opportunities should be considered core curriculum in a nation that values and harbors a tradition of innovation. Some kids were born to create better than they learn. For them, in particular, the discovery of the right medium, the acquisition of technical skill, and the finding of a nurturing environment within which to try some creative leaps all boost self-esteem and motivation. Parents and educators should band together to combat all the school routines, inflexible requirements, excessive stress on end-of-grade high-stakes tests, and other educational policies that discourage, dampen, or leave little or no time for the cultivation of creativity and brainstorming.

§⤜ THE ROLE OF INTUITIVE THINKING IN INFLUENCING ALL FORMS OF HIGHER THINKING

On one of my many airplane trips, I met a young instructor in mathematics at a leading California research university. We got to talking about undergraduate education, and he recounted his recent experiences in teaching calculus to freshmen (a reward often bestowed upon up-and-coming tenure track math faculty). He claimed he could always divide his students into two categories, those who required total formal instruction in the subject and those who on their own could figure out a sizable portion of the content because it made so much sense to them intuitively. I think we would elicit the very same reflection from faculty in all other subject areas. But the students who unveil the meaning of a poem intuitively may not be the same ones who can apply intuition in calculus. In other words, like other forms of higher thinking, intuition is stubbornly specific. Your child therefore may display powerful social, political, scientific, aesthetic, or athletic intuition. The person who tracks down the leak from the bottom of my Dodge Dakota four-wheel-drive pickup may not have to depend upon the repair manual to understand why it also keeps stalling in cold weather; he has an intuitive ability to pinpoint and treat vehicular flaws. This same person, on the other hand, may not be able to tell you what the subject of a simple declarative sentence is.

I have been struck by the large number of teenagers with learning problems who have extraordinary psychological intuition when it comes to helping their friends sort out personal problems. One teenager from Charlotte, North Carolina, confided, "I wish I understood books as well as I understand people." Positive interpersonal intuition doesn't quite bail you out, though, when you need to get to the root of a trigonometry problem. Intuition prefers to specialize.

Intuition is a dark mystery; no one knows how or why it works. It certainly entails a form of cognitive X-ray vision and an instinctive ability to penetrate to the inner core of some subject area, so that you can understand, even make predictions within and about it that would escape others. Intuition allows a subject to come naturally. It makes a learner less dependent on rules and on memorization in general (so-called formalism). Intuition may exert a direct impact on the five forms of higher thinking. Your child may be an intuitive problem solver in math, an intuitive conceptualizer in Sunday school, an intuitive rule applicator in Latin, an intuitive critical thinker in philosophy, or an intuitively creative designer when it comes to scenery for a class play. In getting to know their sons or daughters, parents need to find those special areas in which intuition works positively for a child. They well may represent potential areas of talent that need to be brought out and nurtured over the years. So I always like to ask, especially when a kid is struggling in school: Can you think of any areas in which his mind seems to get a real intuitive boost?

Intuition is magical. It is not possible to induce intuition. We're unlikely ever to offer a high school course called "Introduction to Intuition." It wouldn't surprise me, however, if we found out that every individual on earth has unique areas in which her or his intuition is fantastic. Also, it is possible that when we become experts in an area, strong intuition is a dividend we gain over time. Like most other pediatricians I believe we can walk into a room and tell nearly immediately if a baby is really sick or not—just by looking. Yet, we can't tell you how we know. We just know. That's acquired intuition. A computer support technician may exhibit remarkable diagnostic intuition when your PC is acting ornery. Our responsibility as kid-oriented adults is not to hope to train intuition formally but rather to watch it and help it emerge.

A word of caution: intuition when overused and unchecked has some potential to lead a child astray. There is such a thing as negative intuition, intuition that is misleading or downright wrong. Negative intuition can bring with it bias, prejudicial thinking, and misguided beliefs. Sometimes a child needs our help in making use of good critical thinking to evaluate her own negative intuitions. Of course, we always want to cultivate *positive* intuition, intuition that appears to work constructively for a student. Also, a kid should be discouraged from relying exclusively on intuition; it is a valuable but far from infallible asset. Intuitive thinking has to be supported and verified by fact.

❧ THE HIGHER THINKING SYSTEM AND THE OTHER NEURODEVELOPMENTAL SYSTEMS

Some of the most perplexed and frustrated parents I have encountered have been those who have kids with phenomenal higher thinking that seems disconnected from one or more other necessary brain functions. In these instances, a child's tantalizing ideas and insights may not translate into any accomplishments. For instance, a student may be highly creative in composing music but lack the attention controls to stay focused on the task of writing a song for the school musical. Another may be a great conceptualizer with poor sequential ordering and time management problems, so he never submits his perceptive essays in time to meet deadlines or else leaves their completion to the last minute and produces a substandard rush job. Weak memory function may make it hard for a student to recall rules on the spot, even when a student has an excellent grasp of how those rules work. Such unsupported higher thinking is like a country rich in natural resources while lacking the highways, railroad tracks, and airports needed to get the ores and the crops to where they need to go. I don't know how often I've heard a parent or teacher bemoan, "He is so brilliant, so smart, so clever in the insightful and original way he thinks and expresses himself, but you'd

never know it to read his papers or inspect the teacher comments on his report cards. He just can't seem to deliver on all that promise he shows. It's as
if he's teasing us with his intellectual gifts!"

ᔏ᷁ MINDS OVER TIME: KEEPING A WATCHFUL EYE ON HIGHER THINKING AS CHILDREN AGE

Creativity is a higher order thinking function that makes an early debut on
the academic stage. As early as kindergarten kids may showcase their preferred creative outlets; some may be great storytellers or comedians, others
artists, others musical performers. With the years these creative abilities naturally evolve or change. The challenge is for parents to maintain a creativity
watch and ignite these important sparks of originality. They become the
forerunners of brainstorming ability and innovative thinking.

During the course of their educational careers children show an increasing capacity to conceptualize, engage in critical thinking, and make good
use of rule-based learning. A parent can track a child's growth in these three
critical areas of higher cognitive function. Early on, these capacities are
tapped in very concrete everyday life situations. During a trip to the supermarket, a six-year-old may begin to grasp the concept of good value, the
concept of a balanced diet, or the concept of waiting in line. A shopping
parent can model for a child this age how products are critically analyzed.

In late elementary school, concepts like good sportsmanship, charity,
and politeness bridge the transition from mainly concrete conceptualization
(like predators, stock cars, and breakfast foods) to the highly abstract
concepts that saturate high school books (like taxation without representation, valence, and isomers). Parents should derive a sense of a child's comfort with current concepts in school by discussing them and gauging the
degree to which the child is either grasping or groping. They may discover
that their Gabriela has given up on sense making and is operating exclusively on memory in school. Or, they may find out that Robert is a conceptual specialist; he forms concepts beautifully in social studies but is
consistently concrete and paralytically memory-bound in science and mathematics.

As children pass through elementary school they meet up with a steady
flurry of rules. Initially these are behavioral rules, things that are permissible
or impermissible. And some children who have behavior problems at age
five or six actually show a lack of understanding of the rules and how they
work. Rules invade the formal curriculum at every grade level. In a steady
progression, students are able to understand rules and to demonstrate their
understanding not just by applying them but also by being able to explain

how they work. By middle school students combine critical thinking with rule awareness and make a practice of condemning the rules as "useless" or "unfair." That's actually a helpful if irritating stage in understanding rules.

It is possible to monitor critical thinking over time. We expect to see this function emerge by mid–elementary school and rise rapidly (sometimes much too rapidly for their own good) by eighth grade. Using some of the guidelines I provided earlier in this chapter, beginning as early as second grade, a parent can ask a child to critique a TV commercial, a teacher, a product in the supermarket, or even a good friend to derive an impression of where the child may stand on the continuum that extends from naïveté to cynicism.

✒ PRACTICAL CONSIDERATIONS

• Although higher order thinking is buried deep within many a textbook and lesson plan, I feel strongly that schools should teach explicitly the five components of higher thinking within coursework. Students should be told, for example, "We've now started working with a really key nonverbal abstract concept. It's called an exponent. Why don't we talk about this concept and then map out the critical features of exponents." These direct approaches are especially helpful to students facing the barrage of abstract concepts in secondary school, although some of this can begin in third or fourth grade. While students are learning concepts they should be learning about conceptualization. In general, secondary school students should be given problems to solve in a documented step-by-step fashion, concepts to map out, critical thinking to engage in, and so forth. That is, they should be informed clearly that they are refining these specific higher thinking abilities as they work. This thinking about their higher thinking is sometimes referred to as metacognition and is well known to energize and deepen learning.

• Students should be forewarned when a particular form of higher thinking is to be called into the game. For example, a teacher might say: "Be prepared, this chapter contains a whole bunch of ideas that you may or may not agree with, so you better unpack your critical thinking tools" or "There are some rules here you need to follow to make this job easier; so before you tackle it, figure out which rules would work here." This planning or anticipation of higher thinking needs can be introduced by the middle of elementary school.

• Parents and teachers should always seek a child's zones of effective intuition, which may have revealing implications for that kid's ultimate career pathway. Your child who is so intuitive when baking cakes and pies may be an embryonic cordon bleu chef.

• Brainstorming is worthy of special encouragement. Kids who are overdosed with highly structured after-school activities, infatuated with electronic games, and hypnotically glued to television screens may have little or no chance to let go and dispatch their brains along imaginative, divergent, or elaborative flyways.

• In courses that are predominantly rule-guided, kids can keep their own personal rulebooks. They should log in new rules and also practice making up rules of their own that seem to work for them. Rule creation is an active and productive way of learning. There is evidence that the most successful students in a class are prolific rule makers. A student might recognize, "If my teacher lists some points on the board, then they're probably going to be on the test" or "If my answer to this math problem doesn't make sense, then I better go back and see where I made my mistake." Some children concoct rules that promote home life survival as well: "If my mom stays up late at night, then I know she's going to be in a very ugly mood the next day" or "If I ask my dad for money when he's in a hurry to get to work in the morning, then I have a much better chance of getting it" or "If I tell my big brother I think he's cool, then he'll take me to the movies tonight." There are rules to be thought up everywhere.

• Events in history, episodes in a novel, and current issues in the news all lend themselves to the use of step-by-step problem-solving processes and to critical thinking experience. Explicit activities fitted to these areas serve to build knowledge at the same time that problem solving and critical thinking undergo strengthening.

• As part of being a parent who also educates, you can and should examine closely the five areas of higher thinking and consider how these vital mind functions can be tapped and practiced at home—in fun ways. For instance, sports can be used to think about how rules work, to problem-solve before a game, and to analyze critically the strengths and weaknesses of an opposing team. Before attending a UNC basketball game, one local Chapel Hill family actually talked through various strategic problem-solving issues that arise when there's a high-pressure tournament contest. The two children gave suggestions that they would offer the coach. Then throughout the actual game, their father kept asking the kids for alternative strategies and had them keep an eye on specific players to monitor how they were doing. He was teaching problem solving (knowingly in this case). This father, himself a psychologist, told me that after the game they discussed whether the three-point-shot rule should be changed. He also made sure his kids understood the concept of a zone defense. They also critiqued the coach's judgment (he managed to come out looking okay). This sly father then asked the kids what new rules they would introduce to make basketball more exciting to play and watch. His twelve-year-old son said he would vary the height of the basket during the game—randomly. He also suggested they use different-sized balls in different quarters. Wow, creativity, problem solving, concept formation, rule analysis, and critical thinking all wrapped together in one potentially ordinary basketball game.

• Both parents and teachers need to be vigilant for difficulties a child might be having with one or more of the forms of higher thinking. Sooner or later neglected deficits take a bite out of school performance. Parents are in the best position to be the earliest detectors of a higher thinking dysfunction, one that may be confined to a particular subject area or spread across the curriculum. They can alert the school and also institute activities, such as the ones described in this chapter, to repair, bypass, or at least partially patch up the breakdown. I recall one patient of mine who was having a horrible go of it in seventh-grade algebra. Up until that point most of his math work had reflected obedient memorization and rote imitation. But he really wasn't getting by in his algebra class.

Finally, his teacher gave this boy a list of all the concepts, including, for example, the notion of a balanced equation. Then for a week, instead of completing homework problems, he was asked to go home and think about the concepts, talk to his parents about them, and think of things each concept reminded him of. For example, he came up with the idea that balancing an equation was like eating a balanced diet or trying to shift your weight from one foot to the other while using a balance beam in physical education. This child liked thinking in analogies, a technique that can help many kids. He reported his analogies in class, and his classmates added some of their own. The teacher then put up a massive analogy chart based on what his students came up with. The boy himself told his teacher, "This is the way I like to learn. I have to decide what things remind me of, like from my real life. When I could do this in algebra, it helped me a lot. It made it more fun and more real." By the way, the students also talked about the ways they could use algebra—in the supermarket, in building a fort, in deciding how much grain you need to buy to feed four horses for two weeks. Thinking through real-world applications helped them capture the runaway concepts.

9

Relating to Relating ✒

Our Social Thinking System

A friend may well be reckoned the masterpiece of Nature.

RALPH WALDO EMERSON, "Friendship"

A strapping girl of fifteen asked me if I "used tobacco," meaning did I chew it. I said no. It roused her scorn. She reported me to all the crowd and said, "Here is a boy seven years old who can't chew tobacco." By the looks and comments which this produced, I realized that I was a degraded object, and was cruelly ashamed of myself. I determined to reform. But I only made myself sick; I was not able to learn to chew tobacco. . . . I remained poor and characterless. I longed to be respected, but I was never able to rise. Children have but little charity for each other's defects.

MARK TWAIN, Autobiography

The idea that men are created free and equal is both true and misleading: men are created different; they lose their social freedom and their individual autonomy in seeking to become like each other.

DAVID RIESMAN, The Lonely Crowd

WHEN your child arrives home from school feeling and looking about as downtrodden as an adult who has just been fired, chances are good that your despondent kid has suffered a penetrating social wound. The tumultuous ups and downs of relationships with their friends, their peer group, and their adversaries heavily preoccupy all kids throughout their years at school. Some handle the stress better than others.

There's a new kid on the block. Kevin would like to make friends with him, so he offers to show him where the lunchroom is and asks if he'd like to sit with him during lunch today. Ralph and his friend Hackett disagree about what to do tonight; Ralph wants to go to a movie and Hackett wants to play computer games. Ralph cleverly suggests they rent a video and play computer games for a little while instead of all evening. In both of these instances students are exercising their social strengths. Kevin has demonstrated his ability to start up a new relationship, while Ralph knows how to resolve incipient social conflict without having to resort to aggression. Social initiation and conflict resolution are both examples of neurodevelopmental functions that play a significant role in relationships among kids. The strength or weakness of these and other functions that comprise social ability help determine whether your child's life at school and in the neighborhood will be fulfilling or traumatic.

We all know that kids can be exceedingly cruel to one another. Most often their mean-spirited actions and statements are vented upon well-meaning pathetic peers who lack the know-how, the social functions, needed to establish meaningful friendships and enjoy a decent reputation within the cultures of school and neighborhood. On the other hand, highly accepted and respected children make use of excellent social functions, and these innate abilities keep on growing stronger as kids amass life experience and wisdom. But when social growth fails to occur, your child's life can be a study in daily humiliation, rejection, and isolation.

Many kids who have more than their share of trouble with learning also suffer social wounds at school. I get to see and try to help many such students at the Center for Development and Learning in Chapel Hill. Sometimes I'm asked to consult regarding a kid who gets very good grades but has no friends. I invariably discover underlying defects in specific social functions. Doug was a prime example, a boy accustomed to being unpopular. Doug's parents brought him to see me to get help with his interpersonal misery. They drove in from Washington, where Doug was a student at a prominent, high-powered independent school known for educating the children of our national leaders—ostensibly super-kids with great kinds of minds. Mostly, his mother and father wanted me to demystify this boy, to help him gain insight into his specific social shortcomings. Hopefully, a big dose of personal insight would inspire Doug to work on building his social abilities.

Doug was small for an eleven-year-old. He also was conspicuously chubby with a nearly spherical face. Because an unfair amount of his weight was misallocated to his chest, he appeared to have unusual breast development—which wasn't the case. But this anatomical dirty trick of fate was readily observed and a favorite topic of his peers, especially during physical education. Nothing hurt Doug more than all those cruel comments about his body. The other kids had never taken to Doug. They called him names, bullied him, and walled him off like an infected abscess. At the bus stop, a favorite pastime was known as "Let's bug Doug the bug." Sometimes when teased, Doug would become incensed and explode into cursing and fighting. Some of the other kids found his inflammatory reactions hilariously entertaining and actually derived gleeful exhilaration in detonating him.

Doug would come home every day feeling awful. He once enjoyed school, but not anymore. Despite the fact that he was recognized with all manner of certificates for attaining honor grades, he lived with queasy tension and apprehension, sometimes even terror, from Monday through Friday. No one dared sit next to him on the bus or at lunch out of fear of some bizarre social contamination virus!

Doug's parents were justifiably proud of his wide-ranging talents and interests. He was enthusiastic about science fiction, video games, and computers. He harbored a passion for collecting rocks and comic books. In fact, he loved buying comic books almost more than anything else. He would read his collection over and over again and had become an expert on all comic book characters. Other kids considered Doug's interests totally, unacceptably weird. Many of them talked mostly about clothes and music. Doug was not the least bit interested in what kind of clothes he wore, in how he looked, in buying CDs at the mall, or in talking about sports. Doug's sister, Becky, who was very popular, wanted Doug to act more cool and less like a dork. Doug, however, didn't understand what she meant.

To add to his predicament, Doug had a penchant for saying the wrong things, at least from a social ingratiation standpoint. Or he would express things at the wrong times. When other kids are dead serious, Doug will crack a joke. When peers are having a ball, Doug will say something gravely serious or sad. He was out of step; he could never match moods with others. When Doug got going on a topic that interested him, he never knew when or how to put the brakes on his monologue. Everyone else would become visibly peeved and bored while he, unaware of their reactions, filibustered away. Doug seldom picked up social feedback. Also, when Doug said or did something that made others think that he was strange, he had no insight into what they were thinking.

Yet, Doug liked himself the way he was. Doug's guidance counselor had explained to him that he lacked social skills. A school psychologist told his parents that Doug must have Asperger syndrome, a mild form of autism. The parents rejected this notion, insisting that having weak social skills shouldn't be thought of as a disease, any more than being a poor Ping-Pong player or having trouble carrying a tune should be incorporated into some stigmatizing syndrome. Many people are using the designation "Asperger syndrome" for kids like Doug, but I had to agree with Doug's parents. I have seen no convincing scientific evidence that it exists as a discrete disorder of some kind like a strep throat. I worry when we try to make every little cluster of traits into a syndrome, ignoring the toxic stigmatizing effects of being so designated, which can last a lifetime. We could help Doug without forcing him to become a pathological specimen!

After isolating his specific social gaps, I spent a lot of time talking to Doug, demystifying him. After an extended discussion of his many strengths, we made a list of Doug's particular social weaknesses. I taught him the names of the functions he needed to work on (after all, how can you work on something if you don't even know what it's called?). We discussed ways he could practice such things as picking the right topics to talk about at the right times with other kids and how to gauge their moods so you don't seriously conflict with them. Initially Doug denied he had any social problems, which is common. Soon, however, his defenses seemed to dissolve, and he became riveted on our discussion.

Over the ensuing months, Doug got some targeted advice on these issues from a school counselor. Also, the headmaster of his school cracked down on verbal and physical abuse among kids. His parents had social coaching sessions with Doug a couple of nights a week at bedtime. They came back to see me a few times in North Carolina, and I was impressed by Doug's newly assimilated understanding and willingness to acknowledge and work on what he called "my social trouble."

Then there's Rita, a girl I met at a school we work with in New Jersey. She portrays the opposite social pole; when Rita crosses her school's threshold each morning, she is treated with honor like an internationally renowned rock star. Friends crowd around this mid-puberty idol, competing for her attention like frenzied autograph seekers. At home the telephone rings incessantly for Rita, often bearing newsbreaks of soon-to-be-announced party invitations. Rita's middle school years have been buffeted and turbocharged by her many friends and her high level of popularity. In contrast, I was informed that Rita has a twin brother, Jerome, for whom the telephone never rings. It has been three or four years since he was last invited to a party. At thirteen he is a certified loner. When he does venture into groups, he invades the space of others without realizing it. He frequently gets into altercations. He is constantly made fun of, in part because of his gaunt, "geeky" appearance and thick spectacles but also because he lacks the tools that are needed to relate to other kids, and because he is so klutzy in gym class. The most widely heralded, popular boys and girls in his class lead a relentless defamatory campaign against poor Jerome. You see, ironically and unjustly, popular kids get even more popular by acting tough and putting down those like Jerome in front of everybody.

And finally, at a high school not very far from my farm in North Carolina, Karl and Susan are the most sought after duo in ninth grade. These inseparable friends are attractive, athletic, and socially captivating. In fact, they have received so much overt admiration and attention from peers that nothing else much matters to them. Both are failing in school. Blissfully unaware, neither of them seems to care much about the future or about meeting any academic expectations. They have given themselves over to friendship and popularity to the exclusion of all other priorities in their lives, including their families and their schoolwork. The two have bonded with a behavioral style as showy and graceful as a pair of amorous trumpeter swans.

What do these students have in common? They are all engaged or perhaps entangled in the social melodramas staged every day in every school, within the life of every schoolchild. Their tales represent real episodes within a series of steadily unfolding interpersonal sagas. Kids are on display, and they experience a compulsion to keep displaying for one another. Their classmates are ruthlessly evaluating, observing, and auditioning them for various social roles. There's no place to hide. Showcasing in the social marketplace all day long, most students strive to act and appear cool and to be salable to the group.

Most students will tell you that social pressure exceeds academic pressure by a long shot. Some of them are up to it. They happen to be socially well endowed, equipped to handle the social tests their peers administer. They know how to play the popularity games, and they play them for all they're worth. Social gratification and acceptance are the trophies. Protection from humiliation and a strong sense of belonging represent additional dividends. For others the social part of school is a source of anguish. In fact, chronic rejection by one's peers is one of childhood's saddest stories.

A multitude of factors contributes to the social success or failure of a school-age child. Physical appearance, self-confidence, and credible social role models all exert their influence. But most important are a student's own social capacities. From the case summaries I have cited, it should be obvious that social functioning varies dramatically from kid to kid. By understanding the specific dysfunctions that can be seen in a socially unsuccessful person, we can help him or her put the pieces together and derive some social satisfaction at long last.

❧ THE BIG THREE SOCIAL MISSIONS

The social challenges children face can be separated into three daily missions:

The Friendship Mission

Your child's friends are unquestionably among her or his most coveted possessions. Friends are so much fun, so reinforcing, so supportive, and so protective. Friendship formation and maintenance is our first social mission. Having a friend demands that your child relate successfully on an individual basis. This is relatively independent of overall reputation among your peers (i.e., popularity). Rather, friendship involves starting and keeping up a succession of mutually rewarding experiences with another individual. Of course, it is common to form any number of such working bonds culminating in a nice collection of stable and positive relationships.

Friendship involves intimacy, sharing, and mutual support. Not everyone seeks exactly the same benefits from having friends, and there exist some highly significant gender differences. Most often, boys cultivate friendships around activities. In other words, at least on the surface, friendships serve largely recreational purposes. So a boy seeks companionship with another boy because they like to play baseball, go fishing, or play electronic games together. Your son might even select a prospective friend from among other candidates because he has a basketball hoop in his driveway (what more could you ask?). In many studies, this activity-sharing justification has been found to be a direct contrast to the basis for girl-girl relationships. Girls look for friends with whom they can share inner sentiments, communicate, and generally feel comfortable. They are much less compelled to justify a relationship on the basis of shared recreational agendas. Interestingly, this difference persists well into adult life when men get together to play golf, go fishing, or play touch football, while women have lunch together so they can share their thoughts and feelings. It is not that boys don't want to communicate intimately with other boys, nor is it true that girls shun joint activities. To the contrary, both needs pertain to both groups, but there are significant differences in the extent to which they determine and frame relationships.

A great many of the social functions and dysfunctions we are about to examine in this chapter influence how children form these kinds of close alliances and sustain them over time. Having "my best friend" can be gratifying to a child. Kids take pride in having such a relationship, often referring to "my best friend" as if it were some precious collectible. Your child's friends represent a visible and portable badge of his or her social performance. The relationship also is perceived as long-term security, insurance against loneliness and self-doubt.

The Popularity Mission

Your children may want popularity more than anything else in the whole world. That drive constitutes the second engaging social mission. It differs from friendship in that popularity consists of having a positive reputation among a larger circle of peers. It is possible for your offspring to be popular without having strong friendships. It is just as possible to have some very solid friendships and not be notably popular.

Social psychologists have found that students within the community of a school can be divided into definite popularity subgroups. While these categories shouldn't be viewed rigidly, they represent reality in most school social settings. They are summarized in the following (modified from the work of Stephen Asher and John Coie).

POPULARITY SUBGROUPS IN SCHOOL

Subgroup	Characteristics
Popular Kids	Well liked and respected by most or all of their peers
Controversial Kids	Well liked by some groups and quite unliked by others
Amiable Kids	Not known well in the school but socially acceptable
Neglected Kids	Unnoticed by anyone (some have chosen to be neglected)
Rejected Kids	Actively excluded, possibly bullied, or verbally abused by classmates

Popular children manage to do all the right things. Later in this chapter I will describe verbal and behavioral traits that these gifted socializers are able to parlay gracefully. In contrast, those who become rejected are somehow uploading and downloading the wrong messages, possibly committing a chain of social errors that have managed to alienate them from their peers and gain them their negative reputation. Peer rejection and abuse take a heavy toll. Often rebuked children become depressed and angry. It is not unusual for a victim, following an all-day skein of social setbacks, to arrive home and brutally bully his kid sister or act in an oppositional belligerent way toward his parents. The poor kid has painfully frayed feelings that he has had to suppress all day long, only to let them explode on the domestic scene.

The Political Mission

The quest for political good fortune is the third social mission. It may seem a bit disconcerting to ponder, but childhood is political. Kids have to learn to interact advantageously with individuals in a position to help or hurt them. They need to figure out and influence those who are influential. They do so by forming constructive bonds with such individuals. Their political moves are seldom calculated maneuvers; they are more likely to be unconscious, to seem like the right thing to do or say. Probably the earliest political lessons are learned through sibling rivalries, power struggles within a family that play out as kids seek preferred or privileged treatment from their parents.

You might want to inform your children at some point that they will derive their most lasting and potent political experience by practicing on their teachers, the people who evaluate them on a daily basis. In fact, it has been shown that while children during early elementary school perceive their teachers as surrogate parents, by middle school they come to view them mainly as evaluators and as people of influence. Since teachers continuously reward or demean you as a person, they occupy positions of political power. So it makes good sense to court their favor. In fact, I recently discovered that many early American primers read in schools contained a chapter entitled something like "How to Get Your Teachers to Like You." It was core curriculum and construed as part of "decorum." Perhaps uncharitably, this activity also has been called "apple polishing," or worse. In the real world, however, it satisfies the need to gain the respect of those whom you respect. More pragmatically, even if you don't respect the target of your political actions, you are still aware of the personal benefits that accrue from embellishing that relationship.

Some students seem to acquire a knack for developing suboptimal interfaces with adults. They either are oblivious to the interactions, or find self-destructive ways to sabotage them—often without realizing what they are doing.

In relating to teachers your children first of all must realize that they need to take the initiative. A teacher may have thirty or fifty or a hundred and fifty students, but each student has far fewer teachers than that. Therefore, it is somehow up to the child to craft a positive relationship with a teacher. In part, this process requires a child to realize that teachers are human, that they need to be praised, helped to feel good about the job they're doing, and reinforced by their students. If you tell your history teacher you think history is really boring, you are really telling him you think he's a bore! Your political career, at least in that arena, is in hot water. On the other hand, if you project a genuine interest in history, you nourish the relationship you have with an adult who has devoted his career to history!

Demonstrating an interest, complimenting a teacher, and trying not to alienate or intimidate that person represent key political strategies. Today's teachers are tomorrow's bosses or supervisors. In both cases they determine whether you get promoted. If the relationships are positive, your teacher or your boss will give you the benefit of the doubt.

I have met quite a few kids with learning problems who have as one of their strengths the fact that they get along splendidly with adults. I've always believed that this is no meager asset for a kid to carry with him into adulthood. One such student, a tenth-grade boy, recently confided in me, "I'm at my best when I'm with adults. I feel as if I have more in common with people who are older than I am. I feel more tense with kids my age. Maybe I try to compete with them too much. But I also think they're kind of boring." It may be a little hard to interpret statements like these. The boy was having serious problems with his social abilities and had never gotten along with his peers. Often such students find it far easier to charm adults than to win over their compatriots. Nevertheless, facility with adults serves a useful purpose when you're a kid.

Well-applied political skills are not confined to child-adult interactions. Some peers are highly influential and therefore deserving of political attention. It might be desirable to gain the confidence and trust of the class president, the captain of the basketball team, or the leader of a prestigious clique. Alternatively, one might need to have the wisdom to stay out of his way! Pulling this off calls for deft political agility. It can be especially triumphant to gain the favor of powerful kids without submitting meekly to their oppression and becoming their loyal henchperson, bodyguard, public relations agent, or personal servant. The challenge is to be a skilled kid politician without ceding your own freedom, individual tastes, and integrity.

SOCIAL FUNCTIONS AND DYSFUNCTIONS

The social thinking system consists of a repertoire of partly overlapping neurodevelopmental functions that equip kids to become socially acceptable, indulge in durable friendships, and make the grade politically in and out of school. I think it's helpful to divide the social thinking system into social language functions and social behaviors. That's because I've encountered students who have trouble with the verbal parts of interactions but not the behavioral and vice versa. I think as a parent observing the social side of your child's existence, you are in a position to take note of both how well he communicates with other people and how effectively he acts with them. Students who are popular and who form sound friendships are strong in most or all of the key social functions.

Social Language Function

Every time Chris opens up his mouth, he succeeds in alienating all those within twenty-five feet of him. He sounds abrasive, antagonistic, and boastful without realizing it. Over his decade-long life he has managed to turn off gaggles of his peers. He has no inkling that the way he talks is the reason for his consistent rejection by classmates. Then there's seventeen-year-old Lola, who can't seem to carry on a conversation with anyone. With her, there's never any verbal give-and-take; it's as if she's forever delivering monologues or solo arias—with no recognition or response to any points or ideas brought up by anyone else. Other teens have begun to avoid Lola. She is devastated over the fact that she was recently snubbed and not invited to the graduation party of one of her best friends. Chris and Lola both are inadvertently navigating toward social exclusion through their social language or, rather, their lack thereof.

Social language functions differ from the literate language functions described in Chapter 5. So your child might be as smooth as cashmere with social language but downright coarse when it comes to the linguistics of formal learning. In many respects, social language comprises the highest, the most complex language mode. The study of patients with serious head trauma has provided some evidence for this view. Individuals who have been in calamitous motor vehicle accidents often go through a period in which many of their language functions become seriously compromised. A year later, most of them have recovered the major part of their preaccident language capabilities. But most have not gotten back and often never regain their social language functions. Acquaintances comment, "No one's been able to get along with him since his car crash." We often witness the progressive erosion of social language functions in the elderly. Hence we apply the term "old grouch" or "old codger" to characterize the abrasive, abrupt, negative vernacular of many older individuals. They're not as unpleasant as they sound. Some of their social language sheen has simply worn off with age.

A vital social resource for your child is the ability to express accurate feelings through language, those feelings she or he would like to convey or should convey. Many individuals with social language dysfunctions are forever being misinterpreted because they, like Chris above, have trouble regulating their tone of voice, choice of words, and rhythm of language to convey their feelings accurately. As a result, they sound angry when they're not. Parents need to be alert for this common variety of social dysfunction, which can start to manifest itself as early as age five or six. Affected kids need constant feedback from their parents and they should be given more socially acceptable ways of saying things.

Weak social language abilities also may interfere with interpreting the feelings of others when they speak. A kid with social language dysfunction may have trouble telling when you are joking and when you're serious. He may infer from your speech you're angry with him when actually you're not. In other words such a child has trouble interpreting and communicating the feeling part of language. Parents can help with this too. During or after watching a movie, they can talk about the characters and ask a child to identify the different feelings expressed by each. Such discussions of things people say that reveal how they feel need to be a recurring theme for some kids.

Fourteen-year-old Joe from western North Carolina is a memorable example of misread and miscommunicated feelings. He had been a patient of mine for about six years. In the middle of eighth grade (the social dark ages), he came to my office, and I inquired about what he'd been up to in school lately. Joe responded tersely in a characteristically gruff voice, "What do you think?" With this verbal encouragement, I asked further, "Are there any subjects that are a struggle for you at this point?" Joe snorted, "That's a dumb thing to ask. Of course not." I responded, "Well, that's terrific; it sure sounds as if you are on a roll these days." He yawned rudely and uttered, "Yeah, you could say that, I guess." His intonation and curt replies resembled hostile fire in the face of my friendly approach. Yet, when I confronted Joe and asked why he was so bitter, he looked at me surprised, astonished that I would think he was feeling or coming across as negative. Like so many others with social language weaknesses, Joe could not match his feelings (which were mainly positive toward his pediatrician) with his verbalization (which often came across as antagonistic).

Later that year I referred Joe to an understanding and compassionate counselor, a professional who worked with small groups of kids having social difficulties. Several times she saw Joe alone, and the rest of the time he was part of her group. Over a period of three months she videotaped a series of conversations she had with Joe and also recorded his interactions with some other students. At regular intervals she and Joe reviewed the tapes and discussed them using a checklist of social language functions (such as the ones listed on page 232). Joe couldn't believe how he was coming across—as he put it, "how mean and ornery I keep sounding." He asked his parents to let him know whenever he was sounding "wicked." The feedback helped correct a severe social blind spot in Joe's case. A year later in the middle of ninth grade, during a follow-up visit, it was apparent that this boy had taken the bull by the horns and worked on the way he talked. He was so gracious, I almost couldn't recognize him. His father told me that Joe was actually getting invited to parties, something inconceivable twelve months earlier.

I feel sure there are adults who regularly get passed over for promotion because whenever they express their thoughts, they manage to put off everyone around them—without even seeking to be disagreeable and without realizing they are being disagreeable! I know some of them. You certainly would not want your child to have to live with this insidious kind of handicap. The social costs are high when you're unable to regulate the feelings part of language.

Code switching is another essential social language function. Code switching means simply that you don't talk in the same manner with everyone. Your child is expected to talk differently to his parents from how he speaks to his little sister from how he converses with the cat from how he communicates with his best friend from how he verbalizes ideas to his math teacher from how he expresses himself to a policeman.

There are children who stall out when moving from code to code. They don't know how or when to switch codes or else they speak but one code all the time. That was true of a really cute little kid named Jake, who sounded just like a scholarly little professor whenever and wherever he orated (which was most of the time and in most places). He loved lecturing on prehistoric mammals and holding forth on the more timely topic of modern-day marine invertebrates. Unfortunately, this was the only way that he could speak. He couldn't turn off that intellectual spout when he was with his peers, who had little tolerance for his way of speaking and choice of topics. He was passionate about archaeology and expounded on this esoteric affinity on occasions when classmates were joking around, launching paper planes, and dispensing age-appropriate slapstick humor. His words could not have been more out of step. Thus they rejected him for his inability to switch into their language code. Jake did not have the vaguest idea of what he was doing to put off other kids. When his older brother tried to explain it to him, when he pointed out to Jake that he talked like a "weirdo," the feedback made no sense to him. Jake even uttered something about freedom of speech. But Jake was seriously starved for social acceptance; he had no idea where and how to go look for it.

Other critical social language signposts to watch for in your children include regulation of humor (children need to know when and how to joke around depending upon current circumstances and the people they're with), requesting skills (knowing how to ask for things without alienating everyone), mood matching (being able to match feelings with those of others, so you show some sadness when they're telling you something sad), complimenting (the ability and willingness to say something that makes another person feel good), and lingo fluency (the ability to use the terminology and speech mannerisms of the contemporary culture).

Social Language Functions

Social Language Function	Explanation
The communication and interpretation of feelings	The ability to use and understand word connotations, intonation, and forms of expression so a speaker's true feelings are not distorted
Code switching	The ability to change your way of speaking to fit the people you're with
Topic selection and maintenance	The ability to know what to talk about when and how long to keep it up
Conversational technique	The ability to engage in a two-way discussion, truly sharing communication
Humor regulation	The ability to understand humor and the ability to use it appropriately at the right time and place
Requesting skill	The ability to know how to ask for something without alienating people
Perspective taking	The ability to assume the perspective of the listener and know how he's feeling while you're speaking
Affective matching	The ability to match moods with someone through language, so that, for example, you're not too serious when they're clowning
Complimenting	The ability (and willingness) to praise another person
Lingo fluency	The ability to speak credibly the language of your peers (when you want and need to do so)

Good social language means effective communication, and effective communication goes a long way toward forming meaningful and uplifting relationships with others. So we should help kids think about the impact of their words upon others.

Social Behaviors

Dressing appropriately for an occasion, making good eye contact when meeting someone for the first time, showing sympathy when someone informs you his dog was hit by a car, and collaborating smoothly with other members of the refreshments committee are samples of competent social behavior. Social capacity takes in a collection of such actions or behaviors that speak louder than words. These behaviors are transparent in a wide spectrum of social settings. Some individuals have more trouble with social behavior than with social language, while others exhibit the opposite pattern. There are many facets of social behavior; here we will consider a small group of especially important ones: conflict resolution, the interpretation of feedback, marketing oneself to others, collaborating with peers, and making use of social information.

Resolving serious conflict without resorting to aggression is a real social accomplishment. Many students with social cognitive gaps have no idea how to deal with the setbacks, the impasses, and the interpersonal glitches of day-to-day human interactions. There is no such thing as a social relationship immune from conflict. The real issue is how well people patch up the differences and repair dented egos. Some kids, however, can't handle social conflict without unleashing verbal or physical social grenades.

Here's a classic social behavioral drama: A little girl visits her friend's house and hops and skips into the friend's bedroom, which happens to be where she houses her prized doll collection. She wants to play with her friend's number one very favorite Barbie. No one is authorized to touch that doll, not even the proud owner's blood relatives. What does she, the passionate collector, do at that point? How does she resolve the conflict? Which is worth more to her, that doll or the friendship? No one should have to face such a no-win predicament. Fortunately, a socially capable child rises to the occasion. She is likely to substitute adroitly a far less precious doll or else call for an instantaneous change of venue, perhaps recommending, "Let's get out of here and go have some ice cream." Or, alternatively, she may conclude that a lasting friendship is more important than any doll and explain to her friend, "You can handle my best doll, but first you have to go wash your hands. I don't want that doll getting dirty." These are excellent preventive and therapeutic social solutions. But if you don't have the tools to deal with social conflict, then aggression may be your only alternative. The socially inappropriate kid raises her voice when that friend is presumptuous enough to reach for the plastic idol: "No way. Don't touch that doll. Only I'm allowed to play with her. Besides, your hands are always dirty." She then shoves her friend (now possibly a former friend) out of her bedroom. This girl has employed aggression to resolve conflict. It's a quick way to lose friends and have no influence over people.

When children can't seem to resolve conflict and instead display outbursts of violence or tears, parents need to work with them to keep reviewing alternative actions that they might have tried. Discussions of conflicts should take the emphasis off who started it or who was the culprit and, instead, stress what might be tried the next time such a negative scene takes place. We need to teach kids the art of no-fault conflict resolution. It's a great asset to take with you through life.

In relating to one another, kids constantly have to absorb and interpret social feedback. They need to pick up the sometimes subtle cues etched on the facial expressions or body movements of those with whom they are interacting. If a boy lets loose with a hostile shove or slap, something that really bothers or pains his neighbor, that perpetrator ought to arrive at the instant realization that he said or did something hostile. After an accurate reading of social feedback cues (painted in living color on his friend's face), he can self-correct and recover (e.g., "I was only kidding—I didn't really mean to do that"). Of course, if you are insensitive when it comes to social feedback, as is the case for many kids with social cognitive dysfunctions, you don't even notice that you are infuriating the person you're with. You keep on rubbing salt in the wound, sinking deeper and deeper into social jeopardy with that individual.

Not surprisingly, many kids with weak attention controls have difficulty with self-monitoring; they fail to notice their social faux pas just as dependably as they make unnoticed careless errors in their academic work. In other words, they don't watch what they're doing.

A tool kit of social thinking behaviors enables a kid to "market himself" to others. He is able to create a demand for his presence. First, there is an awareness of the image he is broadcasting to others. He can sense how he is coming across. The way he dresses, the way he acts, and the tastes he manifests create deep impressions. How acutely aware is he of how he's perceived by others? To what extent is he able to shape and project a self-image that others are attracted to and respect? The answers to these questions have a strong bearing on social acceptance.

Some kids have no notion of how to assemble their image. Consequently, they fail miserably at marketing themselves to their peers. There can be many reasons for this—some subtle and some obvious. Strange as it may sound, there are those who have some trouble producing socially acceptable body movements. They move awkwardly or they invade other people's space. Their movements somehow repel their classmates and sometimes adults too. This has actually been characterized as a neurological condition called dyssemia, a state in which individuals lack control over the ways they navigate their bodies through space. As a result, they come across as clumsy, awkward, or unappealing. Sadly and without any justification, during childhood these socially misguided movement styles offend others, who don't even realize why they are feeling so uncomfortable. Commenting on such a student, a teacher once told me: "You can just watch him out in the corridor. He lumbers along awkwardly and moves from side to side as much as he goes straight ahead. He seems to be occupying a lot more than his share of space. And you'd think the kid was carrying a two-hundred-pound backpack. There's something so unattractive about how he moves, and the other students all seem to sense it. You can see them kind of back away. He has no friends as far as I can tell."

In addition to invading other people's space too readily kids with dyssemia have problems using hand gestures appropriately. For example, the movements of their hands may contradict what they are saying. One child I knew was observed pounding on the table while telling a joke. The regulation of facial expressions can also be an issue. The same kid who pounded on the table often looked angry or had a scowl on his face when he really wasn't intending to appear morose or hostile. His mother also mentioned that sometimes when talking about something sad or very serious, it almost looked as if he was smiling. That chronic mismatching between his facial expression and his true feelings in all likelihood put off some people, even though they probably were unaware of what it was about him that was bothering them.

Some students, on the other hand, overdo their self-marketing, overselling themselves in a manner far too direct, aggressive, and obvious—showing off, boasting, displaying ostentatiously. I was told that one boy, a very lonely seven-year-old with extreme social cognitive weaknesses, out of quiet desperation would give away his Tootsie Rolls at lunch and also offer modest financial support (i.e., bribery) to those willing to play with him. Classmates accepted his donations greedily, but the purchased relationships were both tenuous and short-lived.

Collaboration is another key ingredient of social behavior. Students vary considerably in the extent to which they are team players. Nowadays many schools appropriately stress collaboration, since the bulk of productivity in our adult operations entails teamwork on the job. But some children have trouble assuming a collaborative role. They seek too much control or they fail to do their share and thereby alienate others. They lack the sensors needed to make the determination of how assertive and how helpful to be in a coordinated collaborative activity. Often kids with weak collaborative abilities have difficulty giving up any control. They feel compelled to dominate every relationship and to try to take all the credit for positive accomplishments while blaming others for setbacks. They lack a sense of fair play and have great difficulty taking the perspective of fellow collaborators, meeting some of their needs at the same time that all are working toward a joint goal. Children who lack collaboration skills shy away from team sports, committees, and other combined campaigns in school. It is also common for them to be rejected as prospective lab partners or teammates because of their reputation as soloists or unequal sharers.

Many kids I've evaluated for social problems struggle to interpret social information. They can't seem to gather the myriad moment-to-moment social cues and use those data to understand what's going on so they can make appropriate responses. I think the classic example of applied social reading can be seen on a Saturday at a shopping mall anywhere across the land. Just picture some early adolescent girls having lunch together in the food court and engaging in a phenomenon I call mood matching. Here's how it goes: The first girl talks about her mother and how mean she is, how her mother won't ever take her shopping and only cares about her job. The girl sitting adjacent to her senses the sadness and matches it by complaining about her father and how he only cares about her little brother. Then the kid across the table picks up on the tragic quality of the themes and condemns her little brother, whom she hates and who is always getting her into trouble. Then participant number four deftly augments the despair by bringing up a boy in school who's spreading rumors about her; she breaks into copious tears, bottoming out in the depths of depression. Next, quiet prevails; a respectable period of mourning ensues. Then suddenly one girl starts to giggle and says something slightly amusing. The next young lady adds to the newly initiated reverie and laughs heartily. By the time the fourth child has matched hilarious moods with the others, all four are laughing. These girls are all phenomenal at reading moods and matching them. In contrast, a less perceptive socializer might encounter the girls in a state of total mania and say, "Oh, we have that big test tomorrow, don't we." Or else they may all be commiserating over their tragic life circumstances when a social misreader comes by and tells a joke—flagrant misreading and mismatching of moods, an early adolescent big-time taboo.

Before he started to make social progress, Doug's teacher reported to his mother a revealing tidbit. She picked up on the fact that whenever somebody bumped into him in the corridors, Doug had no way of determining whether it was intentional or not. In other words, Doug could not read the evidence, the multiple signs that would tell him whether or not the collider in the hallway was out to get him or whether that fleeting body contact was just an accident. Social information processing includes reading people's true intentions, their feelings, their facial expressions. It also takes in the ability to interpret upper limb gestures, the hidden meanings in the way other people move their hands and their arms—pretty subtle but highly revealing. On my farm in North Carolina, I love to watch the way my swans communicate with their necks; different positions connote anger, threat, apprehension, or sheer vanity. People are no different, but we use our limbs and facial expressions instead of our necks to transmit nonverbal social messages.

Children like Doug also are prone to difficulty conceptualizing friendship and popularity. They simply don't understand what such terms entail and require from them. As a result they sorely lack the internal blueprints they need in order to build and solidify relationships. The table below summarizes some important social behaviors.

IMPORTANT SOCIAL BEHAVIORS

Function	Explanation
Conflict resolution	The ability to resolve conflicts with other people without resorting to aggression
Monitoring	The ability to watch how you're doing while relating or interacting with someone
Self-marketing and image development	The ability to maintain a good public image and "sell yourself" to others appropriately
Collaboration	The ability to cooperate and work with others as a partnership or team effort
Reading and acting on social information	The ability to interpret social incidents, people's actions, and gestures and to comprehend concepts such as friendship

Additional Influential Factors

We don't really know how kids become effective social thinkers. Like other features of a neurodevelopmental profile, this is the end product of environmental, cultural, social, familial, and genetic influences. It is common for a family of four children to include one offspring who is phenomenally popular, one who happens to be somewhat socially controversial, a third child who appears indifferent to the social scene, and a fourth whose life is a continuing saga of brutal peer rejection. It is always tempting to assume that children learn all their social skills from their parents or older siblings. But we now know social equipment is encoded from the moment we're born, and some little babies have it, while others are destined to grow up hearing, "Sorry, this seat is saved." While it's not the whole story, a substantial amount of social ability is inborn.

Your child's social thinking system often joins with some of his or her neurodevelopmental systems. For example, tight control of attention is needed to stop and think about friendship and avoid committing impulsive acts that might alienate potential pals. Attention also allows for the close monitoring of what you're saying and doing socially—you can tell when you're starting to irritate your friend. It shouldn't come as a shock that a sizable number of kids with weak attention controls also experience peer rejection and social desolation.

As I mentioned in discussing social language, a child's verbal capacity never ceases to affect interpersonal transactions and relationships. Motor prowess can be a big social marketing plus; athletes often have an easier time making friends. By integrating these contributions from the other systems with its own closetful of tools, social cognition can enable a student in school or an adult doing a job to mobilize the people skills that dramatically increase his effectiveness and quite often his happiness as well.

Some kids actually voluntarily resign from the social scene. They don't particularly care to make use of any of the social cognitive functions we have mentioned. Not every individual needs or wants to be popular. Some children tread a pathway toward rugged individualism; there are those who enjoy being loners. I was very much that way as a kid and remain so as an adult. In fact, recently a colleague described me as "a loner with good social skills" (one could do worse, in my opinion). I vividly recall as a young child having neighborhood children come to our door and ask my mom, "Can Melvin come out and play?" Meanwhile I'd be at the top of the stairs, whispering fervently to my mother, "Tell them I'm not home." In high school I never attended football games. I think I've only been to one or two basketball games in Chapel Hill (from both of which I fled prematurely). I don't attend class reunions. Weddings are outright torture for me; I try to feign illness when constrained to attend such doings. Cocktail parties are unbearable. When entertaining at our own home, my wife expresses indignation over the fact that I inconspicuously retire to bed long before our guests have left. In all of these contexts it's not that I don't like the people, it's the formats I'm unable to tolerate. I enjoy other people—in tightly regulated doses and in small groups.

Now back to the world of children: sometimes kids reject the values or culture of their classmates. Others pull out because they don't want to emulate a popular brother or sister, and still others secede from the social union because they enjoy being by themselves. I for one love to hear about kids who can "entertain themselves for hours on end." My own mother said this about me—with mixed feelings. Such autonomy has to qualify as a possible strength. In any case, it is reassuring for us rugged individualists (kids and adults) to feel that we are not being forced to retreat out of a lack of social capacity, that we do have the wherewithal (if not the stamina) to relate well when and if we have the inclination to do so. Effective social language and behavior have the potential to make life easier and more gratifying for most individuals.

Parents have to hope that a child's social success doesn't come at too high a price. In my opinion, the very best social capacity gets put to its best use without a child or adolescent sacrificing or undermining her unique identity or individuality. At all ages children are under intense peer pressure, which has the potential to bring with it stifling conformity. The pressure motivating kids to be just like all the others gets turned up especially high during middle school, which is when many surrender individuality and free will to garner acceptance. They feel compelled to talk, walk, act, and dress like everyone else. They may become enslaved to rigid standards of coolness, which then take precedence over competing values (including sometimes the quest for academic excellence). In so many respects, to be cool requires a kid to be pretty ordinary. What a waste, what a tragedy, when potentially extraordinary individuals select that pathway. Kids with insufficient social capacity may have an especially hard time coping with peer pressure, knowing how much to capitulate and how much to be oneself. They need our help and understanding and they all should be demystified to understand how social pressures and social cognition carry on their active dialogues in school all day.

✎ ARE SOME KIDS TOO SUCCESSFUL SOCIALLY?

I know some strikingly affable youngsters who suffer mega-overdoses of interpersonal glorification. They experience so serious a case of social euphoria that little else matters in their lives. Some become globally socially distractible, unable to concentrate on anything other than the latest arriving love notes or fan mail. Their social obsessions can divert them from work and from all previous interests and intellectual or athletic pursuits. Such overwhelming preoccupations are especially common among adolescents, particularly some with academic underachievement. We witnessed the unfolding of this in the case of Karl and Susan earlier in this chapter. They clearly have become addicted to each other and to their peers and are likely to awaken at age nineteen or twenty only to realize that their friends are gone and that they are left with little or nothing (perhaps not even each other) to show for their recent years of social ecstasy. They paid way too high a price.

One of the sharpest changes is seen when a child who has never been particularly popular in elementary school becomes either physically attractive or more socially effective in seventh or eighth grade. That interpersonal rookie of the year suddenly experiences a power surge of high-voltage social gratification. This almost orgasmic sense of acceptance can become so intensely pleasurable that she or he gives up on all other values in life and seems to become totally preoccupied with popularity. Among other complications, it can lead an early adolescent to reject her family and become resentful and critical of parents. This is not an unusual scenario. Social attainment can be too hot to handle when you've never had it before.

Interpersonal ventures during adolescence not only feel right to kids, they also comprise ironclad protective armor. Anyone who has ever observed a group of teenagers prowling around a shopping mall can't help but notice how powerful, how invulnerable each member feels as part of a group. They are willing to say and do things when they are part of the group that they would never consider as individuals. Many teenagers are overwhelmed with fears and trepidations that temporarily vanish when they merge themselves into a group. The protection is helpful—as long as they don't pay too high a price for it.

The social tides do not always flow predictably and evenly. Children can have their interpersonal ups and downs over the course of their school years. Caring adults should certainly keep an eye on the evolving pressures that students impose on one another as they age. Let's understand these developmental trials.

ﾓ MINDS OVER TIME: KEEPING A WATCHFUL EYE ON SOCIAL THINKING AS CHILDREN AGE

During the first several years of school, kids reveal their growing social thought processes. If social development is occurring on schedule you should see some give-and-take in their interactions with friends, in contrast to the parallel play and monologues commonly observed in much younger children. It is possible and desirable to keep an eye on your five- to eight-year-old while she is interacting with peers and note whether she can communicate with social appropriateness, show some insight into a friend's feelings and needs, resolve the inevitable conflicts with friends smoothly, and do some reasonable sharing of experiences and possessions. Throughout elementary school kids strengthen their friendships, are able to call friends on the phone, and have serious discussions with and about them. By fourth grade some students start to emerge from their social larval stage as popular, while others get progressively neglected or rejected. Bullying may rear its grotesque head at this point. Parents need to be aware if and when their kid is developing a negative reputation, becoming rejected or bullied, and try to understand which of the social function(s) described in this chapter she or he may need to work on.

Children in late elementary and middle school come to recognize how thoroughly and often ruthlessly the juries of their peers are judging them. Most live in a state of constant precaution out of fear of exclusion or open repudiation. They feel compelled to watch their step, realizing that they can be disparaged for wearing outmoded garb, hanging out with the wrong kids, listening to unacceptable music, or unfashionably styling their hair. It is much like living in a tyrannical society; the ruthless dictators are the other kids. The pressures are especially intense from fourth through ninth grade. Of course, there are some very special heroes in this age group, children who know how to resist the pressures and just be themselves.

Peer pressure is always on the verge of triggering a self-esteem implosion during middle and high school. Many students in secondary school are wondering whether to play the game or buck it—seek popularity or be yourself. It's a tough decision, a common personal dilemma. Happily, most of them resolve the quandary in a healthy manner; they eventually gain a healthy level of social acceptability while still managing to be true to themselves. But the social pressure never abates.

§➥ PRACTICAL CONSIDERATIONS

• Parents should serve as sympathetic and open-minded social sounding boards. Kids should sense that they can confide in caring adults and tell them about any social setbacks or dilemmas they are facing. When children confess their interpersonal glitches, their mothers and fathers should be all ears, suppressing their parental instinct to swoop down and preach or offer glib (usually unhelpful) advice or bland reassurance. It is actually preferable for a parent to say, "Wow, that must have been incredibly embarrassing for you" than to say, "Whenever that happens, just ignore those guys." He can't. Kids crave empathy, a secure sense that they are not in the fray alone when they deal with what they consider earthshaking social disasters.

• Parents need to provide social tutorial support for all kids. Children need to hear about their parents' social and political career problems. They need to discuss ways of nurturing good relationships with teachers and peers. Parents should provide some informal social feedback. For instance, after going to a concert or a ball game with a child and her friends, the parents can offer a few privately communicated insights regarding any social conflicts that arose among the peers and encourage the child to elaborate on her perception of what took place.

• Parents have a right and an obligation to inform the school when a child is being actively repudiated, made fun of, or bullied by classmates. If the school is unresponsive, the parents may need to appeal to the school board or, in a worst-case scenario, consider taking legal action. I have been involved in several such avoidable dramas. In one case a twelve-year-old was being called a "fag" by others of his age group because he didn't play sports, liked classical music, loved making pottery, and dressed more like "some kind of grown-up." This kid was subjected to punishing physical and verbal abuse nearly every day. His parents finally appealed to the principal, who assumed a "boys will be boys" attitude and was openly unsympathetic, and unwilling to take any action. The parents and I, as their pediatrician, were outraged. They hired a lawyer and threatened to sue the principal in a civil suit. Soon after, the school adopted a zero tolerance rule for bullying. All schools must aggressively outlaw and if necessary punish all bullying, absolutely banning all weapons of verbal and physical abuse. All students should be helped to recognize the shameful immorality of bullying and conspicuously rejecting others, of intentionally causing someone to suffer misery. They should know the difference between teasing (which is pretty natural and often friendly) and the infliction of humiliation (which is morally unacceptable).

• Dangerously low levels of social capacity represent weaknesses that a lot of people contend with (most without realizing it). However, they should not be thought of as diseases or disorders. They are deficits that need work. Therefore, terms like Asperger syndrome (commonly applied nowadays to kids with social gaps and strong areas of interest) are needlessly pathological in their connotation. Let's say instead that a good kid needs some social assistance.

• All students should learn formally about social cognition and social behavior. Throughout this book I have stressed the need for kids to learn about learning while they are learning. Equally salient is the need to learn about socializing while socializing. Students should have a chance to review case studies of individuals with varying patterns of social success and frustration in and out of school. They should be taught the terminology (such as "code switching" and "conflict resolution") contained in this chapter. My book *Jarvis Clutch—Social Spy* is being used as a textbook in some middle school classes, which I think can go far to aid social understanding and to sensitize kids to the values and abilities that come together in their interpersonal lives.

• One or more popular kids can mentor a student who is enduring widespread rejection. In some cases it may seem less threatening if the socially accepted student is at a higher grade level in school. I know of a case where a patient of mine who had managed to suffer one social shutout after another in his fifteen years was sent off to boarding school. During the first semester there, Tim managed to reestablish his friendless existence in a new setting. The headmaster of the school, one of the most deservedly prominent educators in America, called in the school's number one premier athlete-scholar, had a very long talk with that boy and requested that he room with Tim and "help him get along." He explained how deeply unhappy Tim was, which really touched the very popular boy, who agreed to the change in roommates and became almost a big brother to Tim. The two grew quite close over the next couple of years. Tim was allowed to come out of his shell. Peer social tutoring had triumphed in the end.

• Some children benefit from counseling or a formal curriculum in social skills. There are many effective programs that can be investigated by parents and teachers of kids who feel the pain of loneliness. One successful model of social training encourages children to undertake group activities (sports or field trips) and then return to discuss at length the social episodes and interchanges that took place. Videos of the actions and dialogues can also be helpful.

• Children who seem too socially conscious might benefit from some short-term educational counseling regarding the potential downside of their social preening. In many cases, however, they may not welcome this dampening input. There are adolescents who need to explore every possible limit of relationships before they can develop some perspective.

• Everyone should support and celebrate kids who crave and plead to "march to their own drummers," those who are willing to paddle against the tides of social conformity. Probably every child should try this to some extent, since they all should assert a degree of social independence. A couple of years ago, I met an eleven-year-old girl in California whose pediatrician wanted to put her on Ritalin because she was missing social cues and was therefore too isolated. But Laura insisted she didn't want to take medication. When I asked her why, she answered, "Because I'm eccentric. I like being eccentric. I like sitting on that rock reading poetry during recess. That's the real me. People think I'm out of it. But I'm not. I'm just plain eccentric and doing my thing. Ritalin might make me like everyone else. Why can't I be Laura, the real thing?" Ritalin aside, if your child enjoys reading poetry atop a boulder, encourage her, even at the risk of her reputation. If your son passionately loves collecting moths but that makes others think he is a totally weird thirteen-year-old, you might still help him expand his impressive moth collection anyway! Let's empower kids to arrive at these self-affirming conclusions. We must celebrate their distinctiveness—to say nothing of their valiant social courage.

10

When a Mind Falls Behind ✑

The habits of a vigorous mind are formed in contending with difficulties. Great necessities call out great virtues.

ABIGAIL ADAMS, quoted in David McCullough, *John Adams*

"It kinda looks like I was born to lose."

"I don't do anything right when it comes to school."

"I just can't wait till I grow up—when I only have to do what I'm good at."

"School makes me feel completely and totally worthless."

"All my friends catch on to stuff faster than I do."

"The other kids in my class are smarter than me."

"Here's what keeps happening: I get a little behind, but I don't feel like dealing with it, so I put it behind me. Then I get more behind and I don't feel like bothering with it. And then I'm too far behind to do anything about it. And that's the way it happens every year."

"I think my parents would trade me in if they could."

As these self-deflating, melancholy quotes suggest, repeated frustration has the potential to downgrade a kid's estimates of self-worth. At any distance along the academic track, your child's mind could derail. For example, a college student may discover that the heavy dose of terminology in zoology is more than she can handle, despite the fact that she was in the top 10 percent of her high school class. Well into adult life, a certified transmission specialist may plummet into a career tailspin when having to incorporate some brand-new automobile computer technology. An effervescent six-year-old who has consumed the early phases of kindergarten like a hot fudge sundae suddenly may develop a school phobia because he can't seem to match up sounds with the right symbols for reading words. So it is that as the demands increase and change over time, different kinds of minds are likely to prosper or founder.

Most kids simply lack the insulation to handle repeated frustration and personal failure. Some simply surrender. Some become permanently anxious or depressed. Others act out, cause trouble, get themselves pregnant, or take drugs. Still others become transformed into conservative non–risk takers, shutting down and decisively writing themselves off at an early age. Or else they keep criticizing and putting down whatever it is they can't succeed at: "Algebra's useless; I'm never going to use it" or "There's no way I'll ever need to speak Spanish."

None of the frustration complications has to occur. As parents, you want to make sure they don't occur. The first preventive step involves understanding your child's neurodevelopmental profile and being able to anticipate the demands that will be made on it. As one mom stated to me, "She's doing okay in school now, but what worries me most is the future. Latisha has to work so hard to get her thoughts on paper, and it's too difficult for her to commit any set of facts to memory. Next year the writing and memory demands are going to explode in our faces. I'd like to do something about it now—before she fails and gets totally frustrated or loses every bit of her desire to learn."

❦ Constructing Neurodevelopmental Profiles

As I've said, step one in helping any struggling kid is to have a decent picture of her neurodevelopmental profile plus the current state of her academic skills and her knowledge. Search for highly specific strengths and weaknesses, which may or may not be obvious. Direct observations by parents and teachers and the use of multiple sources of information can be like developing a photograph of your son or daughter. I've looked to my own undergraduate education for inspiration in this regard. As a junior I took a class on the American novel, during which Professor Van Nostrand stressed over and over again that if you wanted to understand the author's true intentions in writing *Moby-Dick* or *The Scarlet Letter,* you were obliged to search for recurring themes, patterns that keep coming back in different chapters at different points in the unfurling plot. In the very same manner, this search for recurring patterns should take place whenever we want to understand a child's brain wiring. When we think about a child, we integrate the results of specific tests with the observations of parents, the reports of teachers, direct discussions with the student herself, and a close analysis of samples of her schoolwork. No one source of information is ever admissible as the final word, the ultimate answer, the twenty-four-karat-gold standard. It is only by weaving the strands of evidence that consistent themes emerge sharply, much like the emerging patterns on a sweater in the process of being knitted. At that point we feel confident we have a reliable imprint of a child's profile. We may then work out ways to help that child come to terms with current academic needs.

Clarence was a seven-year-old from Tulsa whom I saw at our center several years ago. He was strikingly handsome and very skinny, tall with long blond hair and a four-inch ponytail. His arms were encircled with various homemade shoelace, cord, and lanyard bracelets, as were both ankles. This boy was exceedingly shy. I usually have little or no trouble establishing rapport with kids, but I just couldn't connect with Clarence. His parents confirmed he was a man of few words. He was brought to me because he had serious problems with writing and spelling. He was often hesitant in his speech, and when he spoke tended to use single words and phrases. In class he sometimes looked confused or disoriented. He was also a daydreamer. Yet Clarence could and did concentrate on his work and always finished all of it. He was never overactive or impulsive in school or at home. He slept well and was well organized in keeping his room neat and in getting things done on time. Additionally, Clarence loved working with his hands; he was a terrific artisan, creating his own jewelry, and tinkering with found objects he would redeem from neighborhood trash cans and other equally exotic repositories.

When he warmed up (a bit), Clarence told me he loved artwork of all kinds and wanted to design toys when he grew up. He confessed that he hated reading and writing and didn't like being called on in class. Because of his shyness, Clarence was a fairly isolated kid; he neither sought nor had close friends and tended to be in the neglected category at school. Clarence avoided competitive games and was perceived as clumsy. When we tested Clarence, we uncovered extraordinary abilities in fine motor function, spatial and sequential ordering, and all the facets of his memory that we examined. On the other hand, Clarence was obviously struggling with language, more so expressive than receptive. This was confirmed by studying some writing samples from him; they were typical of a child with language difficulty. His uneven reading comprehension further confirmed language delays. We observed excellent attention controls, although mental fatigue and poor focus on detail were evident during and only during language testing.

This suggested that his language-processing struggles were eating away at his otherwise good attention. It was also clear from his history that Clarence was manifesting social thinking problems, especially involving the verbal requirements for relating to other people. From his history and from our own observations we could see that Clarence was becoming a good problem solver, a strong conceptualizer, and a highly creative kid; in other words, he displayed solid strengths in some all-important higher thinking areas.

Everyone who knew Clarence reported that he was an anxious child, lacking in self-confidence. That's not at all unusual among kids his age with underdeveloped language. So it was that by pooling information from his parents and teachers and from Clarence himself and then combining this with our observations on testing and in samples of his work, we were able to assemble a neurodevelopmental profile of Clarence. The quest for recurring themes enabled us to account for his problems in writing and spelling, while helping us plan for ways to keep emphasizing his impressive array of strengths.

ஃ IDENTIFYING THE BREAKDOWN POINTS

Problems with learning can be divided into six sometimes overlapping areas of weakness:

1. Trouble mastering skills
2. Trouble acquiring facts or knowledge
3. Trouble accomplishing output
4. Trouble understanding
5. Trouble approaching tasks systematically
6. Trouble with the rate and amount of demands

Trouble Mastering Skills

We are all expected to become proficient in the venerable three Rs, reading, riting, and rithmetic. In keeping a well-informed eye on your child's academic fortunes or misfortunes, you need to be aware that skill learning also takes place in threes, namely the skill layer, the subskill layer, and the neurodevelopmental function layer.

Academic skills are composed of groups of specific subskills. For example, reading contains two subskills: decoding (figuring out the individual words) and comprehension (getting the overall meaning). The subskills of writing include letter formation, spelling, use of good language on paper, mechanics (punctuation and capitalization), organization, and the generation of ideas for writing. Subskills like these, in turn, result from various mixtures of the neurodevelopmental functions I have discussed throughout this book. Different neurodevelopmental systems become involved in attaining various subskills. So language plays a dominant role in learning to decode words during reading and the memory system is our cleanup hitter when it's time to take on the multiplication tables.

Neurodevelopmental functions become stronger the more your kid uses his subskills. So it takes good language functions to learn to read, and if you read enough, those very same language functions grow ever stronger. By exercising your memory to learn math facts, not only do you assimilate those evasive facts, but also your memory gets stronger. Regrettably a very different plot, a much sadder one, unfolds when a child has trouble acquiring a skill. Let's suppose you have a child who has some specific language deficits that have impeded reading. Reading becomes a struggle, and even when it improves, it may be that your child doesn't much like to read, reads as little as he can get away with, and, when reading, doesn't really have his mind sufficiently engaged. Meanwhile his friends are reading with gusto and commitment. And as they read, their language abilities are strengthening, whereas your minimally reading son fails to get any real language boost from his life with books. Then, say at age fourteen, he has two reasons for language problems: he still has the gap he started with plus he never got the verbal acceleration that comes from active reading experience.

Similarly, if you have some gross motor dysfunction, you will most likely shy away from sports, in which case your gross motor abilities will stagnate rather then strengthen over time. Meanwhile, your next-door neighbor with the awesome biceps, cool jock that he is, has been playing basketball for all it's worth, so his gross motor coordination is getting better and better. The gap won't stop widening.

One of the redemptive features of reading and writing is that as you climb upward in school, the curriculum in these skill areas does not mandate any totally new subskills. Obviously, you need to get better at using the ones you picked up earlier, but there is an implicit promise that there'll be no add-on subskills. Unfortunately, this kindly pledge is not forthcoming in the case of the third R, arithmetic, for in mathematics, virtually every time you turn your brain around they challenge or, maybe better said, taunt you with a new potentially ego-threatening subskill to conquer. To make matters worse, new math subskills have old math subskills sequestered within them. Accuracy in the subskill of multiplication is your pay-as-you-go admission fee for the more advanced subskill of division. Moreover, you need both multiplication and division to qualify for entry into the subskill of algebraic equation solving. (One often hurtful way communities let kids know they don't have a lot of respect for their intelligence is by informing them they will have to take "business math" instead of algebra.)

Once we pin down a lagging subskill, however, we can launch our search for recurring themes, for bits of evidence that come together and reveal which neurodevelopmental dysfunctions are getting in the way.

Let's suppose your third grader is struggling and faltering in some aspects of mathematics. In this case we discover that a subskill, namely the ability to solve word problems, is the primary mathematical obstacle for this student. We then can ask our informed selves: Could she be fostering a dysfunction within the capacity of language, a gap that makes it hard for her to understand the wording of word problems (Chapter 5)? Does she have trouble with recognition memory, a dysfunction preventing her from recognizing familiar words or phrases that suggest the need for multiplication or subtraction (Chapter 4)? Is it hard for her to recall facts or processes while solving word problems (Chapter 4)? Does she manifest signs of weak problem-solving thinking (Chapter 8)? Or, alternatively, could it be a case of weak attention to detail? The mystery is likely to be solved by sifting through these multiple sources of evidence:

INFORMATION SOURCES IN THE SEARCH FOR RECURRING THEMES
Background information from parents (parents should always be part of the assessment team).
Observations made by teachers (teachers have front-row seats as observers of neurodevelopmental function in action).
Examination of typical samples of a student's work (examples of writing, math, and artwork are open windows offering spectacular views of a student's neurodevelopmental systems).
Educational history in the earlier grades and preschool (revealing clues are found in a student's earlier performance).
Direct testing of relevant neurodevelopmental functions (including neurodevelopmental examination, neuropsychological assessment, motor evaluation, and/or language testing).
Achievement testing (especially analyses of specific subskills and their breakdowns).
Intelligence testing (but not if IQ gets used—abused—as the so-called gold standard).
Asking the student (don't ever forget to have the student evaluate or diagnose himself).

It should be clear that specificity is important. We can and should identify precisely which are the weak links in the way of learning skills.

Trouble Acquiring Facts or Knowledge

Some students struggle in vain to amass the background knowledge to make sense of a particular academic arena. There are those who can't conquer the content of invertebrate biology, the leaders of European countries, or Spanish semantics. Such specific knowledge abysses lead to disenchantment and anguish for many kids. Having a well-stocked storehouse of knowledge makes new learning more meaningful and relevant. Knowledge provides attachment points for new information. Kids who don't know very much have to start reading the newspaper!

In investigating knowledge shortcomings, we need to consider first of all whether the student is sufficiently focused, whether his attention controls are operating for learning. We also should be aware that some students lack knowledge as a result of their incomplete understanding of the content. This consideration dramatizes the intimate connection between understanding and remembering. It's much tougher to remember facts that you don't understand than it is to store those you do. We can also see content-specific deficits of knowledge (affecting, say, only dates in history or parts of the human body) in students who are having problems filing and accessing information in long-term memory (Chapter 4). One or another form of memory dysfunction can dramatically slow down and reduce the accumulation of factual information. Here's a good example:

There is a kid named Max whom I observed in a school I've been working with. Everyone likes Max. In addition to possessing a coterie of dependable friends, he is widely popular at school and in his neighborhood. He is also a clever artist who draws whimsically surrealistic cartoons. He is a confirmed animal lover. His golden retriever, Beethoven, is his twin. Beethoven won't leave home without him.

In a class discussion, Max always can be relied upon to introduce some of the most incisive ideas. When you converse with him, he seems incredibly smart, with his expansive vocabulary and keen analyses of complex ideas. Despite all these pluses, Max manages to earn very poor grades in school.

Some subjects are particularly trying for Max. Although he understands and likes mathematics, he runs into trouble taking math tests because he works too slowly. He told me when I chatted with him in the lunchroom that he knew the multiplication tables but that it took him a long time to remember them. While doing a problem, he has to think too hard and too long about facts like how much 8 times 9 is. Important bits of knowledge don't exit automatically from his memory.

Max puts it this way: "I know I'm good at thinking but there's stuff in school that I can't ever remember. I'd rather figure out something than have to remember a whole lot of things. It's real hard for me to remember things quickly, like on a test. In science the teacher gave us a test on the periodic table and I couldn't remember most of the elements and their symbols. I thought I knew them, but I guess I didn't. I like science classes and doing experiments and stuff like that, but, boy, did I bomb out on that test—and loads of other ones too."

Max's candid reporting would make me suspect he might have a neurodevelopmental problem with factual long-term memory. Such a memory crevasse may have been preventing the accumulation of knowledge in certain school subjects. We'd want to do further testing of his memory and undertake some careful evaluation of Max's test papers to confirm that hypothesis. If a memory deficit turned out to be the case, then we would demystify Max about his specific breakdown and help him develop a personal bag of tricks to enhance his remembering. Too often in the past kids like Max were given only diagnostic labels, told that they had LD or weren't studying hard enough. It's only in recent years that we have been able to go well beyond the labels and identify specific obstructions to success. To do so requires open-mindedness and, as we have seen, the close collaboration of teachers, parents, clinicians, and the child.

Trouble Accomplishing Output

Over the years I have been especially interested in a group of students who do not so much have difficulty with learning but instead have trouble with output. I call the phenomenon developmental output failure. Affected students are seemingly lazy individuals with low academic productivity. They have baffling trouble completing homework assignments, difficulty studying for tests, and problems meeting deadlines. Their overall output in school can be disappointingly minimal. Work is too hard for them. In evaluating such puzzling students, I have come to the unequivocal conclusion that there is no such thing as a lazy kid. When a child is manifesting low levels of productivity, there are substantial underlying reasons for the phenomenon. The output problems could be the result of any of a number of neurodevelopmental dysfunctions that we have described in the earlier chapters of this book.

Trouble Understanding

A perfect example of chronic misunderstanding can be found in Sue, whom I've known for about a year. When teachers call on Sue, a sweet, well-dressed sixth grader from northern Virginia with long jet-black hair, she often has trouble figuring out what to say. That's because most of the time she doesn't fully understand the question despite the fact that she knows the answer. She has plenty of ideas, but she has trouble putting them into words and sentences.

Her parents and her teachers firmly hold that Sue is intelligent, but all feel let down when they encounter what she says and writes. She loves to think about politics and current events—Hillary Clinton is her role model—but she can't translate that passion and focused knowledge into fluent speech. This saddens her, because she believes it will wreck her chances for a successful career in public service. This girl feels terrible about her school performance; she believes she has let everyone down. Nobody dislikes Sue or makes fun of her; they just don't know her very well because she's so reserved.

Sue has just as much trouble getting her ideas onto paper as she does transmitting them orally; so reports and tests earn her a steady tide of negative feedback. While much of school is difficult for Sue, there are some things that come easily for her. She is, in fact, an instinctive musician. She plays the clarinet and composes her own music. She's also great at sports and computers.

Although Sue is fully competent when it comes to reading out loud, she is superficial at understanding and weak at remembering what she has read. She has only a minimal grasp on the meanings of hard words.

Sue's caught in a dangerous vortex: her reading and writing weaknesses are making her language problem even more of a problem. According to her teacher, "Poor Sue seems to get further and further behind every day." So it is that Sue's language dysfunction is thwarting comprehension.

However, some very good things were done for Sue. First, the school's language consultant saw her on several occasions, observing Sue in class a couple of times. Then he met with Sue's teacher, and then separately with Sue and her parents. All were helped to understand Sue's language deficits and the impact they were having. Sue kept a small spiral notebook and marked down things in class that were confusing to her. Each evening she would e-mail her teacher with the points she found hard. Her teacher was diligent about sending her back some clarification, which Sue's parents helped her understand. This modest intervention has helped Sue tremendously. She is feeling more confident and faring a lot better academically in seventh grade. Her mom mentioned to me over the phone recently, "I think it has also helped Sue a lot to know that she has a language problem. Before that she had convinced herself that she was mentally retarded. At least now she feels she has a problem she can do something about."

As mentioned earlier, besides language, a wide range of dysfunctions also inhibit a child's ability to understand his schoolwork. For example, if your child has trouble with her attention controls, she may fail to understand what the teacher is saying because she regularly tunes out and so misses out on important details. If you have a child like Max with weakness of long-term memory, he may have a problem mobilizing the correct stored knowledge needed to interpret a new morsel of information. Students with tenuous concept formation may become confused when confronted with subject matter that contains some key concepts.

Trouble Approaching Tasks Systematically

School presents students with an ever-expanding smorgasbord of tasks for completion. Worksheets to be completed at home, three-inch-thick books to be read in two weeks, examinations that demand careful preparation, creative projects in art, science, and social studies all compete with one another for time and space in the minds of students. Happily, most students discover effective ways of tackling tasks, methods that combine efficiency with quality. But some students never get there.

Children with weak attention controls often fail to acquire effective approaches to tasks. Take Stan. With his unruly red hair, bright blue eyes, and infectious smile, my patient Stan has a clever sense of humor and an imagination that knows no limits. On some days he does well in school; he hands in his homework and gets good grades on tests. But on other days he just can't seem to do anything right. He can't remember how a pulley operates or crucial facts about the Oregon Trail. Stan's parents and teachers tell him that they know he's smart, that they know he can do the work when he tries. Stan thinks he's always trying, and is truly confused when he is told that he is not.

When Stan attempts to sit and listen in class, his mind drifts away like a tide. Last week the teacher said something about the sky being cloudy. Stan started to think about the sky, and within two minutes, Stan was becoming socially accepted on a distant planet while his teacher had switched to math and was explaining the word problems from yesterday's assignment.

Even when on task, Stan is unsystematic and his work is error-filled. His teacher wrote on a questionnaire we sent her, "Sometimes I have to stand there and slow Stan down. Otherwise, he acts as if every assignment, every worksheet, every book he reads is some kind of frenzied speed trial."

Because it has the potential to slow him down, you won't be surprised to hear that Stan hates to check over his work; he declares such quality control way too boring. When he tries to stay focused, Stan will sit in his seat with his right arm extended over his head so that his hand is playing with his earlobe. He will tap the desk with the five fingers of his left hand while wagging his two feet like a pair of dog tails—anything to try to concentrate, which is difficult.

"You know, my head's the same as a television set except it has no re-mote control so I can't choose the channel I get. All the programs turn on inside my head at the same time." That must have made it hard for him to have a clear enough mind to do things in a systematic fashion. Stan added, "I hate schoolwork because I always make a mess of it. To tell you the truth, half the time I don't even know what I'm doing—I just do it, that's all. What-ever comes in my head I do. And you know what? I mostly mess up. There's lots of stuff I don't know how to do, and nobody ever tells me how to do it." Stan worries about himself. "Sometimes I hate myself," he once told me. "I think about dying a lot. Dying would be easier than going to school. I hate school. And school hates me." Stan was obviously depressed, and I referred him to an excellent child psychologist in his hometown. And because Stan had not acquired his own personal manual of approaches to tasks, he needed to be shown and supported over time. I am happy to report that Stan attended a truly great school and got the support he needed. Among other things, a special educator taught him some good study skills and guided him to perform tasks slowly, one step at a time. In high school, Stan, along with several of his zany friends, has been publishing a monthly satir-ical comic book. He also devotes a lot of time to his own Web site, which is loaded with his far-out ideas and drawings. He says he wants to study jour-nalism in college. There's no sign of any depression in the new Stan.

Even when they don't contend with attention control problems like Stan's, some students just plain don't seem to know how to go about doing things. They have no techniques for studying for tests, planning a report, accomplishing projects in a reasonably systematic and efficient manner. Some of them, in turn, are what I call "nonmethodologists"; they are devoid of strategies that might make work easier and more successful for them. Thomas typifies this very prevalent pattern.

Several years ago, Thomas, a seventeen-year-old high school junior, was struggling academically. This adolescent was a svelte athlete, a nearly myth-ical figure on the varsity basketball and track teams. He was a potential Olympic decathlon contender. He was the "all American boy" so many moms dream of. He was likewise an object of heavenly reverie for a train of his female followers. But Thomas was experiencing unsettling academic discomfort despite the fact that he was motivated and diligent. I interviewed Thomas as part of our evaluation of his learning difficulty. I made use of our standardized interview called STRANDS (Survey of Teenage Readiness and Neurodevelopmental Status), which we administer when trying to get at the neurodevelopmental profiles of kids over fifteen. The interview is based on the premise that through a carefully orchestrated discussion with a high school student, you can find out where his educational breakdowns are occurring while also uncovering his strengths. The following is a revealing, brief excerpt from my interview with Thomas:

LEVINE: "Thomas, if you had a history quiz tomorrow, how do you suppose you would study for it tonight? Please don't tell me how you *should* study for it. Tell me how you actually *would* study for it."

THOMAS: "I guess I would go over the stuff."

LEVINE: "Thomas, can you please tell me what you mean by 'going over the stuff'?"

THOMAS: "Yeah, I would just go over it all."

LEVINE: "Excuse me, Thomas, but what does that actually mean, just going over it?"

THOMAS: "I'd go over it. Like I'd go over like my notes and maybe the book."

LEVINE (in one final attempt): "What does going over it involve specifically?"

THOMAS: "I don't know. I just like kinda go over it."

If I were to ask the same question of an honor student, I would hear the following answer: "Well, let's see. I think I'd go over all the material in my notes, the textbook, and recent homework assignments. Then I would try to figure what's most likely to be on the test tomorrow [selection control], then I would figure out how to make it easier to remember, how I could put all of this in a form that makes it not so hard to learn [filing systematically in long-term memory], then I would try to find out whether or not I knew what I thought I needed to know. I mean I would test myself. I would probably have to do that testing before I went to bed and then again when I got up in the morning. I could also get a friend or my mom to quiz me."

What's the gaping difference between those two responses? It's pretty obvious. The honor student is a master strategist. He carries around a satchel of tactics for approaching tasks. Thomas just does things. He doesn't think in terms of methods, clever devices, and ways of making schoolwork less painful and cumbersome.

You can divide a class of students or maybe even your own children at home into the methodologists and the nonmethodologists among them. The methodologists are the ones who pause and ponder the best available techniques before they do something. The nonmethodologists just do things. As we have seen, strategies are at the core of all systematic problem-solving processes. It turns out that for some kids strategies are a deeply engrained habit of mind, while others reveal no such tendencies.

The parents of disorganized students have to help their children become methodologists. Parents may need to guide a student through the steps of test preparation. For some kids strategies feel natural; for others they never seem to fit right. The latter need to be taught some clever tactics and perhaps even bribed or coerced to deploy them. When taught mind-saving techniques some students I've met have insisted they aren't helpful. Britt, a nineteen-year-old patient of mine, admitted one day, "Dr. Levine, I'll tell you the truth. I have taken so many courses on study skills I think I could teach them to anybody who'd listen. I just don't happen to use any of them myself." This heavy partying undergraduate was fresh from having failed two subjects in the first semester of his freshman year.

Strategic teachers promote strategic planning throughout the curriculum. They are able to model effective techniques and also encourage students to experiment and develop personal methods that work well for them. They convey the notion that in the long run, it is more important to employ a good strategy than it is to arrive at the correct answer. They have kids describe the methods they've used or plan to use, so that other children in the classroom can share their strategies. I observed one middle school science teacher who had everyone submit study plans before preparing for an end-of-semester test. The students had to delineate the steps they were going to follow in learning and making sure they knew the material. They then shared their plans in a class discussion and together they developed a master study plan that included a checklist they all could use while studying for the test. Parents were informed of this, so they could reinforce the need to stick to the checklist. The principal told me that this teacher had been implementing this process for several years and that most of the students used the checklist (with personal modifications) in other subjects. Parents should assist in grafting on methodological approaches to tasks. Hopefully, some affection for strategy can be instilled. Sooner or later, the nonstrategists in your family could be converted.

Trouble with the Rate and Amount of Demands

Samantha was a painfully slow information digester, yet no one could stop her on ice, where she elegantly displayed precision balance, elastic agility, and jetlike velocity. But Samantha's gross motor exploits on the rink contrasted dramatically with her labored and clumsy forays into classroom performance.

In school Samantha was forever striving to catch up and often tripping in her efforts to recover lost ground. In sixth grade she was feeling mentally depleted as the accelerated information flow overtook her brain's processing speed. Samantha's mind maintained a rhythm of slow processing. She was a competent student when she could work at her own rate, but frequently she was outpaced on tests and during classroom instruction. Understandably, watching her classmates thinking and producing work at a much faster clip made Samantha feel awful.

Certain students, much like Samantha, have minds calibrated to function at a slower than average pace. In some cases accuracy, incisive in-depth thinking, and a commitment to quality output in place of mass production more than compensate for slow processing. Without realizing it, people who think relatively slowly eventually may trade off speed for quality—not a bad swap unless you're penalized for failing to answer all thirty questions on a quiz in thirty minutes. Many students I know have learned to use various strategies to deal with their slow processing. They borrow a friend's notes after class, or they go home and do a lot of reviewing of what they didn't quite get during class. Others just give up.

Often, like Samantha, the students are thought to have attention deficits and get placed on Ritalin or some other stimulant. Regrettably, they get labeled ADD, while the unrecognized issue is that they can't process data quickly enough. Even worse, the kiss of academic death, some get called "slow learners," a term frequently deployed to write a kid off as having "low potential."

I think teachers need to reevaluate the speed demands they impose on students. There are hardly any careers where you need to think as fast about entirely new subject matter as you do in school. Within a career relatively redundant information gets conveyed and dealt with from day to day. That makes it fairly easy to interpret those messages that exceed the speed limits of your processing. In fact, you can figure out most things before you even listen to them or look at them. That's the value of experience in a career. Kids lack that duration of experience in social studies or chemistry. They are likely to feel inadequate when their brain's rate is calibrated to operate more slowly than the inputs are arriving and the outputs are expected to be departing.

It is vitally important that teachers and parents identify students who are slow processors and not consider them abnormal or deviant persons. That just happens to be the way their minds are set. We need to ensure they are not being humiliated, and that those who don't have coping strategies are taught some so that they can avoid scholastic calamity. Parents should be able to observe that their child is being left behind by the rapid flow of information in one or more subjects in school. Such students need a great deal of review at a slower pace.

As I mentioned earlier, the sheer amount of input and output doesn't level off throughout a student's school career. Therefore, there is a need to process and produce ever-heavier information loads. Bridgett was a girl whose kind of mind much preferred to deal with smaller chunks. I recently evaluated Bridgett. This was an intellectually sharp kid who was a classic underachiever in sixth grade. During her assessment, we read Bridgett some complex sentences and had her interpret them, since sentence comprehension is a revealing window on language competency in elementary school. Bridgett's performance was nothing short of awesome. She could interpret speedily the most convoluted sentences; syntax that would confuse most fifteen-year-olds was transparent to her. But then I read her a rather lengthy story containing language far less challenging than that of the sentences. I asked her to summarize the story I had read to her. Bridgett was unable to do so with any coherence whatsoever. She omitted key details and was ponderously disjointed in her retelling. Also, she was unable to answer the most basic questions pertaining to the lengthy passage. Later she became confused in the middle of a multistep math problem, losing her place.

Bridgett buckled under the load when required to handle large amounts of input or output. Her learning difference was a quantitative one: the quality and speed of her processing and production were better than average but broke down when faced with a lot of material. As students go on in school, volume demands expand like watermelons during their growing season. Reading assignments stretch out in their page length alongside expectations for extensive writing, ever lengthening lists of new vocabulary words, and a proliferation of large-scale science projects. Students like Bridgett often need help dividing tasks into manageable, bite-sized chunks if they are to tame the volume giant. And schools need to reexamine their curricular demands while asking whether it is the case that more is always better. Pascal, in corresponding with one of his compatriots, once wrote apologetically, "I have only made this letter longer because I have not had the time to make it shorter."

So here are two additional sources of vulnerability in a child's development during the school years: Can she or he keep pace with the *rate* demands? Can she or he deal with the ever-growing *amount* requirements? These are questions that have fairly obvious solutions: we can adjust the rate, and we can either reduce the volume or break it into more manageable chunks. It is also true that over time kids can improve spontaneously in both the rate and the volume of information they handle and synthesize. Tragically, sometimes the rate and volume demands outpace the growth of a student's capacity to handle them. So, even though she is improving, the gaps are widening.

❧ WHEN BAD THINGS HAPPEN TO GOOD PROFILES

Up until this point I have discussed students whose neurodevelopmental profiles make it hard for them to handle the demands of the curriculum. Their abilities don't fit with mandated requirements. But there is another aggravating mismatch that creeps up and may be even more prevalent. This occurs when a student's neurodevelopmental profile collides with a particular teacher or (even worse) a particular parent or (still worse) a particular pair of parents—often because they are too demanding. When a child is struggling, we must always evaluate the fit between him and his adult bosses at home and in school.

What takes place when a teacher's ways of teaching clash with a learner's ways of learning? No matter how good each of them is, they were not meant for each other. Chaos, discord, accusation, and anger often ensue. Stan, our redhead with attention deficits described earlier in this chapter, drove into an oversized academic pothole in the person of his third grade teacher, Mrs. Browning. This was a highly compulsive, meticulous, perfectionistically driven, bottom-up model of a woman, a stickler for detail. When she asked a question there was one and only one acceptable answer (not good for a kid like Stan with his free-ranging mind). And Mrs. Browning demanded strict disciplinary compliance. One parent characterized Mrs. Browning's class as "boot camp for nine-year-olds." Some mothers and fathers admired this teacher, convinced that she was offering kids the firm structure they needed at this age. Others deplored her rigidity. All agreed that Mrs. Browning, just two years short of retirement and in her thirty-fifth year of teaching, was no softy. As might be expected, there was a total mismatch in the relationship between Stan and Mrs. Browning. She had no tolerance whatsoever for the boy's inconsistent work output, his daydreaming, and his free associations. She mercilessly got on him for changing the subject during class discussions. She often put him down in front of other students, calling him a space cadet. Other kids laughed, and Stan felt humiliated. Stan hated school that year, sometimes heading for bed weeping the moment he got home. Mrs. Browning was earnestly trying to help Stan "shape up" (as she put it to his mother).

When asked to write a poem during class, Stan submitted an uninhibited verse criticizing Mrs. Browning. She was not amused and Stan was sent to the principal's office.

In direct contrast, Stan's fourth grade teacher adored him. She loved his sense of humor. She ran a rather unstructured classroom, a platform in which creativity and risk taking were rewarded. Stan sparkled, and came into his own in that more flexible and accepting milieu.

Max, our patient with memory dysfunctions, bumped heads with a science teacher who equated learning with memorization. The kids had to learn and repeat the chemical elements, various phyla in biology, and the different configurations of cloud formations in their unit on the weather. Spot quizzes were the rule. Max got two warning letters for being "unprepared." He suffocated in science during a year in which he was a star in his religion class, which focused on morality and ethical issues. Max said he hated his science teacher (who was not much of a Max fan either) and worshipped his religion teacher (a fitting relationship).

Sue, our girl with language dysfunctions, pretty much hit the wall in fifth grade with Mr. Collins, who loved to lecture. He almost never went to the board (his handwriting was illegible); visual clues and direct experience were absent on his unisensory professorial platform. All of his tests were essays, as were most homework assignments. Sue was sunk, dwelling in constant fear of being called on in class. Her ways of learning were at loggerheads with Mr. Collins's ways of teaching.

Disconcerting mismatching also occurs between kids and their parents. Stan is an example of this. At home Stan was always late. His room was a mess. He procrastinated when it came to chores and was never ready to leave the house with other family members. Meanwhile, Stan's father was neat, punctual, and fastidious in his work habits. Stan's sister was a copy of her father. His mother was somewhere between the two but generally productive and organized. Stan's father was exasperated with Stan and embarrassed by him too. Stan was aware that he was letting down his dad, a feeling of guilt peculiarly fortified by the knowledge that he was an adopted child. His dad once confessed that he loved Stan but didn't like him, and was convinced that Stan would never be able to hold down a job. This was not what he had in mind for a son. There was constant tension between the two.

In facing these conflicts, should we be trying to rewire the child or instead should we modify the environment and alter our expectations? Or should we do both? We have to keep in mind the many modes of success, gratification, and accomplishment that are possible in the adult world. A family or a classroom containing a mind that can't seem to go with the prevailing flow needs at least to consider accommodating a different sort of flow.

Often no one is at fault when the styles of parents or teachers are counter to the learning patterns of a kid. Both sides need to put some work into the relationship and try a healthy dose of compromising and mutual acceptance. The very same transactions must occur among adults in the workplace. It is not at all unusual for an employee to have a manner of working that clashes with a supervisor's expectations or managerial style. Dealing with these disparities during childhood and adolescence is good practice for later life.

ᑌ MINING A CHILD'S PRECIOUS ASSETS

In the process of channeling our well-motivated inquisitive zeal toward uncovering breakdowns in the learning process, we must never neglect the ultimately far more important mission of diagnosing a child's notable strengths and special knacks (such as an interest in music or American history or coins). Such positive attributes can become the levers that help kids make the grade in school and beyond. All children harbor such gifts. We can't neglect them. I'll elaborate on these priceless qualities in my final two chapters.

Giftedness

Some children are described by their parents and teachers as "gifted." Presumably they are among the lucky few who possess super-neurodevelopmental profiles. The extraordinary functioning of their minds is often documented by a high IQ score. They are often eligible to take advanced placement courses or to participate in a program reserved for the gifted. I have a few problems with this. First of all, there's no such thing as a perfect mind. Therefore, every gifted child has some discrete areas of weakness that could cause problems someday. Furthermore, every child I've ever met has had at least one area of potential or actual giftedness as part of his or her neurodevelopmental profile.

ᑌ IDENTIFYING AND UNDERSTANDING EMOTIONAL COMPLICATIONS

When I give talks to parents, teachers, or clinicians I am accustomed to being asked, "How can you tell whether a child has a real learning problem or some kind of emotional problem?" I have to remind people that kids can and often do have both. Additionally, there's a well-traveled two-way street: emotional problems can erode and weaken neurodevelopmental functions, and neurodevelopmental dysfunctions frequently lead to emotional turmoil and behavior problems. If your child is chronically anxious, his or her anxiety will weaken attention and also memory over time. If your child is depressed and withdrawn, he may not express himself and elaborate, a tendency that can stand in the way of expressive language development. Conversely, if your child suffers language difficulties and doesn't realize it, and experiences repeated failure in school, his frustration can lead to anxiety, depression, or a tendency to act out and become defiant, perhaps in a vain effort to save face.

Repeated failure inflicts penetrating wounds in a child's psyche. I have found that four states of mind are especially susceptible to harm in the face of academic frustration: motivation, feelings and moods, self-esteem, and behavior. I'll describe these separately, although they often are jointly affected when children are led to believe that they are disappointing their parents or teachers.

Motivation and Its Depletion

It is not unusual to hear the comment that a particular kid would start doing well in school if he could get himself motivated. I tend to respond to this statement with lightly veiled indignation: "I believe this kid will get motivated when he starts doing well in school!" Motivation is complicated. Success nourishes motivation and motivation makes further success more likely. Failure dampens motivation and a lack of motivation makes continuing failure a near certainty. The neurodevelopmental systems require constant exercise if they are to stay in good shape. Such persistent use is partly dependent upon motivation to learn, that is, a willingness to absorb and endure the risks that go with new and ever more demanding brain challenges. For some kids, motivation is spontaneous. Others don't experience it at all. Some simply give up. Those who have surrendered have been described as experiencing "learned helplessness." Such individuals come to feel that their fate is not in their own hands, that factors beyond their control determine what will happen in school. Believing that you're just not smart enough or that you were born to lose or that you're an unlucky person wipes out any motivation and eradicates all academic incentive.

Generally speaking, an individual is motivated if he finds the goal attractive. He is motivated if he believes he can attain the goal. It is hard to get up for something if you're pretty sure you're going to fail at it. On the other hand, you become motivated if you believe that a desirable goal is achievable without superhuman effort. If it's going to take too much work to get somewhere in life, it may not seem worth the expenditure of energy. Thus, a student may lack motivation because he doesn't particularly see the attractiveness of learning a subject or succeeding at a skill. Even more commonly though, a kid exhausts all motivation by believing he will never be able to make the grade or somehow measure up in one way or another. Why try if you're not going to do as well as your big brother or your younger sister? Why try if you can never meet the standards or the example set by your parents? (Mothers and fathers need not even declare openly that they want you to do as well as they've done or perhaps better; it is power-fully implied by the example they set and/or the values they espouse.) Why try if your teacher always finds fault with what you do?

When an academic skill is not yet fully automatic and takes too much time and energy to do, then motivation may be extinguished. We frequently see this among students with writing problems. Their output difficulties are so formidable that they conclude that a homework assignment is just not worth attempting. In a strange, almost bizarre mind trick, they may even believe that they have done it. They are then accused of lying by their parents and teachers. Somehow they deceive themselves into thinking that if they just forget about it, the work is somehow done (by gnomes?). This is a sure sign of serious motivational loss. Motivational drainage also commonly takes place among kids who have trouble mobilizing mental effort. They fly into a dark cloud of mental fatigue when they set out to accomplish a tax-ing school task.

Distinctions have been made between internal and external motivation. Internal motivation stems from a genuine desire to accomplish something for its own sake. For example, a kid might be internally motivated to learn more about venomous snakes because that is an area of interest to him. External motivation is motivation that has some outside incentive associated with it. For example, a sixteen-year-old may lack any heartfelt desire to learn a foreign language, but an honor grade in German will help her to be accepted at a good college. That external stimulus fuels her motivation.

Nearly paralyzing pessimism can undermine external motivation. A child may hold a dim view of his future and its possibilities. He may react by giv-ing up. Some students deal with their lost motivation and pessimism by seeking alternative pathways toward gratification. Often this entails forming abnormally close attachments with groups of peers, many of whom may be just as academically disinclined, disenfranchised, and disillusioned. Also, it is not unusual for an unmotivated student to denigrate anything or anyone making him feel inadequate. Typical refrains include: "Nobody else likes that teacher," "I'm never gonna use Asian geography anyway," and "School is full of useless stuff they make you learn." Tragically, an individual who expresses these sentiments may travel through adulthood excusing himself from work by knocking the work. A lifetime of eloquently rationalized in-action may unfold.

Obviously, we would like kids to possess both internal and external mo-tivation. Sometimes attractive role models can instill internal motivation as well as ambition. Parents should expose a child to such individuals, espe-cially when that child is short of motivation.

Kids do not normally suffer inborn motivation deficiencies. I like to think that all kids enter the world prepared to become motivated. When we encounter one who is unmotivated, the questions focus on where, how, why, and when motivation was depleted. The job is to restore that force by making the goal more attractive, by seeing to it that the goal is somehow attainable, and by easing the effort required through effective strategies and sensitive teaching. We also can intervene by identifying those areas of life in which a child seems motivated and exploiting those realms energetically. When it comes to motivation, it is safe to say, "When there's a way, there's a will!" If a student can find a way to succeed he is more likely to have the willpower to succeed.

Feelings and Moods that Interfere

Moods play an important role in the drive toward success and satisfaction in school. Some kids are handicapped by dangerously high levels of performance anxiety, as they take every learning event or test too seriously. As one high school freshman confessed to me, "I'm so busy worrying I have no time left to study." For a student like her, each exam seems like the acid test of her competence and the final word on her worth and destiny. Excessive anxiety can interfere with attention and also with memory. Some kids become so anxious they develop flagrant school phobias. They either refuse to attend school or develop troublesome bodily symptoms on school mornings, resulting in a high absenteeism rate.

Anxious students have to be taught to cope with stress more effectively. They need to learn how to stay cool while taking an exam. Somehow they have to convince themselves that single isolated events in school are not the ultimate determinant of success in life. A test, assignment, or class period is trivial in the long run. This obvious point is not evident to kids with stultifying levels of performance anxiety.

Some students don't have enough anxiety. They are simply too "cool," much too laid back. A reasonable level of tension actually is beneficial when taking examinations or responding to other academic and social pressures. Students who are too uptight and those who are not uptight enough are all at a disadvantage. Sometimes kids are medicated to help them overcome the negative effects of anxiety. In the long run, it would be preferable for children and adolescents to be helped to regulate their own moods, to stabilize these feelings and to become more reality-bound rather than having to consume a drug to cushion their apprehension throughout their lives. Parents have a tremendous role to play in preventing the onset of anxiety and depression, largely by helping kids feel good about themselves, by providing an optimal family life, by showing their offspring that they respect their strengths, and by infusing a powerful sense of optimism about their future. Although this approach may not always work, it is likely that it will decrease significantly the amount of antidepressant medication that is prescribed each year.

When anxiety becomes chronic and out of control, an individual may start to exhibit signs of depression. The symptoms include self-critical comments, a loss of interest, extreme sadness, sleep problems, and even thoughts of suicide. While some individuals may be deemed genetically predisposed to depression, it is important for parents, teachers, and clinicians to uncover any underlying neurodevelopmental dysfunctions that may be inciting anxiety and, ultimately, depression. Quickly placing all these kids on antidepressant medication is not the answer. It's a Band-Aid, sometimes just a cosmetic coverup. Medication may be helpful, but there is a compelling need to seek out possible sources of a child's or adolescent's feelings of inadequacy. One of the earliest warning signals may be a loss of self-esteem, often in the form of expressed feelings of inferiority or a tendency to give up on oneself too easily and too soon.

Self-esteem that Dwindles

Pride is basic. We all have a well-entrenched need to believe in ourselves, an inner drive that manifests itself early in life. There are many ways in which people can feel good or bad about themselves. Thus, a child can hold negative feelings about her ability as a student but feel great about herself socially. Adults can compartmentalize their self-esteem as well, perhaps feeling good on the job and inadequate as a family member (or vice versa). Intellectual self-esteem, feelings a child experiences regarding how "smart" she is, tends to be brittle throughout every student's years in school.

It has been shown that sometime in middle school kids decide whether or not they possess intellectual ability. Before then they can't quite make up their minds about their own smartness. During high school their opinion changes surprisingly little. Kids who think they're not too bright keep on thinking that way. Kids who have confidence in their intellectual abilities continue to believe so. These kinds of self-perceptions often become self-fulfilling prophecies. If you truly believe you have intellectual ability, you are more likely to demonstrate intellectual ability than if you think you don't have any. Solid confidence in one's own learning ability is what I like to call intellectual self-esteem.

Some kids with neurodevelopmental dysfunctions that are interfering with learning become convinced that they "have no brains." In this way, they overestimate the permanence and the extent of their imperfections. This is really a shame because everyone is intelligent in one way or another.

Each individual should come to appreciate that she has one or more intellectual specialties, applications of brain function for which she is admirably wired. Many kids require counseling to recognize that some people are well rounded in their intellectual abilities while others are much more specialized. Both kinds of minds are needed and worth valuing.

When kids suffer from perilously low intellectual self-esteem, they can become internally enraged. They feel trapped. Day after day the formal educational process humiliates them, a daily reminder of their cognitive inferiority. Children have very little tolerance for these buried negative sentiments, for these abysmally low feelings about themselves. In some cases, those with deficient intellectual self-esteem are condemned to daily embarrassment in the classroom, and they may become emotional powder kegs that could ignite at any time. These students are exquisitely susceptible to all the dreaded adolescent/young adult catastrophic outcomes, including serious substance abuse, depression, juvenile delinquency, teenage pregnancy, and dropping out of school. Obviously, a lot is at stake. Therefore, a high priority for every family, for every school, and for our society in general has to be the fostering of some type of intellectual self-esteem in every kid. Kids who grow up feeling that their minds are globally defective are definitely in peril.

Every student has a fundamental need to respect his own particular kind of mind and its potential ways to shine. In seeking such routes toward gratification, parents should stress to the child that he is using his mind exactingly. For example, if a child becomes proficient at restoring cars, he should realize that the effort has a very heavy intellectual component, that it is mind work, not just body work. If a kid loves animals, she should be helped to see that her affinity represents an achievement of her mind.

Behavior that Thwarts Learning

It is well beyond the scope of this book to provide a comprehensive overview of the wide range of behavior problems that can be found in students who are not succeeding. Instead, I would like to cite some of the common mechanisms underlying such misbehavior.

Some children get in trouble because they contend with a dysfunction that not only impairs learning but also reduces their self-control. This is often the case among kids with weak attention controls. A student so affected may commit an aggressive act or say something totally indiscreet because he failed to preview before acting or speaking (page 77); his "bad act" was actually an eruption of impulsivity. This occurred repeatedly in the life of Stan. In fact, even he often couldn't believe that he did or said the things he did or said.

We have seen how some children with expressive language problems reveal rather violent or at least unstable behavior because they can't use language to cool themselves, slow down, and think through stresses or behavioral decisions; they lack verbal "self-coaching" of their behavior.

Many children with low social-thinking capacity (Chapter 9) are perceived as having behavior problems. In reality these are kids who simply may not know how to resolve conflicts with others or how to converse in a socially ingratiating tone of voice. They are frequently misread as being defiant, arrogant, or rude.

Some students feel driven to act out simply to save face. They would much rather be perceived as a bad boy (or girl) than as a dummy. Or a child who feels totally inadequate in the classroom may assume the role of the class clown. By volunteering to be the hilarious jester, he diverts attention from his shame caused by delayed oral reading ability. In such instances, the class clown is truly a sad clown.

HOWS INSTEAD OF WHYS: FOCUSING ON IDENTIFYING AND FIXING THE BREAKDOWNS INSTEAD OF THEIR CAUSES

The stress should be on *how* a child is the way she is rather than *why* she is the way she is. I don't think schools and parents should be investing a lot of time, effort, and resources speculating about why a kid is having trouble processing language, playing sports, or making friends. As a mother or father, you should not be wasting your time wondering, "Is all this my fault?" "Could it be from all those ear infections he had as an infant?" "Is he a 'chip off the old block'—stuck with his dad's worst genes?" Instead, you should observe and think about the relevant neurodevelopmental functions, the mechanisms rather than the causes for his woes. All too often searches for causes are biased. People seek and find either what they were trained to find or that which they find most interesting. Also, you can seldom prove a cause, and speculation can be harmful. If I suggest to a mother that I think her kid is having language problems as a result of the ear infections he had as an infant, that mom will suddenly recall all those times she failed to give the amoxicillin for the full ten days or neglected to bring her infant back to her pediatrician for an ear check. She will blame herself—needlessly believing she damaged this child's delicate brain. If I state that I think her kid's problem is mostly genetic, she could conceivably say to herself, "They told me not to marry into that family. I guess I should have listened." Or she might lament quietly, "We never should have adopted her." So, since you can never prove with certainty that any cause was *the* cause, you should skip the whys and instead devote sensitive thinking to describing and understanding your child's neurodevelopmental status and the best way to care for that profile.

As we have seen, brain functions are conditioned by a multitude of influences. If an eighth grader has trouble expressing herself, the cause could be cultural, biological, environmental, anxiety-based—or, most likely, the product of a blending of factors. Think of these functions as main highways; many roads flow into them during the school years. How directly the functions are able to get you to where you want to be depends upon all the converging influences we have described.

Once we have sketched the relevant features of a neurodevelopmental profile we can color in the portrait with other useful information regarding that child's current functioning and needs. These additional factors are enumerated in the list below:

The child's emotional status
The presence of any serious family problems
The child's physical health
The quality of education the child has received
The condition of the child's skills and subskills

❧ THE BENEFITS AND DANGERS WHEN A CHILD'S MIND IS TESTED

It is common practice for struggling kids to undergo detailed assessments of their performance either in or out of school. Because I personally am heavily involved in many of these diagnostic evaluations, I may be biased, but I do think well-conducted, open-minded, and thorough evaluations can be vital in helping parents and teachers unravel and address the complexities of disappointing school performance. However, such diagnostic dissections sometimes can be especially hazardous to intellectual health and well-being. Parents and schools have to be vigilant because so many assessments harbor built-in biases. First and foremost, it is important that a *team* of individuals, not just a single clinician, examine kids. The lone clinician may have serious limitations in his or her professional education. There is an overriding tendency for people to see in a child either that which they were trained to detect or that which they are interested in. So if a clinician has a fascination with depression, there is a likelihood that a large proportion of the kids he evaluates will appear depressed to him. But maybe they're not!

Oftentimes when a school evaluates a child, budgetary limitations and special education laws distort the diagnosis. A school may not want to uncover a problem that it lacks the funds to deal with. Such conflicts of interest are widespread, so parents need to shield students from their effects. They can do so by suggesting that if a kid is complicated, if his problems are not readily apparent and soluble, there should be an outside team evaluation. All Kinds of Minds, the institute I founded, has been working to organize and train objective assessment teams across the United States to work within Student Success Centers. These eclectic multidisciplinary evaluation programs are highly specific in identifying breakdown points, strengths, affinities, and dysfunctions in children with learning difficulties. They then formulate recommendations that fit within a system we call Management by Profile (Chapter 11).

It is common for a school to evaluate a student in order to determine if she or he is eligible for special education services. That child presumably will be served if and only if testing uncovers a significant difference between an intelligence level (IQ) and achievement test scores, evidence that she is not "living up" to her "potential" (for what, I might ask?). Such formulas have been shown to be invalid in multiple recent research investigations. Also, as a parent you should be aware that having your child evaluated to find out if he is eligible for services is not really a full evaluation of his strengths and weaknesses; a lot of important findings can fall through the cracks. Ironically, children who do not qualify for services have been found to be nearly identical in their needs to the ones who do qualify.

IQ testing is a mixed blessing. So often parents have related something like this: "He tested low on his IQ test but we can't believe it. He has so many good ideas and seems so bright to us." This may sound like some kind of rationalization or denial of reality, but quite a few academic psychologists of the mind now acknowledge that there are many different kinds of intelligence. Intelligence tests test relatively few of these. Also, parents and teachers beware: the vast majority of neurodevelopmental functions I have described in this book are *not* brought out on any of the standard intelligence tests in common use. Therefore, many key deficits and strengths can go undetected when there is too much reliance on intelligence testing. I know some kids who ought to exercise a right not to have their intelligence tested. They run the high risk of having their minds misrepresented by a score.

I have encountered many students who have had their IQ measured four or five times as their parents shopped around for evaluations. I am often struck by how inconsistent these test scores tend to be. Pity the kid who had but one intelligence test. A repeat test two years later might have looked like a test of a different person's mind. Maybe all kids should have either no such tests or many of them (take the highest score). On the other hand, I've worked with many skilled psychologists who make excellent use of intelligence testing to arrive at highly perceptive and relevant observations about a child's patterns of learning and coping without overrelying on overall scores. Additionally, results of the subtests of an intelligence test can help us in our search for recurring themes.

❧ Roadblocks and Outcomes in Adulthood

This book has focused mainly on neurodevelopmental variation during the school years. I have thus far mostly neglected the challenges faced by adults. This seeming oversight results largely from the fact that this is a book about the minds of children. Nevertheless, I have been told repeatedly that my lectures cause many adults to experience a case of painful neurodevelopmental flashback. That is, mothers, fathers, teachers, and clinicians keep recognizing themselves as I describe their children. Most readers must have experienced some sharp pangs of self-recognition. Consistent with the structure of *A Mind at a Time,* I offer a gallery of small portraits that testifies to the continuing influence of neurodevelopmental variation well into adulthood. Most often, the origins of these adult struggles can be traced back to specific breakdowns during the school years.

John recently lost his job. He is a master automobile mechanic at a General Motors dealership. He has been fired for excessive absenteeism and showing up late for work. This was his sixth job in two years. Wherever and whenever he gets a job, he soon starts thinking of jobs he'd rather be doing. He has always been a night owl and has had trouble getting up for work in the mornings; he had the same problems on school mornings as a kid. His manager reported that John was unreliable and erratic. When he was on, there was no one better at troubleshooting a defective car. But there were days when either he wouldn't show up at all or else he would be there and would accomplish almost nothing. John had many signs of adult attentional dysfunction.

Louise has often felt totally inadequate. At age forty-nine she was comfortably employed in the claims department of a major health insurer. But late last month the company converted to an entirely new computer system. She has had a difficult time with the new program and is resentful of the change. Down deep in her heart, she wonders why she has been unable to acquire the new skills. Her self-esteem at work has been decimated. It feels like déjà vu as she remembers enduring very similar levels of agony learning new processes in mathematics when she was in middle school. Procedural memory limitations remain a haunting hindrance in her life.

Merrill was close to the top of his class in medical school. He was the first pick of Metropolitan Hospital for its intern group. Now seven months into his internship year, the hospital faculty fears they've made a costly error. Merrill is seriously behind in writing up daily notes on patients. He is four months delayed in dictating discharge summaries. It takes him forever to work up a patient. He is driving the nurses into a state of hostile delirium. His patients admire and take to Merrill because he is so caring and spends a great deal of time with them. But the staff and his fellow interns are distressed with his unacceptably low level of productivity. Merrill has an adult form of output failure. By the way, I regularly receive telephone calls, e-mails, and faxes regarding such disappointing interns and residents from medical centers all over the country. Most of them were highly successful medical students, particularly affable and also deft with rote memory. In medical school you can excel by deploying colossal memory function and astute political acumen. The latter is used to convince the orthopedic faculty that you love bones, the dermatologists that you find the epidermis fascinating, and the ear, nose, and throat professors that you are heavily committed to nasal passages! Such political aptitude is of little value in preparing orders and writing up cases on the hospital wards as an intern or resident.

Corey alienates everybody around her every time she says anything. There is something about her tone of voice and choice of words that comes across as callous and abrasive. She works hard and is productive in her position as an administrative assistant at a large accounting firm. But she is forever letting everyone know how hard she works. She insistently and incessantly promotes herself, talking about the formidable jobs she is doing, inserting such personal commercial messages most recently at the office Christmas party. Nobody is interested in what she's saying, but Corey is unaware of this. What she can't fathom is why it is that she has applied for promotion to office manager four times over the last six years and has been passed over on each occasion. This fifty-one-year-old woman is totally unaware of her own wide gaps in political and social cognition.

Pam and Roger enjoy a pretty decent marriage. They have three teenage kids, and have good jobs. She's a paralegal, and he teaches high school music. Their home life is chaotic. Roger can never find anything; as soon as he puts something down, it vanishes. He usually blames his spouse or one of the children for the disappearance. His closet and dresser drawers are stuffed and unorganized. His wife is much neater, but she is in a perennial time warp. Pam is late for everything. She lacks any instinct regarding the passage of time, how long anything will take to complete, or what to do when. Her temporal disorientation has been a slight problem at work and a mammoth one at home. She goes off shopping at 4:00 P.M. and returns at 7:45 to find a starving throng who were about to call out the National Guard to track down a lost mom. Here's a question: Is it better if a married couple have opposite organizational problems (like Pam and Roger and the author and his spouse, Bambi) or the same organizational problems? What happens if one spouse displays organizational disarray and the other is fastidiously organized in every way? Finally, there is the all too common scenario in which both parents are reasonably organized and they are trying to live with a son or daughter who is hopelessly disorganized. Tolerance is called for, although it seldom comes easily.

These examples are not terrible ones. We know that serious tragedies befall many individuals who have experienced too much failure early in life. Our prisons and mental health facilities are filled with defeated egos. In talking to a woman who runs a drug rehabilitation program for addicted adolescents, I asked her, "What is it that these kids have in common?" Her response was, "None of them could do the work in high school." Indeed it is common for success-deprived kids to seek escape and refuge in a world of induced ecstasy or perhaps to savor gratification chemically if they can't access that feeling through accomplishments.

Devastating problems are most likely to ensue when learning difficulties are combined with other risk factors, such as poverty, excessive exposure to violence, and serious family turmoil. Lest we dwell too heavily on the negative side, however, I should point out that there are many instances of neurodevelopmental conquest in adulthood. To portray a few:

Penny was an insatiable child who grew up to be a highly ambitious entrepreneur. She was utterly oblivious to fine detail in school but eventually started up a brilliantly successful Internet business, took plenty of clever risks, and has been remarkably innovative. She cannot handle the day-to-day financial details, but she has a great administrative staff, none of whom are creative thinkers. Unlike Penny, they are in no danger of producing original ideas for the business. She wishes she had had them in school helping her with all the minutiae that used to defeat her.

Young Pablo was a restless student all the way through school. From the early grades, he was hopelessly distractible. He would sit in class and glance around at every accessible irrelevant visual stimulus. He loved to doodle. Pablo felt compelled to draw bizarre figures and refused to desist despite repeated admonishment from his teachers. Eventually this boy became one of the great artists of his century. If he were in school now, there is a strong chance he would be labeled "oppositional defiant disorder" because he would not stop drawing. Or, his distractibility could lead to his labeling as "ADD." Or, because he was so fixated on artwork, he might be described as having "obsessive compulsive disorder" or Asperger syndrome. There's a fair chance he would have submitted to normalization with large doses of frequently changing medication. It's unclear what that would have done to his artistic flair.

I recently saw a twelve-year-old boy with spatial ordering problems, along with graphomotor dysfunction. This student had markedly deficient nonverbal thinking; he could only reason and conceptualize with language. He showed gaps in spatial memory too, but he was a world-class linguist. His verbal understanding and output were comparable to those of a high school student—and then some. When I explained my findings to Kenny's parents, his father insisted I was also describing him to a T: "I've always been just like that. To this day I can't put together the simplest jigsaw puzzle." I responded, "That seems pretty implausible to me. You have been so highly successful in your career designing fiber optic networks. You told me that's how you made your fortune—by accomplishing something no one has been able to do. It seems to me setting up a vast fiber optic network takes remarkable spatial thinking." He interrupted: "No, Dr. Levine, not at all; I did what I did with my strong language ability. Unlike so many others I know, I have the ability to explain complicated things in a way anyone can understand. I'm a great communicator. That's how I attracted all the venture capital I ever needed. I knew how to convince the investors that it was worth doing and that I was the one to do it. And you know I never graduated from high school because I just couldn't get anything down on paper. We didn't have laptops back then."

Here's a personal fallibility fable: I have never had acceptable spatial ordering, but I've always been a competent linguist. I undertook my first year of medical school at Oxford in England. Over there, anatomy was stressed with somber intensity. Every week we had a quiz at the site of our compliant cadavers. My lab partner, Malcolm, a very quiet dignified Eton graduate, never said much (in retrospect I'm sure he had trouble with expressive language), while I never could be muted. His superb visual motor abilities and my two left hands led to the tacit concurrence that he would do most of the dissecting. When we had our oral quiz (called a "viva") on the arteries of the lower limbs, Malcolm pointed out each blood vessel to the professor while I named it. He could never remember their names, and I absolutely could not picture where any of them went. We both got honor grades in anatomy. He's now in some operating theater in London, and I'm at home writing a book. I'm pretty sure there's a moral to that story.

Another first-person account: a couple of years ago I was about to take off on a flight to San Francisco when a portly, balding man wearing blue jeans and a polo shirt bearing words something like "Blue Sky Natural Gas Pipelines" entered my row. He wore several small portable phones on his wide black belt. The man was carrying an oversized, scraped and dented aluminum attaché case. He managed to fit more than snugly into the window seat adjacent to mine, with some lateral abdominal invasion of my territory. He urgently ordered a Bacardi and Coca-Cola from the flight attendant and then opened his clandestine vault. I, an incurable sociological voyeur, could not help spying on its contents. Inside were one pair of multicolored spotted polyester pajamas, a well-worn toothbrush, a disposable razor, multiple esoteric meters, some tangled black and yellow wires, several impressively fat technical manuals, and three fairly typical airport newsstand paperback novels, one of which he removed and started reading with laserlike intensity. This person was the very model of a modern, highly successful techie. We took off, and after three to four hefty rum infusions (versus my lone tomato juice with lime), with little or no eye contact, he started to converse with me about how much he was loving the novel. Then Dr. Mel Levine, the ever probing neurodevelopmental intelligence agent, asked, "Have you always loved to read?" "No, not at all. I could hardly read when I was a kid. Then at age twenty-six I got into natural gas and had to read manual after manual for my equipment. I subscribed to three different natural gas and pipeline magazines or bulletins and I read them too. Then out of the blue, I got to be a damn good reader. Now I love to read. I read every story I can get my hands on. I learned how to read by reading stuff I really needed, stuff that was interesting to me too. Now I read everything. I read everywhere, like even when I go to the bathroom." There are many individuals who ultimately develop strong skills and functions by doing so within their niche, their chosen specialty. Eventually their expertise provides the nutritious loam for growing some skills. This is the way out of a neurodevelopmental wasteland for many individuals who ultimately make it.

There are lessons to be learned from these vignettes. The stories expose the ongoing saga of neurodevelopmental profiles and their impacts on careers. We have not dwelt on the effects of these differences on family life, including marriage and parenting. What is it like to be the child of a parent who has trouble expressing himself? If you're a disorganized kid but your mom is even more disorganized, what happens to your organizational troubles? Might difficulty with social language or social behavior encroach on marital stability? The effects of neurodevelopmental functions and dysfunctions quite obviously play into the overall life and happiness of every adult. Matters can become tragic when an adult is struggling without understanding what that struggle is all about. An undiscovered neurodevelopmental breakdown is far more hazardous than it needs to be. It is especially tragic when a person consumes large doses of antidepressant medication because she chose the wrong career pathway, one in which there was a precarious mismatching of her profile of strengths and weaknesses to the demands of the job. Drugs don't mend problems with communication, memory, or social cognition, although they may cover them over for a while. Chasms between demands and capacities keep on damaging egos, sometimes irreparably. Those affected need sensitive and knowledgeable help and should try to get it from mental health specialists and others who have a well-informed grasp on neurodevelopmental variation. There is so much to gain and too much to be lost. Failure to get help can be catastrophic. Your child has possibilities for authentic gratification and fulfillment in life. It is our job to interpret and celebrate his or her particular kind of mind.

11

Getting a Mind Realigned (but Not Redesigned) ᔥ

Our chief want in life is somebody who shall make us do what we can.

RALPH WALDO EMERSON, *The Conduct of Life*

ᔥ MANAGEMENT BY PROFILE

How do we get minds to work? How can we make sure that different kinds of minds work in ways that are right for them? How do we immunize our kids against the complications that follow a losing streak in school? How do we rescue those who are not liked the way they are? And how should we respond when they don't like the way they are? Answering such questions requires a logical and systematic approach to the educational care of kids. Over the years, my colleagues and I have developed what we call the Management by Profile system. I like to use the term "management" because we are not aiming for a cure nor do we particularly care to totally rewire any developing mind. Rather, I as a clinician and you as a parent should want to manage a kid's profile without necessarily striving for radical reform (which may not be a possibility anyway). Good management ensures that the problems won't worsen, that we will be preventing complications, that we will do our best to fix important breakdowns, and that we will be helping a kid get the most from the way he is. The word "profile" comes into play as we have made use of it throughout *A Mind at a Time*. We don't manage in isolation loose attention control, a reading delay, or material disorganization. Instead, we manage a profile, a defined balance sheet of our children's strengths and weaknesses. The educational needs of a child with mental energy control problems and superb language skills are going be different from those of one who has similar attention problems but additionally carries the burden of receptive language dysfunctions. That is why we have to manage profiles rather than isolated weak spots.

Management by Profile can be divided into phases, although they can be implemented in any sequence. The phases are listed below:

Demystification—helping kids understand themselves
Accommodations—sometimes bypassing their weaknesses
Interventions at the breakdown points—trying to repair the gaps
Strengthening strengths and affinities—cultivating a kid's assets
Protection from humiliation—preventing public embarrassment
Other services—using professional therapies

Demystification

Kids need to know themselves, and they need to know what to work on to help themselves. They need and deserve to understand clearly the reasons for any academic problems they are experiencing. Too often students fantasize about their deficiencies, and their unguided fantasies tend to be far too global, fatalistic, and self-damning. Struggling students feel a sense of relief when they have a clear picture of their personal strengths and weaknesses. As one boy said to me, "Sometimes I used to think I had real bad problems and I couldn't do anything about them. Then other times I thought I had no problems and was just plain lazy. Now I know I have a problem, a real problem that's not my fault and it's not so bad."

It is soothing and empowering for students to have the exact terms, the specific words that describe their assets and deficits. It's really hard to work on or even think much about something when you don't even know what to call it. As a ten-year-old demystified girl pointed out to me during a return visit, "I can always tell I'm going to get mixed up when the teacher starts talking in sequences."

There are many techniques that can be used for demystification. Sometimes I make use of diagrams, such as the concentration cockpit illustrated in Figure 11-1.

In this case, attention is likened to the controls in the cockpit of a jet plane. A cockpit is presented to a child in the form of a plastic-coated poster. He is given a felt-tipped pen, and after an adult explains each atten-

PROCESSING CONTROLS (INTAKE)

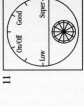

8 MIND ACTIVITY CONTROL
(Being able to get your mind to be active but not too active)

9 WANT AND EXCITEMENT CONTROL
(Being able to do well without lots of excitement or things you want)

6 CONCENTRATION DEPTH CONTROL
(Being able to concentrate deeply enough)

7 CONCENTRATION TIME CONTROL
(Being able to concentrate for the right amount of time)

5 IMPORTANT INTAKE CONTROL
(Being able to pay most attention to what's most important; having good noise filters)

MENTAL ENERGY CONTROLS

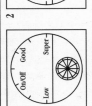

1 ALERTNESS CONTROL
(Being able to have enough brain energy to concentrate without feeling tired)

2 CONSISTENCY CONTROL
(Keeping up steady good work each day)

3 MENTAL EFFORT CONTROL
(Being able to get mind work done)

4 SLEEP CONTROL
(Being able to fall asleep and stay asleep at night)

PRODUCTION CONTROLS (OUTPUT)

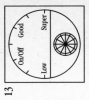

10 PREVIEW CONTROL
(Being able to look ahead and think before saying or doing something)

11 SPEED CONTROL
(Being able to move around and do things at the best speed)

12 PAST EXPERIENCE CONTROL
(Being able to use what happened in the past to decide what to do now)

13 POSSIBLE CHOICES CONTROL
(Being able to think about possibilities instead of acting before you think)

14 MONITORING CONTROL
(Being able to know how things are going or how they just went)

Figure 11-1. Concentration central: attention controls for behavior, learning, and getting along with people.

tion control (in the form of a meter within the cockpit), the child draws in where he thinks his needle usually is, with "low" signifying that he has low control over that aspect of attention, "on/off" meaning sometimes he can control it and sometimes he can't, "good" meaning he is in firm control, and "super" meaning he is in complete control. The kids really get into rating themselves while learning about the specific controls of attention. You know you're getting somewhere when a kid, instead of saying "I'm ADD," says, "I need to work on my intake controls, figuring out what's important when I concentrate, and also I need to get my brain more active when we're learning stuff in class."

Demystification can be accomplished either one-to-one with a child or else in small groups. The process is very upbeat, always nonaccusatory, always optimistic. It contains no preaching or sermonizing. The demystifier speaks to the child's strengths and their importance while pointing out specifically any dysfunctions and breakdown points.

In conversing with a child about her weaknesses, the aim is to impose borders around the deficiencies, so that she is empowered and doesn't come away feeling overwhelmed, pervasively defective, or mentally retarded. An adult might say, "Antonia, there are two things you need to be working on. One is called sequencing, getting things in the right order, and the other is called expressive language, which means putting your ideas into words when you speak or write." Instead of believing she is helpless, Antonia starts to think, "Okay, I guess I have to become a lot better handling all those darned sequences and talking better, then I'll improve a lot in school." That's just how we want her to think. Some realistic possibilities for her future are mentioned—infused with the information that many adults find it easier to have a career than it was to be a kid in school. Finally, it is helpful for the person transmitting the message to let the child know that he wants to be of continuing help; we call this alliance formation.

Children can start to learn about their own minds from the earliest grades in school. In the case of very young children, it is helpful to use many concrete examples and analogies (possibly referring to animals as examples). An informed clinician or educator can perform demystification. Parents should not conduct the activity initially. That's because kids know that their parents love them and are subjective. That detracts from credibility in this process. They should get the word from some outside, objective, and knowledgeable adult. Ideally, as a parent you ought to be present during the discussion with your child and subsequently provide booster doses, reinforcing and reviewing whatever she was told during the session(s).

Accommodations

Accommodations are practices used to work around a kid's area of weakness, but they don't purport to fix it. They resemble the detours we take when road construction blocks a highway. A student may need such alternative routes so he can go where he needs to while we're working on his basic problem, such as trouble with active working memory. Accommodations circumvent the problem or breakdown point, enabling a student to keep on learning and feeling reasonably good about himself without risking humiliation. A host of these potential bypass routes are always available.

Here are a few typical hypothetical examples:

- Your child works slowly, so the school gives her extra time on tests or allows her to complete fewer problems in the allotted time.
- Your child has some receptive language deficiencies, so her teacher puts lists and diagrams on the board rather than just relying on oral instructions.
- Your child has serious graphomotor dysfunction, so his teacher lets him submit an audiocassette instead of a written report.
- Your child has significant long-term memory problems, so his teacher lets him use his notes during a test (she might well allow all the kids to do this to communicate that understanding is more important than memorizing!).
- Your child has always had language problems in English, so the school waives its foreign language requirement for her for this year.

I often think it's a good idea to ask a child for a payback for accommodation, in which case the student may take on some form of additional work to compensate for a reduction of demands in an area of difficulty. Here are a couple of examples: "Julio, because it's so hard for you to finish math tests on time, I'm going to let you solve eight problems instead of ten. But then I want you to do two extra problems on your homework tonight." "Dina, you can have an extra week to work on your term paper because of your writing problems. You are so splendid at art that I would like you to repay me for the accommodation by creating a poster we can hang in the front of the room showing the different forms of mental representation." The payback system helps students sustain their pride, and is fair to the others for whom no accommodation was made.

Some teachers consider accommodations to be ethically questionable. As quite a few teachers have complained to me after reading my recommendations for students, "It's not really fair, you know. Why should I treat him differently? The others are going to complain when they realize Jonathan doesn't have to write as much as they do, and I'm inclined to agree with them." In fact I once listened to this declaration espoused loudly and clearly by a science teacher at a middle school in Fayetteville, North Carolina, where I was involved in teacher education. Then one of the other teachers in the audience catapulted from her seat and shouted, "Honey, you are wrong, just plain wrong. Let me tell you what I do. Each year during the first week of school I tell all the kids in my science classes, 'I'm not going to treat any two of you the same way. And I don't want to hear anything about it. Some of you might have to write long reports and some of you are allowed to do shorter ones. Some of you may have to read long articles and some of you shorter ones. And that's just the way it is. Everyone learns different. If there's ever any special thing any of you need you can let me know, and I'll think about doing it for you. But I don't want to catch you complaining about what I'm doing for anyone else.' " I wholeheartedly agree with that teacher's policy and philosophy and with the need to declare it openly to the students.

Interventions at the Breakdown Points

You and your child need not give up when it comes to the weak areas of function. Interventions at the breakdown points can be effective. These measures consist of specific activities or tasks designed to mend or at least improve a dysfunction. While accommodations work *around* the problem, interventions at the breakdown points work *on* the problem. Here are some typical examples of this phase of Management by Profile:

- Your child has trouble with the language sound system (phonology), so he gets drilled intensively and repeatedly on the individual language sounds (like "th" and "sh") and the letter combinations that stand for them and/or the sounds get represented in multiple ways (i.e., visually, through auditory channels, via touch, and so forth).
- Your child still doesn't know his math facts automatically in seventh grade, so he drills on these and/or uses software for mastering math facts for ten minutes a night just before bedtime (when long-term memory filing works best).
- Your child has trouble with intake control, so he gets practice underlining the main idea in a paragraph and summarizing stories he watches on TV.
- Your child is totally adrift when he undertakes tasks, so he is helped

to develop a step-by-step plan for studying for a test or doing a project in geography.

- Your child has trouble learning dates in history but is an excellent
  artist, so she practices learning dates by making a large illustrated
  poster with a timeline on it.
- Your child has difficulty forming concepts in science class, so she is
  helped to make maps of the relevant concepts using computer software designed for that purpose.
- Your child keeps forgetting things on tests, so she is taught memorizing strategies and learns how to test herself the morning of a test.

One of the teachers enrolled in our training program reported back a
year later: "Guess what, all those spiffy techniques I learned to use for kids
with learning problems, I'm now using with every single kid in my class. It's
a little weird, but they seem to benefit everyone." So often an intervention
technique we deploy to help a struggling class member will indeed help
everybody else in that class and at home as well! Many remedial maneuvers
may represent nothing more than superb teaching, and who would not
benefit from a transfusion of that? Also, kids with a specific dysfunction are
invariably jousting with a function that is an issue for everyone in the classroom. It's just a bit more of a problem for the student who is having trouble
with it. Therefore in a roundabout way, kids with learning problems inadvertently perform a service for their school. They are spotlighting specific
steps in various learning processes, the ones they are having the most trouble with. This accentuation can make teachers more aware of the steps in
learning, which will help teachers understand how best to teach. The same
zealous teacher I just quoted stated, "I've learned so much about learning
just by understanding what breaks down in kids who aren't learning. In a
way, they're all in the same boat; every single one of them is struggling to
make his mind function."

Strengthening Strengths and Affinities

No child's educational plan is complete without suitable provisions and a
substantial commitment to strengthen strengths. Sometimes this part of the
mission requires a search for hidden skills. But once a child's pluses are ac-
counted for, they must never be neglected. It is indeed tragic when a kid has
strengths he has no chance to use, strengths that somehow are not of any
value within his educational sphere. There have to be opportunities for
every kid to feel that his strengths are continuing to grow stronger and that
they are being celebrated. Every school has to make a firm commitment to

all kids guaranteeing that no one's neurodevelopmental high points are being overlooked—more about this in Chapter 13, our plan for a model school. Affinities are especially relevant. These are topics or subject matter toward which a child is drawn. Take the case of AJ, who so plainly illustrates the magic of affinities.

AJ had language problems that were anything but subtle. This fifteen-year-old perspired as he struggled to get his words out in the classroom. Although his automatic everyday language skills worked well for him, his ability to use language to express complex ideas was significantly underdeveloped. He seldom entered into class discussions and he had a hard time with written language as well. He failed Spanish two years in a row. Fortunately, AJ found redemption in science, in mathematics, and in the school orchestra, where he was the distinguished first cellist. His math and science teachers used a lecture format, and, for better or worse, only minimal verbal participation was demanded of students.

What so fascinated me about this boy was the fact that his expressive language dysfunctions vanished when he was discussing his most passionate interest, stock-car racing. Actually named after the star driver A. J. Foyt, this AJ had attended all the NASCAR races he could get to. He pored over racing car magazines and dreamed of becoming a stock-car driver himself someday. Whether he was recounting last Saturday night's competition or else some technical issues regarding distributor caps, AJ was fluent, articulate, and organized in his car rhetoric. AJ was counting the days until someone would let him work with a pit crew. He practiced for this opportunity by putting on and removing the tires of his father's Dodge minivan, while timing himself with a stopwatch. AJ revealed what I call domain-specific strengths. His language difficulties were conspicuous everywhere except within the automotive racing domain. This phenomenon, as common as it is inexplicable, has robust implications for Management by Profile. We should never miss a chance to capitalize on a child's strengths and affinities. AJ should keep building his language functions, such as reading and writing, within the domain of cars. He should use cars as a springboard for solid skill acquisition.

Affinities have been a powerful force in my own life. When I was no more than eighteen months old, my parents recalled that I would ascend into a state of euphoria at the sight of a dog or a cat. I came to love animals and identify with them, perhaps a bit too strongly. Now, countless decades later, I live on a farm in North Carolina that is a refuge for more than two hundred geese, twelve swans, ten peacocks, four donkeys, one horse, one mule, seven dogs, about ten Maine coon cats, as well as some uninvited beavers. I feel an inner sense of fulfillment when these highly communicative denizens engulf me and compete for my affection after work each day. I am fascinated by my own relationships with each of them and by the behaviors they deploy with one another. This enthusiasm is called "biophilia." My male geese and pheasants display for one another and for their coy hens in ways that are perfect replications of scenarios in the corridors of any middle school! My interest in animals is an affinity. No one knows how it got there. Nobody else in my family showed any passion for animals. (My wife maintains that it's out of control.)

In the best of all possible worlds, affinities are fed so that they can develop into passions and those passions also become zones of expertise. Depth of knowledge is a bountiful dividend for a developing mind. For example, one of the best ways to learn to read well is to read about something you know a lot about. I loved reading animal books as a child. The same boost pertains to writing, organizational skills, and many of the brain functions that are needed for success in life. In many respects it is best to nurture and groom functions within an area of affinity or expertise. Adults do not get to select a kid's affinity, so we have to be attentive and open-minded. Then we can recognize, respect, and deepen children's self-selected areas of interest.

The young have a basic right and a need to develop their affinities over time. We have to provide the fertile soil in which that growth can take place, especially in cases where a kid keeps meeting up with academic demands that don't jibe with his kind of mind at all. I remember a mother informing me, "My son has so much trouble getting it all together in school. But Ahmad is infatuated and totally on task when it comes to his computer games. They fascinate and enthrall him. We have subscribed to two computer game magazines, which he devours like vanilla fudge ice cream. He is so incredibly knowledgeable about these things. And recently we've noticed his interest in computer games spreading into other kinds of technology gadgetry. He loves working with computer graphics and the digital camera we got him for Christmas. I feel certain that his mind is tailor-made for technological challenges, and we'll keep right on encouraging him. And, by the way, my spouse and I are technologically incompetent and useless. He sure didn't acquire his specialized brain from us!"

After following large numbers of my patients and watching them become adults, I am convinced that many students who appear to have significant learning problems (and in a real sense they do) in reality have highly specialized minds, brains that were never designed to be well rounded. After seeing endless examples of such misunderstood, often widely condemned kids, I have become convinced that their proper and humane management must include opportunities for early specialization. They need to practice their calling on a part-time basis as soon as the preferences become evident. Parents and our educational system must provide opportunities for kids to utilize and strengthen their strengths and their affinities—no matter what those assets happen to be. To deny a developing mind access to its specialty is cruel. To judge one's worthiness in the specialties of others is equally inhumane. And it's asking for serious trouble.

Protection from Humiliation

From the moment a kid gets out of bed in the morning until she is securely tucked into her quilt at night, she has one central overwhelming mission, the avoidance of humiliation at all costs. By the middle of elementary school, most kids are on a mission to save face. School offers virtually no privacy. Students swim within a fishbowl, constantly under surveillance by their teachers, school administrators, and, more than anything else, by their peers. Nothing creates a more deeply penetrating wound to pride than embarrassing exposures or encounters before an audience of judgmental peers. Consequently, any plan to help a kid must include provisions for safeguards from public humiliation. Those who feel ostracized are highly vulnerable to a wide range of negative outcomes throughout their lives. Their humiliation must be prevented at all costs. Happily, the cost of protecting them is not at all great. We can warn a child with a language dysfunction that we intend to call on her tomorrow to tell us what she knows about the differences between Catholicism and Protestantism. We can tap the shoulder of a boy with attention deficits to remind him that he is tuned out, instead of calling on him in class when he hasn't been paying attention.

Other Services

No list of management steps would be complete without a category called "other services." In this case other services might include tutoring or educational therapy, social skill training, counseling, language therapy, or some interventions to improve motor skills (such as physical or occupational therapy). Fortunately, in most cases, these resources are not necessary. We can hope that if students are well managed in the classroom and at home, fewer of them will require specialized services.

It is advisable for a parent or educator to become a wise and slightly skeptical consumer of services. That's because there exists a multitude of unscientific and ethically dubious interventions that are readily available (for a price). All can cite anecdotal evidence, testimonials that make their methods sound as plausible as they are infallible. Potent placebo effects may be seen; anything seems to help in the short run. But many alternative therapies, such as dietary supplements or restrictions, elaborate exercises involving one or another anatomical regions, and other quick fixes may mask underlying neurodevelopmental dysfunctions and delay or displace optimal management. Perhaps one day some of these therapies will be found to be scientifically valid, although none will ever work in all kids— there are too many kinds of minds for any treatment to be effective universally. Ultimately, when questionable treatments fizzle out (which they usually do after a period of initial euphoria), the child has accumulated yet another defeat and her parents have endured a waste of resources and time.

ᔥ ACCESSING SPECIAL SERVICES IN SCHOOL

There are students whose learning breakdowns are severe enough to warrant intensive individualized help. Often this assistance needs to be provided within the school setting. Fortunately, the field of special education and some related disciplines (such as school psychology; speech, language, physical, and occupational therapy; and guidance/social work) have provided highly effective, targeted services to struggling children and adolescents. For example, students with significant delays in reading may be taken out of their regular classrooms for part of each day and offered intensive training in language sounds and their pairing with letter combinations. Others may get specific assistance in sentence comprehension or language production. Some unsuccessful children may receive counseling to help them overcome anxiety, improve their social thinking, or control their aggressive behavior. Many of the children I have described in this book do not require intervention at this level of intensity, but some clearly need it to ensure they do not become hampered by a mind that's too far behind.

Sometimes it is hard for parents to access school-based services for their children. Legislation exists that entitles students to the services they need. However, they must "qualify" for in-school interventions and accommodations. Before help can be offered, testing is used to demonstrate a sufficient delay and generate a narrowly defined label. Regrettably, there are many kids who could use the services but fall through the cracks in the system. Their deficiencies may not fit the rigid criteria for receiving remediation in school. For those who qualify, the services can be academically lifesaving. In my opinion, the entitling legislation must be preserved and, in fact, strengthened and expanded, so that more kinds of minds can be understood and helped. At the same time we need to keep on improving regular classroom teachers' knowledge of differences in learning, so that kids can get as much understanding and help as possible within regular classroom settings.

There are a number of advocacy groups that represent the interests of children with differences in learning and their parents. These associations monitor legislation and are helping to inform policy makers, including state and national legislators, so that struggling students are appropriately served. The groups, including the Learning Disabilities Association of America (LDA), the International Dyslexia Association (IDA), Children and Adults with Attention Deficit Disorders (CHADD), and the National Center for Learning Disabilities (NCLD), can also serve as informative resources for parents.

One of the most common "other" services nowadays involves pharmacology, medication for kids. Prescribing drugs to help with learning, behavior, and feelings raises many medical, political, and ethical issues.

❧ THE USE OF MEDICATION

More and more kids are being put on medication to help with their learning, their attention, their moods, and, in some cases, their behavior. In many instances these drugs can be helpful. When I started working with these children in the early 1970s, mainly psychostimulants were prescribed. These drugs, including nowadays primarily Ritalin, Dexedrine, Concerta, and Adderall, exert their effects primarily on the attention controls. They help kids slow down, focus on detail, fend off mental fatigue, and self-monitor more effectively. They don't work on all kids with attention deficits, but they can have a dramatic positive impact on many. But you should realize that these chemical remedies alleviate some of the symptoms but they're certainly not the ultimate cure.

More recently large amounts of wide-ranging medications have been prescribed to help kids overcome anxiety, depression, and other mood problems. Drugs are also being used to control behavioral acting out, obsessive-compulsive tendencies, and poor sleep. Once again, in some cases the medication has been beneficial and has helped with the management of some clinical problems that otherwise may have gone unsolved. However, there is a great deal of evidence to suggest that medication is prescribed too liberally and with inadequate diagnosis and follow-up. Therefore, some guidelines need to be formulated and followed if we are to have a set of best practices for the use of medication in kids. I believe the following list of drug caveats should be included in any such set of standards:

- No one should believe that a drug is the final answer to a child's learning problems.
- Medication works best in the long run when it is part of a multi-

pronged treatment plan, one that might include appropriate mentoring, coaching, or counseling, educational help, and the components of Management by Profile.

- Medication should be prescribed only after a thorough evaluation, one that includes careful assessment of the status of a child's neurodevelopmental systems and academic performance, his physical health, the emotional and motivational issues that cut across the capacities, the student's family and social milieu, and his skill attainment.
- When drugs are prescribed, there should be regularly scheduled follow-up visits with a physician to monitor physical health (with periodic complete physical examinations) and to adjust dosage or modify the medication in some other way.
- Whenever feasible a conservative approach is warranted; if at all possible, a child should be on only one medication and stay on drugs for as brief a period as possible.
- Teachers and parents should be actively involved in monitoring the effects of medication.
- Caution is advised with some high school and college students, who may abuse or distribute the medication.
- After a thorough evaluation, it is often possible to avoid or at least delay the use of medication, as other therapeutic possibilities present themselves.

ॐ COACHING AND MENTORING

It can be hard to go it alone when you're feeling inadequate. Many struggling students can benefit from an interaction with a professional who can offer them ongoing advice and advocacy. The choice of courses for next year, strategies for resolving a conflict with a teacher, and techniques for managing time and prioritizing activities are among the subjects that can be shared with a mentor. The alliance can provide a source of security, coaching in troubleshooting problems that come up, and plain old praise and encouragement. If possible this service should be long lasting, continuing over a period of years, so that a strong alliance can be forged. A mentor might be a physician (I think I do a fair amount of this), a mental health professional, an educator, counselor, or member of the clergy. Whoever assumes this role must communicate that he or she is on the side of the student, there to provide support and guidance, a collaborator and a safety net, someone who is going to be around when needed.

✌ RAOUL: AN EXAMPLE OF A CHILD WHO WAS MANAGED BY PROFILE

You met Raoul earlier in this book. He was a boy who, at the end of third grade, possessed a dreadfully illegible handwriting despite the fact that his fine motor function was highly respectable, even praiseworthy. After careful evaluation, our assessment team concluded that this boy had problems with graphomotor implementation (assigning specific muscles to push and pull and grab hold of the utensil to form letters). This was also a boy with commendable language output, a kid who was phenomenal at generating ideas and getting his thoughts into words. Here's how we used Management by Profile with Raoul:

First, I spent a good bit of time demystifying Raoul, helping him understand himself. The process was aided by his strong language abilities; it was relatively easy to explain complicated mechanisms to him. As with all kids, I made use of a lot of concrete metaphors in explaining the problem. The following highly condensed excerpt will give you an idea:

LEVINE: Raoul, I just wanted to talk to you a little about what we found out today on your tests and what we learned from your mom and your teacher. I hope this doesn't make you feel weird—you know you could bring in any kid in your class and we could tell him all about his strengths and weaknesses. That's because everyone has strengths and weaknesses, including other kids, your parents, your teacher, and me.

RAOUL: Okay, that sounds pretty cool.

LEVINE: First of all, we found out that you have a ton of strengths, things you're great at, Raoul. You have super language ability; you're great at understanding words and complicated things people explain to you and you're just as super at putting ideas into your own words when you talk. You also are good at picturing things in your mind and figuring out stuff in space. In addition, you are a really excellent people person and a leader; other kids respect you and look up to you.

RAOUL: I know that. Everybody follows me around. They think I'm funny and they like the games I invent. I even think I'm funny.

LEVINE: But like everybody else, Raoul, you have some weaknesses, things you need to be working on. Raoul, there's one thing that's become a big problem for you, and it's not that serious—but it could get to be more of a problem if we didn't know about it and didn't do anything about it. As you know writing is a big problem. That's because you have what we call a graphomotor weakness [I wrote it down for him]. Even though you have super ideas and neat ways of saying them, you can't get your thinking on paper.

RAOUL: That's for sure, and when I do it's a mess, a total mess.

LEVINE: That must frustrate you.

RAOUL: Yup.

LEVINE: The reason you have this problem is that your brain has trouble telling your finger muscles what they need to do during writing. You know, Raoul, when you write, different teams of muscles do different things. Some make circles, some make straight lines that go up, others make straight lines that go across, and others have the job of holding the pencil so you don't drop it while you're signing your name. Your brain can't seem to decide who should do what and get the right muscles doing the right things at the right times.

RAOUL: Bummer! Oops. Yeah, I sometimes can feel that in my head. It's like my brain gets all confused when I write.

LEVINE: Yes, and then it can't send good signals down to your fingers. Sometimes you try to make up for the confusion by holding your pencil very very tight and near the point. That makes things even worse for you, but it's not your fault.

RAOUL: It makes my hands hurt—real bad sometimes. And also I have to work so hard with my hands that lots of times I forget what I was going to write. That makes me mad at myself.

LEVINE: A lot of very smart people have graphomotor problems; it doesn't mean you're dumb or lazy.

RAOUL: A lot of time I think that [Raoul had tears in his eyes at this point, and he wouldn't look at me].

LEVINE: This problem can be very embarrassing.

RAOUL: Other kids laugh at me when they see how I write. I try to lean over my work, so no one can see it. But the other day we had to correct each other's papers. Mark made fun of my writing—he called it "retard writing"—and showed it to all the other kids. That night I told my mom I don't ever want to go back to school. I couldn't get to sleep because I was very very sad.

LEVINE: Raoul, there are things you can do and we can do to help with your writing problem. I'm going to get these things down in a report for your parents and teachers. They will go over it all with you when the time comes. But I want you to know one important thing: you have all the strengths you need to grow up and become a very successful and happy person. With your personality and great ways of thinking, understanding, and talking, there are so many great jobs and careers you can have. Also,

Raoul, your writing is going to improve steadily, especially if you work on it—and, besides, when you grow up you can pick a job where you don't have very much writing to do. There are lots of those.

RAOUL: Sometimes I can't wait till I grow up.

LEVINE: I know how you feel. Lots of people say it's easier to be a grown-up than it is to be a kid. That's because when you grow up you can stick to things you're good at. The trick is not to let yourself get hurt too bad before then.

RAOUL: I think I'll ask my dad to lock me in the freezer and thaw me out when I'm twenty.

LEVINE: Oh, and one other thing, Raoul. I want to be able to help you over the coming months and years in school. I would like you to return to see me from time to time as you grow up so I can check on how you're doing and help you if you need it. You're a great kid. I'm really interested in you and in helping you.

After I finished trying to help Raoul (and his parents) understand his plight and his assets, we went right to work developing accommodations for Raoul. Since third grade had just about ended, and fourth grade is often a perilous experience for kids like Raoul, we went about setting up a fourth-grade plan that included some ways of bypassing writing at the same time we were trying to fix it. To circumvent Raoul's writing obstacles, we recommended the following measures:

- Letting Raoul submit some oral reports on a cassette—instead of always having to write.
- Permitting him to print instead of using cursive writing (which was much harder for Raoul).
- Giving him more time for writing in class (his writing was most illegible when he tried to write fast).
- Teaching him keyboarding skills and allowing him to do much (but not all) of his writing on a computer.
- Giving him separate grades on his papers for neatness and for content.
- Asking Raoul to pay back for his accommodations by drawing some posters for the class and also by reading one extra library book at the end of the semester.

His soon-to-be fourth-grade teacher did not see these accommodations as a problem and mentioned that there were two other students in her class who needed much the same adjustments. Raoul also liked these ideas, but he was a bit apprehensive about being treated differently from other kids. He did comment that it would be cool to be able to say that he had read more books than his friends. Fortunately, this fourth-grade teacher, much like the science teacher I quoted earlier in this chapter, always let the kids know that she wasn't going to treat everyone in the class exactly the same way anyway, since different kids' minds work differently in school.

We formulated some specific interventions at the breakdown points to help Raoul overcome his graphomotor dysfunction. Each night Raoul was to practice for five to ten minutes writing in a journal using a better (tripod-type) way of holding the pencil. This is the garden-variety normal pencil grip and is most efficient for most people. A special educator was to help Raoul talk through letters as he wrote them for several sessions a week. Raoul would say to himself, "Go up, then go across, then go down" while forming an oversized letter. Such verbal cueing is often helpful in getting letter formation to be more consistently executed. Finally, Raoul would have plenty of opportunities to write about things that most interested him. He very much wanted to be the author of a joke book; that project would motivate him to concentrate on letter formation while exploiting his wit and perhaps his artistic bent as well.

To shelter Raoul from public humiliation, it was agreed that his teacher would avoid having students correct each other's work. She also said she would not be publicly critical of Raoul's messiness on paper as long as she felt he was working on the problem.

Raoul's many strengths were to be strengthened. Taking advantage of his strong political abilities, his teacher gave him a leadership position in the class—an extended term as head monitor, which involved some vigilance in the playground as well as taking attendance and several additional presti-gious micromanagement responsibilities. He also was to be cast in a starring role in the fourth grade's Christmas play, since Raoul clearly loved perform-ing, especially when there was some comedy involved. We suggested to Raoul's art teacher (one of the boy's steadfast fans) that he make use of his keen drawing abilities and wry sense of humor to learn some cartooning. Each month one of his cartoons could be on display in the classroom. That would instill in Raoul some motor gratification and add some buoyancy to his self-esteem.

To round out the process of Management by Profile, one additional serv-ice was sought. Raoul was to be seen by an occupational therapist, who would offer some ideas for finger activities that might help Raoul improve the motor aspects of his writing. His parents would implement these exer-cises, and the therapist would check his progress every three or four months. By the way, I could see no reason to put Raoul on Ritalin, even though he did at times have trouble staying focused in the classroom. His inattention was not severe, and while out of focus he often was fabricating original and exotic thoughts. We had much that was far more appropriate to offer this boy. Besides, we didn't want to stifle his kind of mind in any way.

So it was that Raoul was Managed by Profile. He came back to see me approximately every four to six months for the next three years, and we kept reviewing the demystification and also refining the accommodations and interventions. I served as his mentor. His gains outpaced my optimistic expectations, and he reported his progress with beaming pride. While Management by Profile doesn't always work as well as it did in Raoul's case, it can provide a stable framework for helping any child or adolescent overcome barriers to learning and accomplishment.

I believe that every student in a school would benefit from one or another version of Management by Profile. We even need plans to deal with kids who are too successful; we don't want those golden boys and girls to peak prematurely in life. There are students who succeed but have to work too hard to do so. Others make the grade with little or no effort but seem to be learning very little despite their adequate report cards. Still others just get by and derive no inspiration or excitement from their school experience. All such students are at risk. They need to be better understood and they need to understand themselves better. They are on thin ice, precarious, as we all are, at least from time to time.

12

Raisin' Brain ✒

Homes for All Kinds of Minds

Home is the place where, when you have to go there,
They have to take you in.

ROBERT FROST, "The Death of the Hired Man"

Arriving home fresh from the maternity ward closely clutching a newborn is like taking delivery of a jet plane without knowing how to fly. Unfortunately in the case of an infant, there is no instructor, no toll-free number to dial for instructions. So parents are left to determine how this newest model of a mind is supposed to be operated and maintained. Parents, for better or worse, don't get to shop to pick their child's kind of mind.

Here's a lyric from the musical "The Fantasticks":

> Plant a radish get a radish
> Not a brussel sprout.
> That's why I love vegetables
> You know what they're about.

When we plant a child we don't really know what he or she is going to be about. It follows that children need to live in homes that can love and support the growth of their unique minds, including even those kinds of minds parents don't understand. How can that be pulled off? I'll offer some thoughts on homes for all kinds of minds in this chapter.

✎ KNOW THY CHILD

Becoming familiar with a particular growing mind can be like watching a daffodil bloom or a peach blossom transform itself into a fruit of lush ripeness. But how does a parent observe that budding brain as it gradually seeks to bloom? How do we understand a child's evolving neurodevelopmental profile? Actually, abundant clues are available. We see how he takes on the challenge of reading, how he strives to get thoughts on paper, how he relates to others, how he manages time, how he controls his attention. Equipped with some knowledge and open-mindedness, parents can and should become well-informed mind watchers.

Every parent rearing more than one child comments on the striking differences between offspring. These contrasts are authentic, and significant. Therefore, parents must view each child as unique, as a distinct and distinctive individual. And parents need to respond intelligently and compassionately to what they are seeing and sensing in their children. Sooner or later every kid proclaims what it is he is wired for as well as what he is miswired for. Is anybody watching and listening? Is anyone responding positively to these sometimes desperate declarations of identity?

Parents must take seriously their assignment as informed and vigilant observers of their children. By becoming generally familiar with our eight neurodevelopmental systems a parent can become an informed observer of a child, taking note of her strengths and dysfunctions, as well as emerging affinities, positive intuitions, and special knacks. Here are a few examples of what you might observe:

• Arthur, a shy and sensitive child with weaknesses of social cognition, is reserved during the earliest phases of his elementary school life. He mostly plays alone. When he's with other seven- and eight-year-olds, he acts silly, but no one seems to mind. Suddenly in the middle of fourth grade this longtime loner is showing signs of despondency and timidity at school. Arthur has reached the common developmental social stage where kids are starting to be competitive and judgmental, a time when as a parent you should keep a close eye on your child's social performance. His fellow bus passengers are now actively rejecting and making fun of this socially awkward child whom they used to tolerate or perhaps ignore. Arthur's parents knew that fourth grade would represent a critical test for their son. Having raised two other children, they knew how ferociously mean kids can be to one another when they get to be Arthur's age. They had a feeling he was vulnerable socially, but kept hoping he would outgrow it the way his sister did. But, if anything, things got worse for him. Fortunately, they were alert to this possibility as soon as he started fourth grade. They observed their son's stormy interactions keenly during this year and concluded early on that he needed social skills training.

• Twelve-year-old Beth, at one time an honor student, has fallen from academic grace early in seventh grade. She now loathes school, earns dismal grades, and insists the work has gotten too hard for her. Her well-informed parents have been vigilant, however, knowing how the workload expands in middle school and how much help they have been giving their daughter with homework. Mrs. Bryant told her husband, "Hers was a bubble that had to burst. I just knew she could fall apart in middle school—and she has. Fortunately, because I'm a teacher, I'm more aware of the demands and the pitfalls as kids wend their way through school."

This mother was acutely aware that early adolescents have to reach up into higher language function. They need to hold more data in their active working memory. They are required to think about and use many more abstract concepts than they ever guessed would have existed. They must relate, interrelate, and consolidate a massive amount of unfamiliar detail. And all of their previously conquered subskills (such as math facts) have to become entirely automatic. Early on, the Bryants thought about their daughter against this backdrop of what was to come and strongly suspected that she might stall in her language growth; in fact, as a middle schooler, she was tripping over all the subject matter that required higher language functions. The Bryants approached the school and requested help from a speech and language therapist, who observed Beth in class and made suggestions to her teacher. The therapist also conducted a series of one-to-one language therapy sessions with Beth. At home, her parents rose to the occasion by trying to conduct more high-level discussions at the dinner table and in the car as well as suggesting heavier doses of intelligent reading for all family members. Importantly, Beth herself was helped to understand her lack of higher language and how it was hurting her self-esteem and diminishing her academic record. Beth was relieved to discover that she wasn't doomed to fail forever.

• Edwin appeared competent and confident throughout his career in preschool, behaving and relating admirably. He was entirely upbeat in his interest in all activities. Edwin loved listening to and telling stories, and he relished chances to exhibit his motor skills along with leadership qualities (i.e., his overbearing bossiness) during outdoor games. Now, late in first grade, this boy is foundering. He can't seem to read, spell, or write with the others. He's in the middle of the pack in arithmetic. His parents know that this is a time when phonological awareness, a reliable sense of the language sound system, displaces most other neurodevelopmental functions. The Fowlers therefore suspect that their offspring may be lacking in his appreciation of language sounds (despite obviously good language function on other levels). They point this out to his teacher, who is young and new to the school this year. An evaluation team soon confirms their hypothesis. Reading tutoring begins promptly. The parents request and receive intense basic training for their son in language sounds and matching up sounds with letter combinations. This is accomplished through the special education program in the school. Also, each night at bedtime his mother or father drills Edwin on which letter combinations go with which sounds. Everyone feels confident that once he is over the phonological hurdle, Edwin will succeed linguistically in school because he is strong at the sentence, discourse, and semantic levels of language.

The three examples I've provided above showcase parents who were aware of the twists and turns that make up the obstacle course known as the school years. These mothers and fathers knew about the changes within minds must occur at specific points in their kids' educational lives. Their background knowledge alerted them to know what to look for and when. More important, it made them wise consumers of their children's education, well-informed advocates for their kids. So often I have found that a parent is in a better position to detect the early manifestation of a dysfunction (or a strength) than is the school. So that's one reason I feel strongly that parents who know what to be looking for are parents for all kinds of minds. They know when they might need help in responding to the assets and the deficits of a mind that they see.

Communities should offer parents educational programs about child development and neurodevelopmental variation, stressing the implications for observing and fostering intellectual growth at home. Courses might be offered by local schools or other community agencies or perhaps online. Well-informed parents can then learn about the unique needs of each unique child. At present, I'm not aware of the existence of such programs, but there is certainly a need for them.

⮞ Responding to Gaps

In Chapter 11 we described some ways neurodevelopmental dysfunctions can stubbornly prevent academic success and satisfaction. I can remember an instance where a divorced single mother brought her eleven-year-old, Jennifer, to see me for learning problems. Before they arrived at our center, I looked over questionnaires filled out in advance by the girl's well-respected private school. Her teacher reported that Jennifer was earning solid Bs and that her standardized achievement test scores were "nicely above average." The school implied strongly that Jennifer's highly successful trial attorney father (whom she saw on alternate weekends) and prominent pediatrician mother were exerting unreasonable pressure on their daughter as they strived to make her a straight A student. Before even meeting this child, I assumed the school must be right—pushy parent, victimized kid. Her teacher and the head of her school had no idea why Jennifer's mother sought an evaluation. School personnel adored Jennifer, who was well behaved, affable, and the very model of an academic plugger. I felt put upon that these parents would take up one of our valuable appointment slots and squander our scarce clinical time.

But this mother was right on. I found that her child had suboptimal language function and very tight space in active working memory. Jennifer was holding her grades up but only because of heroic maternal rescue missions every evening at homework time, and she was working much too hard in her battle to keep up in school. Moreover, her mother reported, "Jennifer shows absolutely no joy whatsoever in learning, no, not a glimmer of academic pleasure ever." Higher language and active memory dysfunctions were destined to result in Jennifer's academic bankruptcy in middle school when extended discourse and heavy writing demands would prevail.

Jennifer's parents both felt the presence of their daughter's burden. Her father reported, "Whenever I see Jennifer on my weekends with her, I feel deeply uneasy. She never talks about school, and if I mention it, she automatically changes the subject or else promptly zones out. I couldn't put my finger on it, but I've had a sense that she's been on a narrow precipice when it comes to learning; she could fall off at any time. And, sure enough, Dr. Levine, you've confirmed my deepest instincts and my uneasiness about her." Both parents wisely wondered, "Why should we wait until she's in serious trouble to get her the help she needs?" A good question. They shouldn't wait. I've often told Jennifer's story over the years because it makes my point that parents are in a prime position to suspect or detect vulnerability and early glimmers of failure. They can do something about such weaknesses before too many tough-to-fix emotional complications take hold.

✒ FOSTERING STRENGTHS, KNACKS, TALENTS, INTUITIONS, AND AFFINITIES

A child's natural strengths and affinities are a key part of his unique mind. Once these powerful pluses are identified, parents must actively support them. Strengths have to undergo strengthening on the home scene. Even when a child's strong points don't coincide with what a mother or father would have chosen from a prenatal menu, parents must see to it that there are plenty of opportunities to nurture them. Children never stop yearning for applause, especially from their parents. Parents must never offer false praise; accolades should reward what a kid clearly excels at.

Neglected or suppressed strengths are like infections under the skin; eventually they cause serious damage. Some years ago I evaluated Mark, a seventeen-year-old boy who had been incarcerated twice in a juvenile detention center for drug dealing and other antisocial offenses. This teenager had a long history of frustration and humiliation in school because of unremitting dysfunctions of his attention production controls, temporal-sequential ordering, and receptive language. He suffered delays across the board in reading, written output, spelling, and math. The very thought of writing elicited his rage. Mark spoke well and conveyed the impression that he was very bright yet not the least bit inclined to succeed in school. Somehow I must have won his confidence because, during our interview, Mark allowed me access to his private sketchbook. I was astounded, totally taken with his artistic talent and originality. Mark's drawings had never been on display anywhere. Furthermore, he had never received an art lesson. He was ingenious at designing and building forts as a kid; he built and rebuilt his own and was a leading fort consultant in the neighborhood. This boy showed remarkable intuition when it came to problem solving in the domain of construction. Nobody ever picked up on this. His mind was telecasting what it was wired to do well, but nobody tuned into the program. His family never particularly noted or strengthened his artistic and spatial abilities.

Happily, I can report that Mark eventually succeeded. We managed to get him to attend a community college, where he took some art and computer classes. One young faculty member developed an interest in Mark and served as a powerful mentor, offering this kid the encouragement and praise that was so long overdue. Eight years later Mark is a highly successful designer of Web sites for obstetricians, having launched his own business. In addition, Mark has been taking night courses as possible preparation for becoming an architect (a triumphant rerun of his earlier fort designing). A close call, Mark's life was on the brink of futility, partly due to long-standing strength neglect complicated by chronic success deprivation and a near total loss of motivation.

I receive a steady stream of mail from young adults I saw as kids. These letters and e-mails have come to represent the most gratifying dividend of my career. Here's an excerpt from two pages Mark wrote to me a year ago:

> Dear Doc:
> I keep thinking about all the things you told me. I used to pretend I wasn't listening to you, but I was. And I'm sorry, real sorry; I gave you

such a hard time and acted as if I hated you. I didn't. I sure was screwed up when I was a teenager. I didn't think there was any hope at all for me. Everywhere I turned, I saw failure written on the walls and ceilings. It never occurred to me that the answers to the riddle of my life were on my sketch pad and way up in the amazing forts I used to build when I was a little kid. You were the first one ever to let me know how important and strong my strengths were. It was you who mentioned that the best part of growing up was being able to practice your mind's specialty, not being forced to do other people's specialties. You said that the cure for me would arrive when I could find my niche. Well, Doc, I've found it. I've got my specialty. I'm on a roll. The future looks real rosy. Also, I have a fantastic girlfriend, and we'll be married pretty soon. When we have kids, I intend to help them find out what they're wired for (as you would say). Thanks, Doc.

Your friend forever,
Mark

I have stressed the boosting and bolstering of your child's neurodevelopmental strengths, but content affinities, those focused interests in specific subject areas, also need nourishment. I think a mind grows through the pursuit of deep interests, the following of its inclinations. An affinity can bring on expertise. I would like to see every kid become an expert on something, accumulating more knowledge and insight on particular topics than anyone else in the immediate vicinity. Parents can make this happen. Schools should insist on it (see the next chapter). Betty can qualify as the local authority on rocks and gems. Peter can be a well-respected grasshopper, cricket, and praying mantis consultant. Claude's interest in weather should be encouraged. Such interests can be fortified with appropriate reading materials (including magazine subscriptions), parent-led field expeditions, discussions in the car, family projects, summer jobs, a Web site, and the accumulation of oversized, overdone, overboard collections. Over time kids could accumulate impressive portfolios within their domains of expertise.

Affinities should seed passions, intimately felt connections with the subject matter. One word of caution: an affinity is not synonymous with a recreational activity. It is instead an area of deep or potentially deep focused knowledge and interest. For the most part, therefore, soccer, tennis, and track are not what I mean by affinities, although sports are important and healthy activities. Kids thrive when they connect with both—intellectual affinities plus recreational pursuits and talents. In addition to sports or some other mode of pure entertainment, a child also needs those heavy-duty content affinities. His parents and his teachers should aid him in locating one or more such heartfelt semischolarly interests.

ᔰ TRYING NOT TO HARM

In taking the venerable Hippocratic Oath, we physicians pledge *"primum non nocere."* In English that means "first, do no harm." Parents should submit to a similar oath. A child's ego is fragile. There is no one, absolutely nobody on earth that children yearn to please and impress more than their parents. If children come to feel that they are a disappointment to their parents, kids become emotional powder kegs. Children who believe they've let down their parents may become pathologically dependent on their peers (whom they are overly careful not to let down). They may withdraw, live only in the present, show aggression, or languish in anxiety and feelings of hopeless inadequacy. Such pessimistic states decimate academic and career motivation as well as self-esteem.

So parents have to be careful not to be excessively and monotonously critical of any child. Kids can be held accountable for their behavior and academic work without being toxically overdosed with negative feedback. The ledger of praise and criticism should always be weighted toward praise. Parents should always demonstrate respect for their children. Children and adolescents usually feel pretty secure that their parents love them, but they may often wonder whether their parents respect and admire them, whether they might ever overhear their parents boasting about them to friends and relatives. This is particularly a concern for kids who endure the pain, the fear, and the confusion that is brought on by underachievement due to the effects of neurodevelopmental dysfunctions.

Parents should avoid comparisons between siblings. Mothers and fathers need to convey that they firmly believe that kids are all different from one another, and they would like to see their kids succeed in different ways because they have different kinds of minds. Don't ever underestimate the potency of sibling rivalry. Whatever we parents do, brothers and sisters will keep comparing themselves to each other. And nothing is more taxing than having to live with a brother or sister who has been noticeably more successful than you. It is the often unspoken form of torture that accompanies school failure. It plays a principal role in the life scenarios of these children. Consequently, parents have to find ways that these kids can demonstrate their unique claims to family citizenship. That means making sure that they are shining in their own individual strengths and affinities, ways of succeeding that are different from those of their brothers or sisters.

Parents should watch their words with care, since kids can take them much too literally and seriously. If an irate father says to his son, "You know, you're never going to amount to anything," that glum prophecy may well come true. Also, it can be seriously damaging to be torn down by your parents in front of your siblings or friends. Private feedback is far more humane and less likely to have lethal long-term side effects.

Parents have to build their "listening-to-kids" skills. School-age children have a lot bottled up within them—pent-up feelings, anxieties, perceptions, conceptions, misconceptions, and misperceptions, all of which are worthy of being expressed. But kids won't talk frankly unless they feel it is safe to do so. A part of that safety stems from their sense that true confessions will not trigger canned lectures. Often it is preferable just to listen and say relatively little (or perhaps even nothing) than to sermonize, criticize, trivialize, or stigmatize in response to a child's true confessions. Kids need parental sounding boards, mothers and fathers who know how to listen with care and take seriously what children are saying.

✎ Supporting Education

Parents should partner with schools. Neither can educate a child without the collaboration of the other. Such joint efforts may be especially hard to implement within modern dual-career or single-parent families, but nevertheless, the need is there. Parents should acquire a clear idea of what the school expects from a student and then support him or her in meeting those expectations—assuming the requirements make sense. Collaboration is especially warranted when a student is struggling in one or more important areas, in which case the parents and the school need to use the same terminology to talk about and demystify the relevant issues while deploying compatible strategies to help him succeed. I remember an ever-giggling twelve-year-old, Shantel, whose school had concluded that she wasn't "putting in any effort"; her mother maintained she had a learning problem while her father had concluded his daughter simply wasn't smart. The mixed signals impinging on this girl ultimately turned out to be far more toxic than her learning problems. Shantel sensed the disagreement and confusion surrounding her ability. In eighth grade she confided to one of her teachers, "I don't know why I failed that test. I keep on failing. I don't know why. And my mother and my dad, they don't know why. They don't agree with each other anyway. I just get all mixed up listening to them. A lot of times I think I have some kind of bad brain damage, and no one will tell me." Her confusion scared her, even terrified her. She came to perceive school as part threat and part blind dark alley. Shantel wrote off her mind; she became pregnant and dropped out of school in the middle of ninth grade.

Close parent-school communication works. With input from teachers, parents can serve as willing educational consultants to their kids. They should never actually do the work for them, but instead be available to offer advice, assist in finding and correcting mistakes, and carve out very well defined explicit roles. They can help with selecting topics, finding resources, organizing, getting started, and coming to the rescue when their kid gets stuck.

Parents should be responsible for the ongoing automatization of skills and facts. There should be drill on math facts, letter formation, basic vocabulary, or spelling each night at bedtime (the best hour in which to consolidate new information in long-term memory). School affords virtually no time to achieve automatization and in instances where kids have problems with automatic memory, parental assistance can be the only thing to prevent a student from acquiring that dangerous and disheartening feeling that he is too far behind to catch up.

I think schools should assume responsibility for teaching kids how to learn, and parents need to have the assignment of teaching kids how to work! Mothers and fathers can legitimately assume the roles of taskmasters (as opposed to their current oft-assumed positions as child entertainers and recreation coordinators). A powerful work ethic has to permeate a home. Countless kids have learning capacities that far outstrip their actual work output. Homework and studying represent golden opportunities to build students' working capacities. Parents should require a set duration of brain activity at least five evenings per week. They should help their children understand that keeping your mind in shape is just as vital as keeping your body in shape—both call for daily workouts. Kids should be given an incentive not to rush through their homework, since they need to work for at least a specific amount of time (the exact duration dependent upon age and other variables). Parents don't have to hand in their fun licenses, but they do need to take seriously the often neglected role of taskmaster.

In extreme cases parents have found that partnering with the school is nearly impossible. At such times it has become increasingly common to opt for home schooling. This choice is often made when a parent feels the need to protect a child from the negative aspects of the educational system—in general or locally. The values and hazards of the school may be seen as threats to the child's learning and overall well-being. Parents may feel that they can do a better job. In many instances, they may be right. Students with significant differences in learning sometimes are prime candidates for home schooling. Their parents believe that the school is rubbing salt in the wounds, failing to understand the needs of their boy or girl and perhaps not providing a suitable education. Home schooling has some disadvantages. A parent may not be in a position to deliver the rigorous education a child needs. There may also be some sacrifice in much needed social and political experience for the student. But I have seen many instances in which home schooling, at least for a year or two, has been beneficial. Finally, I should add that all kids should be home-schooled and most are—part time.

✍ MAINTAINING AN INTELLECTUAL LIFE AT HOME

In addition to fostering love, sensible decision making, moral and spiritual values, discipline, sound physical health, and security, family life should provide for a child's neurodevelopmental well-being. A home doesn't have to replay the intellectual rigor of the school, but it can be a site where mind growth takes place and a love of learning is instilled and nourished. Specific measures can be taken to ensure this:

- Parents should demonstrate a powerful interest in what their child is learning. Kids should have an opportunity to describe school-acquired subject matter to a parent. After all, the best way to learn something is to teach it! If the parents show excitement over what a child is learning in school, the student can feel more inspired and committed to the content. And parents can reveal that they themselves are still interested in learning.
- Passive activities, such as television viewing, should be limited to certain set times and not allowed to dominate the home environment.
- Adults at home can model intellectual activity by discussing ideas, problem solving, and other thorny issues with their kids. Events in the news or problems at work or home can be good focal points.
- Kids need to witness their parents reading—newspapers, magazines, novels, whatever.
- Limits should be placed on heavily structured activities (such as soccer Monday, clarinet Tuesday, kung fu Wednesday, and so on), so that kids get a chance to brainstorm, exercise creativity, and engage in imaginary play. Also, they need some downtime.
- Parents should reward a kid's productivity rather than his grades on a report card. Children deserve the most praise when they work hard, hand in all their assignments, and study with sufficient duration and intensity. Grades should be secondary and thought of as at least in part a matter of luck!
- Parents need to keep on seeking ways to offer a child genuine praise for the work of his or her kind of mind. Such kudos often

comprise the highest-octane fuel for intellectual activity during childhood.

⧉ Fostering Optimism and a Positive View of the Future

Children's minds flourish when they feel upbeat about their prospects for the future. They should keep thinking about and regularly discuss pathways to fulfillment. This is especially true when and if they have had a difficult time coping with present demands. It can be soothing for a kid to hear from a parent what I have mentioned earlier in this volume, namely, that there are countless individuals who find it much easier to be an adult than they found being a child. As one child said to me, "My dad told me that when he goes to work in the morning, he doesn't even feel as if he's going to work. That's because his work is so much fun for him—and he even gets paid for having fun. Me, I have to go to school. That's no fun, and they don't pay me anything. I can't wait to grow up when my work will be more like a game. That will be cool."

Parents should help children acquire a reasonably optimistic perception of what lies ahead for them. Seizing upon a kid's affinities and neurodevelopmental strengths, they can discuss all the exciting and important things she can engage in someday. Parents can use what they know about their child's profile to etch a plausibly positive engraving of the future, an alluring vision that will sustain motivation and ambition. All children need to grow up believing that what they are heading for is reachable and worth seeking. Then it will be.

13

The Right to Differ ❧

Schools for All Kinds of Minds

If we are to achieve a richer culture, rich in contrasting values, we must recognize the whole gamut of human potentialities, and so weave a less arbitrary social fabric, one in which each diverse human gift will find a fitting place.

MARGARET MEAD, *Sex and Temperament in Three Primitive Societies*

I WOULD like to see schools change in response to what we now know about the legitimate differences in learning that abound among students at every grade level in every community. A child's school experience is known to produce actual changes in brain function and anatomy. That fact alone would suggest that educators and parents are not just influencing the thought processes of our children but actually helping to construct their brains. This also means that we can damage these malleable minds when we misinterpret and therefore miseducate them. To build a mind requires that you understand it. We can use our awareness of the diversity of minds in every one of our schools. Here's how.

Five major considerations come up in our effort to create schools that tolerate, educate, and celebrate all kinds of minds:

1. Teachers: their roles and their training for those roles
2. Parents: their meaningful involvement in a child's learning
3. Students: learning about learning and learning about their kinds of minds

4. Humane schools: protective and nurturing settings for all kinds of minds
5. Pathways: greater availability of options for success.

ஒ TEACHERS: THEIR ROLES AND THEIR TRAINING FOR THOSE ROLES

I would like teachers to become the community's front-line experts on mind development and learning in the age group(s) they work with. Whether he or she teaches honors science, business math, freshman football, or driver's education, a teacher should be knowledgeable about the highly specific neurodevelopmental functions required for success in these realms and the differences in learning that teachers are likely to encounter among any cohort of students. The recent outpouring of research on brain function and learning should flow directly into classrooms. A teacher who acquires background knowledge about neurodevelopmental matters can understand the ways in which different learners have their personal ways of learning. From this, teachers can generate ideas about how to teach.

A memorable example is Marian Victor. A superb teacher at a rural school in Tennessee, she had Schools Attuned training (see page 312). I was visiting her school one day when she was talking to her colleagues about eight-year-old Malcolm at a third-grade faculty meeting. The discussion was conducted around a small table in the media room. Mrs. Victor presented Malcolm's case to the other teachers and went over her thinking about his persistent spelling problems. Here's some of what she told them: "I believe to spell accurately in late third grade my students have to bring together a little cluster of essential ingredients, which include a smattering of language (specifically their knowledge of language sounds, the meaningful parts inside of words, and vocabulary), some parts of long-term memory, a dash of sequential and spatial ordering, and a reasonable level of attention control. In Malcolm's case language hasn't seemed to be the problem because he reads so well, is perfectly fluent in literate English, quickly picks up on any of my verbal directions, and loves listening to stories. Also, I've never witnessed any evidence of attentional dysfunction or sequential or spatial ordering problems. But I have discovered that memory burdens constantly defeat Malcolm. For example, he understands the concepts and vocabulary in mathematics but has been unable to learn his facts reliably. And here's something worth noting: Malcolm's spelling is vastly more accurate when he spells words in isolation than when he tries to put them in a sentence or paragraph. His accuracy deteriorates noticeably when he needs to recall spelling at the same time that his mind is engaged in letter formation, capitalization, punctuation, and recalling facts. So it seems to me that Malcolm's spelling difficulties might stem from a memory overload—especially visible during sentence and paragraph writing. I discussed this with our learning specialist, who agrees and is willing to do some testing if Malcolm doesn't improve."

Mrs. Victor was aware that overloaded memory space, resembling a stuffed and cluttered closet, was a common neurodevelopmental affliction within the age group she taught. She was planning to demystify Malcolm (and the rest of the class) regarding the memory load and its possible troublesome effects on the learning of some students. Malcolm was told not to think about spelling very much while he was writing sentences and paragraphs. A day after each writing assignment he was given back his paper just to check over the spelling. He would earn a sticker for each error he could find and correct. Meanwhile, his parents were given some guidelines for drilling him on basic spelling words, so that some spelling might become more automatically accessible for him. They were already doing this for his math facts. Malcolm's teacher demonstrated the kind of expertise and problem-solving ability that all teachers should possess.

Not only should teachers become thoroughly knowledgeable about brain development and natural learning routes in the age group they teach, but, as I have implied, they also should be adept content analysts, probing the ways in which their subject matter draws on particular sets of neurodevelopmental functions—or, in the case of some students, fails to do so. That means teachers should dissect what it is they're teaching as well as how they're teaching it, so that they can identify such ingredients as the kinds of memory required to pass one of their geography tests, the attention controls operating during silent reading, and the extent to which word retrieval or sequential long-term memory might be exerting an influence on a child's ability to summarize information in class. The process has been called task analysis; in essence you diagnose the activity instead of the kid. I prefer to think of it as "expectations analysis," the way a teacher identifies the specific neurodevelopmental functions he is expecting a student to deploy. Once that teacher starts thinking in this manner, he can then reflect not only on a mind at a time but also on his methods of teaching. For example, a high school teacher I worked with in California confessed, "I never realized how much rote memory I was imposing on my students. But when I analyzed my neurodevelopmental expectations, it was obvious that the exams I was giving, our discussions in class, and my lecturing style were delivering the resounding message 'You gotta remember all this stuff' rather than how important it is to understand the concepts and their relevance to present-day life. I can tell you, I've changed my whole approach. I give the kids more open-book tests or let them use their notes during a quiz and I'm placing a lot less emphasis on pouring facts into their memory banks!"

As teachers gain neurodevelopmental expertise, they are in a far better position to understand students who are struggling to keep up. Once familiar with the kinds of memory and spatial ordering needed in fifth grade math, a teacher can inspect a student's quiz paper and determine whether his mistakes reflect problems with pattern recognition, factual recall, procedural recall, nonverbal thinking, active working memory, or automatization. A teacher then has the option either to bypass the student's area of difficulty or intervene and seek to repair the student's breakdown—or, even better, do both. Equally empowering, that teacher can demystify the student so that she comes to understand why math is such a threat to her. Such revelations inspire a student to work on her weak links rather than resign herself to mathematical failure.

The Teacher as Lead Observer

The great baseball catcher Yogi Berra has been quoted as saying, "You can observe a lot by watching." Teachers have nearly exclusive access to what I call the observable phenomena, the windows that offer an unobstructed view into a child's learning mind. Parents also have their windows, as I pointed out in the last chapter. Here are a few examples of observable phenomena.

An astute second-grade teacher reports that when Fred copies from the board, his head goes up and down four or five times as often as the other students. She suspects Fred is struggling with short-term memory; he can't hold a sufficient chunk of information in short-term memory firmly enough to transfer it to paper. His head movements during copying constitute a telling observable phenomenon. Overlooking it might have had harmful consequences.

An observant high school basketball coach notices that Steven appears dazed and then clowns around whenever he listens to an explanation of a multiple-step motor task. Steven also has trouble dribbling a basketball. These are lucid observable phenomena. The coach wonders if Steven might be encountering some obstructions in temporal-sequential ordering. He checks with Steven's American history teacher and learns that Steven gets mixed up about dates and sequences of events. Over the telephone his mother comments almost bitterly that Steven still doesn't know the months of the year in their correct order and is a "lost cause" when it comes to allocating time for schoolwork, meeting deadlines, and returning home at a decent hour on Saturday nights. The observable phenomena tell the story of a competent boy in danger of being eaten alive by his unmanaged weaknesses of temporal-sequential ordering.

Sarah is perpetually shy and withdrawn. As a result, this thirteen-year-old from Los Angeles has no friends. In school she is barely distinguishable amid the hordes in the hallways, and in class she seems to fade into the classroom walls. Although a credible performer on tests and quizzes, Sarah is a noncontributor to exchanges of ideas. When called upon, she is stingy in her responses. Her writing resembles uncooked stew; there's a lot of stuff in it, but it needs more preparation to be palatable. Of late Sarah has become severely depressed. Her physician has prescribed an antidepressant, which helps her feel a little better. Sarah's health teacher has taken an interest in her and, after calling on her in class and reading a very brief report she wrote on triglycerides, Mr. Stanley reported to the school psychologist at lunch one day, "You know that girl Sarah we were discussing last week? I've been thinking about her and I've come to believe that a substantial portion of Sarah's angst and inhibition in life stems from problems she has generating language. Her verbal output is abysmally low. It's funny because a language problem has been so plainly conspicuous, parading before all of our eyes and ears, almost as if it has been too obvious to notice!"

I have often found that such neglected transparency is true of many lethal dysfunctions. It's possible to be so close to a problem that you can't see it or relate it to anything else. Sarah's health teacher happens to be correct. By the way, a psychologist in the community evaluated Sarah two years earlier and found no "learning disability." Unfortunately, the tests most often used by psychologists fail to explore the major components of expressive language. A classroom teacher enjoys free and unlimited access to language production; no one else reaps this harvest to such a rich extent.

Observable phenomena provide insights that are unavailable on the standardized achievement or diagnostic tests commonly used in schools and clinics. We know the phenomena exist because we witness their unfolding every single day, despite the fact that many of them can't be captured succinctly with a test score. That makes direct well-informed observation indispensable. Sadly, there has been an entrenched and dangerous tradition, one that has seriously hurt countless children, namely that if a problem doesn't surface on a test, you can't have it. What a fallacy! A sizable number of the dysfunctions described in this book are not detectable on any test. But we know they're there because we can see them.

Teacher Education
How do we prepare teachers to become the lead observers, describers, and builders of neurodevelopmental function? How can educators be

helped to see the implications of neurodevelopmental function for teaching all kids and, in particular, for salvaging the ones who are floundering due to their undetected weaknesses or else suffering from chronic neglect of their strengths? And how do we assist teachers to derive instructional strategies based upon their direct observations and descriptions of the observable phenomena? The answer is plain. The way we prepare teachers must change. Courses and direct experience in managing neurodevelopmental variation should be provided before teachers enter the classroom and should be an integral part of their professional development throughout their careers. My colleagues and I in All Kinds of Minds have been working toward this goal since 1987 through Schools Attuned, a program funded originally by the Geraldine R. Dodge Foundation in New Jersey. There are now regional training centers located around the world striving to educate educators about different kinds of minds. The current features of Schools Attuned are summarized in the following table. The project has been expanding rapidly and is becoming a significant influence in many school districts. Other professional development programs accomplish similar goals for reading, mathematics, and other areas, but Schools Attuned is probably the broadest and most comprehensive training experience. More such programs are needed to translate the latest research on learning into methods that can be introduced and maintained in schools for students of all ages and all kinds of minds.

The Components of Schools Attuned

Component	Content
Training	Teachers undergo intensive education about neurodevelopmental function and variation, most often in weeklong summer courses or through the year.
Ongoing assistance	Teachers have mentors who help them renew and apply what they've learned throughout the school year.
Networking	Teachers have regularly scheduled "grand rounds" to discuss their work with students; also, they have access to the Schools Attuned Web site facilities.
Tools	Teachers use computer-based instruments, the Views Attuned, to observe systematically and help struggling kids from kindergarten through twelfth grade; also they apply various classroom management guidelines we provide.

(continued on next page)

Component	Content
Consultation	Teachers receive help with specific children working with a specially trained "profile advisor," who helps them interpret profiles and derive plans.

Schools Attuned teachers become zealous advocates very rapidly. They say that the program has enhanced their understanding of kids' minds and of the learning process. Many also say they have become much more tolerant of differences in learning and are far less likely to accuse or condemn a student who daydreams or appears lazy and unmotivated. Many tell us that they manage such phenomena far more effectively. One teacher commented on a form evaluating Schools Attuned, "This program actually saves me time. By dealing more knowledgeably with the kids who are struggling, I have far fewer discipline problems in my class, and they were the ones who really were taking up too much of my time. Also, Schools Attuned has changed the way I treat and teach everyone. It's fascinating, and with this kind of knowledge I feel more like a professional."

It will be equally important for schools of education to prepare teachers in training to be among a community's experts on childhood neurodevelopmental function and variation. For the most part, aspiring teachers do not learn very much about differences in the way students learn and are unprepared to deal with the immense challenges those differences pose each day in the classroom. Also, I am often amazed to discover how minimally teachers are taught about learning. Many discussions about raising teaching standards identify a need for math teachers to know more math and Latin teachers to know more Latin, but little mention is made of the need for all teachers to become more knowledgeable about minds and, more specifically, about all kinds of minds.

The Teacher as Informed Advisor

Teachers can serve as student advisors, academic coaches, or mentors. This practice has been common in many independent schools, although often the teacher's advisory functions are neglected as a result of other responsibilities. A mentor should stick with a kid for at least several years. That advisor/coach/advocate should be on top of a student's evolving neurodevelopmental profile and educational needs. She or he can advocate for the child in school and, when necessary, even outside school. A well-trained teacher-mentor can be a highly informed spokesperson and coach for a student. Incidentally, there is no reason to limit this role to teachers. Isn't it possible that some qualified individuals in the community might volunteer to become trained as neurodevelopmental advisors for one or more students? Kids have trouble making it alone. They need to sense that there's at least one adult out there beyond the family who knows them well and cares how they function, how they feel, and where they're headed.

❧ PARENTS: THEIR MEANINGFUL INVOLVEMENT IN A CHILD'S LEARNING

As I stressed in the last chapter, parents should become their children's educational allies. This active role is reassuring to a child, knowing that his parents also are his learning partners. He takes comfort in the belief that they can and will go to bat for him when it comes to his specific educational needs.

Many children view their teachers as daytime parents; as well, they ought to recognize their parents, in part, as night and weekend teachers. There should never be a vast divide between school life and home life. Every kid is partly home-schooled and every kid is partly school-homed! Issues discussed in school should be pursued further at the dinner table or on a car trip. The school should assign homework for parents. That homework should consist of activities parents can conduct with their children to reinforce what they are learning in school. Teachers can readily transmit such expectations through e-mail to all parents whose children are in their class. Who knows, moms and dads might even be able to update or upgrade their own knowledge and skills while helping their sons and daughters.

While mothers and fathers rightfully have to advocate for their kids in school, they need to be cautious in representing their children's best interests without fighting all their battles for them. Kids should resolve their own conflicts with teachers or with other kids whenever possible. Such coping skills and conflict resolution is a core part of a child's education. Parents ought to serve as consultants, offering advice on how to deal with a tough situation and seeing to it that problems are properly resolved by the children themselves at school. When one of my patients had a personality conflict with his middle school science teacher, his mother insightfully told me, "He gets so worked up over his relationship with her and wants me to call the principal and complain for him. But I won't do it. In fact, my husband and I believe this conflict he is having with his science teacher is a key part of his education. I told him last night that someday he may have a boss or co-worker he has trouble with, someone who reminds him of his seventh-grade science teacher. We're willing to offer him advice and moral support, but he has to get in there and work things out with that teacher. He'd probably learn more from doing that than he could from reading any science textbook." This is the right approach for parents to take in such situations.

Finally, parents should influence policy in the school and in the community. Mothers and fathers pack more educational policy clout than any other constituency, especially when they band together. Therefore, broad participation in well-run parent groups is essential for the well-being of education. A group of parents on behalf of children with attention deficits has been instrumental in getting laws changed so these kids can be accommodated in classrooms. The parents of schoolchildren in several schools I've worked with have come together to make sure their school provides adequate remedial services to their struggling students. Parent groups have rallied and lobbied for special education funding, for safeguards on end-of-grade testing, for the use of accommodation strategies, and for summer school programs. Those who believe in the philosophy of *A Mind at a Time* can join forces to develop plans to create neurodevelopmentally attuned schools in their communities and cooperate with educators to find models that meet their educational standards and mesh with the cultural values of their communities. Your child's school can become a demonstration site for realizing the ideas and ideals I am setting forth in this volume. It's already happening. I work with many school systems in which the parents have come together and lobbied to have teachers trained in our Schools Attuned program and to implement programs to help kids learn about learning.

Ꮓ STUDENTS: LEARNING ABOUT LEARNING AND LEARNING ABOUT THEIR KINDS OF MINDS

In a school for all kinds of minds, students can be taught about their attention controls and be reminded of the need to keep strengthening them by thinking about them periodically while they study or take notes. To help them get ready for examinations students should be acquainted with tactics that foster in-depth understanding and make memory work best. They should be learning about the levels of language function while they study English or a foreign language. Their coaches should help them understand the motor functions that operate during long-distance running or throwing a Frisbee or swimming. Finally, as they strive to interact meaningfully with peers, they need explicit knowledge regarding social thinking. While your children learn about learning they are also getting to know themselves as individuals, making the acquaintance of their kind of mind.

All schools should be offering formal courses on how our minds grow and work. This form of education need not dominate the curriculum, but its presence should always be felt. At certain points (possibly second, sixth, eighth, and eleventh grades), students should take mini-courses in neu-rodevelopmental function and learning. In fact, my colleagues and I have actually designed and implemented one such eight-unit program called "The Mind That's Mine," which is currently being used with fifth or sixth graders. Meanwhile, throughout the curriculum, teachers can keep referring to the specific functions and their roles in learning. A physics teacher can point out, "Mass is a really key nonverbal concept in this class; you should be making a concept map of it for your concept atlas." A seventh-grade English teacher can be instructing and warning her early adolescents about the need to combine multiple kinds of memory with language during writing. She can help reluctant or overwhelmed writers to write in stages. A first-grade teacher can make life easier for all her novice readers by taking the time to explain to them how phonological awareness works and how words are built from little sound bricks called phonemes (see Chapter 5).

As teachers become knowledgeable about the neurodevelopmental systems, they can become aware of the ways in which their instruction of students can explicitly strengthen key brain functions. Educators can then set some neurodevelopmental goals as shown in the following table.

THE NEURODEVELOPMENTAL SYSTEMS
AS THEY TRANSLATE INTO AIMS OF EDUCATION

Neurodevelopmental System	*Aim of Education*
Attention: Mental Energy Control	To educate students so they can reliably concentrate their mental resources and be capable of expending adequate work effort.
Attention: Intake Control	To educate students to think about what's important, to delay gratification, and to become active processors of information.
Attention: Output Control	To educate students to be reflective, to slow down and think through alternatives, to unite previous experience with foresight and vision.
Sequential Ordering	To educate students to be wise consumers of time, to understand how to think and act in a step-by-step fashion.
Spatial Ordering	To educate students to make good use of mental imagery and analogy, to engage in some productive and attractive nonverbal thinking.

(continued on next page)

Neurodevelopmental Capacity	Aim of Education
Memory	To educate students to be thoughtful and systematic in managing their memory files and be able to merge understanding with remembering.
Language	To educate students to derive gratification and knowledge from language input and to become effective verbal communicators.
Motor	To educate students regarding the ways in which they can achieve a satisfying level of motor effectiveness.
Social Thinking	To educate students to understand and practice effective interpersonal skills and to be tolerant of differences in social values and styles.
Higher Thinking	To educate students as thinkers, so they become adept conceptualizers, creators, problem solvers, and critical analysts.

As a parent or educator one can feel ecstatic about a seventeen-year-old who is firmly in control of his attention controls and is, in his own unique manner, a deft operator of the other neurodevelopmental systems as well! In fact, a version of this table, with appropriate local supplemental aims, could be etched upon a bronze plaque displayed in the front hall of every school.

Teachers can target specific neurodevelopmental functions and incorporate them into tasks or activities. When they do so, they should use what is called "explicit instruction"; they need to inform their students about the function being stressed in the exercise. A social studies teacher might ask his students to bring in a newspaper article in which they have underlined the most important points. He should explain that this activity is being assigned to strengthen one of their attention controls, namely the detection of importance. Too often kids miss the point of an assignment because its specific mind-building quality hasn't been explicitly described. A biology teacher could say to his class, "Look, it isn't so crucial that you learn these invertebrate names, but the way in which you go about trying to learn them trains your mind to prepare for an important upcoming event [a test] and also helps you organize your long-term memory filing system for scientific terminology."

๑ HUMANE SCHOOLS: PROTECTIVE AND NURTURING SETTINGS FOR ALL KINDS OF MINDS

To accommodate all kinds of minds, schools should be safe zones in which kids feel free to assume some intellectual risks. In class a student should sense that it's okay to go out on a limb and make statements that might be inaccurate, controversial, or inconsistent with the teacher's views. Some students I know have a way of learning that necessitates thinking out loud ("How can I know what I think until I hear what I say?"). They should be able to do so comfortably. It should also be perfectly safe to make mistakes without fear of peer ridicule. A kid should not be disgraced for giving the wrong solution to an algebra problem in class. In fact, the teacher should seize the occasion to congratulate that student for committing an error or revealing a misunderstanding that is actually helpful in boosting everyone's grasp of a procedure. In this way errors become steps in the learning process. Students should also always have the opportunity to correct their own errors—even on a test they have taken. Some recovery points should be granted to those who correct their errors and try to account for the reasons for their mistakes. Examinations should be viewed in part as powerful tools for learning from mistakes.

ELIMINATING HARMFUL PRACTICES

Immunity from fears of impending academic doom extends to many school practices. Retention in a grade has to qualify as one of the most malignant setbacks for a student. It has been demonstrated in many studies that this archaic practice is ineffective; it does not help kids improve in school, especially when implemented after first grade (there is some evidence that kindergarten or first-grade retention may work sometimes and isn't as lethal). I've read psychiatric case studies that portray adults in their mid-forties who still endure bad dreams about having been retained in fourth or fifth grade. Many studies have revealed that most dropouts are kids who've been held back in a grade. Nothing can leave a deeper scar on a young ego than having to ride the bus in September with your little sister, who is now in the same grade you are. Since the punitive practice of grade retention doesn't help kids achieve and inflicts harm, it should cease. It should not be viewed as the only alternative to so-called social promotion. After all, there are summer schools and tutorial programs that can help kids catch up without subjecting them to humiliation.

Grade retention is malignant in another serious respect: it often communicates to a child that her problematic school performance is entirely her own fault. How ironic, since in most cases it's the fault of the school for not understanding and meeting the educational needs of that child, for never having uncovered the obstructing neurodevelopmental dysfunctions. I remember a boy named Charley whom I saw for the first time when he was nearly seventeen. Charley had been retained in eighth grade and felt terrible about it. When we evaluated Charley, I explained to him that he was having serious problems with various parts of his retrieval memory (which I explained in detail to him). When I finished the demystification, Charley looked up at me and asked in a choked-up, hoarse voice, "How come nobody ever told me about that? When I was held back in eighth grade, I guess it was because of my memory problems. And the school didn't even know anything about them. That meant, Doc, I couldn't go to school with my friends anymore. That means I was being punished because the school wasn't smart enough to know I had memory problems. That makes me mad, real mad." We need alternatives to grade retention, including additional help for students, summer schools, and perhaps a somewhat longer school day for those who are delayed in their skills. In conforming to the policy of eliminating social promotion schools run the risk of creating damaging social demotion among the oppressed few that are not promoted.

Equally cruel is the practice of punishing a kid for his weakness by banning the use of his strengths. Here's an example of this totally irrational practice: Wilbur, a six-foot-three fourteen-year-old, was a promising forward on his middle school basketball team in New Jersey. As a result of his failing grades in English and Spanish, he was suspended from the team for the remainder of the season. Not surprisingly, he didn't use the free time to immerse himself in the stacks of the local public library. Rather, he headed for the streets. Months later he commented bitterly to his probation officer, "Those guys ripped off my basketball life, the only thing I ever could do that made me feel good about myself." I would rather have seen the school get him some remedial help and explain to Wilbur and the coach that while he is working on improving his academic skills, he will only be able to attend basketball practice three times a week instead of every afternoon. That would keep Wilbur accountable and provide some incentives to improve without sentencing him to long-term success deprival.

Iatrogenic diseases are a group of common afflictions caused by medical care, such as a streptococcal infection a young child picks up in the hospital, the side effects of an antibiotic, or psychological trauma stemming from hospitalizing a toddler. I think it is fair to say that education can and does cause its share of iatrogenic disease. Chronically humiliated kids, those whose differences go unrecognized and untreated, and individuals who are not permitted to make use of their strengths are all at risk for iatrogenic depression, maladjustment, and motivational loss. And it's all so preventable.

PRESERVING ACCOUNTABILITY

In responding humanely to neurodevelopmental differences, however, we have to make sure we don't inadvertently abolish or even diminish student accountability. A somewhat arrogant thirteen-year-old patient of mine from Manhattan proclaimed to his teacher with intense fervor, "I don't have to do that assignment; it's loaded with too many sequences, and I've been told by Dr. Mel Levine that I have a malfunction in my sequential ordering system. So it's unfair to make me do that stuff. It's like a civil rights violation." I of course did not tell him he could use his weakness as an excuse for not trying. Nothing doing; we can't allow kids to avoid responsibilities on the basis of their dysfunctions. If anything, once students have been demystified and understand themselves, they can and should be held *more* accountable than ever. We would not want to found a community of neurodevelopmental invalids. A teacher can and should respond, "Okay, now that you know all about your sequencing problems, what are you doing about them?" and, of course, "How can I help you?"

In Chapter 11 I explained Management by Profile, our systematic approach to redeeming kids who are diminished and perhaps even demolished in school. As part of the discussion of accommodations for differences in learning, I mentioned a form of payback, which deserves further emphasis here. Whenever kids are allowed to do less of something, they need to be held responsible for doing more of something else. In this way we preserve and even heighten personal accountability. In the long run, this can prevent kids with learning difficulties from feeling like second-class citizens in school and in life. Everyone is expected to be a highly productive student but they do not all need to be turning out the same products.

EASING SOCIAL PAIN

As discussed throughout, verbal and physical derision or abuse in school should be considered a form of criminal behavior and punished accordingly. Peer cruelty is unacceptable and a clear violation of kids' rights. Most of the time, students are made fun of because of things over which they have little or no control—their appearance, their name, certain features of their neurodevelopmental wiring, the faux pas they commit due to dysfunction of social cognition. In particular, students with limitations in social thinking capacity need our protection and support. Their lack of social awareness can bring on the peer predators. As recommended in Chapter 9, all kids should be taught about social cognition and the tough road ahead facing those who were born without enough of it.

A school for all kinds of minds should be a microcosm in which students come to tolerate and respect one another, a young society in which the words "weird" and "cool" lose much of their meaningfulness. It should be a place where social conformity and peer pressure are dampened in favor of the celebration and encouragement of healthy differences. One middle school principal sighed as he told me, "One of my greatest challenges is to do something about the destructive things kids do to one another. Our politicians keep blaming teachers and parents for everything. But no one ever wants to deal with the toxic effects students can have on one another. I'm concerned about the oppressive power of peer pressure. I've been an educator for a long time, and the intensity of peer pressure seems to be increasing every year. My seventh and eighth graders sometimes are living in a totalitarian government with little or no freedom to be themselves. The brutal dictator is their peer group, which they fear so much. We have started talking to the kids about these social issues, which are so potent in their daily lives. We're trying to encourage kids to liberate themselves, to be themselves, and to let other kids be who they want to be without ridiculing or excluding them."

৯ PATHWAYS: GREATER AVAILABILITY OF OPTIONS FOR SUCCESS

We can help all kids fit in by making the system more accepting of them, by finding ways for all children to have their place in the sun. Here's a worthy example of that: Ricky at age eight and a half has hit the wall when it comes to reading. His writing and spelling are holding stubbornly at a basal kindergarten level. Math facts, concepts, and procedures seem not to penetrate his mind. Ricky lives on a busy dairy farm in North Carolina and has always enjoyed communicating with animals. In recognition of this affinity in a diminished boy, Mr. Weld, his adamantly pro-kid principal, officially appointed Ricky the director of animal feeding for the entire kindergarten to fourth grade. He now takes pride in this prestigious title and carries out with flashy showmanship the major responsibilities it entails. His high-profile job in school is making him feel like a first-class citizen; he perceives himself as valued and respected. This extraordinarily sensitive intervention is cushioning the pride-annihilating impact of Ricky's learning problems. Ricky has a way of fitting in with his kind of mind. He has prestige.

I interviewed Ricky for a video library on learning that we made with WGBH, the public television station in Boston. He was reticent when I inquired about his learning differences. Then suddenly this shy and withdrawn boy looked up at me and smiled. "But you know what? I'm a water hose technician." "A what?" I asked. "A water hose technician," he responded. "You see, we have lots of dogs on our farm, like more than fifty of them, I think. And every day after school I go home and fill all their water pails with the hose. My daddy told me I'm a water hose technician," Ricky boasted.

How then can we create more arenas that lead to educational gratification for more children? First, every child (whether or not he or she presents plainly visible problems in school) should have an educational plan, one that sets goals and customizes learning to the individual needs and natural pathways of that student. The plan should consider what (if anything) to do about weaknesses and how to keep uncovering and strengthening strengths. The plan should be revisited and revised every few years, since kids change and keep on revealing more about themselves and their needs. The student and her parents should be major co-authors of the plan, the child playing an increasingly influential role over the years. Let's consider some of the directions to take.

Students need diverse forms of successful endeavor. Ideally, these triumphs should include becoming an expert in at least one domain, experiencing some mode of motor success, finding a medium for creative expression, experiencing the satisfaction of helping others, and demonstrating skills and a reasonably broad base of knowledge.

Many schools have had the policy of tracking children by ability. While sometimes this is necessary, it is always done at a price. As one child I knew said to me, "I'm in nothing but dummy classes." Such inferior educational placements can convey to kids the notion that not much is expected from them. I would rather see a school in which every single student is eligible to take one or more advanced placement classes. Such classes may be in areas such as math, music, history, physical education, or psychology. In one way or another, every student should think of herself as an honor student. Each one should have at least one pathway along which he can feel accelerated.

Supporting Expertise

Children's content affinities need to be exploited in school as at home. Every student should select (or be helped to select) a topic upon which to become "the world's leading expert" (or, at the very least, the acknowledged authority in Ms. Bundy's sixth-grade history class at the East Plainview Middle School). The topic would be pursued for a minimum of three years, at the end of which that kid would know more about, for example, pachyderms than any member of the student body and possibly even the faculty!

In the next phase of his education he could select a new topic or continue to pursue the existing one. After three years, he would have: a) completed several hefty pachyderm art projects; b) read all the relevant elephant books and articles in the library; c) finished two science projects in addition to reports on various subtopics; d) taught others about elephants; e) made three videos of elephant behavior at the local zoo; f) written several elephant stories; and g) started planning for his very own www.pachyderm.org. In this way intellectual initiative would be practiced and rewarded, and kids could experience intellectual depth. All of this independent study would run alongside the regular curriculum and be supervised by an advisor with whom the student would meet periodically. The advisor might be the child's mentor, an expert from the community, a teacher, or a school administrator. The child scholar would compile his own reference library and amass his personal collected works on the subject. It is likely that his reading, writing, higher thinking, and organizational skills will have undergone impressive growth, catalyzed by his expanding expertise.

Expertise kindles intellectual self-esteem; it helps a kid feel smart. Also, knowing a lot about something instills a sense of what it is like to be thorough, to dig into knowledge in depth, to become more than an inquisitive sampler and dabbler. Parents can collaborate by setting up experiences that enrich expertise (such as that excursion to the zoo to observe elephant behavior and an interview with a keeper). As part of their high school curriculum, all students should complete a major twelfth-grade project that represents the culmination of their most passionate pursuit.

Fostering Motor Success

Opportunities to enjoy motor mastery should be written into the plan for every student. Be it a team or individual sport, a musical instrument, a mode of dancing, or a technical skill or craft, there have to be opportunities for a student to connect his motor neurons to muscles in a way that makes him feel like an effective doer.

But kids need protection from the negative effects of motor humiliation. There should be a ban on making fun of children during sports activities. Some students would sell their souls to be part of a team sport but they lack the gross motor capacity to make the team. We should consider offering these individuals administrative or managerial positions, perhaps as assistant coaches. Athletic programs in school should all offer a managerial track to kids who love sports but lack athletic talent.

I will never forget Bertram, a lanky kid who reminded me of a creaky old wooden ladder. He was referred to me for evaluation when applying for admission to boarding school. When I first met Bertram he suffered with prominent facial acne and was painfully reserved, making little if any eye contact with me. He was accepted at the school of his choice, but it turned out later he seemed sentenced to incarceration as a loner at his New England boarding school. Implacably stigmatized as a classic "geek" with conspicuous "dorky" features, no one was willing to be his roommate, a universal reluctance blamed on his allegedly horrible hygiene. His situation wasn't helped by the fact that his neurodevelopmental toolbox lacked some vital social thinking equipment (both verbal and behavioral), and he was unable to compete in any sport due to problems with motor sequencing. But Bertram was a whiz at a computer monitor; his flat personality would percolate when he was expounding upon the latest electronic frontiers or coming up with solutions to the aggravating impasses of information technology. However, his social isolation drove his self-esteem ever downward. It diminished steadily until Greg Collins, the school's inspired football coach, approached Bertram and asked him to become the team statistician.

Bertram took to this role as if he were born for it. He generated statistics the likes of which had never before been quantified—last-quarter performance by player weight, percentage of successful point-after kicks correlated with weather conditions, and so on. At the end of each game, a throng of athletes would surround their beaming, meek-geek statistician clamoring for the latest data on their performance. Yes, Bertram had become a statistics jock.

The basketball, soccer, and track coaches soon recruited this teenage "mathlete." He also was asked by the drama teacher to handle the lighting and audio for the school's performance of *The Music Man*. For the first time since first grade, Bertram started to feel good about himself. He began to dress better. Over Christmas he asked his mom to take him to Abercrombie & Fitch. She was astounded. He now felt like a product worth packaging. He visited me during those holidays, and I could barely recognize him. Bertram was gushing with anecdotes about school and lecturing me about changes he would like to see in his school's lunch program. He also described some technological advances he had initiated in the school's audio capabilities. I feigned interest but had no idea what he was talking about. All I knew was that I was sitting across from a restored ego. I had trouble containing my own high tide of excitement.

All students need to feel valued. Carefully thought-out cameo roles, such as those fulfilled by Bertram, salvage a diminished kid. The football coach deserves a niche in the Hall of Fame. Robert Frost, a continuing rich source of inspiration in my life, wrote a poem called "The Oven Bird." This is one of the last New England birds to head south in late autumn. It's not a very attractive bird, nor does it trill the most melodious sounds. But I have always been touched and strongly influenced by the last lines of this poem:

But that he knows in singing not to sing.
The question that he frames in all but words
Is what to make of a diminished thing.

I guess I've spent my career trying to decide what to make of the patients I've seen. So many of them are like diminished things. It's our responsibility as adults who care about children to figure out just what to make of them—and what to do for them.

Creating Possibilities for Creativity

Having a creative product line can be like an essential vitamin for a growing mind. For example, there are endless potential hookups linking motor effectiveness to creativity. Blooming artists, photographers, and crafts people need to have their works prominently displayed. Others are ready to share their musical talent. Still others should be recognized amply for having an impressive aptitude for building model planes, rocket ships, and the like. We might even make a conspicuous fuss over kids who have been able to outsmart every electronic game on the market. I think in planning any child's education we should seek one or more suggested routes toward creative fulfillment and recognition. Once launched on a creative pathway, students need to build rigorous technical skills within their chosen media, so that they can keep growing as disciplined creators. I know of many students with substantial learning problems who happen to be remarkably skilled and clever cartoonists. Yet few if any elementary or even high schools offer lessons in cartooning.

Creative writing can be an ego oil strike for some students. So many kids have potent feelings and strong views of the world bottled up inside them but discover no expressive channel. Danny comes to mind. At eighteen he started writing vividly visual poetry. I had known Danny for six years, having evaluated him for serious graphomotor and expressive language delays. Throughout his education, Danny hated writing and often just boycotted written assignments. Now he was creating free-form poetry. I wished we had thought of that medium sooner. Poems became the mode of expression for this writing-phobic student. He had had such a hard time achieving legibility, keyboarding speed, and grammatical construction that he felt relieved to discover a way to express himself on paper without inviting any denunciations or accusations of moral turpitude from judgmental adults.

Creative performing can extend as well to acting in a school play or soloing at a recital. For some students, such stage appearances are vital expressive outlets, often helping them to overcome the negative implications of their neurodevelopmental profiles. There are students with serious memory problems who have no trouble learning all their cues and lines for the school pageant. Their affinity for this form of performing seems to bypass their trouble remembering. As one high school acting teacher informed me when I had lunch with her, "Every year a bunch of my best performers are kids with serious academic problems. So many of them are brilliantly creative and expressive in their quirky, unique ways. Last year we did a version of *Romeo and Juliet*. The eleventh-grade boy who played Romeo was receiving warning letters in English. Yet on stage he was magnificent. He learned his lines effortlessly and showed magical insight into the character he played. It happens all the time. Some kids were born to be on stage. Their minds flourish under the glare of the spotlight."

Helping Kids Become Helpful

Developing minds can expand through altruism or outreach to others. Community service in one form or another should be a part of an educational plan. Volunteer work in a hospital, teaching, tutoring, or coaching younger children, and rehabilitating poverty sites are common outlets for kids' basic but often hidden drive to be helpful to others. More and more schools are requiring this form of unselfish dedication. Service can be a great equalizer; kids with all kinds of minds can collaborate in assisting where they are needed.

Dealing Sensitively with Academic Proficiencies and Deficiencies

We have to find the portals through which all kids can feel smart and be smart. Theories of multiple intelligences, such as those of psychologist Howard Gardner, should help convince us, however, that there is no need for them all to be smart in the same way. School practices and policies must become responsive to this growing realization.

A lofty challenge looms ahead if we try to educate all kinds of minds at the same time that we strive to keep raising educational standards and to prove we are doing it through high-stakes testing of all students. Could these be mutually exclusive aims? I don't think so. I believe all kids should have a strong base of knowledge across a wide range of subject areas. Every citizen should be culturally and scientifically literate. But we should be offering much wider curriculum choices, particularly in secondary schools. Every student should undergo some form of competency assessment. But is it fair to test them all in the same way on the same material? In our school for all kinds of minds students would have some choice in what they wanted to be evaluated in and how they wanted to be evaluated. Alternatively, some core testing could take place and then students could choose one or several areas of strength that they would also like to be evaluated on. Showing excellence in one area should be permitted to offset a low score on the core testing. In other words, everyone should be highly competent, but it would be disastrous if every seventeen-year-old was expected to be competent in the same way.

I know of many students who have a compelling need to learn through direct, hands-on experience. They should have opportunities to be doing bodywork on cars, training horses, repairing computers, working as hair stylists, or setting up audio systems. These activities can be mingled and even neatly integrated with their schoolwork. So it is that we should be encouraging the growth of magnet schools and various forms of early technical education. Some students may only learn to read well by reading electronics manuals! Such practical experience represents the most sensible way to reach some kinds of minds. If a kid chooses to have an education that has a strong technical component, he should be convinced that his interest in fixing cars, for example, need not signify that he will be doing that line of work all of his life. Many people who started out in the oil fields of Oklahoma and Texas are now high-ranking executives at major oil companies. Your interests are not to be equated with your level of aspiration. You can be ambitious in any domain; the sky's the limit!

We need to help rather than punish or embarrass those who are not succeeding. That doesn't mean that we must necessarily expand special education services. To the contrary, there's been great success with so-called inclusionary programs that educate all kids in regular classrooms. Some students require additional educational boosts to acquire basic skills or need special services (such as tutoring or language or occupational therapy), but that can be accomplished unobtrusively.

Enabling Them Without Labeling Them

A school for all kinds of minds will not label any of its students. Terms such as ADD and LD (including the currently trendy term "nonverbal learning disability") lump too many diverse children into one deceptively simple category. Labels are not particularly helpful and are often misleading. In the past the labels served a worthy purpose by communicating that kids' learning problems were not their fault, that they represented distinct neurological conditions. But I hope that we will soon see the decline of the ever-burgeoning practice of labeling kids, of putting the letters "DD" (i.e., deficit disorder) after every puzzling trait, satisfying the compulsion to call most variation deviant. Instead of labeling the children, it is more helpful and humanistic to label the phenomena with which they are contending. So, instead of calling Susan an LD kid, we acknowledge that she is a child who is having trouble with her awareness of language sounds in words, and that that is making it hard for her to acquire reading skills. And, of course, everyone sooner or later has developmental breakdowns. If you drive an automobile, you're going to get a flat tire, but that doesn't mean that you have tubeless deficit disorder!

Labeling is reductionistic. It oversimplifies kids. The practice overlooks their richness, their complexity, their strengths, and their striking originality. Labeling can be dehumanizing; it can consume a person's total identity. It becomes especially scary to me when people can say, "I am ADD." Can you imagine someone proclaiming, "I am bronchial asthma"?

The labels can be pessimistic. They imply you're pretty much always going to be the way you are, that you will have these problems for the rest of your life if you suffer them now. We have absolutely no evidence that this glum prophecy is true. It denies the resiliency we know drives the human central nervous system. And, as we have noted, there always lurks the substantial risk of self-fulfilling prophecy. If we imply to our kids that they are always going to be pathological, in all likelihood they will be.

To some, labels signify that you may only have one problem. A school, for example, may force a committee to decide if a student has LD (learning disability) or BD (a behavior disorder). That often arbitrary decision will exert a powerful influence over the education, self-concept, and stigmatization of a young child. The implication is that if you have a learning problem, you can't be having an emotional problem. You must select one or the other! In reality, if you have one thing, it is more likely that you're struggling with a cluster of problems. Finally, labels are used too glibly, and there is no rigorously validated list of criteria for most of them. The terms are convenient as an excuse for giving kids medication, for getting reimbursement from insurance companies, for making people semipermanently dependent upon clinicians of various types, and for applying some kind of cap, so we can be sure we don't have too many children obtaining services in school. We are all opposed to putting caps on treatment for prostate cancer or AIDS.

Current practices of testing students to determine if they meet criteria for a label in order to help them are totally arbitrary and unfair to those who qualify as well as those who fall within the cracks. In fact, I have described on these pages many serious dysfunctions that need attention but would not ever qualify as legitimate within the mind-set of rigid labelers. A short-term memory problem or poor time management can be vastly more devastating than a delay in decoding multisyllabic words, yet the former may not satisfy testing formulas used by the school system. In other words, labels become a way of preventing kids from getting help—or, in my opinion, of being well understood. The labels are showstoppers; once a clinician comes up with a label, people somehow think they need look no further; they now have a handle on that kid. That's so obviously false.

Labels may be used to justify the profuse use of medication. That is, once you label someone, a vast array of medication options burst forth. When the medication stops working, it's time to change the label. Without labels, we might be more conservative in our psychopharmacology.

Let's just describe children's educational needs without calling the kids any names. Our school for all kinds of minds would guarantee a label-free environment.

Evaluating Performance

A school that welcomes all kind of minds needs to devote serious consideration to how it assesses its students, confronting the thorny issue of testing. In my opinion our educational system suffers from a malignant and rapidly metastasizing evaluation cancer. Often students come to view their teachers as evaluators and judges rather than allies. Their parents then function as evaluation reactors. I believe strongly that a great deal of the disillusionment and sometimes even alienation among teenagers is attributable to the fact that they are being overevaluated. A fourteen-year-old kid spends his entire day under scrutiny, getting tested repeatedly. His Spanish teacher gives him spot quizzes. His track coach evaluates how high he can jump. His math teacher critiques the homework problem he's put on the board. His social studies teacher can't stop talking threateningly about the end-of-year state examinations the students will have to take to prove they deserve promotion to ninth grade (and, more important, to establish him as a competent teacher). His parents keep on finding fault (early adolescents obligingly nourish their parents with plenty of fodder) as they point to the flaws in his manners, personal hygiene, attire, and taste in friends. Finally, his fellow students, in a real sense, are forever grading him rigorously on how cool he is. Many teenagers are seriously victimized by society's evaluation obsession. Life gets excruciatingly hard to take when a kid is not faring very well on some, perhaps even all, of these evaluations. Things have a peculiar way of snowballing. When you start falling short on one evaluation scale, your performance on the others may soon plummet. A failure spiral ensues.

Testing is a necessary evil. But any test format any test maker ever devises will discriminate unfairly against certain kinds of minds. An essay test, a standardized multiple-choice examination, or an oral quiz might be fair to one student and discriminatory against the child seated next to her.

We need to offer multiple options for evaluation, particularly as kids head into the upper grades. Some educators have advocated assessing students based on tangible evidence of their accomplishments at all grade levels. In this model kids are evaluated on the basis of their products. Such a process would salvage and provide incentives for those many kids who don't test well and who know so much more than they can display on traditional measures. This should definitely be one of a series of options granted to students in all courses. Well-maintained archives of your best work would play a big role in a school for all kinds of minds.

The following list provides some cautious guidelines regarding the testing of children and adolescents. These steps will help minimize the iatrogenic effects of tests while enhancing their usefulness as a part of a student's education.

Kids Taking Tests: Some Guidelines and Safety Nets

- Testing can be a useful, uniform, objective way to gauge the extent to which all children are learning.
- Testing when used properly can be an aid to elevating educational standards but not if it creates large numbers of students deemed unsuccessful by our society.
- Not all children can demonstrate their strengths in the same manner; therefore, different kids may need to be tested or allowed to demonstrate their strengths differently.
- Ultimately, students should be given some choice with respect to how they would prefer to be evaluated.
- It is cruel to rub a kid's nose in something he is poor at; in the worst cases this is what testing can represent.
- Students deserve privacy; their test scores should not be posted or publicized, especially if they are disappointing.
- We should be aware that some students who excel on tests might develop a false sense of security and confidence, failing to realize that adult careers tap many abilities that are not on any test.
- We should always place an emphasis on the evaluation of strengths rather than deficits; students should be required to strengthen their strengths and should be graded rigorously in their chosen specialties.
- For some individuals testing may be a poor indicator of ability; such students may be better served through an exhibition of their portfolios, track records, or some form of project as alternatives to formal testing.
- Certain test formats discriminate against certain kinds of minds; so multiple-choice, fill-in-the-blanks, or essay tests are unfair for some kids.

- Some testing may place too great an emphasis on memory and regurgitation rather than true understanding; testing should place less stress on recall and more on analysis, critical thinking, and problem solving.
- We need to avoid the hazards of having teachers programmed to teach to the tests because their performance or their school is judged by kids' scores on examinations.
- We must be sure that kids are not undergoing excessive evaluation, especially during their highly sensitive and vulnerable adolescent years.
- We need to have clear contingency plans for kids who perform poorly on a test; testing should not represent an end in itself—instead, when used properly, it should be a call to action.

Schools should reexamine seriously their most judgmental practices and find ways to contain any testing mania in their region, a change of direction that I think would add more joy to learning, infuse greater trust and respect for students, and substantially reduce adolescent turmoil. Our school for all kinds of minds would place far less emphasis on performance evaluation than is now customary policy.

We expect students to fly away from the school cocoon admirably educated but we worry that many will be casualties in some courses. Consequently, I would allow learners to gain exposure to some subject areas without the pain of being evaluated. This way we could have students who are liberally educated but unwounded.

One humane alternative would be to allow some students to specialize. Even during the elementary grades more choices could be offered. By high school, students might engage in a broad spectrum of courses but be graded only in their area(s) of specialty. Several or all of their nonspecialty classes would be pass-fail subjects. These students would be aware that they are going to be evaluated stringently in their chosen area(s). Another option, a model that has proven effective, is the magnet school devoted to a specific theme or specialty, permitting kids to pursue their strengths and feed their passions without stigmatization.

✒ THE EDUCATIONAL AMBIANCE

A school for all kinds of minds must embrace the conviction that every learner has distinct educational needs. Even success requires sensitive management. Is this renowned student athlete setting himself up for a colossal letdown at the age of twenty-two? Is this girl getting straight As in school mostly because of her phenomenal rote memory? Perhaps she has become a master mimic, having acquired a repertoire of test-taking tactics that will be of no use to her in later life. How will this highly attractive, universally popular girl cope when she's a junior in college and her professors aren't swayed by her charm? So it is that triumphant mastery has to be managed as sensitively as underachievement.

Timing and pacing are murky issues in every school. Are we artificially hurrying developing minds? Should they all be expected to operate at the same (often frenetic) rate? We have seen how the production controls of attention are actually trying to signal us that adolescent brains need to decelerate and transmit their impulses at a far slower rate. Yet as kids progress through secondary school, the rate demands keep calling for faster and faster output. As I pointed out earlier, we know that certain kinds of minds are calibrated to operate more slowly (and perhaps more painstakingly) than others. In adulthood such pensive, reflective beings may have the upper hand—but not when they're young. In the meantime, will some of them get too discouraged and give up on themselves at an early age because they are unable to keep pace? Perhaps. A school for all kinds of minds encourages and assists kids to find the learning and output pace that seems to work best for them.

I've talked to some secondary school educators who hold the view that students should complete their high school years at their own rate. Students would have to acquire the requisite total credits for graduation but could take as long as they would like to do so. One student might attend school during the summers and attempt to graduate in three years. Another might prefer to slow down and go for six years, while holding a part-time job. Someone else may opt for a school-free year or two and work instead of attending college or undertaking serious job training. These should be realistic alternatives that allow kids to find the proper pacing and rate of ripening of their kinds of minds. And by the way, I have seen truckloads of students who needed to take off a year after high school before attending college. They weren't ready for college, and their academic performance as undergraduates vividly reflected their unreadiness. And bear in mind, there's absolutely no need for every kid to attend college. We've all met plenty of successful adults who never attended college. Some never completed high school. Many of them own the kinds of minds that learn and grow best through direct experience—tried-and-true apprenticing and on-the-job training. College may thwart such learners! That's why we need flexible education in the high school version of our school for all kinds of minds.

It is essential that schools keep asking the question, "What actually are we preparing these kids for during their adult lives?" Then they need to weed out those elements of the curriculum that are outdated and not related to contemporary reality and needs. What kids learn should change with the times. At all grade levels we should be getting kids ready for the demands of adulthood and not just for what's coming next year or in college.

Schools should keep on reexamining their curricula, in terms of the amount of information conveyed and learned. Should students know a lot about a little? Or should they learn in depth in fewer areas than they now are exposed to? Cramming more and more questionably relevant factual material into every crevice of a kid's cerebral cortex is likely to be counterproductive. The principal of one school complained, "I don't how much longer some of my teachers intend to keep cramming more and more facts into the heads of our students."

Changing classes every fifty minutes may limit how well students are able to consolidate much of what goes on during a class. One teacher I met wondered out loud, "Sometimes I just marvel at how our students do it, proceeding like drones from one class to the next with no letup. As soon as they get into the groove in one subject, it's time to switch tracks completely. We're almost teaching them not to get too involved in anything, how to disengage rather than how to engage." Block schedules, formats in which students spend several months at a time focusing mainly on one subject area (such as organic chemistry or Asian history) are likely to allow for more complete digestion of content. Fewer and longer classes also help. So our school for all kinds of minds could deploy a modified block schedule, starting in seventh grade.

Ultimately kids should find themselves in educational environments where they can win out over oppressive peer pressure and live as their true selves. This will be our steepest climb. I encounter countless children and teenagers who are being homogenized and/or "mediocritized" by their peers. More than anything else, they become committed to being like everybody else and live with an overwhelming fear of being perceived as different (sometimes termed "weird"). I hope that schools can develop ways to encourage kids to be themselves and not actively capitulate to the socially tyrannical forces that engulf and often suffocate them without their realizing it. By having kids collaborate in activities with classmates whose minds are very different from their own, we can foster more respect for the differences. By conducting open discussions about the pros and cons of different kinds of interactions with peers, a school can initiate a social dialogue that may liberate many students. Schools need to be places where a reasonable level of nonconformity is enthusiastically encouraged.

A school atmosphere richly doused with the philosophy espoused in *A Mind at a Time* should impart highly contagious excitement about learning.

As students cease to see school as an unyielding and brutally judgmental institution, they will be better able to sit back and distill pleasure from academic content and, out of that stimulation, acquire the intrinsic motivation to keep on learning. I remember when my American literature professor at Brown University told us, "The most important book you will read in this course is the one you read two weeks after the final examination!"

I think it's appropriate at this stage to summarize some of the main characteristics of our school for all kinds of minds.

What We Would See Within Schools for All Kinds of Minds

- Teachers who are well versed in neurodevelopmental function and as such serve as the lead local learning experts.
- Teachers who observe, describe, and respond to the neurodevelopmental observable phenomena of their students.
- Teachers who base their own teaching methods on their understanding of how learning works.
- Students who are learning about learning while they are learning.
- Students who gain insight into and are able to track their own evolving neurodevelopmental profiles.
- Students whose strengths have been properly identified and cultivated.
- Students who respect students whose neurodevelopmental profiles and personal backgrounds differ from their own.
- Parents who collaborate with schools and join forces to create and sustain schools for all kinds of minds.
- Schools that celebrate and foster neurodevelopmental diversity.
- Schools in which all students acquire and build unique expertise, maintain collections, and develop their affinities.
- Schools that make available multiple educational pathways.
- Schools that stress long-term projects over rapidly executed activities.
- Schools that help kids blaze their own trails for motor success, creativity, and community service.
- Schools that create and maintain an educational plan for each student.
- Schools that refuse to label their students.
- Schools where kids can learn and work at their own natural pace.
- Schools that offer a range of ways in which students can reveal their knowledge and their academic accomplishments.
- Schools that seek to be far less judgmental of students.

- Schools that provide students with mentors from the faculty or from the community.
- Schools that help to educate parents about neurodevelopmental function and a mind at a time.

❧ RESULTS

No uniform human "product" will ever flow from the pipelines of education. Instead, schools, whether they intend to or not, are producing a diversified assortment of human beings. We hope that education strengthens personal strengths and affinities sufficiently while providing broad exposure to the diverse realms of knowledge and skill. As the superintendent of a large school district wrote to me, "Dr. Levine, I would like you to come and speak to all of our teachers. Please help them understand that we want every kid to be exposed to the widest possible gamut of knowledge, but we also want each and every one of them to have a bulge, one or more things at which they truly excel and about which they feel a sense of excitement and accomplishment." Most of all, we should want students to see possibilities for themselves at the same time that they are enriched by their years of formal education. Consistent with the central theme of this book, a student's neurodevelopmental profile should be healthy enough to prosper in the face of life's challenges.

❧ NEURODEVELOPMENTAL PLURALISM: A MIND AT A TIME AS AN ETHIC

The pages of *A Mind at a Time* are filled with moral and ethical implications. Our awareness of neurodevelopmental variation leads us to ask how much of a right we have to change the way somebody is wired or to stand in ruthless judgment of that wiring. We should question what we are saying when we call an individual "abnormal," in view of our respect for variation and for the differences among the minds of members of a society. In truth, it is normal to be different. Recognizing this, we must make a firm social and political commitment to neurodevelopmental pluralism. We can now see how unjust it is to criticize, to obliterate the self-respect and aspirations of a child you don't understand. Imagine growing up being told you can do better when the person glibly conveying that accusatory message happens to be wrong. It is morally unjustifiable for a child to have to suffer public condemnation for not submitting homework when transforming his ideas into words is an insurmountable barrier for him.

Schools are like airport hubs; student passengers arrive from many different backgrounds and take off for widely divergent destinations. Their particular takeoffs into adulthood will demand different flight plans. Fortified with our understanding of neurodevelopmental functions and differences, we can affirm a new mind-based humanism within a society that values, respects, and preserves all kinds of minds, beginning during early childhood and continuing through our entire life spans.

No mind should have to beg to differ.

Helpful Readings and Other Resources

ONLINE INFORMATION

All Kinds of Minds (www.allkindsofminds.org)

All Kinds of Minds is a nonprofit institute for the understanding of differences in learning. Each month, the All Kinds of Minds Web site explores different areas of learning and learning differences. The site has a libraryful of articles, book excerpts, audio and video clips, a searchable LearningBase of strategies, and many more resources, including up-to-date information about the institute's programs and products.

LD OnLine (www.ldonline.org)

LD OnLine is an interactive guide to learning disabilities for parents, teachers, and children. LD OnLine is the official site of the Coordinated Campaign for Learning Disabilities. LD OnLine provides articles on a wide range of topics, a national calendar of events, a network of resources, artwork and writings by children, parents, and other individuals, and much more.

SchwabLearning.org (www.schwablearning.org)

This site is a parent's guide to learning differences and provides a road map to understanding the language and landscape of learning differences and disabilities. On the site, parents can navigate among such topics as "Identifying Learning Differences," "Managing Learning Differences," and "Connecting with Others."

BOOKS

Aaron, P., and C. Baker. *Reading Disabilities in College and High School: Diagnosis and Management*. Timonium, Md.: York Press, 1991. This book can be especially useful for teachers trying to assist older students with delays in reading skill. It provides good insight into the problems themselves and presents useful ideas for management.

Asher, S. R., and J. D. Coie, eds. *Peer Rejection in Childhood*. Cambridge: Cambridge University Press, 1990. This collection of essays focuses on research into children who are rejected by their peers. There are useful reviews of specific forms of social thinking and their roles as well as papers on social skill training methods.

Asher, S. R., and J. M. Gottman, eds. *The Development of Children's Friendships*. Cambridge: Cambridge University Press, 1981. This volume contains a collection of papers on various aspects of social skill development during childhood. There are excellent discussions of how children succeed or fail in gaining acceptance by peers.

Blythe, T. *The Teaching for Understanding Guide*. San Francisco: Jossey-Bass, 1998. This guide asks teachers to explore what they most want their students to understand, helps them evaluate their current practices, and asks teachers to evaluate how well they know if their students understand what they are teaching.

Brooks, R. *The Self-Esteem Teacher*. Circle Pines, Minn.: American Guidance Service, 1991. This guide offers a systematic approach to helping children maintain their self-esteem in school. Although the book is directed toward teachers, much of the advice is also suitable for parents.

Carlisle, J. *Reasoning and Reading, Level 1 and Level 2*. Cambridge, Mass.: Educators Publishing Service, 1993 and 1983. These two workbooks provide a range of exercises for improving reading comprehension. There is an emphasis on the development of sophisticated thinking skills while also enhancing overall reading abilities.

Chall, J. S. *Stages of Reading Development*. New York: McGraw-Hill, 1983. This classic is a very accessible account of how children normally acquire reading skills as they progress through their school years. The book helps the reader understand why certain children experience reading difficulty at particular periods in their education.

Chapman, R. S., ed. *Processes in Language Acquisition and Disorders*. St. Louis: Mosby Year Book, 1992. This collection of papers provides an excellent and sophisticated overview of issues related to normal language development and to the problems of children with weak language understanding and production. It contains helpful reviews of the literature on these topics.

Clark, L. *SOS! Help for Parents*. Bowling Green, Ky.: Parents Press, 1985. This highly readable book is filled with excellent suggestions for parents about how to manage behavior problems at home. Practical methods of discipline, reward, and time-out are described.

Cunningham, P. M., S. A. Moore, J. W. Cunningham, and D. Moore. *Reading and Writing in Elementary Classrooms: Strategies and Observations*. New York: Longman, 2000. This book presents a balanced approach to reading and writing instruction. Included are accommodations and adaptations to help struggling students as well as technology tips and electronic resources.

Gerber, A. *Language-Related Learning Disabilities*. Baltimore: Brookes Publishing, 1993. This book is a well-written, comprehensive resource for parents, clinicians, and teachers who wish to learn more about the language aspects of learning as well as the specific verbal weaknesses that plague some children and adolescents. It also contains many helpful suggestions for management in school and for language therapy.

Gleason, J. B. *The Development of Language*. 5th ed. Needham Heights, Mass.: Allyn & Bacon, 2001. This book covers language acquisition and its ongoing development from infancy through adulthood, presenting individual differences and recent research findings.

Gunning, T. G. *Creating Reading Instruction for All Children*. 3rd ed. Needham Heights, Mass.: Allyn & Bacon, 2000. This text presents approaches and techniques for reading and writing instruction, including instructional strategies for working with struggling readers and writers.

Harris, K. R., and S. Graham. *Making the Writing Process Work: Strategies for Composition and Self-Regulation*. Cambridge, Mass.: Brookline Books, 1999. This book offers practical strategies for more effective writing, including helping the student become a self-regulated writer, one who understands and is in control of the writing process.

Levine, K. J. *Fine Motor Dysfunction: Therapeutic Strategies in the Classroom.* Tucson, Ariz.: Therapy Skill Builders, 1991. This book includes descriptions of strategies to use in the classroom with students who have difficulty with fine motor and graphomotor function.

Levine, M. D. *All Kinds of Minds.* Cambridge, Mass.: Educators Publishing Service, 1993. This book is written to help younger students (under eleven) understand different kinds of learning disorders. It is a fictitious account of a group of children with specific difficulties in school. The book describes how the children come to understand and deal with their problems. Cassette tapes of the book, read by Dr. Levine, are available. There is also a manual *(Guidelines for the Use of All Kinds of Minds)* to help adults use the book with children.

———. *Developmental Variation and Learning Disorders.* 2nd ed. Cambridge, Mass.: Educators Publishing Service, 1998. This book offers comprehensive information about developmental variations in children that can lead to learning disorders. Research from different disciplines and their interactions is explored. The abundance of information in this reference guide is useful for clinicians, educators, and parents alike.

———. *Educational Care.* 2nd ed. Cambridge, Mass: Educators Publishing Service, 2002. This book provides a practical guide to parents and teachers who are working with students who are having problems with learning and/or behavior. The volume emphasizes collaborative management at home and in school.

———. *Jarvis Clutch—Social Spy.* Cambridge, Mass: Educators Publishing Service, 2001. Dr. Mel Levine teams up with fictitious eighth grader Jarvis Clutch to offer insight and advice on the middle school social scene. Jarvis's spy notes provide a bird's-eye view of the often traumatic social trials that middle school students are bound to encounter. His wry perspective is alternated with commentary and wisdom from Dr. Levine, who provides an analysis of social situations from an expert's perspective and shares the terminology that students need to understand what it is that makes social interactions so difficult. At the end of each chapter, discussion questions and "Jarvis Activities" offer an opportunity to continue discussions on social interaction, and a glossary at the end of the book serves as a helpful reference to "tech talk" presented by Dr. Levine.

———. *Keeping A Head in School.* Cambridge, Mass: Educators Publishing Service, 1990. This book is designed to help older children (ages eleven and up) to understand the nature of their learning disorders and strengths. It reviews issues relating to attentional dysfunction, various kinds of learning disorders, as well as difficulties with motor function, self-esteem, and social skill. Students are given suggestions for working on their problems and using their strengths. Cassette tapes of the book, read by Dr. Levine, are available.

———. *The Language Parts Catalog.* Cambridge, Mass.: Educators Publishing Service, 1999. This "catalog" for students in seventh to tenth grade explains the various aspects of language and how they operate. While learning and reading about language, students can fill out an "order form" requesting the language parts they would like and indicating how much they need the parts. A manual is available to help educators use this book with students.

Lyon, G. R., and N. Krasnegor. *Attention, Memory, and Executive Function*. Baltimore: Brookes Publishing, 1995. This text is a compilation of research and theories about various components of attention and memory, especially as they relate to learning and differences in learning.

Mastropieri, M. A., and T. E. Scruggs. *Teaching Students Ways to Remember: Strategies for Learning Mnemonically*. Cambridge, Mass.: Brookline Books, 1999. This book focuses on how to teach students memory techniques they can use for acquiring basic skills, concepts, facts, and systems of facts.

Meltzer, L. J., B. N. Roditi, D. P. Haynes, K. R. Biddle, M. Paster, and S. E. Taber. *Strategies for Success: Classroom Teaching Techniques for Students with Learning Problems*. Austin, Tex.: PRO-ED, 1996. Written for teachers, this book describes a wide range of teaching strategies that can be used with late elementary, middle, and early high school students.

Middleton, J. A., and P. Goepfert. *Inventive Strategies for Teaching Mathematics: Implementing Standards for Reform*. Washington, D.C.: American Psychological Association, 1996. This book is part of the series "Psychology in the Classroom," which is written for elementary through high school teachers. The user-friendly text includes case illustrations, sample activities, and suggested readings related to mathematics.

Moats, L. C. *Speech to Print: Language Essentials for Teachers*. Baltimore: Brookes Publishing, 2000. This thorough book on language describes ways to recognize, understand, and manage the difficulties students may have when learning to read and write.

Sedita, J. *Landmark Study Skills Guide*. Prides Crossing, Mass.: Landmark Foundation, 1989. This manual offers abundant suggestions on how to improve study skills. The book presents specific methods for reading, taking notes, and organizing time and space. It is geared to the needs of children with learning disorders. There is a Spanish version as well.

Shames, G., E. Wiig, and W. Secord. *Human Communication Disorders: An Introduction*. 5th ed. Needham Heights, Mass.: Allyn & Bacon, 1998. Often used as an introductory text in speech language pathology and audiology courses, this text focuses on understanding the underlying nature of communication problems.

Sugden, D. A., and J. F. Keogh. *Problems in Motor Skill Development*. Columbia: University of South Carolina Press, 1990. This book describes different forms of motor difficulty. The introduction and several of the chapters are especially relevant to the understanding of children with motor problems affecting writing.

Turecki, S. *The Emotional Problems of Normal Children*. New York: Bantam, 1994. Dr. Turecki, a psychiatrist, provides much practical advice on the understanding and management of common behavioral problems in childhood. His wisdom reflects his vast clinical experience, and his philosophy is refreshing, as he stresses that even "normal" children have problems.

Vail, P. L. *Smart Kids with School Problems*. New York: E. P. Dutton, 1987. In this general book about learning styles and learning disorders, the author provides excellent insights into the multiple factors that relate to academic success and failure. The book is equally relevant for parents and teachers.

VIDEO- AND AUDIOTAPES AND CURRICULUM MATERIALS
Developing Minds (2002) (Video)
A production of WGBH Boston (www.wgbh.org) in association with All Kinds of Minds (www.allkindsofminds.org).

Developing Minds is a video resource library for parents, educators, and clinicians on differences in learning. Eight "Theme" videos present the learning problems and successes of children and early adolescents, with a focus on specific subject or performance areas. Eight "Construct" videos provide deeper insight into specific neurodevelopmental breakdowns that contribute to differences in learning. Three "Management by Profile" videos introduce a systematic process for developing an educational management plan based on a student's neurodevelopmental strengths and weaknesses. Three "Introductory" videos provide a brief description of the video library components and present the philosophy and approach of All Kinds of Minds. All the videos feature easy-to-use strategies and include print guides that augment the learning issues and concepts presented. Commentary by Dr. Mel Levine is provided throughout these videos.

Ennis' Gift: A Film About Learning Differences (2000)
Videocassette produced by Hello Friend/Ennis William Cosby Foundation, www.hellofriend.com (telephone orders: 800-343-5540).

Ennis' Gift is inspired by the legacy of Ennis William Cosby, a young man who became a passionate educator dedicated to helping all children find their gifts and learn. The film introduces you to students and adults who have experienced differences in learning and refused to be limited by their difficulties.

How Difficult Can This Be?: The F.A.T. City Workshop (1989)
Videocassette produced by the Learning Project at WETA, Washington, D.C. (telephone orders: 800-343-5540).

This video hosted by Richard Lavoie allows viewers to experience the same frustration, anxiety, and tension that students with differences in learning face each day.

Last One Picked . . . First One Picked On (1994)
Videocassette produced by the Learning Project at WETA, Washington, D.C. (telephone orders: 800-343-5540).

Host Richard Lavoie describes difficulties students can have making and keeping friends due to poor social skills.

Learning Disabilities/Learning Abilities: A New VIDEO Series Dedicated to the Idea That All Children Can Learn (1997)
Videocassette series produced by Vineyard Video Productions, www.vineyard video.com (telephone orders: 800-664-6119).

This series of videos includes nationally recognized experts providing the latest methods for teaching strategies and how they can work in the classroom. Experts include Marilyn Jager Adams, Ph.D., Judith R. Birsh, Ed.D., Martha Bridge Denckla, M.D., G. Reid Lyon, Ph.D., Nancy Mather, Ed.D., Louisa Cook Moats, Ed.D., Joyce Steeves, Ed.D., and many more.

Look What You've Done! Stories of Hope and Resilience (1997)
Videocassette produced by the Learning Project at WETA, Washington, D.C. (telephone orders: 800-343-5540).

This video featuring Dr. Robert Brooks offers practical strategies for helping students develop the confidence and resilience they need to succeed. A teacher's guide and parent's guide are available.

The Mind That's Mine

M. Levine, C. Swartz, and M. Wakely. Chapel Hill, N.C.: All Kinds of Minds, 1995 (distributed by Educators Publishing Company, Cambridge, Mass.).

A program to help upper elementary school students learn about learning. This curriculum is designed to be integrated into the classroom and includes an extensive teacher's manual, student texts, a student video, a teacher's video, a brain poster, and Dr. Levine's book *All Kinds of Minds*.

Reaching Minds (1997–present)

Audiocassette series produced by All Kinds of Minds (distributed by Educators Publishing Service, Cambridge, Mass.), www.allkindsofminds.org.

Hosted by Dr. Mel Levine, *Reaching Minds* is an audiocassette series that demystifies learning and is geared to helping parents, educators, clinicians, and other professionals who work with students with differences in learning. With the expertise and experience of Dr. Levine and other renowned professionals, this audiocassette program describes ways to better understand how to help students who are struggling in school.

When the Chips Are Down . . . Strategies for Improving Children's Behavior (1997)

Videocassette produced by the Learning Project at WETA, Washington, D.C. (telephone orders: 800-343-5540).

Host Richard Lavoie offers practical advice on how teachers and parents can create an environment to help students manage their behavior.

Index